M.s 89/14

18.95

Gender Under Scrutiny
New inquiries in education

by the same editors
Gender and the Politics of Schooling
Edited by Madeleine Arnot and Gaby Weiner

Gender Under Scrutiny

New inquiries in education

**Edited by Gaby Weiner and Madeleine Arnot
at The Open University**

Hutchinson

London   Melbourne   Sydney   Auckland   Johannesburg
in association with

The Open University

Hutchinson Education

An imprint of Century Hutchinson Ltd

62–65 Chandos Place, London WC2N 4NW

Century Hutchinson Australia Pty Ltd
PO Box 496, 16–22 Church Street, Hawthorn,
Victoria 3122, Australia

Century Hutchinson New Zealand Ltd
PO Box 40–086, Glenfield, Auckland 10
New Zealand

Century Hutchinson South Africa (Pty) Ltd
PO Box 337, Berglvei 2012, South Africa

First published 1987

Set in Linotron Baskerville by
Input Typesetting Ltd, London SW19 8DR

Printed in Great Britain by
Richard Clay Ltd, Bungay, Suffolk

ISBN 0 09 172871 1

Preface

This collection of readings has been designed to complement the Open University Master's degree option *Gender and Education*.* The volume has been designed to help students appreciate the theoretical assumptions underlying research on gender and education and to become familiar with different lines of inquiry and different research methodologies. The articles selected provide an extension to the discussion of major theories and frameworks in the study of gender and education and their implications for state policy discussed in the other reader for this course, *Gender and the Politics of Schooling*, edited by M. Arnot and G. Weiner (also published by Hutchinson).

As the reader forms only part of the course (which also consists of a written study guide and cassette material discussing the issues raised in the reader articles), it cannot claim to offer a comprehensive account of research on gender and education. The selection of articles has been designed to highlight specific problems and to develop students' critical understanding. Opinions expressed within articles are therefore not necessarily those of the course writers nor of the university. However, the editors believe that the selection focuses on major issues in the field and will be useful to anyone with an interest in gender and education.

* Further information about the course associated with this book may be obtained by writing to: Higher Degrees Office, PO Box, 49, The Open University, Milton Keynes MK7 6AD.

Contents

8 *Contents*

Acknowledgements

The editors and publisher would like to thank the copyright holders below for their kind permission to reproduce the following material. Every effort has been made to obtain permission from the relevant copyright holders but where no reply was received we have assumed that there was no objection to our using the material.

British Educational Research Journal and Alison Kelly for pp. 233–42, reproduced from *British Educational Research Journal*, **II**, no. 2, 1985.

Croom Helm Ltd for pp. 101–13 by Judith Okely, reproduced from S. Ardener (ed.), *Defining Females: The Nature of Women in Society*, 1978.

The Dunmore Press Ltd for pp. 77–89 by Sue Middleton, reproduced from J. Codd, D. Harker and R. Nash (eds.), *Political Issues in New Zealand Education*, Palmerston North, 1985.

Falmer Press Ltd and Christine Griffin for pp. 213–21 by Christine Griffin, reproduced from R. G. Burgess (ed.), *Field Methods in the Study of Education*, 1985.

Elsevier Science Publishers BV for pp. 37–49 by T. Carrigan, M. Connell and J. Lee, reproduced from *Theory and Society*, **14**, 1985.

Feminist Review and Anna Davin for pp. 143–9, reproduced from *Feminist Review*, no. 3, 1979.

Forum – for the discussion of new trends in education for pp. 150–4 by Glenys Lobban reproduced from *Forum – for the discussion of new trends in education*, spring 1974, vol. 16, no. 2.

Sigmund Freud Copyrights Ltd, The Institute of Psycho-Analysis and The Hogarth Press for permission to quote from *The Standard Edition of the Complete Psychological Works of Sigmund Freud*, translated and edited by James Strachey.

Kogan Page for pp. 26–36 by Janet Sayers, reproduced from S. Acker, J. Megarry, S. Nisbet and E. Hoyle (eds.), *The World Yearbook of Education 1984: Women and Education*, 1984.

Longman Group for pp. 155–9 by Jean Northam, reproduced from *Education*, **10** (1), spring 1982.

Macmillan, London and Basingstoke for pp. 187–97 by Julian Wood, reproduced from A. McRobbie and M. Nava (eds.), *Gender and Generation*, 1984.

Routledge & Kegan Paul for pp. 117–33 by *Gill Frith*, reproduced from C. Steedman, C. Urwin, and V. Walkerdine (eds.), *Language, Gender and Childhood*, 1985.

The Open University for pp. 67–76 by June Purvis, reproduced from *Understanding Texts*, E205, unit 15, copyright © 1984 The Open University Press.

Sage Publications Ltd, for pp. 134–42 by Olivia Foster-Carter, reproduced from

Sage Race Relations Abstracts, **9** (4), November 1984. Used by permission of Sage Publications Ltd. Copyright © 1984 by the Institute of Race Relations.
Virago for pp. 90–100, reproduced from B. Byran, S. Dadzie and S. Scafe, *The Heart of the Race*, 1985.

Introduction

In preparing this volume of readings, our aims have been fourfold:

a to give a sense of the strength and diversity of research into gender and education.
b to provide an indication of how research into gender within educational institutions has developed since 1975, the year of the Sex Discrimination Act, especially in relation to issues of race and sexuality.
c to illustrate the range of disciplinary and feminist perspectives used by researchers and the methods of research developed to analyse educational experiences.
d to identify new lines of inquiry and directions for research.

Since 1975 research on gender and education has become increasingly popular among academics, undergraduate and postgraduate students, practising teachers, administrators and advisers. This interest was stimulated by a number of features affecting education policy after the Second World War, especially the Education Act (1944) with its formal commitment to equality of opportunity, the Sex Discrimination Act (1975) and the Race Relations Act (1976), and the development of the new women's movement from the late 1960s. Teachers in particular have taken up the debate about sex discrimination in education and either have conducted their own investigations or have focused on gender issues while on initial teacher training, post-graduate or in-service courses.

In the United Kingdom patterns of curriculum provision, subject choice and processes of gender differentiation in schooling have been important topics of research. Coeducation and teacher employment, which directly affect policy-making, have also been key issues for investigation and debate. Initially the problem for many researchers was defined in terms of female and male achievement in education. In 1980, Dale Spender along with others asked whether girls had gained from the development of state education and the ideology of equal opportunities. Was equality of opportunity a myth? Were girls, in effect, 'learning to lose'?

By the mid 1980s, as a result of recent research, the questions and indeed the criticisms of the educational system have become more extensive and detailed. Although factual information about patterns of female and male educational achievement is still relatively sparse, researchers have tended to concentrate on in-depth and often small-scale analyses of educational processes and structures. (This is partly due to the current lack of availability of funding for research into gender and education.) The assumption that equal access to education was sufficient to ensure equality between the sexes has now been challenged by evidence that more fundamental reforms are needed to reshape the unequal relations between the sexes. Increasingly, the need to ensure equal *outcomes* of schooling has been recognized, despite the fact that the mechanisms involved are at early stages of being understood. Attention has thus focused increasingly on the process of schooling, on male–female power relations within educational institutions and on the relationship between class, race and gender divisions in education and in society.

Researchers have taken up the challenge of investigating male and female experiences of schooling. They share a commitment to finding ways to transform gender relations – a commitment that has focused attention on the role that schooling plays in reproducing gender difference and male power in society. Such commitment has led to investigations of taken-for-granted aspects of school life and professional understandings about the nature of equality of opportunity.

Despite such similarity of purpose, there are also considerable differences in perspective, research methodology and the interpretation of data among researchers. In this volume, it is impossible to do justice to the wealth and diversity of research in this field of educational analysis. The range of disciplinary perspectives adopted, for example, by academic sociologists, historians, psychologists and cultural theorists as well as by teachers of different subjects makes a representative sample difficult. Our contributions come from researchers working in the United Kingdom, Australia, New Zealand and the United States, reflecting, we hope, the international interest in these issues.

In the first part of the reader we present a theoretical discussion of the main theories of gender development and gender difference. We suggest that the topics academic researchers choose (as well as policy-makers and practitioners) are structured by their assumptions about how individuals acquire their gender identity and how they are prepared for life within a sex-segregated world. Assumptions are also made about the processes involved in gender development, determining the nature of research projects and the interpretation of evidence.

There a number of theories of gender development now available – however, the dominant theory in educational research has been that of sex-role socialization (or social learning theory for developmental psychologists). Sex-role theory, as Carrigan, Connell and Lee (in this volume) describe, developed in the United States in the 1950s and was within the positivist structural-functional tradition of social science, itself not without critics. Research questions shaped by such theories of learning concentrated upon the messages children receive by way of approval or disapproval of gender appropriate behaviour. Education was researched in terms of its role in preparing individuals for their separate gender identities and gender roles – for separate and complementary male and female spheres.

Other theories of gender development such as cognitive-development theory or Freud's theory of male and female sexuality have had less impact on educational research (although one can glimpse the latter's impact in Wood's research (in this volume)). More recently, gender difference has become the focus of theoretical debate. Gender categories and relations have been analysed as historically and culturally specific. Further, attention has focused upon power relations between men and women, its material basis within the economy and other social divisions. Also the relations *within* masculinity and femininity (e.g. between dominant and subordinate forms of masculinity) as well as *between* the male and the female have now become important research topics. Carrigan *et al.* (in this volume) in raising such issues, describe the emergence of theories of male homosexuality and the assumptions about heterosexuality within gender theories.

Other new critiques of theories of gender development include that of race. Ann Phoenix challenges the assumptions behind the psychological theories of social learning, cognitive development and psychoanalysis in so far as they assume a white middle-class 'normal' family – a family form that excludes black people and which characterizes them as deviant and 'outside' normal processes of gender development.

The impact of different theoretical perspectives on gender differences in framing research questions can be explored by comparing the articles within each section of the reader. For example, Frith's analysis of the school story, in terms of the ideologies of female subjectivity and the subcodes of femininity offers a clear contrast to the content analysis of Lobban or Northam. Similarly Wood's explorations of male sex talk differs considerably from that of Randall or Stanworth.

We have selected articles for the reader on the basis of specific areas of study and have brought together examples of research illustrating different theoretical and methodological traditions within each area. The first line of inquiry (Part Two) includes studies which explore the past as a means of understanding the relationship between gender and educational experiences. Here, through autobiographies and life histories, researchers have attempted to 'capture' and analyse individuals' and groups' personal lives. Through subjective accounts of family and school life, we can glimpse what it is like to grow up male or female, in particular eras and in particular class or ethnic cultures.

Such research has become particularly important in the development of feminist ideas, frequently concentrating on the principle that the 'personal is political'. Life histories and individual or collective biographies offer women, in particular, a 'voice' to express in their own words how their lives have been shaped as women. Such accounts offer opportunities for understanding how individuals negotiate the structures and ideologies of schooling and how they make sense of often contradictory messages about gender and gender relations.

Purvis discusses the problems of interpreting autobiographies or life histories and Middleton provides examples of life histories of feminist educationalists, offering insights into the subcultures of schooling and the forces which shape girls' critical awareness of gender relations. The autobiographical articles by Okely and by Bryan, Dadzie and Scafe contain personal, though analytic accounts of female education; Okely on girls' private schooling, and Bryan *et al.*, on the education of black girls and women since the 1950s.

Our second line of inquiry (Part Three) pursues the problem of how to evaluate texts. This area of research has developed only gradually, despite the clear need for the consideration of implicit messages contained within learning materials. Research flourished in the early 1970s (particularly in the United States), yet there are few substantial textual analyses currently available in the United

Kingdom. This may be explained in part by the failure of the Sex Discrimination Act to include scrutiny of educational materials in its brief, thus disqualifying the Equal Opportunities Commission from extending the concept of sex discrimination to include literature and textbooks. The reasons why, perhaps, such textual analysis has flourished in the United States is that there has been greater acceptance among politicians of the impact of discriminatory texts on social inequalities.

We have chosen examples from the field of children's literature and popular culture to illustrate important theoretical and methodological questions which any researcher of texts might encounter. Frith, Foster-Carter and Davin relate the ideological messages of the texts to economic and class relations, and to gender or race relations. Concepts of sex stereotyping, on the other hand, have framed the research of Northam and Lobban and interestingly here more quantitative methods are employed.

The third line of inquiry (Part Four), into the processes of schooling, broadens the analysis of gender relations in education. Investigations of gender interaction in schools and classrooms, of female and male cultures, and of the different school experiences of male and female pupils, all explore the complexities of the schooling process. Sociologists have investigated gender dynamics, especially in coeducational school settings. Here the relations between the sexes and between male and female students and their teachers have been of special interest.

The examples of empirical research we have selected show how different research methods have been used to explore schooling processes – classroom observation, interviews with participants, questionnaires and ethnographic studies. Randall, Wood and Stanworth, for example, focus on the relations between female and male pupils and their teachers in particular contexts. Cecile Wright's research, on the other hand, challenges assumptions that classroom gender relations can be accurately portrayed without reference to race. Griffin's discussion of how she set up her research on girls' cultures and their experience of leaving school and finding work, shows some of dilemmas facing those wanting to use ethnographic and cultural analysis, while Trenchard and Warren, in their survey of young lesbians and gay men, make visible the specific problems that these young people face in the school system.

Our final choice of a new line of inquiry (Part Five) has been to consider the different ways in which teachers have become involved in the research process either as research subjects or as researchers themselves. Research on teachers' attitudes to equal opportunities has taken the form either of major surveys comparing male and female teachers' responses or of comparing the views of teachers in different subjects (see Kelly *et al.* in this volume). Alternatively, academic researchers have set up action research projects working with small groups of teachers, planning interventions into girls' and boys' education, or researching and monitoring individual schools or classrooms. In the latter set of projects the relationship between research and practice, between academic and teacher has been critical. The forms of investigation and the methods used have been shaped by the process of collaboration as well as by the contingencies and limits set by the research topic. The variety of evidence produced by the different teacher research approaches indicates the complexity of gender issues in school.

The impact of 'feminist' ideas on educational research is of particular interest. Criticisms from feminists about existing hierarchies of research, their challenge to positivism and the moral and ethical questions raised by research of a personal nature, have informed researchers in the design of their studies. Questions have been asked about the ethics of the research process – who does research, for what reasons, upon whom? Need research necessarily be exploitative of the research subject? What can research on gender and schooling offer to pupils and teachers? These questions are touched on by Griffin, Chisholm and Holland, and by Millman in this volume.

The four lines of inquiry we have selected offer insights into the problems of gender relations in schooling yet none in itself provides a definitive analysis. Rather they are complementary, each contributing more information on the nature of the relations between the sexes in education and each suggesting new directions for research.

Finally, another consideration has shaped this collection of readings. We have indicated through our choice of material, examples of two major themes within educational research on gender; race and sexuality. The development of anti-racist strategies within the women's movement and the awareness of gender within the study of race relations has led to increased interest in integrating research on these two different sets of power relations and patterns of social inequality. For many black people, the concerns of white researchers about gender have not addressed the issues which directly confront their experiences in the educational system and in the community. Thus gender research has been pressed to frame research questions not merely on the basis of the lives and experiences of white men and women, but also to take into account black people's lives. The articles by Ann Phoenix, Beverley Bryan, *et al.*, Olivia Foster-Carter and Cecile Wright share a common perspective by placing race on the agenda in theories of gender development, in describing educational experiences, in the evaluation of texts, and in observations of classroom dynamics respectively.

The theme of sexuality has also become of increasing interest in the 1980s. Some local education authorities, for instance, particularly in metropolitan areas, have begun to consider how sexual relations (especially the relations between heterosexuality and homosexuality/lesbianism) are dealt with in educational insti-tutions. Concern has been expressed about the educational experiences of young gay male and lesbian students (see Trenchard and Warren this volume). The discussion by Carrigan *et al.* in this volume suggests that research on gender should consider the relations between heterosexual definitions of masculinity and femininity and those which apply to homosexuals or lesbians. Middleton and Wood explain why sexuality, not just gender, shapes school experiences. Middleton explores the different subcultures of 'academic' and 'non-academic' girls and Wood analyses male sexual fantasy and sex talk.

We hope that the chapters in this book provide researchers with useful resource material on specific methods of research and the opportunity to consider whether the processes described in research reports can be found in other educational institutions. As Millman (in this volume) argues, the development of the teacher as researcher model for the study of gender issues has been particularly important in bridging the gap between academics and practitioners. We hope that the examples of research projects published here will provide sufficient material for students and teachers to conduct their own projects along similar lines. It is crucially important that inquiry into gender and education is open to all levels in the educational system, and the different ranges of skills and expertise are utilized. It is the diversity of research as well as political will that has given research on gender and education its momentum.

Part One

Theories of Gender Difference

1 Female sexuality

Sigmund Freud

During the phase of the normal Oedipus complex we find the child tenderly attached to the parent of the opposite sex, while its relation to the parent of its own sex is predominantly hostile. In the case of a boy there is no difficulty in explaining this. His first love-object was his mother. She remains so; and, with the strengthening of his erotic desires and his deeper insight into the relations between his father and mother, the former is bound to become his rival. With the small girl it is different. Her first object, too, was her mother. How does she find her way to her father? How, when and why does she detach herself from her mother? We have long understood that the development of female sexuality is complicated by the fact that the girl has the task of giving up what was originally her leading genital zone – the clitoris – in favour of a new zone – the vagina. But it now seems to us that there is a second change of the same sort which is no less characteristic and important for the development of the female: the exchange of her original object – her mother – for her father. The way in which the two tasks are connected with each other is not yet clear to us.

It is well known that there are many women who have a strong attachment to their father; nor need they be in any way neurotic. It is upon such women that I have made the observations which I propose to report here and which have led me to adopt a particular view of female sexuality. I was struck, above all, by two facts. The first was that where the woman's attachment to her father was particularly intense, analysis showed that it had been preceded by a phase of exclusive attachment to her mother which had been equally intense and passionate. Except for the change of her love-object, the second phase had scarcely added any new feature to her erotic life. Her primary relation to her mother had been built up in a very rich and many-sided manner. The second fact taught me that the *duration* of this attachment had also been greatly underestimated. In several cases it lasted until well into the fourth year – in one case into the fifth year – so that it covered by far the longer part of the period of early sexual efflorescence. Indeed, we had to reckon with the possibility that a number of women remain arrested in their original attachment to their mother and never achieve a true change-over towards men. This being so, the pre-Oedipus phase in women gains an importance which we have not attributed to it hitherto.

And indeed during that phase a little girl's father is not much else for her than a troublesome rival, although her hostility towards him never reaches the pitch

Source: Extracted from Freud, S., *Three Essays on the Theory of Sexuality*, Vol. 7 of *The Standard Edition of Complete Psychological Works of Sigmund Freud* translated and edited by James Strachey, London, The Institute of Psychoanalysis and the Hogarth Press 1977, pp. 372–88.

which is characteristic of boys. We have, after all, long given up any expectation of a neat parallelism between male and female sexual development.

I began by stating the two facts which have struck me as new: that a woman's strong dependence on her father merely takes over the heritage of an equally strong attachment to her mother, and that this earlier phase has lasted for an unexpectedly long period of time. I shall now go back a little in order to insert these new findings into the picture of female sexual development with which we are familiar. In doing this, a certain amount of repetition will be inevitable. It will help our exposition if, as we go along, we compare the state of things in women with that in men.

First of all, there can be no doubt that the bisexuality, which is present, as we believe, in the innate disposition of human beings, comes to the fore much more clearly in women than in men. A man, after all, has only one leading sexual zone, one sexual organ, whereas a woman has two: the vagina – the female organ proper – and the clitoris, which is analogous to the male organ. We believe we are justified in assuming that for many years the vagina is virtually non-existent and possibly does not produce sensations until puberty. It is true that recently an increasing number of observers report that vaginal impulses are present even in these early years. In women, therefore, the main genital occurrences of childhood must take place in relation to the clitoris. Their sexual life is regularly divided into two phases, of which the first has a masculine character, while only the second is specifically feminine. Thus in female development there is a process of transition from the one phase to the other, to which there is nothing analogous in the male. A further complication arises from the fact that the clitoris, with its virile character, continues to function in later female sexual life in a manner which is very variable and which is certainly not yet satisfactorily understood. We do not, of course, know the biological basis of these peculiarities in women; and still less are we able to assign them any teleological purpose.

Parallel with this first great difference there is the other, concerned with the finding of the object. In the case of a male, his mother becomes his first love-object as a result of her feeding him and looking after him, and she remains so until she is replaced by someone who resembles her or is derived from her. A female's first object, too, must be her mother: the primary conditions for a choice of object are, of course, the same for all children. But at the end of her development, her father – a man – should have become her new love-object. In other words, to the change in her own sex there must correspond a change in the sex of her object. The new problems that now require investigating are in what way this change takes place, how radically or how incompletely it is carried out, and what the different possibilities are which present themselves in the course of this development.

We have already learned, too, that there is yet another difference between the sexes, which relates to the Oedipus complex. We have an impression here that what we have said about the Oedipus complex applies with complete strictness to the male child only and that we are right in rejecting the term 'Electra complex' which seeks to emphasize the analogy between the attitude of the two sexes. It is only in the male child that we find the fateful combination of love for the one parent and simultaneous hatred for the other as a rival. In his case it is the discovery of the possibility of castration, as proved by the sight of the female genitals, which forces on him the transformation of his Oedipus complex, and which leads to the creation of his super-ego and thus initiates all the processes that are designed to make the individual find a place in the cultural community. After the paternal agency has been internalized and become a super-ego, the next task is to detach the latter from the figures of whom it was originally the psychical representative. In this remarkable course of development it is precisely the boy's narcissistic interest in his genitals – his interest in preserving his penis – which is turned round into a curtailing of his infantile sexuality.

One thing that is left over in men from the influence of the Oedipus complex is a certain amount of disparagement in their attitude towards women, whom they regard as being castrated. In extreme cases this gives rise to an inhibition in their choice of object, and, if it is supported by organic factors, to exclusive homosexuality.

Quite different are the effects of the castration complex in the female. She acknowledges the fact of her castration, and with it, too, the superiority of the male and her own inferiority; but she rebels against this unwelcome state of affairs. From this divided attitude three lines of development open up. The first leads to a general revulsion from sexuality. The little girl, frightened by the comparison with boys, grows dissatisfied with her clitoris, and gives up her phallic activity and with it her sexuality in general as well as a good part of her masculinity in other fields. The second line leads her to cling with defiant self-assertiveness to her threatened masculinity. To an incredibly late age she clings to the hope of getting a penis some time. That hope becomes her life's aim; and the phantasy of being a man in spite of everything often persists as a formative factor over long periods. This 'masculinity complex' in women can also result in a manifest homosexual choice of object. Only if her development follows the third, very circuitous, path does she reach the final normal female attitude, in which she takes her father as her object and so finds her way to the feminine form of the Oedipus complex. Thus in women the Oedipus complex is the end result of a fairly lengthy development. It is not destroyed, but created, by the influence of castration; it escapes the strongly hostile influences which, in the male, have a destructive effect on it, and indeed it is all too often not surmounted by the female at all. For this reason, too, the cultural consequences of its break-up are smaller and of less importance in her. We should probably not be wrong in saying that it is this difference in the reciprocal relation between the Oedipus and the castration complex which gives its special stamp to the character of females as social beings.[1]*

We see, then, that the phase of exclusive attachment to the mother, which may be called the *pre-Oedipus* phase, possesses a far greater importance in women than it can have in men. Our interest must be directed to the mechanisms that are at work in her turning away from the mother who was an object so intensely and exclusively loved. We are prepared to find, not a single factor, but a whole number of them operating together towards the same end.

Among these factors are some which are determined by the circumstances of infantile sexuality in general, and so hold good equally for the erotic life of boys.

---

* Superior figures refer to the Notes at the end of chapters.

First and foremost we may mention jealousy of other people – of brothers and sisters, rivals, among whom the father too has a place. Childhood love is boundless; it demands exclusive possession, it is not content with less than all. But it has a second characteristic: it has, in point of fact, no aim and is incapable of obtaining complete satisfaction; and principally for that reason it is doomed to end in disappointment and to give place to a hostile attitude.

Another, much more specific motive for turning away from the mother arises from the effect of the castration complex on the creature who is without a penis. At some time or other the little girl makes the discovery of her organic inferiority – earlier and more easily, of course, if there are brothers or other boys about. We have already taken note of the three paths which diverge from this point: *a* the one which leads to a cessation of her whole sexual life; *b* the one which leads to a defiant over-emphasis of her masculinity; and *c* the first steps towards definitive femininity. It is not easy to determine the exact timing here or the typical course of events. Even the point of time when the discovery of castration is made varies, and a number of other factors seem to be inconstant and to depend on chance. The state of the girl's own phallic activity plays a part; and so too does the question whether this activity was found out or not, and how much interference with it she experienced afterwards.

Little girls usually discover for themselves their characteristic phallic activity – masturbation of the clitoris; and to begin with this is no doubt unaccompanied by fantasy. The part played in starting it by nursery hygiene is reflected in the very common fantasy which makes the mother or nurse into a seducer.

A prohibition of masturbation, as we have seen, becomes an incentive for giving it up; but it also becomes a motive for rebelling against the person who prohibits it – that is to say, the mother, or the mother-substitute who later regularly merges with her. A defiant persistence in masturbation appears to open the way to masculinity. Even where the girl has not succeeded in suppressing her masturbation, the effect of the apparently vain prohibition is seen in her later efforts to free herself at all costs from a satisfaction which has been spoilt for her. When she reaches maturity her object-choice may still be influenced by this persisting purpose. Her resentment at being prevented from free sexual activity plays a big part in her detachment from her mother. The same motive comes into operation again after puberty, when her mother takes up her duty of guarding her daughter's chastity. We shall, of course, not forget that the mother is similarly opposed to a boy's masturbating and thus provides him, too, with a strong motive for rebellion.

When the little girl discovers her own deficiency, from seeing a male genital, it is only with hesitation and reluctance that she accepts the unwelcome knowledge. As we have seen, she clings obstinately to the expectation of one day having a genital of the same kind too, and her wish for it survives long after her hope has expired. The child invariably regards castration in the first instance as a misfortune peculiar to herself; only later does she realize that it extends to certain other children and lastly to certain grown-ups. When she comes to understand the general nature of this characteristic, it follows that femaleness – and with it, of course, her mother – suffers a great depreciation in her eyes.

At the end of this first phase of attachment to the mother, there emerges, as the girl's strongest motive for turning away from her, the reproach that her mother did not give her a proper penis – that is to say, brought her into the world as a female. A second reproach, which does not reach quite so far back, is rather a surprising one. It is that her mother did not give her enough milk, did not suckle her long enough. Under the conditions of modern civilization this may be true often enough, but certainly not so often as is asserted in analyses.

When we survey the whole range of motives for turning away from the mother which analysis brings to light – that she failed to provide the little girl with the only proper genital, that she did not feed her sufficiently, that she compelled her to share her mother's love with others, that she never fulfilled all the girl's expectations of love, and, finally, that she first aroused her sexual activity and then forbade it – all these motives seem nevertheless insufficient to justify the girl's final hostility. Some of them follow inevitably from the nature of infantile sexuality; others appear like rationalizations devised later to account for the uncomprehended change in feeling. Perhaps the real fact is that the attachment to the mother is bound to perish, precisely because it was the first and was so intense; just as one can often see happen in the first marriages of young women which they have entered into when they were most passionately in love. In both situations the attitude of love probably comes to grief from the disappointments that are unavoidable and from the accumulation of occasions for aggression.

We shall conclude, then, that the little girl's intense attachment to her mother is strongly ambivalent, and that it is in consequence precisely of this ambivalence that (with the assistance of the other factors we have adduced) her attachment is forced away from her mother – once again, that is to say, in consequence of a general characteristic of infantile sexuality.

The explanation I have attempted to give is at once met by a question: 'How is it, then, that boys are able to keep intact their attachment to their mother, which is certainly no less strong than that of girls?' The answer comes equally promptly: 'because boys are able to deal with their ambivalent feelings towards their mother by directing all their hostility on to their father'. But, in the first place, we ought not to make this reply until we have made a close study of the pre-Oedipus phase in boys, and, in the second place, it is probably more prudent in general to admit that we have as yet no clear understanding of these processes, with which we have only just become acquainted.

A further question arises: 'What does the little girl require of her mother? What is the nature of her sexual aims during the time of exclusive attachment to her mother?' The answer we obtain from the analytic material is just what we should expect. The girl's sexual aims in regard to her mother are active as well as passive and are determined by the libidinal phases through which the child passes. Here the relation of activity to passivity is especially interesting. It can easily be observed that in every field of mental experience, not merely that of sexuality, when a child receives a passive impression it has a tendency to produce an active reaction. It tries to do itself what has just been done to it. This is part of the work imposed on it of mastering the external world and can even lead to its endeavouring to repeat an impression which it would have reason to avoid on account of its distressing content. Children's play, too, is made to serve this purpose of supplementing a passive experience with an active piece of behaviour and of thus, as it were, annulling it. When a doctor has opened a child's mouth, in spite of his resistance, to look down his throat, the same child, after the doctor has gone, will play at being the doctor himself, and will repeat the assault upon some small brother or sister who is as helpless in his hands as he was in the doctor's. Here we have an unmistakable revolt against passivity and a preference for the active role. This swing-over from passivity to activity does not take place with the same regularity or vigour in all children; in some it may not occur at all. A child's behaviour in this respect may enable us to draw conclusions as to the relative strength of the masculinity and femininity that it will exhibit in its sexuality.

The first sexual and sexually coloured experiences which a child has in relation to its mother are naturally of a passive character. It is suckled, fed, cleaned, and dressed by her, and taught to perform all its functions. A part of its libido goes on clinging to those experiences and enjoys the satisfactions bound up with them; but another part strives to turn them into activity. In the first place, being suckled at the breast gives place to active sucking. As regards the other experiences the child contents itself either with becoming self-sufficient – that is, with itself successfully carrying out what had hitherto been done for it – or with repeating its passive experiences in an active form in play; or else it actually makes its mother into the object and behaves as the active subject towards her. For a long time I was unable to credit this last behaviour, which takes place in the field of real action, until my observations removed all doubts on the matter.

We seldom hear of a little girl's wanting to wash or dress her mother, or tell her to perform her excretory functions. Sometimes, it is true, she says: 'Now let's play that I'm the mother and you're the child', but generally she fulfils these active wishes in an indirect way, in her play with her doll, in which she represents the mother and the doll the child. The fondness girls have for playing with dolls, in contrast to boys, is commonly regarded as a sign of early awakened femininity. Not unjustly so; but we must not overlook the fact that what finds expression here is the *active* side of femininity, and that the little girl's preference for dolls is probably evidence of the exclusiveness of her attachment to her mother, with complete neglect of her father-object.

The turning-away from her mother is an extremely important step in the course of a little girl's development. It is more than a mere change of object. We have already described what takes place in it and the many motives put forward for it; we may now add that hand in hand with it there is to be observed a marked lowering of the active sexual impulses and a rise of the passive ones. It is true that the active trends have been affected by frustration more strongly; they have proved totally unrealizable and are therefore abandoned by the libido more readily. But the passive trends have not escaped disappointment either. With the turning-away from the mother clitoridal masturbation frequently ceases as well; and often enough when the small girl represses her previous masculinity a considerable portion of her sexual trends in general is permanently injured too. The transition to the father-object is accomplished with the help of the passive trends in so far as they have escaped the catastrophe. The path to the development of femininity now lies open to the girl, to the extent to which it is not restricted by the remains of the pre-Oedipus attachment to her mother which she has surmounted.

If we now survey the stage of sexual development in the female which I have been describing, we cannot resist coming to a definite conclusion about female sexuality as a whole. We have found the same libidinal forces at work in it as in the male child and we have been able to convince ourselves that for a period of time these forces follow the same course and have the same outcome in each.

Biological factors subsequently deflect those libidinal forces (in the girl's case) from their original aims and conduct even active and in every sense masculine trends into feminine channels. Since we cannot dismiss the notion that sexual excitation is derived from the operation of certain chemical substances, it seems plausible at first to expect that biochemistry will one day disclose a substance to us whose presence produces a male sexual excitation and another substance which produces a female one. But this hope seems no less naïve than the other one – happily obsolete today – that it may be possible under the microscope to isolate the different exciting factors of hysteria, obsessional neurosis, melancholia, and so on.

Even in sexual chemistry things must be rather more complicated. For psychology, however, it is a matter of indifference whether there is a single sexually exciting substance in the body or two or countless numbers of them. Psychoanalysis teaches us to manage with a single libido, which, it is true, has both active and passive aims (that is, modes of satisfaction). This antithesis and, above all, the existence of libidinal trends with passive aims, contains within itself the remainder of our problem.

Note

1 It is to be anticipated that men analysts with feminist views, as well as our women analysts, will disagree with what I have said here. They will hardly fail to object that such notions spring from the 'masculinity complex' of the male and are designed to justify on theoretical grounds his innate inclination to disparage and suppress women. But this sort of psychoanalytic argumentation reminds us here, as it so often does, of Dostoevsky's famous 'knife that cuts both ways'. The opponents of those who argue in this way will on their side think it quite natural that the female sex should refuse to accept a view which appears to contradict their eagerly coveted equality with men. The use of analysis as a weapon of controversy can clearly lead to no decision.

2   Psychology and gender divisions

Janet Sayers

Introduction

Sociologists (Barrett, 1980)* and biologists (Wilson, 1978) have variously sought the historical and biological determinants of current sexual divisions in society. Psychologists, in contrast, have been less concerned with the determinants of these divisions, than with how individuals come to be located psychologically in relation to them. Some have been strongly influenced by biological determinism, others variously by social-learning, cognitive-developmental and psychoanalytic theory. This chapter evaluates these approaches and proposes a missing element in them all.

Biological determinism

Any adequate explanation of psychological sex differences must take into account the fact that the sexes differ biologically from each other. One way of doing this is to argue that biology directly determines these psychological differences. It has been argued, for instance, that the 'female' hormone oxytocin makes women more nurturant and therefore better equipped psychologically than men to look after children (Rossi, 1977). Others have claimed that boys are more aggressive than girls, and that this psychological sex difference is determined by the higher levels of circulating androgens in boys which, it is claimed, fits them as men for the competitive struggles of occupational life (Goldberg, 1977; Wilson, 1978).

One problem with the above arguments is that the evidence for sex differences in nurturance and in aggression is not conclusive (see Maccoby and Jacklin, 1974, and Tieger, 1980, respectively). Rossi's argument is also flawed because it rests on the dubious assumption that because oxytocin stimulates nipple erection preparatory to breast-feeding it thereby makes women nurturant. The argument that aggression facilitates occupational success is similarly flawed. Aggressive individuals are indeed more often marked by their occupational failure than by their occupational success. (See Sayers, 1982, for a more extended discussion of these arguments.)

A biological determinist account of psychological sex differences that is gaining currency in education concerns girls' relative lack of science attainment. This sex difference has been linked to the oft-repeated finding (Orsini *et al.*, 1982) that, on average, girls perform less well than boys on psychological tests of visuo-spatial

Source: Acker, S., Megarry, J., Nisbet, S. and Hoyle, E. *World Yearbook of Education 1984: Women and Education*, London, Kogan Page, 1984.
* Full references quoted in the text can be found in the Notes and references at the end of chapters.

ability (Gray, 1981). In turn, this difference has been linked to the fact that boys' brains seem to be more specialized than girls' for visuo-spatial function (Levy, 1972; Jones and Anuza, 1972; de Lacoste-Utamsing and Holloway, 1982). Selection for this biological sex difference, it is suggested, occurred over the course of human evolution because it aided species survival by fitting men for territorial defence and hunting thus protecting women and leaving them free to care for children (Gray, 1981).

Whatever the virtues of this evolutionary and functionalist account of existing sex differences in visuo-spatial ability, it cannot adequately explain the current under-achievement of girls in science. In the first place, there is no evidence that specialization of spatial function within one hemisphere of the brain is causally related to spatial ability (Jacklin, 1979). Second, there is no evidence that the ability measured by visuo-spatial tests is necessary to science achievement (Saraga and Griffiths, 1981). Third, sex differences on these tests are minuscule by comparison with the large differences between boys and girls in their attainments in science. Last, the research on sex differences in the science attainment of 14-year-old boys and girls on which Gray bases his argument did not control for the number of science-based subjects currently being taken by these teenagers. Where such controls are introduced, as in a related study of sex differences in mathematical ability (Fennema, 1980), few sex-related differences emerge. It has accordingly been suggested that sex differences in mathematics and science attainment might be related more to social than to biological factors – to the apparent irrelevance to girls of science and mathematics for their anticipated roles as women in our society, so that they feel less enthusiastic about, and less eager to opt for, courses in these subjects (Fennema, 1980; Saraga and Griffiths, 1981).

The general inadequacy of existing biological determinist hypotheses concerning the psychological correlates of sexual divisions in society has led many psychologists and feminists to favour a socialization account, and in particular a social-learning explanation of psychological sex differences.

Social-learning theory

According to social-learning theory, the child acquires his or her knowledge and repertoire of sex-typed behaviours on the basis of observation. He or she observes the behaviour modelled by parents, teachers, other children, etc. (Raskin and Israel, 1981), and on the basis of the sex-typing of behaviours depicted, for instance, in picture books (Weitzman *et al.*, 1972; Ashton, 1983), television (McGhee and Frueh, 1980), reading schemes (Sharpe, 1976), and in school subjects such as history and geography (Scott, 1980).

Whether the child actually imitates these behaviours depends on whether or not he or she has observed that rewards are experienced when the behaviour is performed by someone of his or her sex (Mischel, 1966). Evidence that children are quickly given the chance to learn the sex-linked rewards of particular behaviours comes, for instance, from research indicating that parents show approval of their children's sex-appropriate and disapproval of their sex-inappropriate behaviour; that 3- and 4-year-old children criticize, and are less willing to play with, other children who indulge in activities associated with the opposite sex, and from the finding that nursery school teachers criticize their pupils for playing with opposite sex-typed toys (Archer and Lloyd, 1982). Mischel also suggests that children learn the sex-linked rewards of particular activities in the process of learning about sex-role stereotyping; that is, through learning that such activities are socially labelled as appropriate for one sex but not the other.

The stereotyping of school subjects as male (for example, science) might explain reported differences between girls and boys in their explanations of their school successes and failures. Girls, it is said, typically attribute their failures to lack of ability, boys to lack of effort (Etaugh and Hadley, 1977; but see Frieze *et al.*, 1982). Furthermore, teachers appear to contribute to this process through their assumption that, unlike boys, girls are well-behaved and work hard at school, so that girls are made to feel that errors in their school work reflect lack of ability rather than lack of effort (Dweck, 1978). As one teacher expressed this attitude: 'On the whole you can generally say that the boys are more capable of learning. . . . Although the girls tend to be good at most things, in the end you find it's going to be a boy who's your most brilliant pupil' (Clarricoates, 1980, p. 33). Parents convey a similar message to their children, viewing their daughters as having to work harder than boys to reach the same level of attainment in mathematics (Parsons *et al.*, 1982). The general message seems to be that boys have a natural aptitude for mathematics which girls can only equal through hard work. And this is reinforced by the attitude that attributes girls' mathematical successes, unlike boys', to rule-following rather than to reasoning ability (Walkerdine, 1982). There is an interesting parallel here with racial divisions in society, where one finds some educationalists (Jensen, 1969) viewing school work among blacks as properly a matter of rote-learning, and among whites as a matter of intelligence!

Perhaps the differences in the attributions that parents, teachers and children make about the school successes and failures of boys and girls reflects the male-typing of the intellectual processes involved in education. However, although social-learning theory draws attention to the importance to child development of the sex-typing of activities such as school work, it does not address the source of this sex-typing. One possible source lies in the fact that reason and education have for many centuries been regarded as irrelevant, or even as downright harmful to girls' future roles as wives and mothers (Walkerdine, 1982; Walden and Walkerdine, 1982), so that they have come to be viewed as men's natural sphere – one in which girls can hope to succeed only through hard work. The extreme male-typing of subjects such as science might then be due to their particularly strong association with social production (Rose, 1982) – a sphere that has come to be regarded as a male preserve as it has become progressively divorced from social reproduction within the home.

Social-learning theorists (Bem, 1981) have typically not addressed themselves to the origins of sex-typing nor how it is that particular activities have come to be viewed as male- or female-typed. However, as I shall indicate later, this is crucial to the explanation of patterns of gender development, and the psychological centrality of sex in child development. The more usual objections raised against social-learning theory are: first, that parents do not reward their children differentially according to sex to the degree anticipated by the theory; and, second, that children's sex-role concepts and behaviour are not an exact model of those around them (Maccoby and Jacklin, 1974; Constantinople, 1979). These two objections are avoided by cognitive-developmental theory which provides another, equally influential, framework for current psychological research on gender development.

Cognitive-developmental theory

According to cognitive-developmental theory, it is neither biology nor society but their conceptualization by the child that determines gender development. This development, as the Piagetian psychologist Lawrence Kohlberg (1966) has argued, is initiated by the child's ability to correctly categorize itself as either a boy or a girl – an ability that is normally acquired by the age of 3 years (Thompson, 1975). Having correctly categorized itself by sex, the 3-year-old's egocentrism leads it to value the objects and activities associated with its sex. Evidence on this point, and on the linkage of gender identity with sex-role stereotyping in pre-school children comes, for instance, from Albert and Porter (1983) and Kuhn *et al.* (1978).

Kohlberg accounts for young children's avoidance of sex-inappropriate behaviour, not in terms of reinforcement contingencies but in terms of Piaget's account of the development of object constancy. Conservation experiments reveal that the nursery and infant school child lacks a stable sense of object constancy, and that, at this age, the child wrongly thinks that the volume of a liquid expands when it is poured from a fat into a thin glass because its level is now higher up the glass. Similar evidence shows that children of this age can wrongly believe that if a child dresses or plays in a sex-inappropriate way its sex thereby changes (Emmerich *et al.*, 1977). According to cognitive-developmental theory, the child's cognitive need to maintain a stable gender identity leads it to vigorously avoid cross-sex behaviour and to condemn such behaviour in other children (Damon, 1977) until gender constancy is firmly established at about 5 or 6 years of age (Marcus and Overton, 1978). It is in these terms that this theory explains the peaking of sexism at this age – a sexism that contrasts with the generally more liberal sex-role attitudes of older children, parents, and teachers (Garrett *et al.*, 1977; Meyer, 1980; Urberg, 1982).

Kohlberg maintains that, consistent with the concrete-operational level of the 5- and 6-year-old's conceptual structures, it is found that the sex-role concepts of children at this age are based on obvious physical differences between the sexes. Since men are clearly bigger than women they are viewed by young children as more powerful and older, and therefore as more intelligent than women. And, just as the child of this age regards moral and social rules as absolute and God-given (Piaget, 1932), so the child of this age also regards sex-role norms as absolute; the 10-year-old child, in contrast, tends to view them as more a matter of social convention than of biological imperative; while the teenager, just as he judges social conventions in terms of their correspondence with general principles of equity and justice (Piaget, 1932), likewise assesses and questions sex-role norms in these terms (Kohlberg and Ullian, 1974; Ullian, 1976).

Although cognitive-developmental theory avoids some of the problems of social-learning theory, it raises other problems. It has been pointed out, for instance, that even if boys come to make moral judgements in terms of justice and natural rights, girls come to make these judgements in terms of their bearing on relations between people and not in terms of abstract rights (Gilligan, 1982). If this is the case, and sex-role development parallels moral development (as Kohlberg claims) then it is unlikely that girls' sex-role development proceeds in the way described by Kohlberg and Ullian. Others (for example, Mischel, 1966) have objected to Kohlberg's theory in that it fails to explain individual differences in gender development (except tendentiously in terms of individual differences in IQ – see Kohlberg and Zigler, 1967). Nor can Kohlberg explain the very early appearance of sex-typed behaviour as evidenced, for instance, by the fact that babies look more at pictures of other infants of the same than of the opposite sex (Lewis and Brooks-Gunn, 1979) for he assumes that such sex-typing depends for its appearance on the acquisition of gender identity at 3 years of age. Lastly, Kohlberg does not explain the acquisition of gender identity, nor why it becomes so crucial in the child's subsequent development. Recent attempts to make good this flaw in cognitive-developmental, as in social-learning theory, have suggested that the centrality of sex as a basis of social classification and hence its centrality to child development derives from the obviousness of sex difference (Lewis and Weinraub, 1979; Martin and Halverson, 1981). But this does not explain why this physical difference becomes crucial while other obvious physical differences (such as hair colour) do not become crucial in psychological development. Freudian psychoanalysis, on the other hand, does address this problem.

Psychoanalytic perspectives

Freud argued that psychological differentiation between the sexes is initiated by the 3- and 4-year-old's interpretation of genital sex difference in terms of castration and lack. Prior to this, he claimed, boys and girls are equally masculine and feminine in their attitudes and behaviour; they both equally entertain active as well as passive oral, anal, and genital strivings toward their primary care-giver, the mother. It is, he said, the genital eroticism of the phallic phase, and the significance that the child places on genital sex difference on account of this eroticism, that leads boys to become primarily masculine, and girls primarily feminine, in their subsequent behaviour.

The dawning of genital eroticism, at around age 4 says Freud, leads the boy to desire his mother genitally, thus bringing him into direct rivalry with his father. The boy dreads that his father will retaliate against his genital desire for the mother by castrating him. This dread now gives the genital difference between the sexes – previously ignored or denied – a new significance. Girls, it now seems to the boys, literally have been castrated. This interpretation fuels his castration anxiety and leads to the destruction or repression of his Oedipus complex, and to his identifying with the father and the masculine values he represents (Freud, 1977).

In girls, too, argues Freud, genital eroticism leads to their putting a new construction on the genital difference between the sexes. The penis, says Freud, 'strikingly visible and of large proportions', now seems on this account to be 'the superior counterpart of their small and inconspicuous organ'. Girls, claims Freud, accordingly 'fall a victim to envy for the penis' to which they respond either by giving up their phallic activity and their sexuality in general, or by clinging to the fantasy of being a man (that is, developing a 'masculinity complex'), or by following the 'very circuitous' path of 'normal' femininity in which they blame the mother for their genital lack and – drawing on the passive (feminine) trends of their bisexual constitution – turn instead to the father (Freud, 1977).

Feminists have generally objected on ideological grounds to Freud's argument that psychological sex differences originate in the child's erotically determined construction of the penis as superior to the clitoris. Instead, they have argued that this construction is socially, not biologically, determined (de Beauvoir, 1972; Friedan, 1965); for instance, that the construction is determined by the centrality given the phallus within male-dominated societies (Mitchell, 1974; Rubin, 1975). A more telling empirical objection to Freud's account of the development of psychological sex differences is that these differences appear well before the age at which Freud locates the first appearance of phallic eroticism and the castration complex. Nevertheless, there are some feminists who remain sympathetic to psychoanalysis, because its account of the unconscious and of the infantile roots of behaviour, unlike social-learning theory, seems to address the deep-rootedness of women's and men's psychological acquiescence in existing sexual divisions in society. Given the inadequacy of Freud's explanation of psychological sex differences in terms of the Oedipus complex, they have sought instead an explanation of these differences in terms of psychoanalytic accounts of the pre-Oedipal phase of development.

Post-Freudian accounts of this phase stress that it is initially marked by a sense of psychological fusion between mother and infant out of which mother and infant gradually come to individuate themselves as infancy progresses. Mothers, says Nancy Chodorow (1978), being the same sex as their daughters, tend on this account to merge more with them and therefore to prolong in them the experience of personal relations in terms of fusion. On the other hand, being the opposite sex from their sons, mothers tend to relate to them as separate and different, and hence propel them relatively early into the individuation process. As a result, claims Chodorow, boys and girls grow up with differing relational capacities: boys with the sense of separateness in personal relations that fits them for the impersonal demands of the labour market; girls with the sense of mergence and empathy in personal relations that fits them for the demands of childcare. In effect, Chodorow, unlike Freud, argues that psychological sex differences are initiated in infancy by the mother's, rather than by the child's, psychological response to the fact of biological sex similarity and difference.

The subtle sex differences in emotional dynamics between mother and infant postulated by Chodorow are neither addressed nor easily handled by social-learning or cognitive-developmental theory (Ingleby, 1981). Nevertheless, there is now considerable evidence for the early appearance of differences in the way women handle girl and boy babies (Moss, 1967; Smith and Lloyd, 1978). It might well be that one reason girls do so well in primary, as compared to secondary, schools is that the former are mainly staffed by women teachers who, like mothers, identify more on grounds of sex with girls, thus facilitating their school progress.

Chodorow's account of psychological sex differences, however, raises a recurrent problem with psychological perspectives on sexual divisions in society. Like biological determinist and social-learning theorists, Chodorow assumes that psychological sex differences smoothly fit men and women for existing sexual divisions in society. And this assumption is equally made by those who assume that education effectively functions to socialize girls and boys for the roles allotted to them as women and men by our society. But the very existence of the women's movement attests to the fact that neither psychology nor education smoothly conditions women into a primarily maternal and domestic role: women are even now vigorously protesting their discontent with this role. Neither biological determinist, nor social-learning, nor Chodorow's perspectives on psychological sex differences address the fact of resistance to existing sexual divisions. In contrast, Freud (1973), in his account of everyday errors and neurotic symptoms, drew attention to the way individuals both conform with and resist social, including sex-role, conventions. His theory of the unconscious, by which he explained these phenomena, provides a means of conceptualizing the contradiction between women's and men's psychological resistance to, and simultaneous acquiescence in, existing sexual divisions (Sayers, 1983) – something that is not provided by any of the other theories of gender development considered above.

Sex, society and gender development

I have sought to provide a critical, albeit brief, introduction to perspectives currently guiding research on the way individuals come to be situated psychologically in terms of existing sexual divisions in society. None of the theories outlined above is concerned with the origins of these divisions. This is not seen as problematic by those who adhere to biological determinism; they assume that gender development is directly determined by biology unmediated either by the child's construction of its gender identity, or by behavioural sex differences. Nor is it a problem for Freudian theorists who explain the acquisition of gender identity, and its centrality to the development of these differences, as an effect of the development of genital eroticism and the child's construction of genital sex difference.

However, as I have indicated, neither of these two theories adequately explains gender development. By contrast, social-learning and cognitive-developmental theorists, and Chodorow's use of post-Freudian psychoanalytic theory, assume, but do not explain, the psychological salience of biological sex to parents and children. Chodorow, as we have seen, assumes that mothers relate differently to boy and girl children because of the significance they attach to biological sex similarity and difference. Similarly, social-learning theorists assume that children quickly come to classify behaviours by sex, and to imitate these behaviours in accord with their own self-categorization by sex. Likewise, cognitive-developmental theorists assume, but do not explain, the acquisition of gender identity by the 3-year-old, and the centrality of this acquisition to the child's subsequent psychological development.

This centrality can only be explained by examining the way that social relations have come to be structured historically by sex. It is here that biology is important.

Biology does not directly determine sexual divisions. It does not entail, as some suggest (Firestone, 1970), that women be primarily tied to the home and dependent on a male breadwinner. The biological fact that women bear babies does not prevent them from participating substantially in 'breadwinning' activity, either in industrial or non-industrial societies (Slocum, 1975; Land, 1975). However, the way in which the biological fact of women's childbearing has interacted with forms of social and economic organization has had a significant impact on sexual divisions in society. The social and historical elaboration of this biological fact has resulted in a particular family household system that structures sexual divisions in social and educational institutions, and determines the direction of the sex-typing of educational and occupational activities (Coote and Campbell, 1982). It is because of the all-pervasive dichotomizing of social relations in these terms that sex is psychologically so salient to parents, teachers, and children, and hence is so central to psychological development (Bem, 1981). Any psychological theory must accordingly take into account the historical development of existing gender divisions if it is adequately to explain the psychological importance of sex in child development, and the current patterning of sex-role stereotypes.

References

Albert, A. A. and Porter, J. R. 'Age patterns in the development of children's gender-role stereotypes', *Sex Roles*, **9**, 1983, pp. 59–67.

Archer, J. and Lloyd, B., *Sex and Gender*, Harmondsworth, Penguin, 1982.

Ashton, E., 'Measures of play behavior: the influence of sex-role stereotyped children's books', *Sex Roles* **9** 1983, pp. 43–7.

Barrett, M., *Women's Oppression Today*, London, Verso, 1980.

Bem, S. L., 'Gender schema theory: a cognitive account of sex typing', *Psychological Review* **88**, 1981, pp. 354–64.

Chodorow, N., *The Reproduction of Mothering*, Berkeley, University of California Press, 1978.

Clarricoates, K., 'The importance of being Ernest . . . Emma . . . Tom . . . Jane. The perception and categorization of gender conformity and gender deviation in primary schools', in Deem, R. (ed.) *Schooling for Women's Work*, London, Routledge and Kegan Paul, 1980.

Constantinople, A., 1980, 'Sex-role acquisition: in search of the elephant', *Sex Roles*, **5**, 1979, pp. 121–33.

Coote, A. and Campbell, B., *Sweet Freedom: The Struggle for Women's Liberation*, London, Picador, 1982.

Damon, W., *The Social World of the Child*, San Francisco, Jossey-Bass, 1977.

de Beauvoir, S., *The Second Sex*, Harmondsworth, Penguin, 1972.

Deem, R. (ed.), *Schooling for Women's Work*, London, Routledge and Kegan Paul, 1980.

de Lacoste-Utamsing, C. and Holloway, R. L., 'Sexual dimorphism in the human corpus callosum', *Science* **216**, 1982, pp. 1431–2.

Dweck, C. S., 'Achievement' in Lamb, M. E. (ed.), *Social and Personality Development*, New York, Holt, Rinehart and Winston, 1978.

Emmerich, W., Goldman, S., Kirsh, B. and Sharabany, R., 'Evidence for a transitional phase in the development of gender constancy', *Child Development* **48**, 1977, pp. 930–6.

Etaugh, C. and Hadley, T., 'Causal attributions of male and female performance by young children', *Psychology of Women Quarterly*, **2**, 1977, pp. 16–23.

Fennema, E., 'Sex-related difference in mathematics achievement: where and why', in Fox, L. H. *et al.* (eds), *Women and the Mathematical Mystique*, Baltimore, Johns Hopkins University Press, 1980.

Firestone, S., *The Dialectic of Sex*, New York, Morrow, 1970.

Fox, L. H., Brody, I. and Tobin, D. (eds), *Women and the Mathematical Mystique*, Johns Hopkins University Press, 1980.

Freud, S., *Introductory Lectures on Psycho-Analysis*, Harmondsworth, Penguin, 1973.

Freud, S., 'The dissolution of the Oedipus complex', in *On Sexuality*, Harmondsworth, Penguin, 1977.

Freud, S., 'Female sexuality' in *On Sexuality*, Harmondsworth, Penguin, 1977.

Freud, S., *On Sexuality*, Harmondsworth, Penguin, 1977.

Friedan, B., *The Feminine Mystique*, Harmondsworth, Penguin, 1965.

Friedman, R. C., Richart, R. M. and Van de Wiele, R. L. (eds), *Sex Difficulties in Behaviour*, New York, Wiley, 1974.

Frieze, I. H., Whiteley, B. F., Hanusa, B. H. and McHugh, M. C., 'Assessing the theoretical models for sex differences in causal attributions for success and failure', *Sex Roles* **8**, 1982, pp. 333–43.

Garrett, C. S., Ein, P. I. and Tremaine, I., 'The development of gender stereo-typing of adult occupations by elementary school children', *Child Development* **48**, 1977, pp. 507–12.

Gilligan, C., *In a Different Voice: Psychological Theory and Women's Development*, Cambridge, Mass., Harvard University Press, 1982.

Goldberg, S., *The Inevitability of Patriarchy*, London, Temple Smith, 1977.

Gray, J. A., 'A biological basis for the sex differences in achievement in science?', in Kelly, A. (ed.), *The Missing Half: Girls and Science Education*, Manchester, Manchester University Press, 1981.

Ingleby, D., 'The politics of psychology: review of a decade,' *Psychology and Social Issues* no **2**, 1981, pp. 4–18.

Jacklin, C. N., Epilogue in Wittig. M. A. and Petersen, A. C. (eds), *Sex-Related Differences in Cognitive Functioning*, New York, Academic Press, 1979.

Jensen, A., 'How much can we boost IQ and scholastic achievement?', *Harvard Educational Review* **39**, 1969, pp. 1–123.

Jones, B. and Anuza, T., 'Sex differences in cerebral lateralization in 3- and 4-year old children', *Neuropsychologia* **20**, 1982, pp. 347–50.

Kelly, A. (ed.), *The Missing Half: Girls and Science Education*, Manchester, Manchester University Press, 1981.

Kiger, J. A. (ed.), *The Biology of Behaviour*, Corvallis, Oregon, Oregon University Press, 1972.

Kohlberg, L., 'A cognitive-developmental analysis of children's sex-role concepts and attitudes', in Maccoby, E. E. (ed.), *The Development of Sex Differences*, Stanford, Stanford University Press, 1966.

Kohlberg, L. and Ullian, D., 'Stages in the development of psychosexual concepts and attitudes', in Friedman, R. *et al.* (eds), *Sex Differences in Behavior*, New York, Wiley, 1974.

Kohlberg, I. and Zigler, E., 'The impact of cognitive maturity on the development of sex role attitudes in the years four to eight', *Genetic Psychology Monographs* **75**, 1967, pp. 89–165.

Kuhn, D., Nash, S. C. and Bruchen, L., 'Sex role concepts of two- and three-year-olds', *Child Development* **49**, 1978, pp. 445–51.

Lamb, M. E. (ed.), *Social and Personality Development*, New York, Holt, Rinehart and Winston, 1978.

Land, H., 'The myth of the male breadwinner', *New Society*, 9 October 1975, pp. 71–3.

Levy, J., 'Lateral specialization of the human brain: behavioral manifestations and possible evolutionary basis', in Kiger, J. A. (ed.), *The Biology of Behavior*, Oregon, Corvallis, Oregon University Press, 1972.

Lewis, M. and Brooks-Gunn, J., *Social Cognition and the Acquisition of Self*, New York, Plenum, 1979.

Lewis, M. and Weinraub, M., 'Origins of early sex-role development', *Sex Roles*, **5**, 1979, pp. 135–53.

Lloyd, B. and Archer, A. (eds), *Exploring Sex Differences*, London, Academic Press, 1976.

Maccoby, E. E. (ed.), *The Development of Sex Differences,* Stanford, Stanford University Press, 1966.

Maccoby G. E. and Jacklin C. N., *The Psychology of Sex Differences*, Stanford, Stanford University Press, 1974.

McGhee, P. E. and Frueh, T., 'Television viewing and the learning of sex-role stereotypes', *Sex Roles* **6**, 1980, pp. 179–88.

Marcus, D. E., and Overton, W. F., 'The development of cognitive gender constancy and sex role preferences', *Child Development* **49**, 1978, pp. 434–44.

Martin, C. L. and Halverson, C. F., 'A schematic processing model of sex typing and stereotyping in children', *Child Development* **52**, 1981, pp. 1119–34.

Meyer, B., 'The development of girls' sex-role attitudes', *Child Development* **51**, 1980, pp. 508–14.

Mischel, W., 'A social-learning view of sex differences in behavior', in Maccoby, E. E. (ed.), *The Development of Sex Differences*, Stanford, Stanford University Press, 1966.

Mitchell, J., *Psychoanalysis and Feminism*, London, Allen Lane, 1974.

Moss, H. A., 'Sex, age, and state as determinants of mother-infant interaction', *Merrill-Palmer Quarterly* **13**, 1967, pp. 19–36.

Orsini, A., Schiappa, O., Chiacchio, L., and Grossi, D., 'Sex differences in a children's spatial serial-learning task', *Journal of Psychology* **111**, 1982, pp. 67–71.

Parsons, J. E., Adler, T. F., and Kaczala, C. M., 'Socialization of achievement attitudes and beliefs: parental influences', *Child Development* **53**, 1982, pp. 310–21.

Piaget, J., *The Moral Judgment of the Child*, London, Routledge and Kegan Paul, 1932.

Raskin, P. and Israel, A., 'Sex-role imitation in children: effects of sex of child, sex of model, and sex-role appropriateness of modeled behavior', *Sex Roles* **7**, 1981, pp. 1067–77.

Reiter, R. R. (ed.), *Toward an Anthropology of Woman*, New York, Monthly Review Press, 1975.

Rose, H., 'Making science feminist', in Whitelegg, E. *et al.* (eds), *The Changing Experience of Women*, Oxford, Martin Robertson, 1982.

Rossi, A., 'A biosocial perspective on parenting', *Daedalus* **106**, 1977, pp. 1–32.

Rubin, G., 'The traffic in women: notes on the "political economy" of sex', in Reiter, R. R. (ed.), *Toward an Anthropology of Women*, New York, Monthly Review Press, 1975.

Saraga, E. and Griffiths, D., 'Biological inevitabilities or political choices? The future for girls in science', in Kelly, A. (ed.), *The Missing Half: Girls and Science Education*, Manchester, Manchester University Press, 1981.

Sayers, J., *Biological Politics: Feminist and Anti-Feminist Perspectives*, London, Tavistock, 1982.

Sayers, J., 'Is the personal political? Psychoanalysis and feminism revisited', *International Journal of Women's Studies* **6**, 1983, pp. 71–86

Scott, M., 'Teach her a lesson: sexist curriculum in patriarchal education', in Spender D. and Sarah, E. (eds) *Learning to Lose*, London, Women's Press, 1980.

Sharpe, S., *Just Like a Girl*, Harmondsworth, Penguin, 1976.

Slocum, S., 'Woman the gatherer: male bias in anthropology', in Reiter, R. R. (ed.), *Toward an Anthropology of Women*, New York, Monthly Review Press, 1975.

Smith, C., and Lloyd, B. B., 'Maternal behaviour and perceived sex of infant', *Child Development* **49**, 1978, pp. 1263–5.

Spender, D., and Sarah E. (eds), *Learning to Lose: Sexism and Education*, London, The Woman's Press, 1980.

Thompson, S. K., 'Gender labels and early sex role development', *Child Development* **46**, 1975, pp. 339–47.

Tieger, T., 'On the biological basis of sex differences in aggression', *Child Development* **51**, 1980, pp. 943–63.

Ullian, D. Z., 'The development of conceptions of masculinity and femininity', in Lloyd, B., and Archer, J. (eds), *Exploring Sex Differences*, London, Academic Press, 1976.

Urberg, K. A., 'The development of the concepts of masculinity and femininity in young children', *Sex Roles* **8**, 1982, pp. 659–68.

Walden, R. and Walkerdine, V., *Girls and Mathematics: The Early Years*, Bedford way Papers 8, University of London Institute of Education, 1982.

Walkerdine, V. 'Gender and the production of rationality in the family and at school', paper given in Manchester at the British Sociological Association Annual Conference, 'Gender and Society', 1982.

Weitzman, L. J., Eifler, D., Hokada, E., and Ross, C., 'Sex-role socialization in picture books for preschool children', *American Journal of Sociology* **77**, 1972, pp. 1125–50.

Whitelegg, E. *et al.* (eds) *The Changing Experience of Women*, Oxford, Martin Robertson 1982.

Wittig, M. A. and Petersen, A. C. (eds) *Sex-Related Differences in Cognitive Functioning*, New York, Academic Press, 1979.

Wilson, E. O. *On Human Nature*, Cambridge, Mass., Harvard University Press, 1978.

3 The 'sex-role' framework and the sociology of masculinity

Tim Carrigan, Bob Connell and John Lee

The upheaval in sexual politics of the last twenty years has mainly been discussed as a change in the social position of women. Yet change in one term of a relationship signals change in the other. From very early in the history of Women's Liberation it was clear that its politics had radical implications for men. A small 'Men's Liberation' movement developed in the 1970s among heterosexual men. Gay men become politicized as the new feminism was developing, and Gay Liberation politics have continued to call in question the conventional understanding of what it is to be a man. Academic sex-role research, though mainly about women in the family, was easily extended to the 'male role'. From several different directions in the 1970s, critiques and analyses of masculinity appeared. Quite strong claims about the emergence of a new area of study, and a new departure in sexual politics, were made. The purpose of this article is to bring together these attempts [and to] evaluate them.

The political meaning of writing about masculinity turns mainly on its treatment of power. Our touchstone is the essential feminist insight that the overall relationship between men and women is one involving domination or oppression. This is a fact about the social world that must have profound consequences for the character of men. It is a fact that is steadily evaded, and sometimes flatly denied, in much of the literature about masculinity written by men.

It is necessary to face the facts of sexual power without evasion but also without simplification. A central argument of this article is that the theoretical bases for doing so are now available, and a strong radical analysis of masculinity has become possible. Three steps open up this possibility. First, the question of sexual power has to be taken more seriously and pursued *inside* the sex categories. In particular the relations between heterosexual and homosexual men have to be studied to understand the constitution of masculinity as a political order, and the question of what forms of masculinity are socially dominant or hegemonic has to be explored. The writings of Gay Liberation theorists already provide important insights about this problem. Second, the analysis of masculinity needs to be related as well to other currents in feminism. Particularly important are those which have focused on the sexual division of labour, the sexual politics of workplaces, and the interplay of gender relations with class dynamics. Third, the analysis needs to use those developments in social theory in the last decade or so that offer ways past the dichotomies of structure versus individual, society versus the person, that have plagued the analysis of gender as much as the analysis of

Source: Extracted from Carrigan, T., Connell, M. and Lee, J., 'Towards a new sociology of masculinity', in *Theory and Society* **14**, 1985, pp. 531–604.

class. These developments imply a focus on the historical production of social categories, on power as the ability to control the production of people (in both the biological and psychological senses), and on large-scale structures as both the objects and effects of collective practice.

The early sociology of gender and the 'sex-role' framework

'The problem of women' was a question taken up by science generally in the second half of the nineteenth century, at first in a mainly biological framework. This was not simply part of the widening scope of scientific inquiry. It was clearly also a response to the enormous changes that had overtaken women's lives with the growth of industrial capitalism. And, towards the end of the century, it was a response to the direct challenge of the women's emancipation movement.

The political stakes were particularly evident in psychological research. The area usually referred to today as 'sex difference research' has been a major component in the development of social science work on gender. In the view of one prominent observer of the field, this work was originally

motivated by the desire to demonstrate that females are inherently inferior to males. . . . But from 1900 on, the findings of the psychologists gave strong support to the arguments of the feminists.[1]

By the mid[twentieth]-century functionalist sex-role theory dominated the western sociological discourse on women. The key figure in this development was Talcott Parsons, who in the early 1950s wrote the classic formulation of American sex-role theory, giving it an intellectual breadth and rigour it had never had before. The notion of 'role' as a basic structural concept of the social sciences had crystallized in the 1930s, and it was immediately applied to questions of gender. Two of Parsons's own papers of the early 1940s talked 'freely of sex roles'. In the course of his argument he offered an interesting account of several options that had recently emerged within the female role. There was, however, little sense of a power relation between men and women; and the argument embedded the issue of sex and gender firmly in the context of the family.[2]

For the rest of the 1940s Parsons was mainly occupied with the system-building for which he is now famous. When he returned to the theme of sex it was with questions of structure behind him, and questions of how people were fitted into structures – what he called 'socialization' – uppermost in his mind. The main tool he used on this problem was psychoanalysis, and his work thus is the first important encounter of Freudian thought on sexuality with the American sociology of gender – even if it was the rather bland version of psychoanalysis being naturalized in the United States at the time.

In the two chapters of the collaborative volume *Family, Socialization and Interaction Process* (1953) that represent the culmination of this development, Parsons achieved a notable synthesis. He brought together a structural account of kinship, the socialization problem in sociology, psychoanalytic accounts of personality formation, the internal interaction patterns of the household, and the sexual division of labour into a coherent argument.

At a key point Parsons [made] sex-role differentiation the problem, asking how it was to be explained. He rejected the biological-difference argument as utterly incapable of explaining the social pattern of sex roles. Rather, he derived it from a general sociological principle, the imperative of structural differentiation. Its particular form here was explained by the famous distinction between 'instrumental' and 'expressive' leadership. Parsons treated sex roles as the instrumental/expressive differentiation that operated within the conjugal family. And he treated the conjugal family both as a small group, and as the specific agency of the larger society entrusted with the function of socializing the young. Thus he deduced the gender patterning of roles, and their reproduction across generations, from the structural requirements of any social order whatever.

To this *tour de force* of reasoning Parsons added a sophisticated account of role acquisition, in the sense of how the role gets *internalized*. This is where psychoanalysis, with its account of the production of masculinity and femininity through different patternings of the Oedipal crisis, came into play. In effect, sex role becomes part of the very constitution of the person, through the emotional dynamics of development in the nuclear family.

Thus Parsons analysed the acquisition of sex roles as a matter of the production, from one generation to the next, of what we might call *gender personalities*. For example:

relative to the total culture as a whole, the masculine personality tends more to the predominance of instrumental interests, needs and functions, presumably in whatever social system both sexes are involved, while the feminine personality tends more to the primacy of expressive interests, needs and functions. We would expect, by and large, that other things being equal, men would assume more technical, executive and 'judicial' roles, women more supportive, integrative and 'tension-managing' roles.[3]

This notion provided Parsons then, as it provides role theorists still, with a powerful solution to the problem of how to link person and society. But its ability to do so was based on a drastic simplification. As phrases like 'the masculine personality' show, the whole argument is based on a normative standard case. Parsons was not in the least concerned about how many men (or women) are actually like that. Even the options within a sex role that he had cheerfully recognized in the earlier papers had vanished. All that was left in the theory was the normative case on the one hand, and on the other, deviance. Homosexuality, he wrote only a couple of pages after the passage just quoted, is universally prohibited so as to reinforce the differentiation of sex roles.

Apart from being historically false (homosexuality was and is institutionalized in some societies), such a theory fails to register tension and power processes *within* gender relations. Parsons recognizes many forms of 'role strain', but basically as a result of problems in the articulation of the different sub-systems of society. For instance, in his account the relation between the family and the economy is the source of much of the change in sex roles. The underlying structural notion in his analysis of gender is always differentiation, not relation. Hence his automatic assumption is that the connection between the two sex roles is one of complementarity, not power.

The institutional power that role theory enjoyed in sociology, especially in the United States – where as recently as the mid 1970s Komarovsky could describe

it simply as 'the generally accepted arsenal of sociological conceptual tools'[4] –
ensured that feminist questions would be posed in that framework, at least at the
start. Could this framework encompass feminist propositions? Especially could it
incorporate the notion of *oppression*, or as it was more often called in this literature,
the power differential between men and women?

Some feminist sociologists argued that this was perfectly possible; that role
theory had been misapplied, misunderstood, or had not been extended to its full
potential.[5] Yet by the late 1970s, other feminist sociologists were arguing that the
sex-role framework should be abandoned. Not only had the notion of 'role' been
shown to be incoherent. The framework continued to mask questions of power
and material inequality; or worse, implied that women and men were 'separate
but equal'.[6]

These criticisms underlined a more general problem: the discourse lacked a
stable theoretical object. 'Sex-role' research could, and did, wobble from psychological argument with biological assumptions, through accounts of interpersonal
transactions, to explanations of a macro-sociological character, without ever
having to resolve its boundaries. The elusive character of a discourse where issues
as important as that of oppression could appear, disappear, and re-appear in
different pieces of writing without anything logically compelling authors to stick
with and solve them, no doubt lies behind much of the frustration expressed in
these criticisms. As we shall see, this underlying incoherence was to have a
devastating influence on the sociological literature about men.

The 'male role' literature before women's liberation

A sociology of masculinity, of a kind, had appeared before the 'sex-role' paradigm.
Specific groups of boys and men had become the object of research when their
behaviour was perceived as a 'social problem'. Through the 1950s and 1960s the
most popular explanation of such social problems was 'father absence', especially
from poor or black families. The idea of 'father absence' had a broader significance, since the historical tendency of capitalism has been to separate home from
workplace. Most fathers earning wages or salaries are therefore absent from their
families much of the time. This imbalance was the focus of one of the first
sociological discussions of the *conflicts* involved in the construction of masculinity.

Ruth Hartley, in a paper published in 1959, related the absence of fathers and
the overwhelming presence of mothers to a widespread anxiety among American
boys, which was centred in the whole area of sex-connected role behaviours.

an anxiety which frequently expresses itself in overstraining to be masculine, in virtual
panic at being caught doing anything traditionally defined as feminine, and in hostility
toward anything even hinting at 'femininity,' including females themselves.[7]

Hartley's interviews produced a picture of boys who had distant relationships
with their fathers, who had been taught to eschew everything feminine from a
very early age while having to live in an environment dominated by women, and
who consequently constructed an oversimplified and over-emphasized understanding of masculinity within their peer groups. For Hartley, the basic problem
was not 'father absence' as such, so much as a pattern of masculine socialization

rigidly upheld by adults in a society where feminine roles were changing rapidly and the emancipation of women was well advanced.

Other sociologists, including David Riesman, proposed that in the modern male role, expressive functions had been added to the traditional instrumental ones.[8] The idea was clearly formulated by Helen Hacker in a notable paper called 'The new burdens of masculinity', published in 1957:

As a man, men are now expected to demonstrate the manipulative skill in interpersonal relations formerly reserved for women under the headings of intuition, charm, tact, coquetry, womanly wiles, et cetera. They are asked to bring patience, understanding, gentleness to their human dealings. Yet with regard to women they must still be sturdy oaks.[9]

This argument has become virtually a cliché in more recent writing. Hacker's paper is striking in its emphasis on conflict within masculinity. She pointed out that though the husband was necessarily often absent from his family, he was 'increasingly reproached for his delinquencies as father'. To compound the problem, men were also under pressure to evoke a full sexual response on the part of women. The result was the growing social visibility of impotence.

Male homosexuality was also becoming increasingly visible, and this was further evidence that 'all is not well with men'. It is notable that Hacker did not conceive of homosexuality in terms of the current medical model but in relation to the strong differentiation between masculine and feminine social roles.

The 'flight from masculinity' evident in male homosexuality may be in part a reflection of role conflicts. If it is true that heterosexual functioning is an important component of the masculine role in its social as well as sexual aspects, then homosexuality may be viewed as one index of the burdens of masculinity.[10]

Though Hacker probably viewed (more equal) heterosexual relations as the natural order of things, her remark in fact prefigured the perspective reached within the gay liberation movement twelve years later. Almost all subsequent sociological writing, however, has ignored Hacker's brief comments, as well as the gay movement's arguments, and has continued to take the heterosexual definition of masculinity for granted. Hacker never lost sight of the fact that masculinity exists as a power relation. Her appreciation of the effects of power led her to describe the possible range of masculine types as more restricted than that of feminine types. It also led to the suggestion 'that masculinity is more important to men than femininity is to women'.[11]

Lionel Tiger's *Men in Groups* (1969), was also a paradigmatic treatment of masculinity. It extensively documented men's control of war, politics, production, and sport, and argued that all this reflected a genetic pattern built into human beings at the time when the human ancestral stock took up co-operative hunting. Greater political participation by women would be going against the biological grain.

The notion that there is a simple continuity between biology and the social has been very powerful as ideology. So has another important feature of Tiger's argument, the way *relations* are interpreted as *differences*. The greater social power of men, and the sexual division of labour, are interpreted as 'sexual dimorphism' in behaviour. With this, the whole question of social structure is spirited away.

Tiger's scientific-sounding argument turns out to be pseudo-evolutionary speculation, overlaying a more sinister political message. Its drift becomes obvious in the book's closing fantasy about masculinity and its concern with 'hard and heavy phenomena', with warmongering being part of 'the masculine aesthetic', and arguments about what social arrangements are and are not 'biologically healthy'.[12]

[In contrast] Komarovsky's *Blue Collar Marriage* is one of the best pieces of empirical research on any topic produced by American sociology in its heyday.[13] Based on long interviews conducted in the late 1950s, the study yielded a vivid account of the interactions that actually constitute the politics of everyday life. Out of this came a picture of masculinity that was both more subtle, and harsher, than anything else written in its period. Though she did not use this terminology, she painted a picture of masculinity as something constructed in a very complex and often tense process of negotiation, mostly with women, that stretched right through adult life. The outcomes are never guaranteed; and there is a lot of variation in the patterns Komarovsky found. Nevertheless there was a general sense of unease. The working men she found in her American steel town were on the whole an unhappy lot, with little real communication with their wives, and constricted views of the world outside. There was a lot of prejudice and aimless anger around. Ten years later these themes were to be made a centre-piece of the 'men's movement' account of masculinity in general.

The 'male role' literature in the 1970s

The first effect of the new feminism on the study of men's roles was a dramatic increase in its volume. There was also a distinct change in mood. The advent of women's liberation and feminist critiques of patriarchy gave a focus to the literature on masculinity that it had never had before. There was now a degree of coherence to the discussion as a whole, a common set of issues, and for many of the authors, a distinct new genre of writing.

Much of this work could hardly be described as feminist. One of the most prominent themes in the 'male role' literature of the 1970s concerned the restrictions, disadvantages, and general penalties attached to being a man. 'Do men need women's liberation?' was a common question or point of reference, and the response was resoundingly 'Yes' – for the benefit of men. This was sometimes so that men too could become complete, authentic human beings. The title of one early paper, 'The inexpressive male: a tragedy of American society', captured the tone. But there were also more specific hazards in being male, not least being men's high rates of death and illness relative to women's. Problems for men given attention ranged from the threatening nature of their sex role for men as they age, and the role strain experienced by athletes and non-athletes, to the maladaptive effects of men's sexual socialization.[14]

The new literature viewed traditional masculinity as bad for two main reasons. First, it leads men to do nasty things, like compete with each other, oppress women, destroy the environment, and ruin the third world, notably by bombing Vietnam. Second, men are themselves uncomfortable with it. There is 'role strain', a 'male dilemma', a 'crisis of masculinity', men can't live up to their images. This was evidently a deeply felt point. The autobiographical sketches that peppered the 1970s books-about-men regularly remarked how the author had been taught the conventional male role, found it hard to inhabit, and eventually discovered the trouble was not in him but in the role.

Where then does masculinity come from? There were two starkly different views. The minority of authors who continued to reject feminism clung to the idea that masculinity is a product of genetic programming, derived from far back in our evolutionary history. Society might attempt to modify this, but did better just expressing it. The much more common view was that masculinity is the artificial product of conditioning, with biological differences of only minimal importance. Accounts of how this artificial production of masculinity occurs usually relied on a simplified social-learning theory. Parents' injunctions, school curricula, peer example, TV sports programmes, and car and cigarette advertising, were all laid out side by side as influences. They were usually assumed to be all pointing the same way. 'Conditioning', 'modelling', 'influence', were the terms typically used to describe the acquisition of the male role. Psychoanalytic accounts of gender were quite strikingly ignored.

There was a definite tendency in the masculinity literature to psychologize the feminist critique of men's oppression of women, and men's competition with each other. It typically located the source of the trouble in the heads of men, in their character structure, not in a structure of relationships. The feminist critique of the family was generally ignored. There was a very general re-interpretation of feminism to mean women breaking out of their roles, rather than women contesting men's power. The notion of the prevailing relationship between the sexes was therefore often one of 'segregation', not oppression. The personal/political site described by many feminists as 'patriarchy' became 'sex role stereotyping', and the cure, freer thinking.[15]

There was, however, a more positive side to the masculinity literature. It not only argued men are oppressed; it argued they need not be. A good deal of it was in fact devoted to the theme of changes in male character, and to rationalizing the idea of a modernized masculinity. In this, the notion of 'androgyny' came into its own, as a translation to the level of the individual of the earlier idea that the modern male role comprised expressive as well as instrumental elements. The 'healthy' modern man does not possess exclusively gender-consonant traits, but a mixture of masculine and feminine.

Perhaps the most striking feature of this writing was the appearance of a small industry of books about men, the male role, and masculinity. Though most of these books were ephemeral, the 1970s did see some substantial attempts to develop the sex-role perspective. Perhaps the most interesting is the work of Joseph Pleck. Pleck has built an academic career as a social psychologist primarily concerned with the male sex role; he is also one of the most prominent 'men's movement' publicists. His work has three main components: theoretical writing about how to understand sex roles, a programme of empirical research, and practical arguments about gender politics and associated social issues. Pleck's most substantial treatment of these themes is in his 1981 monograph *The Myth of Masculinity*. The title is curiously un-apt; the main argument is not about masculinity, let alone myths, but is a critique of one version of sex-role theory and an attempt to replace it with another.

It is clear enough what he wants to reject: biological determinism, depth psychology, simple masculinity/femininity scaling, and the notion of 'identity' as a key to the psychology of gender. Broadly, he wishes to replace this with a more thoroughgoing role perspective, emphasizing the importance of social expectations, the way both conformity to them and violation of them may be 'psychologically dysfunctional', and the strains arising from the fact that they change in history. Here, as elsewhere,[16] the essentialist understanding of the self common in much of the male-role literature is clear.

The inconclusiveness of all this is partly a result of muddled argument. Pleck tries to grasp historical change, for instance, by contrasting 'the modern male role' with 'the traditional male role'; in the 'traditional' basket are included not only the working-class and American ethnics but also 'primitive societies', making a theoretical category that should have quite a few anthropologists (Margaret Mead not least) turning in their graves. But more generally, the indeterminacy lies in the basic concepts of role theory itself; the more rigorously Pleck applies them, the more their underlying inadequacy appears. In an important paper called 'Men's power with women, other men, and society: A men's movement analysis', he proposes a connection between the subordination of women and the hierarchy of power among men. This hierarchy is maintained in terms of wealth, physical strength, age, and heterosexuality, and the competition among men to assert themselves in these terms produces a considerable amount of conflict.

Thus, men's patriarchal competition with each other makes use of women as symbols of success, as mediators, as refuges and as an underclass. In each of these roles, women are dominated by men in ways that derive directly from men's struggle with each other.[17]

Further, Pleck connects men's power to the sexual division of labour. Discussing the apparent contradiction of men exercising power in their family but enduring jobs where they are relatively powerless and that the great majority find meaningless, he argues that

They experience their jobs and themselves as worthwhile only through priding themselves on the hard work and personal sacrifice they are making to be breadwinners for their families. Accepting these hardships reaffirms their role as family providers and therefore as true men.[18]

Though criticisms could be made of both these formulations, the connections are important and the implications large. Here Pleck was beginning to move beyond 'role' notions altogether. But it was not sustained. Two later papers on the sexual division of labour lost all sense of power in gender relations, talking instead of sex-segregation 'norms'. In the second of these, Pleck had become quietly optimistic that men with working wives are now increasing their share of domestic work. A survey (based on men's self-reporting) found that these men did half an hour more of domestic work per day than other men. Pleck concludes that the 'changing role perspective' is more accurate than the 'exploitation perspective' as an approach to the question of men's domestic work. Comment seems unnecessary.[19]

In most ways Tolson's *Limits of Masculinity*[20] is the best thing yet written on the whole subject. It is, for one thing, a real attempt at a *sociology* of masculinity, concerned with the organization of power on a large scale. Tolson goes through the research literature of family, community, and workplace studies, mining it for evidence about the situation and activities of men; and in consequence is able to make the first serious attempt to explore class differences in the construction and expression of masculinity. The book's central theme, unlike most writing on masculinity, is the social relations of the workplace, and Tolson presents very interesting material on what he calls the 'culture of work' and the ways masculinity is both constructed and undermined by the dynamics of the capitalist labour process. More, he offers an account of the psychodynamics of masculinity, focusing on both father–son and peer relations as sources of the emotional reactions that sustain masculinity.

Not all of this is successful. Though the description of workplaces, and especially working-class daily life, is vivid, the underlying sociology is rather structuralist. Tolson's account of the Oedipal crisis is confused. His notion of masculinity is still mainly based on a trait notion of personality, and the consequence of that is a good deal of stereotyping. But he goes a long way to showing what can be done when the interaction of capitalism and patriarchy, rather than a search for the real self, is taken as the starting point for an understanding of masculinity.

Tolson at least lends support to gay liberation; but it is notable that he treats 'gay' and 'masculine', 'gays' and 'men', as quite separate concepts. In this, he is very much in the tradition of the books-about-men. Works in the genre range between generally ignoring homosexuals and homosexuality, and totally ignoring them. In this evasion is a final confirmation of the political meaning of the 'men's movement' and the books-about-men genre. It is not, fundamentally, about uprooting sexism or transforming patriarchy, or even understanding masculinity in its various forms. What it is about is *modernizing* hegemonic masculinity. It is concerned with finding ways in which the dominant group – the white, educated, heterosexual, affluent males – can adapt to new circumstances without breaking down the social-structural arrangements that actually give them their power.

Broadly, the '[sex-]role' framework has been used to analyse what the difference is between the social positions of women and men, to explain how they are shaped for those positions, and to describe the changes and conflicts that have occurred in and about those positions. At the simplest level, it is clear that the sex-role framework accepts that sexual differentiation is a social phenomenon: sex roles are learnt, acquired, or 'internalized'. But the precise meaning of the sociality proposed by the framework is not nearly as simple as its proponents assume.

The problem here is that the sex-role literature does not consistently distinguish between the expectations that are made of people and what they in fact do. The framework often sees variations from the presumed norms of male behaviour in terms of 'deviance', as a 'failure' in socialization. This is particularly evident in the functionalist version of sex-role theory, where 'deviance' becomes an unexplained, residual, and essentially non-social category.

As social theory, the sex-role framework is fundamentally static. This is not to say that it cannot recognize social change. Quite the contrary: change has been a leading theme in the discussion of men's sex roles by authors such as Pleck. The problem is that they cannot grasp it as history, as the interplay of praxis and structure. Change is always something that *happens to* sex roles, that impinges on them – whether from the direction of the society at large (as in discussions of how technological and economic change demands a shift to a 'modern' male sex role), or from the direction of the asocial 'real self' inside the person, demanding more room to breathe. Sex-role theory cannot grasp change as a dialectic arising within gender relations themselves.

The role framework, then, is neither a conceptually stable nor a practically and empirically adequate basis for the analysis of masculinity. Let us be blunt about it. The 'male sex role' does not exist. It is impossible to isolate a 'role' that constructs masculinity (or another that constructs femininity). Because there is no area of social life that is not the arena of sexual differentiation and gender relations, the notion of a sex role necessarily simplifies and abstracts to an imposs-ible degree.

Gay liberation and the understanding of masculinity

The masculinity literature before women's liberation was frankly hostile to homo-sexuality, or at best very wary of the issue. What is post-women's-liberation is also post-gay-liberation. Gay activists were the first contemporary group of men to address the problem of hegemonic masculinity outside of a clinical context. They were the first group of men to apply the political techniques of women's liberation, and to align with feminists on issues of sexual politics – in fact to argue for the importance of sexual politics.

The gay movement has been centrally concerned with masculinity as part of its critique of the political structure of sexuality. [It] attacked the social practices and psychological assumptions surrounding gender relations, for a prominent theme in [its] arguments is an attempt to explain the sources of homosexual oppression in these terms. The British gay liberation newspaper *Come Together* declared in 1970:

> We recognize that the oppression that gay people suffer is an integral part of the social structure of our society. Women and gay people are both victims of the cultural and ideological phenomenon known as sexism. This is manifested in our culture as male supremacy and heterosexual chauvinism.[21]

Activists argued that homosexual people were severely penalized by a social system that enforced the subservience of women to men, and which propagated an ideology of the 'natural' differences between the sexes. The denial and fear of homosexuality were an integral part of this ideology because homosexuals were seen to contradict the accepted characteristics of men and women, and the com-plementarity of the sexes that is institutionalized within the family and many other areas of social life.[22]

Not surprisingly then, the gay movement has been particularly critical of psychi-atric definitions of homosexuality as a pathology, and of the concern with 'curing' homosexuals, a phenomenon of twentieth-century medicine marked by both theor-etical incoherence and practical failure. Activists readily observed the ways in which notions such as 'gender inversion' were a transparent rationalization of the prevailing relationship between men and women. For the whole medical model of homosexuality rested upon a belief in the biological (or occasionally socially-functional) determination of heterosexual masculinity and femininity. The gay liberation tactic in this and many other areas was one of a defiant reversal of the dominant sexual ideology. In affirming a homosexual identity, many gay liberationists embraced the charge of effeminacy and declared that the real problem lay in the rigid social definitions of masculinity. It was society, not themselves, that needed to be cured.[23]

To understand gay liberation's political responses, we should observe how the gender dichotomy acts to define homosexual men not only as 'outside' of patriarchal sexual relations, but 'within' them as well. In the first case, as we have just noted, homosexual men are penalized for failing to meet the criteria of masculinity, and are told that they are weak, effeminate, maladjusted, and so on. But they have often been defined 'within' patriarchal sexual relations by being divided into 'active' and 'passive' types. Gay activists argued very strenuously that when homosexual men consequently organized a relationship in terms of husband and wife 'roles', they were expressing self-hatred in a futile attempt to win heterosexual tolerance. More centrally, activists attacked sexual 'role playing' or concepts of oneself as 'butch' or 'femme'. The objection was not simply that this was sexist and bizarrely conformist; there was an agonizing personal trap for homosexual men in such a conception.

The most general significance of the gay liberation arguments was that they challenged the assumptions by which heterosexuality is taken for granted as the natural order of things. It is, for example, a fundamental element of modern hegemonic masculinity that one sex (women) exists as potential sexual object, while the other sex (men) is negated as a sexual object. It is women, therefore, who provide heterosexual men with sexual validation, whereas men exist as rivals in both sexual and other spheres of life. The gay liberation perspective emphasized that the institutionalization of heterosexuality, as in the family, was achieved only by considerable effort, and at considerable cost not only to homosexual people but also to women and children. It is, then, precisely within heterosexuality as it is presently organized that a central dimension of the power that men exercise over women is to be found.

The gay movement's theoretical work, by comparison with the 'sex role' literature and 'men's movement' writings, had a much clearer understanding of the reality of men's power over women, and it had direct implications for any consideration of the hierarchy of power among men.

What emerges from this line of argument is the very important concept of *hegemonic masculinity*, not as 'the male role', but as a particular variety of masculinity to which others – among them young and effeminate as well as homosexual men – are subordinated. It is particular groups of men, not men in general, who are oppressed within patriarchal sexual relations, and whose situations are related in different ways to the overall logic of the subordination of women to men. A consideration of homosexuality thus provides the beginnings of a dynamic conception of masculinity as a structure of social relations.

Gay liberation arguments further strengthen a dynamic approach to masculinity by providing some important insights into the historical character of gender relations. Homosexuality is a historically specific phenomenon, and the fact that it is socially organized becomes clear once we distinguish between homosexual *behaviour* and a homosexual *identity*. While some kind of homosexual behaviour may be universal, this does not automatically entail the existence of self-identified or publicly labelled 'homosexuals'. In fact, the latter are unusual enough to require a historical explanation. Jeffrey Weeks and others have argued that in western Europe, male homosexuality did not gain its characteristically modern meaning and social organization until the late nineteenth century.[24]

The emerging history of male homosexuality offers the most valuable starting point we have for constructing a historical perspective on masculinity at large. Conceptually, gay history moves decisively away from the conception that the history of masculinity is the story of the modulation, through time, of the expressions of a more or less fixed entity.[25]

The history of homosexuality obliges us to think of masculinity not as a single object with its own history, but as being constantly constructed within the history of an evolving social structure, a structure of sexual power relations. It obliges us to see this construction as a social struggle going on in a complex ideological and political field, in which there is a continuing process of mobilization, marginalization, contestation, resistance, and subordination. It forces us to recognize the importance of violence, not as an expression of subjective values or of a type of masculinity, but as a constitutive practice that helps to make all kinds of masculinity – and to recognize that much of this violence comes from the state, so the historical construction of masculinity and femininity is also a struggle for the control and direction of state power. Finally it is an important corrective to the tendency, in left-wing thought especially, to subordinate the history of gender to the history of capitalism. The making of modern homosexuality is plainly connected to the development of industrial capitalism, but equally clearly has its own dynamic.

Notes and references

1 L. Tyler, *The Psychology of Human Differences*, New York, Appleton Century Crofts, 1965, p. 240.

2 T. Parsons, 'Age and Sex in the Social Structure of the United States', in *Essays in Sociological Theory*, New York, The Free Press, 1964, pp. 89–103; and, in the same volume, 'The Kinship System of the Contemporary United States', pp. 177–96.

3 T. Parsons and R. F. Bales, *Family, Socialization and Interaction Process*, London, Routledge and Kegan Paul, 1953, p. 101.

4 M. Komarovsky, *Dilemmas of Masculinity*, New York, Norton, 1976, p. 7.

5 See, for example, M. Komarovsky, 'Presidential Address: Some Problems in Role Analysis', *American Sociological Review* **38**, December 1973, pp. 649–62; M. Millman, 'Observations on Sex Role Research', *Journal of Marriage and the Family* **33**, November 1971, pp. 772–6; and E. Peal, ' "Normal" Sex Roles: An Historical Analysis', *Family Process* 14 September 1975, pp. 389–409.

6 See, for example, A. R. Edwards, 'Sex Roles: A Problem for Sociology and for Women', *Australian and New Zealand Journal of Sociology* **19**, 1983, pp. 385–412; S. Franzway and J. Lowe, 'Sex Role Theory, Political Cul-de-sac?' *Refractory Girl* **16**, 1978, pp. 14–16; M. Gould and R. Kern-Daniels, 'Toward a Sociological Theory of Gender and Sex', *American Sociologist* **12**, November 1977, pp. 182–9; and H. Z. Lopata and B. Thorne, 'On the Term "Sex Roles" ', *Signs* **3**, Spring 1978, pp. 718–21.

7 R. E. Hartley, 'Sex Role Pressures in the Socialization of the Male Child', *Psychological Reports* **5**, 1959, pp. 458.

8 D. Riesman, *The Lonely Crowd*, Garden City, Doubleday and Anchor Books, 1953.

9 H. M. Hacker, 'The New Burdens of Masculinity', *Marriage and Family Living* **19**, August 1957, pp. 229.

10 Ibid., p. 231.

11 Ibid., p. 231.

12 L. Tiger, *Men in Groups*, London, Nelson, 1969, p. 209.

13 M. Komarovsky, *Blue Collar Marriage*, New York, Vintage, 1964.

14 J. O. Balswick, 'The Inexpressive Male: A Tragedy of American Society', paper at meeting of American Sociological Association, 1970; C. E. Lewis and M. A. Lewis, 'The Potential Impact of Sexual Equality on Health', *New England Journal of Medicine* **297**, October 1977, pp. 863–9; J. K. Burgess-Kohn, 'A Note on Role Changes that Prepare Men for the Ageing Process', *Wisconsin Sociologist* **13**, 1976, pp. 85–90; P. J. Stein and S. Hoffman, 'Sports and Male Role Strain', *Journal of Social Issues* **34**, Winter 1978, pp. 136–50; A. E. Gross, 'The Male Role and Heterosexual Behaviour', *Journal of Social Issues* **34**, Winter 1978, pp. 87–107.

15 J. Nichols, *Men Liberation*, New York, Penguin, 1975.

16 J. H. Pleck, 'The Male Sex Role: Definitions, Problems and Sources of Change', *Journal of Social Issues* **32**, 1976, pp. 155–64.

17 J. H. Pleck, 'Men's Power With Women, Other Men, and Society: A Men's Movement Analysis', in Pleck and Pleck, *The American Man*, p. 427.

18 Ibid., p. 428.

19 J. H. Pleck, 'The Work-Family Role System', *Social Problems* **24**, April 1977, pp. 417–27; and 'Men's Family Work: Three Perspectives and Some New Data', *The Family Coordinator* **28**, October 1979, pp. 481–8.

20 A. Tolson, *The Limits of Masculinity*, London, Tavistock, 1977.

21 A. Walter (ed.), *Come Together*, London, Gay Men's Press, 1980, p. 49.

22 M. Mich, *Homosexuality and Liberation*, London, Gay Men's Press, 1980; D. Fernbach, *The Spiral Path*, London, Gay Men's Press, 1981.

23 R. Bayer, *Homosexuality and American Psychiatry*, New York, Basic Books, 1981.

24 J. Weeks, *Coming Out*, London, Quartet, 1977; J. Weeks, *Sex, Politics and Society*, London, Longman, 1981; K. Plummer, (ed.), *The Making of the Modern Homosexual*, London, Hutchinson, 1981.

25 P. Hoch, *White Hero, Black Beast*, London, Pluto Press, 1979; J. L. Dubbert, *A Man's Place*, Englewood Cliffs, Prentice Hall, 1979; P. N. Sterns, *Be a Man!*, New York, Holmes & Meier, 1979; F. H. Pleck and J. H. Pleck (eds), *The American Man*, Englewood Cliffs, Prentice Hall, 1980.

4 Theories of gender and black families

Ann Phoenix

A great deal has already been written about gender relations and how women and men come to have gendered subjectivities. However, most of this writing, whether theoretical or empirical, has been based on the experiences of white women and men (or white girls and boys). This chapter first explores the consequence of this concentration on gender relations exclusively in white people, then considers whether existing theories of gender are relevant to black people of Afro-Caribbean origin. Black people of Asian origin are similarly omitted from theories of gender development. However, some of their gender experiences differ from black people of Afro-Caribbean origin and therefore need to be dealt with separately.

Gender relations and colour

Work on gender is usually reported as if colour and class were not salient to gender relations (see for example the review by Henshall and McGuire, 1986). From this it might be presumed that black people and white people develop gender identities in similar ways. If that were the case colour would be irrelevant to work on gender.

However, the reality of racism means that black people have less access to sources of societal power than white people. Black children and white children therefore have different developmental experiences. There is no evidence that gender relations as described in the literature are not specific to the white people who were the subjects of the research on which the theories were founded. In order to understand why black people are omitted from most work on gender relations it is necessary to consider how black people are generally treated in research and academic literature.

When 'normal' processes are being studied, black people are usually excluded from samples for two sorts of reasons. The first set of reasons is to do with the strict control of the number of variables in studies. This is thought to be necessary if the findings of the study are to be clearly interpreted as being due to the independent variables being investigated. Phrases like 'No blacks or Hispanics were included . . . hence some degree of homogeneity was established. . . ' (Sebald, 1986) are indicative of this set of reasons. This exclusion of black people suggests

Source: Commissioned.

that it is white people who develop and behave in normal ways, while black people are exceptions to the norm, deviant or pathological.

The other set of reasons for the exclusion of black people from research samples are the result of what Jennifer Platt (1985) calls 'samples of opportunity'. Researchers frequently study samples that live conveniently near their university departments, or that are visiting the university for some purpose. These localities are frequently white and middle class. This means that the sampling does not ensure that the final sample is representative of the general population of a town or of the country as a whole. Platt points out that samples of opportunity are not adequate when generalizations are to be made from data. This criticism is even more pertinent when generalizations are to be made from a local study which completely omits a significant section of the population, namely black people.

Whatever the reason for the exclusion of black people from certain research projects, the effect is to underline the common-sense view that black people are different from white people. This differentiation is reinforced by studies of pathological or deviant situations which focus exclusively on black people. So for example there are a number of studies of 'teenage' mothers which include only or predominantly black women (Furstenberg, 1976; Field *et al.*, 1980). This focus is especially significant because when 'normal' mothering and 'normal' child development are being studied black women are excluded in the ways already described. 'Teenage motherhood' is highly socially stigmatized and yet this is one of the areas in which black women are made visible. Black households are included in a similar way when 'father-absence' (another stigmatized category) is being studied.

However, this normalized absence/pathologized presence couplet is not the sole constituent of research's contribution to the maintenance of existing power relations between black people and white people. Academic work is conducted within a social context in which racism means that black people are socially devalued and white people are socially valued. Most researchers are white, and as a result are likely not to share the same perspectives as black people. Research therefore must be suspect when conducted within the value systems of a racist society. This means that when comparisons are made between groups of black people and groups of white people research continues to construct white people as the norm and black people as abnormal by comparison. This is equally true of studies which concentrate mainly on white people but include a single section on black people (see, for example, Sharpe, 1976).

The best-known examples of comparisons between black people and white people are probably black–white IQ differences, and differences in educational achievement between black children and white children. It is not that black–white comparisons are in themselves reprehensible; rather the interpretations placed on findings (particularly by those who espouse hereditarian views) are individualistic and locate pathology in black people while leaving social and political causes untheorized and unchallenged in a way that Ryan (1972) calls 'blaming the victim'. (For a more detailed discussion of how black families are pathologized in British society see Parmar, 1982 and Lawrence, 1982.)

The treatment of women in academic literature has paralleled the treatment of black people described above. Researchers on major social issues have in the past omitted women from their samples but made generalizations about the whole population from the data (see, for example, Willis, 1977). Comparisons have also been made between women's and men's abilities and behaviours in such a way that women are presented as being inferior (see Archer and Lloyd, 1982, for further discussion of this). It is therefore ironic that white feminist writings, which have had significant impact on the way that women are treated in academic (and popular) literature, should themselves also exclude black (and working-class) women and hence help maintain the power differentials between black women and white women (see Carby, 1982; the black women's issue of *Feminist Review*, 1984; Brah and Minhas, 1985; Hooks, 1982 and 1984; and Bhavnani and Coulson, 1986, for discussions of how white feminism has refused to address issues of racism, and hence colluded with racism).

Theories of gender development and 'the family'

Human development does not, of course, occur in a vacuum. It occurs within specific contexts. 'The family' is implicitly given centrality in most theories of normal or optimal child development. In studies of child development parents (predominantly mothers), are usually either observed in interaction with or interviewed about their children. This emphasis on parents only occurs because parents are considered to be (and in this society undeniably are) a major influence on their children. The family therefore is a crucial site for the production of the 'normal' child, who among other things shows appropriate gender behaviour and has the gender identity appropriate to her/his sex.

The social construction of the normal family which is thought best suited to the production of the normal children described above is a highly specific one. In the 'normal' family, marriage and the having of children are inextricably linked so that marriage entails having children, and the conception of children should necessarily follow marriage (Busfield, 1974). Once children are born, provision for them is divided between the parents on gender lines.

Fathers are expected to be in a position to make economic provision for their children by having paid employment. By contrast women are expected to stay at home with their children and to be responsible not only for fulfilling their children's basic needs, but also for the ways in which their children develop. This means that mothers need to engage in high quality interactions with their children and to have some knowledge of child development (Urwin, 1985). Mother–child dyads are observed in interaction together as if their homes were isolated from the rest of society. This 'desert-island' approach (Riley, 1983) ignores considerations of how material conditions such as housing and income affect how parents are able to deal with their children. It also has a 'normalizing effect' (Henriques *et al.*, 1984) in that it confirms that it is both right and normal for women and children to be locked up alone with each other all day.

The pervasiveness of this model of the 'normal' family within current dominant ideology means that it is the model implicitly assumed in cultural theories of gender development. (Biologically determinist explanations suggest that gender differences are naturally occurring rather than being subject to environmental influences. They therefore do not require any particular family type for gender development and will not be dealt with here.)

There are three major theories of the processes by which gender development occur. In social-learning theories the child learns gender stereotyped roles through observation and imitation of the same sex parent. In addition parents, by using rewards and punishments, condition children into appropriate gender behaviour. In cognitive-developmental theory (Kohlberg, 1966) the child actively learns that each person throughout life belongs to one of two genders. In psychoanalytic theory it is the awareness of genital sex differences between males and females that eventually leads young children to identify with the same gender parents. (See Sayers, this volume, for discussion of these processes.)

What these three theories have in common is that they assume that children live with both parents. Parents provide the child with the first experiences of what it means to be gendered. So, for example, according to social learning theory parents act as role-models for their children as well as providing them with reinforcement for their gender related behaviour. Similarly, in cognitive-developmental theory parents are an important source of information about gender related behaviours. In psychoanalytic theory children learn gender identification both by observing the behaviour of their parents towards each other, and competing with and identifying with them. This is not to suggest that parents are the only influence on children's gender development. School, other adults and other children, the media, etc. all have an acknowledged role in theories of gender development. The point is that the nuclear family is implicitly included as important in these theories.

The assumed importance of this family type has led to a great deal of research on parental influences on gender development. This research in general has searched for pathological gender development in 'father absent' households (which in reality is frequently synonymous with 'single parent' households), and for the concomitants of normal development, as well as the significance of particular parental behaviours in two parent households.

Many children in western societies do not, however, live in nuclear families. In Britain it is estimated that at any one time 9 per cent of all children under 16 years of age live with their mothers but not with their fathers (New and David, 1985). This percentage represents over 1.25 million children. A large number of children, for some or all of their childhood, do not, therefore, live in the type of family which has been used to construct theories of gender development and which has gained acceptance as the best site for the production and reproduction of gendered subjectivity.

Families without fathers

The occurrence of female headed households is not evenly spread among the population. For a variety of socio-political and historical reasons (including the fact that there are many more black women than black men in the USA) black women of Afro-Caribbean origin in this country, and of African origin in the USA are much more likely not to live with their children's fathers (see Bryan *et al.*, 1985, for discussion of the British situation, and Hooks, 1982; Davis, 1981; and

Marable 1983 for the USA). In the USA 50 per cent of black children of African origin live in female headed households. In Britain the comparable figures are 31 per cent for black women of Afro-Caribbean origin compared with 5 per cent for black women of Asian origin and 10 per cent for white women (Brown, 1984). Black children are thus least likely to live in the family grouping considered most suitable for gender development or development in general.

Black women of Afro-Caribbean origin are not the only mothers who are likely to live apart from their children's fathers. In 1985, 65 per cent of births to women who were under 20 years of age were to single women (OPCS, 1986). This percentage is not solely composed of women who do not live with their children's fathers because some of these women will be cohabiting. However it is an indication that in this age group it is now not normative to follow the pattern expected in dominant reproductive ideologies.

Since different family structures are now not uncommon in British society, it is important to gain some understanding of how this diversity affects children's gender development. Research on 'father absence' has concentrated on comparing children who live alone with their mothers with children who live with both parents. The findings of these studies usually show that children who live in households without their fathers are less academically successful, and have more behaviour problems than those who live with both parents (Lamb, 1976; Biller, 1981). These findings are usually attributed to lack of paternal interaction for children of both genders and to boys' lack of a role model to provide sufficient opportunities for social learning. Boys are considered to suffer more than girls from 'father absence'.

By extension the poor educational achievement of black children of Afro-Caribbean descent is frequently blamed on 'father absence' (Scarr *et al.*, 1983; Swann Report, 1985), which is used as a shorthand for inadequate socialization. Similarly, analyses of urban unrest in the popular media give explanations in terms of the pathology of the West Indian family (Lawrence, 1982). Recent reviews of literature in this area have pointed out the unsatisfactory nature of research in this field, and how it fails to take into account such factors as length of father absence, age of children when absence begins, reason for absence etc. as potentially significant (Henshall and McGuire, 1986; Archer and Lloyd, 1982).

Because research on gender development starts from a theoretical position which presumes that fathers are crucial to good child development it fails to give sufficient consideration to precisely how, when, and what it is that fathers actually contribute to the process of child development. Most people would agree that it is desirable that fathers should share the care of their young children. However a study which compares how much modern fathers do with their 1-year-old children compared with thirty years ago suggests that, contrary to popular beliefs, fathers have not started to interact significantly more with their children than their fathers' generation (Lewis, 1984). More research is required on what inter-active and non-interactive fathers contribute to their children's gender development.

For black people this lack of research, together with the popular definition of black parents as predominantly 'single parent', helps to both produce and reproduce dominant ideological assumptions about the pathology of black families. It also means that black children are not considered to have received proper gender socialization.

Interest in 'father absence' has meant a concentration on parents and the household as primarily responsible for child outcomes. This excludes social network influences and wider social and political influences on gender identity. Children are not, however, monocultural. It is rare for them to be exposed only to their parents and to stay only in one setting. Television, for example, is an external influence and in addition most children eventually go to school where they meet a variety of people. This approach is therefore not 'ecologically valid', to use Bronfenbrenner's (1977) terms.

Ecologically valid attempts to theorize the process whereby all children acquire gendered subjectivity would require developmental researchers to expand the age range they study beyond the current concentration on the very early years. It would also require that children be studied in interaction with other people as well as their parents, and in more than one setting (for instance, Dunn and Kendrick, 1982, study on siblings and mothers; Tizard and Hughes, 1984, study of young children learning at home and in the nursery school). It must also be remembered that children do not learn about gender in isolation. They learn about it as they simultaneously learn about other social facts in their world, like race and class.

So far it has been suggested that the only structural difference between black households which have children in them and similar white households that has been discussed is the greater likelihood that black mothers will be single rather than married or cohabiting. However black women are more likely to be in full-time paid employment than are white women. In 1982, 41 per cent of black women of Afro-Caribbean origin were in paid employment compared with 21 per cent of black women of Asian origin and 21 per cent of white women. If part-time employment and self-employment are included, then 59 per cent of black women of Afro-Caribbean origin were in paid employment compared with 29 per cent of black women of Asian origin and 41 per cent of white women (Brown, 1984).

These figures unfortunately do not tell us how many of these employed women have children, particularly children who are under 5 years of age. However, the Women and Employment Survey showed that 20 per cent of women with pre-school children in Britain work part time, while 7 per cent work full time. 56 per cent of mothers with dependent children are in some form of paid employment (Martin and Roberts, 1984). Thus a substantial proportion of young children receive some care from people other than their mothers. It seems clear that black mothers of Afro-Caribbean origin are more often in paid employment outside the home than are white mothers.

It is thus important to consider issues of ecological validity in research on the acquisition of gender identity. Many children, particularly black ones, are cared for by people other than their mothers. The fact that 'it is almost always women's work to care for and educate children, whether at home . . .' or elsewhere (New and David, 1985) does not mean that children learn exactly the same things from the different women who look after them. Black women know that their structural circumstances mean that they have no choice but to try to be economically independent (see Bryan *et al.*, 1985). This means that black mothers tend to explicitly teach this to their daughters (Joseph, 1981), while the mothers described by Eichenbaum and Orbach (1985) (who are presumably white), subtly encourage their daughters to be emotionally, rather than economically, independent. Moreover the process of gender development may well be different if there is lack of congruence between mother and caregiver about the way boys and girls are treated and expected to behave, than it would be if they were congruent.

There is no substantial evidence that maternal employment outside the home by itself causes children to hold less gender stereotypic views about women's roles (New and David, 1985). This adds weight to the argument that it is over-simplistic for theories of gender development to implicitly assume that the mother necessarily has a privileged position of influence on gender development. This must be particularly so in families where several individuals share the care of children. These families are currently more likely to be black than to be white. The psychic development of children who grow up in these circumstances remains unexplored in psychoanalytic literature probably because therapists are more likely to see white middle-class rather than black working-class women.

Gender differences

While different processes for the acquisition of gender have been theorized, the structure that facilitates those processes (that is, the nuclear family) is, as discussed above, usually implicitly assumed. In a similar way the content that is to be processed is presumed to be obvious and commonly shared. However, societal divisions of race and class mean not only that the process of gender development is different for different groups of people, but also that gender is differently experienced by black people and white people, by working-class people and middle-class people.

Comparing differences between any two groups tends to polarize them and minimize their similarities. A secondary effect of this is that the two polarized groups appear internally homogeneous. However, there are important within-group differences between women and between men which have relevance for theories of gender development. The effects of racism and what this means for the class position of black people means that black children grow up knowing that black women and black men are in a qualitatively different position from white women and white men.

In western patriarchal societies men gain more educational qualifications than women. Even if educational qualifications are controlled, men obtain proportionally more high status jobs (Archer and Lloyd, 1982). These differences are reflected in family relationships. Governments as well as the rest of society accord men the status of 'heads of households' and provide family benefits on that basis. If there are children in a household, it is women, not men, who bear the weight of societal expectations (which they may or may not share) that they will stay at home, care for and educate those children, giving up any paid employment they have in order to do so.

Since stereotypes usually have political implications and can provide a window on how different groups are perceived in a society, it is useful to consider how women and men are commonly stereotyped. Women are stereotyped as being the complementary opposite of men. They are supposed to be nurturant, passive, weak and non-competitive while men are supposed to be aggressive, active, powerful and competitive – qualities which have frequently been used to justify male dominance of society. This is allegedly the content that girls and boys learn in the process of becoming gendered.

Not surprisingly, however, these stereotypes do not fit all women or all men. In fact descriptions of male and female behaviour and dominant/subordinate positions actually relate only to the situation of those who hold most power within society, the white middle classes. This leaves gender relations between black people and working-class people untheorized and invisible.

In general black people of African origin in the USA and of Afro-Caribbean origin in Britain, gain few educational qualifications (Swann Report, 1985; Eggleston, Dunn and Anjali, 1984; and Staples, 1985). When they do gain educational qualifications it is more likely to be women rather than men who achieve these (Fuller, 1983; Hare, 1984). Black people (particularly men) are much more likely than white people to be unemployed. When they are employed it is likely to be in the most menial, least-paid jobs (Brown, 1984; Hare, 1984; Staples, 1985). The realities of racism also mean that black men are more likely to be imprisoned than are white men.

Hence, black men are frequently not in a position to support women and children economically. The choice of being supported by a man while staying at home with children is therefore not a realistic one for many black women (Hooks, 1982). This gives an indication of one reason why marriage is less common for black couples than for white couples. While western marriage is often portrayed as being solely the result of romantic love, there still are (and always have been) economic reasons for the contracting of marriage (Gittins, 1986). Where men cannot fulfil an economic role, there is less incentive for marriage.

Thus black men of Afro-Caribbean origin do not fit the stereotype of the powerful male in western societies. Instead they are stereotyped as feckless, violent, criminal, and oversexed, even to the extent that they are likely to be rapists (see Davis, 1981). It is not that black men are stereotyped as being outside the category 'male' or as emasculated, but as pathological/devalued males who have some stereotypically male characteristics to excess, and completely lack others. The gender positions that black men occupy illustrate the boundaries of stereotypic maleness. While 'normal' males have some degree of aggression and strong sexual drives, to be too aggressive and have too much sexual drive (as black men are stereotyped to have) is not to be a supermale but rather to be bestial. 'Normal' males (who are white) are measured in their maleness and their bestiality is carefully controlled.

Black women similarly are stereotyped as having some 'feminine' characteristics to excess, but also some 'male' characteristics. Thus black women are perceived as being easily available sexual objects who are prone to prostitution. King (1984) calls this the 'depreciated sex object' stereotype. The mythology of black women as having different sexuality from white women has served to permit the rape and sexual exploitation of black women (since they are stereotyped as being more bestial than white women) without public outcry being equivalent to when white women are raped (Hooks, 1982). For this reason it is not surprising (although the researcher does not make this point explicitly), that in a study of one hundred 15-year-old girls in three London comprehensives it is a black girl who reports the most sexist interchange with a male teacher.

He picks me out. 'Jenny', he goes. I go 'Yeah'. 'You little f——'. . . . He's heard from another teacher that I'm cheeky so he goes 'Oh Jenny, cheeky little cunt, ain't you' . . . (Lees, 1986, p. 125).

Black women are also stereotyped as being matriarchs who are tough (as opposed to the weakness assumed for white women who require protection from a strong white male). Such toughness means that black women can be expected to work hard, in a way that would not be expected for white women, and to dominate their households. This stereotype was given academic credence in the United States by Moynihan (1965) who blamed black females and the black female headed household for the emasculation of the black male, and hence all the problems of American black people. Lees (1986) gives a clear example of how this stereotype also operates in the British context in this quote from a white girl.

They look black and somehow stronger. If you got a white girl and a black girl you say 'Oh she looks stronger *'cos she's black*' [italics added] (Lees, 1986, p. 141).

Black children's acquisition of gender identity is therefore qualitatively different from that of white children. Contact with the media and with other societal institutions means that black children cannot help but learn that black people and white people occupy different structural positions. They learn that their parents, and hence they, are excluded from positions of power within society. Black children simultaneously learn that black people are stereotyped in different ways to those in which white people are stereotyped. From this they learn that gender differences between black males and black females are qualitatively different from white female–male differences. Hence black children learn about racism as well as about gender differentiation.

However, in contrast with what they learn from the wider society, black children learn more positive gender models from their own social networks. Black women's participation in the labour market means that black children grow up accepting that mothers can also be employed. The fact that black children are more likely than white children to live with other relatives as well as their parent(s) means that they have a wider variety of people to interact with and with whom to develop close relationships.

While there are undoubtedly gender differences between black women and black men (see Hull *et al.*, 1982), the denial of power to black people that results from racism, and the fact that black women and black men occupy different gender positions from white women and white men, mean that the 'dominant/subordinate model' of sexual power relationships is not applicable to black people in the same way it is to white people (Lorde, 1984).

This does not mean that black people automatically reject the dominant ideological stereotypes of gender roles. Being subject to the same ideological forces as white people means that many black people accept dominant ideologies of gender (see Staples, 1985). This probably occurs for three reasons. First, because being relatively powerless makes people desire the positions, and so espouse the attitudes of those who are perceived to be more powerful (see Fanon, 1952; and Henriques, 1984). Second, because being at variance with accepted societal practice means that individuals are subject to stigmatization. Avowed acceptance of dominant ideology may well be (in Goffman's, 1963, terms) in compensation for the stigma that attaches to individuals who do not fit societal norms. An effort is thus made to reduce the social distance between stigmatized individuals and the rest of society, and hence to remove stigma. The third reason is because the pervasiveness of patriarchal structures means that individual subjectivity cannot help but be affected by them (Thompson, 1977).

It is important to recognize that individuals can simultaneously accept dominant gender stereotypes and actively resist racism because they disagree with the basis on which black people and white people come to occupy different societal positions. It is because black women and white women occupy different structural positions that many young black women actively resist the gender stereotypes that are constructed as 'normal' femininity. So, for example, the passivity and weakness that is meant to elicit a powerful male's protection is redundant for black women (and white working-class women) whose fathers and male peers do not occupy positions of power. It is not surprising then that black female school students and white working-class school students are reported to be more boisterous at school than their white middle-class counterparts, and should be sceptical about the benefits of marriage for them (Sharpe, 1976; Bryan *et al.*, 1985; Lees, 1986).

Race, class and gender

Because racism operates structurally to maintain black people in a state of relative powerlessness in comparison with white people, most black people are working class. Black children and white working-class children therefore have some common experiences of what it means to be gendered – in particular learning what it means to be excluded from and different from mainstream society. The impact of experiences that give working-class children insight into what it means to be a working-class woman or man is unfortunately not theorized in literature on gender, as the following example from a woman who experienced a working-class childhood makes clear.

A sense of dislocation can provide a sharp critical faculty in a child . . . . Working-class autobiography frequently presents, as a moment of narrative revelation, a child's surprise at the humility of a domestic tyrant witnessed at his work-place, out in the world . . . . Beyond the point of initial surprise, none of the literature deals with what happens to children when they come to witness the fracture between social and domestic power . . . (Steedman, 1986, p. 72).

To be a black child, to be a black working-class child, or to be a white, working-class child is to occupy qualitatively different societal positions from white, middle-class children.

Subjectivity as multiple, produced in contradictory and shifting positions, through power and desire, has specific and harmful effects upon those whose lack of fit is rendered pathological (Walkerdine, 1985, p. 237).

Moving between home, school and other contexts provides children who are other than white and middle class with contradictions which lead them to the understanding that they and their parents are outside the social construction of gender, and are relatively powerless. The results are that,

Black daughters learn at an early age that their mothers are not personally responsible for not being able, through their individual efforts, to make basic changes in their lives or the lives of their children (Joseph, 1981, p. 96).

However, racism does not only differentiates between black women and white women. It also differentiates the working class in such a way that in a public context white working-class women are advantaged over black working-class women and over black working-class men. This is graphically illustrated in the following quote from Gail Lewis's description of relationships between her black father and white mother.

Another thing was my Mum's contempt for my Dad because of his humble demeanour in the face of white authority. Throughout their marriage it was agreed that Mum would deal with any authorities that had to be faced . . . . And since they both believed that by 'rights' the man should do this kind of stuff, then it only served to reinforce their shared belief in my Dad's inadequacy. Which led to him having to 'prove' himself by reasserting his dominance over her as a man. It was a situation that was fed by racism and their attempt at overcoming it . . . (Lewis, 1985, p. 232).

Conclusions

By ignoring issues of race and class, current theories of gender, and the research on which these are based, actually address the development of gender identity in the white middle classes. This means that black children (and white working-class children) are rendered invisible in the processes of normal gender development, but visible in pathological categories like 'father-absent' households.

It is not only that the structure of family life presumed by theories of gender development implicitly reinforce race and class divisions but that the content they presume also does so. Black children and white working-class children experience the disjunction between their parents' power over them as children, and their parents', particularly fathers', lack of social power, as contradictions that have to be reconciled as they learn about their social world in the different contexts they experience. This means that the account of their gender development must be different from that of white middle-class children who are less likely to experience such contradictions.

Theories of gender will become ecologically valid (Bronfenbrenner, 1977) if that they take account of household organizations other than the nuclear family, and the different experiences of people of different classes and colours. This must not, however, be an adding-on of an account of black gender development to an unchanged account of white middle-class development, since this would still result in black people appearing pathological by comparison with the familiar account of white gender development.

Instead, theoretical accounts of gender development must centrally include structural factors like participation in the employment market, household structure, the operation of class and of racism. Gender development is therefore much more complex than current theories recognize. To concentrate solely on race would obscure the fact that shared class means that black working-class people and white working-class people have common exclusions from sources of societal power. However the fact of racism means that there are experiences which are exclusive to black people. Structural relations and emotional relations need to be related together so that we gain insights into the psychic development of black children and white working-class children.

References

Archer, J. and Lloyd, B., *Sex and gender*, Harmondsworth, Penguin, 1982.

Bhavnani, K. and Coulson, M., 'Transforming socialist feminism: the challenge of racism', *Feminist Review*, **23**, 1986, pp. 81–92.

Biller, H., 'The father and sex-role development', in M. Lamb (ed.), *The role of the father in child development*, (2nd edition), New York, John Riley, 1981.

Brah, A. and Minhas, R., 'Structural racism or cultural difference: school for Asian girls', in G. Weiner (ed.), *Just a bunch of girls*, Milton Keynes, Open University Press, 1985.

Bronfenbrenner, U., 'Towards an experimental ecology of human development', *American psychologist*, **23**, 1977, pp. 513–31.

Brown, C., *Black and white in Britain: the third PSI survey*, London, Heinemann, 1984.

Bryan, B., Dadzie, S. and Scafe, S., *The heart of the race: Black women's lives in Britain*, London, Virago, 1985.

Busfield, J., 'Ideologies and reproduction', in M. Richards (ed.), *The integration of a child into a social world*, Cambridge, Cambridge University Press, 1974.

Carby, H. V., 'Schooling in Babylon'. In Centre for Contemporary Cultural Studies, *The Empire Strikes Back: Race and racism in 70s Britain*. London, Hutchinson, 1982, pp. 183–211.

Davis, A., *Women, race and class*, London, The Women's Press, 1981.

Dunn, J. and Kendrick, C., *Siblings*, London, Grant McIntyre, 1982.

Eggleston, S., Dunn, D. and Anjali, M., *The educational and vocational experiences of 15–18 year old young people of minority ethnic groups*, Report to the DES, 1984.

Eichenbaum, L. and Orbach, S., *Understanding women*, Harmondsworth, Penguin, 1983.

Fanon, F., *Black skins, white masks*, London, Pluto Press, 1952.

Field, T., Widmayer, S., Stringer, S. and Ignatoff, E., 'Teenage, lower class, black mothers and their pre-term infants: An intervention and developmental follow-up', *Child Development*, **51**, 1980, pp. 426–36.

Fuller, M., 'Qualified criticism, critical qualifications', in L. Barton and S. Walker (eds), *Race, class and education*, Kent, Croom Helm, 1983.

Furstenberg, F., *Unplanned parenthood: The social consequences of teenage childbearing*, New York, The Free Press, 1976.

Gittens, D., *The family in question: Changing households and familiar ideologies*, London, Macmillan, 1986.

Goffman, E., *Stigma*, Harmondsworth, Penguin, 1963.

Hart, N., 'Revolution without a revolution: The psychology of sex and race', in *The best of the black scholar: the black woman* **II**, 1984.

Henriques, J., Hollway, W., Urwin, C., Venn, C. and Walkerdine, V., *Changing the subject*, London, Methuen, 1984.

Henshall, C. and McGuire, J., 'Gender relations', in M. Richards and P. Light (eds), *Children of social worlds*, Cambridge, Polity Press, 1986.

Hook, B., *Ain't I a women: black women and feminism*, London, Pluto Press, 1982.

Hooks, B., *Feminist theory: from margin to centre*, Boston, South End Press, 1984.

Hull, G. T., Scott, P. B. and Smith, B. (eds.), *All the women are white, all the blacks are men, but some of us are brave*, New York, The Feminist Press, 1982.

Joseph, G. and Lewis, J., *Common differences. Conflicts in black and white feminist perspectives*, New York, Anchor Books, 1981.

King, M., 'The politics of sexual stereotypes', in *The best of the black scholar: the black woman* **II**, 1984.

Kohlberg, L., 'A cognitive-developmental analysis of children's sex-role concepts and attitudes', in E. Maccoby (ed.), *The development of sex differences*, London, Tavistock Press, 1966.

Lamb, M. (ed.), *The role of the father in child development*, New York, John Wiley, 1976.

Lawrence, E., 'Just plain common sense: the roots of racism', in Centre for Contemporary Cultural Studies, *The Empire Strikes Back: Race and racism in 70s Britain*, London, Hutchinson, 1982, pp. 47–94.

Lees, S., *Losing out: Sexuality and adolescent girls*, London, Hutchinson, 1986.

Lewis, C., *Fathers of one year olds*, Paper presented to the Annual Conference of the Developmental Section of the British Psychological Society, Lancaster, September 1984.

Lewis, G., 'From deepest Kilburn', in L. Heron (ed.), *Truth, dare or promise: Girls growing up in the fifties*, London, Virago, 1985.

Lorde, A., 'Scratching the surface: some notes to barriers to women and loving', in *The best of the black scholar: the black women* **II**, 1984.

Marable, M., *How capitalism underdeveloped black America*, London, Pluto Press, 1983.

Martin, J. and Roberts, C., *Women and employment: A lifelong perspective*, London, HMSO, 1984.

Moynihan, D. P., *The negro family: A case for national action*, Office of Policy Planning and Research, United States Department of Labor, 1965.

New, C. and David, M., *For the children's sake*, Harmondsworth, Penguin, 1985.

Office of Population Censuses and Surveys, Fertility trends in England and Wales: 1975–1985, *OPCS Monitor. Reference FMI 86/2*, 15 July 1986.

Parmar, P., 'Gender, race and class: Asian women in resistance', in Centre for Contemporary Cultural Studies. *The Empire Strikes Back: Race and racism in 70s Britain*, pp. 236–75.

Platt, J., *What can case studies do?*, Paper presented to the ESRC Field Research seminar on case study research, March 1986.

Riley, D., *War in the nursery: Theories of the child and mother*, London, Virago, 1983.

Ryan, W., *Blaming the victim*, New York, Vintage Books, 1972.

Scarr, S., Caparulo, B., Ferdman, B., Tower, R., and Caplan, J., 'Developmental status and school achievements of minority and non-minority children from birth to 18 years in a British Midlands town', *British Journal of Developmental Psychology*, **1**, 1983, pp. 31–48.

Sebald, H., 'Adolescents shifting orientation towards parents and peers', *Journal of marriage and the family*, **48**, 1986, p. 5–13.

Sharpe, S., *'Just like a girl': How girls learn to be women*, Harmondsworth, Penguin, 1976.

Staples, R., 'Changes in black family structure: the conflict between family ideology and structural conditions', *Journal of marriage and the family*, **47**, 1985, pp. 1005–13.

Steedman, C., *Landscape for a good woman: A study of two lives*, London, Virago, 1986.

Swann Report, *Education for all*, Report to the Department of Education and Science, London, HMSO, 1985.

Thompson, E. P., 'Happy families', *New Society*, 8 September 1977, pp. 499–501.

Tizard, B. and Hughes, M., *Young children learning: Talking and thinking at home and at school*, London, Fontana, 1984.

Urwin, C., 'Constructing motherhood: the persuasion of normal development', in C. Steedman, C. Urwin and V. Walkerdine (eds), *Language, gender and childhood*, London, Routledge and Kegan Paul, 1985, pp. 164–202.

Walkerdine, V., 'On the regulation of speaking and silence: subjectivity, class and gender in contemporary schooling', in C. Steedman, C. Urwin and V. Walkerdine (eds), *Language, gender and childhood*, London, Routledge and Kegan Paul, 1985, pp. 203–41.

Willis, P. E., *Learning to labour: How working class kids get working class jobs*, Farnborough, Saxon House, 1977.

Part Two

Exploring the Past: Autobiography and Life History

5 Understanding personal accounts

June Purvis

Written texts are usually regarded as the province of historians, but sociologists use them too, as well as using the writings and interpretations of historians. Indeed, the relationship between history and sociology is an old and established one, even if there are a number of tensions between these two disciplines. Part of the problem is that there is much controversy about what constitutes 'history' and what constitutes 'sociology'. Some writers even claim that there is no distinction between the two. Abrams, for example, asserts that history and sociology 'are and always have been the same thing' (Abrams, 1982, p. x). While there is a considerable overlap between the two disciplines for some writers, there is also a clear difference between them for many others. Many historians give most attention to establishing as accurately as possible what happened and why. Many sociologists, while also concerned with the so-called 'facts', give more effort to developing theoretical explanations for why things happened in the way that they did. It is important to stress, however, that this difference between historians and sociologists is only a difference of *emphasis*. After all we cannot know facts independent of theoretical assumptions. As the historian E. H. Carr points out, historians 'select' certain facts from the mass that are available and 'interpret' them in some way:

The historian is necessarily selective. The belief in a hard core of historical facts existing objectively and independently of the interpretation of the historian is a preposterous fallacy, but one which it is very hard to eradicate   (Carr, 1978, pp. 11–12).

Though there is controversy about what constitutes 'history' and what constitutes 'sociology', the role of texts in each discipline has tended to differ. For the historians studying the past (especially the distant past), written texts are usually the *main* and often the only source of evidence. A historian will decide, for a variety of reasons, to research a particular issue – perhaps because other historians have ignored it or misunderstood it. Then a wide range of texts will be studied for as long as is possible – ideally, until the researcher decides that the ground has been covered adequately. During the period of collecting evidence, the historian usually develops a 'feel' for the period being studied. When writing up the research, not all the texts consulted will be cited – there are usually too many. The historian will select certain texts as sources for evidence, and if a text is cited

Source: The Open University, *E205*, Unit 15, Understanding Texts, The Open University Press, 1984.

to support a general point, the reader of what the historian has written will have to take on trust that the source cited is typical or representative.

For the sociologist, on the other hand, written texts tend to be just one of a wide range of sources of evidence. This is not surprising since most sociologists study the present and the recent, rather than distant, past. Thus most sociologists combine the use of written texts with other sources of information – such as interviews, social surveys, and participant observation. Though written texts command a much more central place in history than in sociology, both historians and sociologists face the same problems when analysing them.

My main aims in this chapter are to examine the different kinds of texts that historians and sociologists use and to consider some of the problems involved in their interpretation. I shall distinguish between three main kinds of texts – *official texts*, *published commentary and reporting* and *personal accounts*. This classification into three main kinds of texts is only a rough guide, but it does enable us to identify broad categories of texts which share certain things in common.

I am using the term *official texts* to refer to state, bureaucratic and legal texts such as government reports, court reports, memoranda and official letters. *Published commentary and reporting* covers accounts of certain events that may be written without the direct help and assistance of the participants. Such texts include novels, films, photographs, advertisements, the writings of key political and social figures, and newspapers. The approach in *personal accounts* is essentially in terms of one person's subjective experience. They include such things as letters, diaries, photograph albums, autobiographies and life stories.

How might a researcher of education, then, use official texts, published commentary and reporting, and personal accounts? There seem to be two important kinds of information which texts can provide. First of all, and most obviously, many provide accounts of events, people and places in which we are interested. In the case of historical texts, and sometimes even with contemporary ones, we may have no other source of information about these matters. All the different types of texts can be used in this way. For example, if one wished to find out about the nature of schooling in nineteenth-century Britain, one could consult such texts as nineteenth-century government reports, the writings of school inspectors or the autobiographies of teachers and pupils. Equally, though, one might look at the portrayal of schools in nineteenth-century novels.

We can treat the creators of texts as witnesses, and use their descriptions of the world to provide information about events, people and places in which we are interested. Or we can treat them as representative of particular social groupings and use their texts for what they tell us about the perspectives of such groups. We might call the first *descriptive* analysis and the second *perspective* analysis. Though these two types of analysis are analytically distinct, in practice historians and sociologists often blur the distinction between the two. With descriptive analysis, the accuracy of the account is the central concern, and in order to assess this, it is necessary to compare the account with others describing the same phenomenon. In the case of perspective analysis, however, the accuracy of the account does not necessarily matter. What is important is whether it is representative of the perspectives of the social category to which one is assigning the author(s) of the text. Once again, the text will be compared with others, but this time with those produced by other members of that social category.

The two types of analysis are complementary. In particular, perspective analysis may suggest ways in which the description of events in a text may be biased. For example, if we know that the author is a member of a political party, we will evaluate the information given in the light of that author's political perspective. The analysis of texts, whether as descriptive accounts or as representing a particular perspective on education or on society generally, is by no means straightforward. For example, one often finds contradictory statements in a range of texts by a single author, or even within the same text. Equally, the content may sometimes be ambiguous. It is hardly surprising, therefore, to find that the historian or sociologist may interpret texts in different ways.

One of the problems that the researcher using textual evidence faces is not knowing when to stop. As Platt asks: 'How many defunct journals' review sections, secondhand book catalogues or publishers' advertisements in the backs of old books must one read before being entitled to conclude that a further search is not likely to turn up anything new?' (Platt, 1981, p. 39). And when one is engaged in research relating to the past 200 years, one has to rely upon records that have survived the passing of time. Such research, therefore, has relied heavily on texts that have been carefully preserved and stored, e.g. official government documents and other items thought worth saving. Such a reliance may favour certain social groups, such as the middle class, the famous, and men, and under-represent others, such as the working class, those who did not become famous, and women. Also, the texts still available may focus upon some aspects of social life much more than on others.

Using personal accounts

As indicated earlier, the classification of texts into three main types is only a rough guide, and there are some texts which are much more difficult to classify than others. However, in this section I shall concentrate upon two kinds of texts which fall very firmly into the category of personal accounts – autobiographies and life stories. It is important here to define the terms 'autobiography' and 'life story'. An *autobiography* may be defined as the written story of one's life whereas a *life story* is delivered orally to a researcher who may write it down or, in this present time, store it on a tape recording. Sometimes life stories collected in this way are then transcribed into written texts.

Oral evidence in the form of life stories was a common means of data collection in nineteenth-century government reports. Many social observers in the nine-teenth century also collected information through life stories. Henry Mayhew, for example, used this method to find out about the London poor in the 1850s (Mayhew, 1851). Life stories were told to him by a wide variety of people, including street hawkers, such as the costermongers, who sold a range of goods from fish to apples, and men selling baked potatoes. Social observers like Mayhew were living at a time when sociology was in its infancy, but collecting life stories remained a persistent, though not dominant, method among some sociologists during the first half of the twentieth century. W. I. Thomas and F. Znaniecki, for example, used this method, along with other methods – such as the analysis of letters, newspapers, court records and records of social agencies – to collect information that was eventually published in their book *The Polish Peasant in Europe and America*. They claim that 'life records' constitute the 'perfect' type of sociological material (Thomas and Znaniecki, 1927, p. 1832). In the 1980s we are witnessing a revival of interest in both published autobiographies and life stories. The enthusiasm for such accounts is particularly pronounced within historical circles, but sociologists are becoming increasingly interested in such information too (see Plummer, 1983). Sociologists often stress that the life story provides invaluable insight into the subjective meaning of experiences from the viewpoint of one person. The sociologists Annabel Faraday and Kenneth Plummer, for example, state:

In line with the broad tradition of [interpretive] sociology, the life history technique documents the inner experiences of individuals, how they interpret, understand and define the world around them . . . the focus of the life history is paramountly concerned with the subjective meanings of individuals. Most notably it comes to lay bare the 'world taken-for-granted' of people – their assumptions and what it is they find problematic about life and their lives in particular   (Faraday and Plummer, 1979, p. 776).

What I shall do now is look at autobiographies and life stories in greater depth and, in particular, I shall concentrate upon extracts from these texts which tell us something about the experience of schooling.

Autobiographies

The advantages of autobiographies as sources of data for the researcher include the following:

— autobiographies are accounts of individual experience, accounts of events that may be very different from the perceptions of another observer. The event, indeed, may be something that is known only to the individual. Clifford, for example, mentions how Esther Dunn, an American girl, recollected in her autobiography the delight of that moment in school when she knew what it was to be able to read – a moment that her teacher did not 'even know as fact' (Clifford, 1978, p. 192).
— autobiographies may bring together, through the subjective experience of one person, a number of strands of thought that tend to be studied separately by researchers. For example, writing about the experience of being a pupil or student may integrate knowledge relating to one's home background, to one's sex, to the teachers, to other pupils, to the curriculum.
— autobiographical writings may record occurrences that are regarded as irrelevant or unimportant by the researcher and illustrate the inadequacies of certain research techniques. For example, in *Beachside Comprehensive*, Stephen Ball (1981) notes that he asked the pupils to keep diaries and that the information gathered from the diaries demonstrated the shortcomings of some of the sociometric data he had collected:

The sociometric questionnaires failed to pick up the casual friendships that existed between pupils outside school, and made it appear that they had no such contact. In addition, they failed to pick up the cross-sex friendships that were also established at this time. Perhaps the notion of 'friendships' is too narrow and ill-defined to account for these other kinds of adolescent relationships. . . . The entries in the diaries that several of the pupils wrote for me did, however, refer to these contacts. For instance, Kathy Tree's friendship choices of Warris and Payne, which did appear in the previous questionnaire, began to make sense   (Ball, 1981, p. 100).

At the same time, there are disadvantages in using autobiographies as sources of data. As they are subjective accounts of events, autobiographies contain an inevitable bias in the selection and presentation of content. Sometimes this bias may result in errors of information and inaccurate reporting of events. Here, for example, is what Craigie says in her introduction to the 1979 reprint of Emmeline Pankhurst's autobiography *My Own Story*:

A Harvard graduate, Andrew Rosen . . . wrote: 'Produced hurriedly, in 1914, when Mrs Pankhurst was at the height of her fame, *My Own Story* is so replete with errors and glossings-over as to be virtually useless to the historian.' True, there *are* several errors, referred to later, but the 'glossings-over' are no more numerous or misleading than those common to most memoirs. No historian would dismiss, for instance, the *Memories and Reflections* of the Earl of Oxford and Asquith on account of their glossings-over or, for that matter, their errors. In dilating upon the attitude of members of his Cabinet to women's suffrage, for example . . . Asquith states that the opponents consisted of himself, Lord Loreburn, Lewis Harcourt and others, whereas Sir Edward Grey, Haldane and Lloyd George took the opposite view, thereby giving the impression that the supporters of women's suffrage were in the minority. In fact, it was the other way round. Two thirds of the Cabinet professed to be in favour of votes for women; Asquith himself was in the minority. His recollection of the suffragette campaign, which includes four glaring inaccuracies, is devised, understandably, to absolve himself from any responsibility for the women's resort to militancy, and, furthermore, to excuse the shocking treatment inflicted on them in prison. But many MPs, suffragists and even Millicent Fawcett, no lover of the Pankhursts, placed the blame firmly on Asquith's shoulders   (Craigie, 1979, p. vi).

This point, that errors and glossings-over may be common to memoirs, is important. However, while they may weaken the usefulness of a text for descriptive analysis, they do not affect its usefulness for perspective analysis. The war memoirs of Lloyd George or Winston Churchill's account of the Second World War, for example, are of interest not primarily as sources of factual information, but because of their biases and glossings-over and what these reveal about the perspectives of these two key figures in British politics.

Other problems arise in autobiographies – often they are written in later life, and as Clifford has noted, recorded memories, especially of childhood, may be only the 'oft-repeated recollections of others' (Clifford, 1978, p. 188). They are frequently selective in regard to the kinds of topics that are discussed and the factors governing selection are seldom made explicit.

Autobiographies may *over-represent* certain groups in society such as the elderly and that articulate section of the population who have that degree of self-confidence that is probably necessary for such an undertaking plus the time that would be necessary to write about oneself. Conversely, autobiographies may *under-represent* other groups in society, e.g. those who are young, those people engaged in manual occupations rather than occupations that require skill with words (such as school teaching), those people who have experienced only a minimum of schooling, and those people in society who are oppressed in some way (certain racial minorities and women). Bulmer has suggested that the use of written sources by sociologists tends to particularly under-represent the working class and women (Bulmer, 1981, p. 543), and, we may add, especially working-class women.

Autobiographies (like many other texts) may be written in the hope of attaining fame as a writer and the content will therefore be unreliable since it will be selected according to that kind of reading public the author wishes to attract. As Paul Thompson observed:

The printed autobiography is a one-way communication, with its content definitely selected with the taste of the reading public in mind. It cannot be confidential. If it is intimate, it is with the consciousness of an audience, like an actor on the stage or in a film. As a public confession, it is controlled, and rarely includes anything which the author feels really discreditable   (Thompson, 1978, p. 94).

The strengths and limitations of data for either descriptive analysis or perspective analysis can be identified prior to use in research. For example, Irene Payne's 'A working class girl in a grammar school' (Spender and Sarah, 1980) is written from a feminist viewpoint, and an important part of her analysis therefore is to offer autobiographical documentation of how girls are prepared at school for roles in the wider society that reproduce women's subordinate position. One could therefore use her account as *perspective analysis*. In other words, one could use her essay as representative of a particular political grouping – feminists. If using this extract for perspective analysis, we would have to consider whether Payne's essay is representative of feminist writing. Is it representative of a certain variety of feminism? In order to answer these questions, we would have to engage in an extensive reading of feminist literature. Even then, we might not be able to come to a conclusive answer since feminist literature may not be representative of feminism but only of feminists who write.

Payne also provides an excellent descriptive account of the process of schooling, as she experienced it, and one could therefore use her account as *descriptive analysis*. She gives us much interesting information about, for example, the way the grammar school attempted to make its female pupils into 'educated young ladies'. If one were using this essay for descriptive analysis, then one would have to consider whether her account was accurate and how much her experience in later life had coloured her interpretation of her younger days at school, whether class and gender relations were the two most important factors shaping school experience, and whether there are any processes within the grammar school that do not help to reproduce the sexual division of labour. In order to do this, we would have to compare her account with other descriptions of the experiences of working-class pupils, and especially girls, in grammar schools in the 1950s. Overall, I would suggest that Payne's article is a good example of the way perspective analysis and descriptive analysis may complement each other.

For those concerned to find out about schooling as experienced by pupils, autobiographies are an important source of data. They can provide documentation about the experience of schooling where no other evidence might exist.

Life stories

Whereas an autobiography is written by the person himself or herself, the life story is delivered orally to a researcher. Whereas written autobiographies have only one author, the life story is the result of interaction between the narrator and the researcher (Bertaux, 1981, p. 8). The collection of such oral life stories today is especially associated with the Oral History Archives at the University of Essex. However, the interest in the collection of such life stories is now much more widespread and some easily accessible accounts may be found in books such as McCrindle and Rowbotham (1979) and Thompson (1981). The following two life stories, extracted from Thompson's book, reveal Edwardian childhoods as they were lived.

Clifford Hills was born in 1904, in the village of Great Bentley, Essex. His father was a farmworker and the family were poor, having to buy things in 'ha'porths' and 'penn'orths'. Clifford Hills attended the local elementary school until he was 12½ years old:

No, I can't say that I did enjoy school. We were glad to get away from school. We got the cane and we played truant, you know, for no good reason. We played truant when the fox hounds would come on the green and we used to follow the hounds sometimes, all round the fields, be gone all day. We knew what we'd get in the morning. We always got the cane, one on each hand. And another time there was an aeroplane, one of my first sights of an aeroplane, came down in Little Bentley in a big field there. We saw it come down. 'Course we all left school and went to see it. We all got the cane for it though the next morning. See, once we started on anything we didn't try to go back to avoid getting the cane, we just kept away. There's no going back once we started to play truant. . . .

I had so much to do, so many jobs to do before I went to school, so I couldn't help being late sometimes. Clean the knives, clean shoes, sift cinders, clean the dogs' kennels, scrub the bath house, no end of jobs to get in. Pluck birds, pheasants, partridges, skin rabbits, hares. That was when I was kitchen boy and then of course I had the same work to do when I left school, plus going with the farmer in his pony and cart round the farms. . . . I worked as a kitchen boy till twelve and a half and the farmer came to the school one morning and said he wanted me to work regular every day, all day, could I leave school because his gardeners had gone to the war. And I left school and I went to work for him every day from six in the morning until half past five at night and then till five o'clock on Saturdays for five shillings a week, all those hours for five bob, and I was still doing the paper round every night, because when the war broke out there was a big camp at the bottom of the hill, hundreds of soldiers there and I had to take newspapers to this camp, and I sold many more papers, of course, and I got one and three a week then because I was selling so many papers, but I had to work about three hours for it, plus a black eye sometimes, the troops used to put us in boxing gloves to fight the band boys down there   (Thompson, 1981, pp. 54–61).

Esther Stokes was born in 1895. She came from an upper middle-class background since her father was a Chancery barrister. Esther Stokes was one of nine children who were all brought up in the Catholic faith. The family lived in London:

My school was rather unsatisfactory, the whole thing. You see, my parents didn't like boarding schools, of that I'm sure. They wanted convent education and they didn't like the day school side of the convent because, I suppose, they thought that tradesmen's children went there; and so we were allowed to be day girls in the boarding school which was quite a mistake looking back on it, because well we never really belonged. I never felt I really belonged to the school in any sense 'cause we went away just as all the fun and games were beginning, you know the sort of tea-time and then the children play and the homework, and we went home then. So we were just quite isolated being the only day girls in a boarding school. It was in Clapham the boarding school, kept by the Notre Dame nuns and I should think they had about 150 boarders, a very fine house and wonderful grounds, a huge lake on which we used to boat. The teaching I think was very very good. . . .

I don't think I ever learned any Latin. We had the usual algebra and geometry. I loved those. And we had a mild amount of botany, nothing very thrilling and of course a lot of needlework. I was taught a lot of needlework; I can sew very nicely, I really can, a long fine seam and embroider and that sort of thing. We spent a lot of time doing that. There are great gaps in English history that you know I never went through as a child. We seemed to go always round and round and never seemed to me that there was any plan in it. I don't know whether there was or wasn't. We never had a debate or anything like that. It was all just classrooms but I remember getting up *Everyman*. I remember having a part in *Everyman*. That's the only play I can remember them doing, but I've no doubt they did do other plays. We had a science room with some bunsen burners. I can't imagine what we did there, but I supposed we messed about with some very very elementary piece of knowledge. I simply don't remember that that was ever used as an exam subject. We took what were the then exams, they were called Oxford and Cambridge and I think they were called junior and senior, yes I think they were. We took those. And we took all the piano exams. . . .

Deportment was a great thing. There was a curious kind of board, rather like a surf board, which some girls if they had weak backs used to have to spend half an hour lying on this board. And then we had another kind of board, almost like a yoke, which you would hang on. You put it like that and it kept your back up like that, with two handles. And then in a quiet way we had quite a lot of deportment. We had lovely things called Indian clubs. I used to enjoy them madly. We were quite good at swinging them, and I suppose we had marching and skipping but we didn't have any gym. We had no ropes or horses or anything like that. Dancing. Not at school. I don't think we had dancing at the school. My mother used to take us to a dancing class in the town. We had games, we had hockey and we had netball and we had some very feeble tennis because the tennis courts were so bad. Full of daisies but still . . . and there was a certain amount of boating. But that wasn't any good 'cause they didn't teach us to row. They just took turns going and being taken on the water.

I left school at fifteen. I went to Rome that very October and stayed there till May and learned Italian and learned to play the piano quite nicely   (Thompson, 1981, pp. 183–57).

The advantages of autobiographies are also those of life stories, i.e.

— life stories are accounts of individual experience, accounts that may be very different from the perceptions of another observer;

— life stories may bring together, through the subjective experience of one person, strands of thought that tend to be studied separately by researchers;
— life stories may record occurrences that are regarded as unimportant by the researcher and illustrate the inadequacies of certain research techniques.

However, life stories have other strengths which are specific to them alone. They are transmitted orally and can, therefore, draw from a much larger proportion of the population than that literate articulate section that is able to write an autobiography. In particular, life stories can be a means of reaching working-class people who cannot or do not wish to write. Their experience of day-to-day life, in the home and in waged labour, may be recorded in the life story. As Paul Thompson said in 1978:

Owing to the recording work of oral historians, and also the influence of the radio, we now have life-stories from a much wider range of authors: from local as well as national leaders, from the ordinary rank and file, and also from non-unionized workers; from women as well as men; from labourers, domestic servants, sweated and casual workers, as well as from miners and labour aristocrats. Equally important, the content and language have shifted from the public life to the ordinary experience of work and family (Thompson, 1978, p. 71).

Life stories also have an immediacy which autobiographies lack. In particular, the person collecting the life story may ask the respondent certain questions or generally indicate the kinds of subject they would like to see talked about. Life stories can, therefore, 'fill the gap' that the documentary source of the auto-biography leaves.

Some of the disadvantages of life stories are similar to those of autobiographies. For example, there is always the danger that the interviewer's framework of questions may distort the importance or non-importance of certain events in the life of the respondent.

Life stories may also contain errors and bias in the selection of evidence on the part of the respondent. As Seldon has noted, failure of memory is a serious criticism which can be levelled against oral history (Seldon, 1982, p. 10). In addition, he continues, there may be retrospective editing, self-justification, ration-alization, myth-building and other evils. Life stories are usually recorded in later life and may be, as A. J. P. Taylor once claimed, accounts of old men 'drooling about their youth'.

Though the collection of life stories has been particularly associated with historians, sociologists have often engaged in the same activity – though this has been somewhat obscured by the fact that it has often gone under another name – such as 'interviewing'. Of course not all interviews are life stories – but life story interviews have been used by sociologists as a means of collecting data. Such a method has probably been most common in sociological studies of communities. However, within the sociology of education, the most famous study that has used the life story interview is Jackson and Marsden's *Education and the Working Class* (1966). In this study, Jackson and Marsden traced the fortunes of eighty-eight working-class boys and girls who attended grammar school in Huddersfield and collected their information by life story interviews.

Autobiographies and life stories, then, are texts that contain much of value for researchers, whether for descriptive or perspective analysis. Different kinds of texts tend to have characteristic strengths and limitations, as we have seen, though the significance of these will vary according to the nature of the analysis, as will the way in which we seek to check their validity.

References

Abrams, P., *Historical Sociology*, Shepton Mallet, Open Books, 1982.

Ball, S. J., *Beachside Comprehensive: a case-study of secondary schooling*, Cambridge, Cambridge University Press, 1981.

Bertaux, D., 'Introduction' in Bertaux, D. (ed.), *Biography and Society*, London, Sage Publications, 1981.

Bulmer, M., 'Approaches to methodology course content', *Sociology*, **15** (4), 1981 pp. 539–44.

Carr, E. H., *What is History?*, Harmondsworth, Penguin Books, 1978.

Clifford, G. J., 'History as experience: the uses of personal-history documents in the history of education', *History of Education*, **7** (3), 1978.

Craigie, J., 'Introduction' in Pankhurst, E., *My Own Story*, London, Virago, 1979.

Faraday, A. and Plummer, K., 'Doing life histories', *Sociological Review*, **27** (4), 1979 pp. 773–98.

Jackson, B. and Marsden, D., *Education and the Working Class*, Harmondsworth, Penguin, 1966 (revised edn).

McCrindle, J. and Rowbotham, S. (eds), *Dutiful Daughters: women talk about their lives*, Harmondsworth, Penguin, 1979.

Mayhew, H., *London Labour and the London Poor*, London, 1851.

Payne, J., 'A working class girl in a grammar school', in Spender, D. and Sarah, E. (eds), *Learning to Lose: sexism and education*, London, The Women's Press, 1980.

Plummer, K., *Documents of Life*, London, George Allen and Unwin, 1983.

Seldon, A., 'Learning by word of mouth', *The Times Higher Education Supplement*, 20 August 1982.

Thomas, W. I. and Znaniecki, F., *The Polish Peasant in Europe and America*, Chicago, University of Chicago Press, 1927 (2nd edn).

Thompson, P., *The Voice of the Past: oral history*, Oxford, Oxford University Press, 1978.

Thompson, T., *Edwardian Childhoods*, London, Routledge and Kegan Paul, 1981.

6 'Streaming' and the politics of female sexuality: case studies in the schooling of girls

Sue Middleton

This chapter presents three case studies as the basis for a grounded discussion of the complex and often contradictory ways in which family strategies of cultural reproduction are linked to the structural requirements of both capital and the state for certain sorts of labour. It investigates in detail the power of what Althusser has called 'the family-school couple'.[1]

In order to study the mechanics of 'the operation of the sexual division of labour in the creation and the nature of cultural capital,'[2] a case-study approach is necessary. Oral history procedures enable researchers to describe and relate the personal experiences of individuals to structural and historical phenomena, and thus to explore what Plummer has called: 'one of sociology's core contradictions; the interminable tension between the subjectively creative human being acting upon his/her world and the objectively given social structure constraining him or her'.[3]

Sociologists of education have made little use of this approach, and few researchers have asked people to describe and analyse their own schooling. The research project on which this chapter is based is a study of the life histories of twelve feminist educators, all born and educated in New Zealand in the post-war era.[4] The twelve had attended a total of seventeen secondary schools, which included seven single-sex girls' schools (six state and one Catholic), and ten coeducational. Two of the women had taken commercial courses, while the others had been in either top-stream or second-stream academic classes. In so far as these women have entered the female-intensive profession of teaching, their socialization as 'feminine' women has been at least partially successful. During the teacher shortage of the 1950s and 1960s, when these women were at school, there was an effort on the part of the government to recruit one sixth form girl in two to a scheme of teacher training[5] as part of a co-ordinated campaign of 'manpower planning'.

In this chapter I shall explore the process of cultural reproduction in the 'family-school couple' through analysing how three of these twelve women describe their schooling from their perspective as feminist adults. As they are women with university degrees in at least one of the social sciences (sociology, anthropology,

Source: Extracted from Codd, J., Harker, D. and Nash, R. (eds), *Political Issues in New Zealand Education*, Palmerston North, Dunmore, 1985. The article was originally entitled ' "Setting" and the politics of female sexuality: case studies in the schooling of girls'. 'Setting' has been changed to its British equivalent.

or education), the analysis they present in the transcripts is already sociological. The transcripts and theoretical framework in which they are embedded has been checked, corrected and modified by each woman concerned as well as by some of the other women in the wider study. Thus, the perspective presented is a collaboration between the researcher and the subjects.[6]

Bourdieu's concept of 'cultural capital' provides a useful starting point for substantive analysis. He argues that 'each family transmits to its children, indirectly rather than directly, a certain *cultural capital* and a certain *ethos*.'[7] Bourdieu argues that members of different social-class groups internalize the objective chances of a member of their class achieving academic success, so that objective chances become subjective hopes. Subject choice can be seen as conditioned by these internalized hopes; choosing a course in the third form is like 'charting a course' through one's entire academic career, in that:

if success at the highest level of a school career is still very closely connected to the very earliest stages of that career, it is also true that very early choices have a great effect on the chances of getting into a given branch of higher education and succeeding in it. In short, crucial decisions have been taken at a very early stage.[8]

In the process of selecting knowledge for inclusion in the academic curriculum, the school legitimates some knowledge as being of high status and devalues others, and so Bourdieu argues that children from middle-class homes may find their culture legitimated, while those from the working class, or from cultural minorities, may find their world-views invalidated.

'Streaming' and school subcultures

During the 1960s, 'streaming' was the dominant mode of secondary school organization in New Zealand.[9] Sociologists have argued that the practice of streaming leads to a kind of reification of pupil identities – images of 'academic girls' and 'commercial types' are constructed by both teachers and pupils.

In the following case studies, I shall describe the images of academic and commercial girls as the women I interviewed remember and interpret them. In this, the women described their perceptions of their own and other streams, and their (remembered) perceptions of their teachers' perceptions. In the first study I discuss the case of Sharon in terms of how her mother and father influenced her 'choice' of a commercial course, and how that decision has influenced her later career and eventual acquisition of cultural capital as an adult student.

I then describe the case of Margaret, whose school-teacher parents' cultural capital influenced her choice of an academic course and a professional career. Students in the top-stream academic forms took two languages. In city schools, this was usually Latin and either French or German.[10] These streams were often seen as the preserve of the middle upper class.[11]

In the third case, Tahuri, a Maori woman with upper-class ancestry, had been brought up by adoptive parents who did not have any formal educational qualifications. She describes the clientele of '3 Professional A' in the girls high school of her provincial town as:

. . . the most elitist, most exalted third form in the school which included the daughters of the town's professional and business elite. The high school teachers' kids, the doctors' kids, the lawyers' kids, the accountants' kids, the boss of the supermarkets' kids, the research scientists' kids.

Within elite streams of girls, 'intellectual' subcultures developed; in this study one of these will be described by Margaret, who attended a girls' school in a provincial town. Margaret's 'intellectual' girls' subculture was based on a virginal model of female sexuality and affected the dress and mannerisms of university students. Their model of intellectuality was based on their fantasies of an academic/artistic bohemia, partly drawn from their contact with 'university freshmen'; for the girls, however, the development of their intellect was largely aimed at attracting an intellectual/professional husband. In their case, the process of cultural reproduction was, at least in part, one of acquiring the 'know-how' to become the wife of a professional man.

According to the women in my study, girls in the academic streams who either became overtly sexually active or who assumed the outward trappings of 'tartiness' often became outcasts in the eyes of their teachers and the 'straight' academic girls. In this they created 'deviant' subcultures. Tahuri, placed in the top stream because of her high intelligence, was forbidden to do Maori, which was seen as not good enough for the top stream. She and two other outcasts formed what Willis has called a 'culture of resistance' and were eventually expelled from the school.[12]

Commercial-stream girls took subjects which prepared them, not for executive or managerial positions in the business world, but for typing jobs. Although there is little research on this in New Zealand, it may reasonably be surmised that few 'commercial girls' became top secretaries, as few continued their schooling beyond School Certificate.[13] Top secretaries (such as legal or executive secretaries) usually have at least University Entrance and possibly a degree, and learned their short-hand and typing at business college or technical institute. The curriculum of commercial courses has been described by Australian researcher Sandra Taylor as a form of 'apprenticeship in womanhood' in which girls learn not only practical office skills, but also the appropriate mannerism of deference to the boss, 'feminine' dress and grooming. Taylor notes that these courses are taken by a mixture of middle-class and working-class girls and that in her study:

Very few gave office work as their desired occupation at the time of subject choice. There was some evidence of mothers and sisters having encouraged girls to take commercial courses, sometimes because they had done so themselves.[14]

The women in my study noted that commercial streams were perceived by academic girls and teachers as 'dumb classes'. Furthermore, commercial and other 'lower stream' girls were often perceived by academic girls (whether it was true or not) as more sexually active – as 'tarts.'[15]

The case studies reported in the next section describe the typifications of intellectuality and sexuality within adolescent girls' subcultures associated with top academic and commercial streams.

Three case studies

Sharon: a commercial girl

Sharon is a school teacher with a university degree. She took a commercial course at school, passed School Certificate the second time round and worked in a succession of typing jobs. Her tertiary education was undertaken as an adult 'second chance' student.

Sharon's father was a dairy farmer, and her mother had been a primary school teacher[16] before marriage and motherhood. Sharon believes neither of her parents were happy in their careers.

Her 'decision' to take a commercial course at school was made in a family context of contradictory expectations about the nature and role of women. It is important to explore her adult perceptions of the expectations of each of her parents in turn.

Her mother had been strongly encouraged to become a teacher by both of her parents:

... she had a good education. Her parents really saw to it that she studied and she really did well. She did languages and they wouldn't let her do any housework. She couldn't even cook when they got married because they were so intent on her getting a good education.[17]

Sharon believes that her mother had felt disadvantaged by her education when she had married into her husband's family, feeling alienated from the other wives in the farming district:

She married into a farming district. My father had been on the farm. He was the third generation. I think they hated her because of that and they gave her a hard time because she married in. She always resented the fact that they hated her because she was more educated. So for some reason in turn she decided her girls didn't need an education.

Sharon's mother's ambivalence about her own education was transmitted to her. She was denied access to books during her childhood:

Never read anything. Never had any books, that I can remember; my parents never encouraged us to read any books. They were well-off, after a while. We were not wanting for anything. We never had good books at home. We weren't encouraged to do anything like that.

During her childhood and adolescence, Sharon experienced contradictory expectations over her body image. These contradictions reflect the dilemma of many women and girls on family farms. Sharon was expected to be both an unpaid farm labourer and a 'feminine' woman.[18] This contradiction was mediated by *both* Sharon's parents, and exacerbated at puberty.

Sharon notes that her mother had refused to do manual work on the farm, a characteristic which further differentiated her from any of the other wives of the district:

She refused to be like a lot of the other wives around who just sort of helped to muck down. She wouldn't do that, I think fancied herself a bit higher than that.

Sharon's father had no formal educational qualifications. Sharon believes that he held conservative views on the nature and role of women, noting that he had set ideas:

of what you could do at certain levels, and what women could do at certain ages. Because since then (I mean about three years ago) my father told me that he feels women are second-class citizens. So he has certain ideas about the division of labour.

From her father, however, Sharon had learned farming skills. As a child, farm duties had been a normal part of her life. Sex-role stereotyping was not at that stage an issue.

we used to have to help on the farm, which was the *normal* thing with girls. Anybody did on the farm, if you were born a boy or girl you actually worked on the farm. We had to help milk in the sheds. We had rosters; we had to be there in the morning or at night. Before we went to school, and when we came home we had to help clean up. And we had to help feed the cows during the season, and so, you know, we were just part of the work force. And in the summer time we had to help with the hay making. We had to drive the tractor for my father to feed out. One time we had to tether the hay. And we did all that independently so that we split up all the tasks that were easy. We were milking at night or we were doing the tethering.

However, after puberty Sharon was drastically restricted in her physical freedom:

Then we had this confusion. When I was a teenager then there started to be these constraints. I remember the first time getting a hiding, a good thrashing for coming home late one night we'd been around at a friend's place. They had built a tree house. And they were boys, that family. There were a lot of boys in our district and my parents started to be concerned about those sorts of things. So I started off being free. Then at that stage my father started saying things like 'You'll have to watch your nails' and things like that. And you don't realise that those pressures are conflicting. You're out doing things on the farm. And then you're supposed to be looking nice.

For Sharon, adolescence marked a time of restriction. As a physically active girl who excelled at sport, she found this restriction difficult. Sharon's cultural heritage, then, was fraught with contradictions. From her father she had learned to work hard physically on the farm, that girls were as capable as boys at manual labour. Suddenly in her teens she was expected to change her body image – the calloused hands of the farm worker must metamorphose into the manicured elegance of the 'lady'. Climbing trees with local boys was acceptable in childhood, but unrestricted associations with boys exposed the teenage girl to the dangers of pregnancy or 'moral corruption'. From feeling strong and independent in her body image, she was pressured to regard her body as a 'thing' for the pleasure of others, to be looked at and moulded into the current fashions of beauty. The parents' model of a 'young lady' would ensure the reproduction of the family at a comparable, or higher, class status.

From her perspective as an adult, Sharon notes that it was as a result of these contradictory forces in her family that she took the commercial course at her local District High School, noting that her father had been:

. . . the main one to make the decision. Definitely I remember mother thinking that marriage was the only thing – that girls didn't need an education, which is surprising seeing she had a very good one. My father actually made that decision I think finally.

Although they may have combined because my mother was a stronger person than my father. She would have told him to say it to me. That's the way things worked, but they decided secretarial work was enough. Like my cousin, my other first cousin, she was a secretary and that was going to be enough.

Although she was successful in her commercial course, Sharon disliked school, and still feels cheated at her lack of initiation into the subject matter taught in academic streams:

There were no teachers that motivated me at all. The only one that I was impressed with was the typing teacher who was most efficient and I suppose the only role model I had in terms of a woman operating efficiently and well and successfully. She is the only one that comes to mind. She had high aspirations for the girls you see and that came through very much. I was first, second, third. She praised and gave encouragement to those who were successful. So that on my school report – when I finally left the Headmaster put on my report 'Will make a good career in typing'. Well there it was. . . . So that was my only role model, and my cousin who was a typist. Otherwise there were no aspirations. It was just awful. I felt my education was totally lacking. I never had any Shakespeare. So amazingly minimal.

Sharon was aware of the low status of the commercial course, a perspective shared by several New Zealand women in their autobiographies[19] as well as by sociological researchers:[20] 'At school I felt I was in the dumb class.' She had left school and taken a typing job after passing her School Certificate the second time she sat it. She blames her father's ignorance of the workings of the 'system' (i.e. his lack of academic cultural capital) for her first failure:

I had failed School Certificate the first time. But my father had given me the impression that School Certificate was a four-year course, and now when I'm at university I read up on all this educational history, I realise that it was, originally, meant to be a four-year course. And then, of course, it just developed into a three-year course. And my father was operating within the original dates . . . now I get furious to think that put such tremendous pressure on me, not to worry about it in the third year so much, and I did fail it the first time round. And I sat it the next year and didn't do much better. I got, I'm always too ashamed to tell people I only got about seven marks over. So I passed the thing, but appallingly.[21]

At 19, Sharon suffered what she describes as a 'nervous breakdown'. She took a series of casual jobs, devoting much of her time to her sporting interests. After many years of overseas travel, she was encouraged by a friend to apply for provisional admission to the university. After being turned down the first time, she reapplied and was accepted. After a successful year, she applied for Teachers College as a means of gaining 'qualifications'. This provided her with a means of gaining an education and being paid at the same time. Sharon attributes her success as an adult 'second chance' student to the confidence maintained through her exceptional sporting prowess and through satisfying her life-long thirst for travel.

Sharon: I had this big vision of going overseas and I'd had it since primary school where there'd be a map on the wall, and I thought one day I'd go overseas, and that was the only thing that pulled me through, that was having this one thing I wanted to do.

Interviewer: Where did you get that idea from?

Sharon: I don't know. The only place I can think of getting it from was from primary
school, where we had a school photograph taken, and behind us was the world map.
And for some reason that world map is a very important part of my life. Somewhere
it got in and never went away.

Although Sharon's mother had deliberately tried to prevent her from becoming
highly educated, Sharon comments that she had always 'had a hankering to have
an education'. Eventually, she, like her mother and grandmother before her,
became a school teacher. However, the years of denial by her mother, her place-
ment in a commercial stream, and her initial failure at School Certificate have
left her insecure in her identity as an intellectual.

As an adult, Sharon retains a deep-seated sense of intellectual inferiority, despite
some outstanding success academically. She says that she feels her schooling as
a 'commercial girl' gave her an inferior education and that she can never catch
up with her peers who were in academic streams:

I missed a lot of groundwork and, for instance, I didn't know how to put an essay
together. I was so unconfident in those first days at university that I'd be a nervous
wreck. I'd be crying and weeping and wailing over my efforts to get things up to a
standard which I'd never before had to accomplish. I just found the whole thing
traumatic, utterly traumatic. I think there are things that you never actually pick up on,
just basic knowledge, basic general knowledge of how the world operates. All about
religions, all about politics, all about the history of the world. I've had none of that and
I just feel, all the time there's this undercurrent of non-confidence sort of goes along
with me all the time because I just know that even though I can get to a certain standard
now and I've got a good degree, I still have this basic lacking. But I'll never catch up.
I'll never be able to read fast enough, I'll never catch up on all those 'booky' type things
in my whole life.

Margaret: an academic girl

Margaret is a school teacher with university qualifications in mathematics. She
had, upon leaving school, attempted an engineering degree. After failing the first
year of the course, she had taken casual jobs, married and had children. On first
applying for Teachers' College, she was turned down – she was accepted the
following year. Now a qualified teacher she has completed a university degree.

Margaret's parents were both primary school teachers who had taught together
in rural schools throughout much of her childhood. She felt that both parents
had always expected her to succeed academically and 'It was always assumed
that I would go to university.' Both her parents and her grandmother provided
her with academic cultural capital and Margaret had always aimed at a
professional career:

I remember thinking that I was different from other girls, say particularly when I was
in the third form, in a girl-only school because I knew I was going to university and
I felt that going to university was much better than being a secretary. I was actually a
total intellectual snob; I wouldn't have dreamed of doing something I thought as
insignificant as being a secretary or something like that. I used to feel I was more
interesting because I was a female with those kind of ideas, because I knew it was
unusual for a woman. The other thing that was always talked about in my family was

my grandmother was always held up to me. That's my mother's mother, not my father's mother. My mother's mother was very bright and had got a degree in maths and she'd had a big struggle to get it. This example of granny was always held up in front of me. There were strong expectations of me.

The model of female intellectuality that Margaret had grown up with was intertwined with a perception of an appropriate feminine sexual identity. From her perspective as an adult, Margaret notes that during adolescence, part of her professional ambition (engineering) was motivated by marital ambitions. Although her father had wanted to be an engineer, the war had prevented this and he had become a teacher instead. This lost ambition was transferred to Margaret and became a part of her intellectual and sexual fantasy life:

I never could decide what I wanted to do. I ended up heading towards engineering because I couldn't think of anything else. My father kept saying how good it would be. A part of their whole fantasy, I've got to say, was that it was always assumed that I was going to get married and there was a slightly 'snobby' thing I suppose. Obviously if you think you have an intelligent daughter I suppose you don't want her to marry a drainlayer. Part of this thing was that I would go to university, I would have a career on my own which would make me more interesting and all the rest of it. It wasn't so much that I would have a wonderful life myself – that's part of it, but still there was this fact that I would make some brilliant professional man an exciting wife.

As a member of the top academic stream in a girls' school in a provincial town, Margaret and her friends had their own 'intellectual' subculture.

I used to go to the fifth form dancing class which was held from 3.30 to 4.00 and boys came up from the boys' college. You can imagine how innocent I was. It was in the Girls' College assembly hall. . . . The other thing I used to do at school was debating which is what the girls in the academic stream used to do because we could meet the boys; we had a combined Boys' High School–Girls' High School debating team. If you were too superior to hang around the boys' college when the first fifteen were having rugby practice you joined the debating society and met the intellectuals. An aura of ultimate snobbishness, we really were. . . . The highlight of the debating year was that the university freshmen used to send a team up to debate the combined Girls'-Boys' College and of course these people had enormous status just because they were at university.

The girls in this intellectual subculture saw themselves and each other as virgins. 'Dates' were with boys from the same top-stream academic level with similar aspirations and fantasies. They had their own mode of dress (the boys 'affected black jerseys'), no doubt copied from the bohemian atmosphere of university student coffee bar subculture of the early 1960s:

Margaret: As for boyfriends, me and the girls that I was friendly with, our boyfriends all came from our own class level at the Boys' College and the boys were exactly like we were: from the top class and the debating society, high achievers academically. . . . When we were in the fifth form we were all into poetry, candles and stuff like that and we used to go around to Jim's place, the intellectuals amongst us, and lie around in the corner being bohemian. Drinking black coffee with no sugar, which we all hated, but couldn't have asked for some milk or sugar because you had to drink black coffee. The candles would be spluttering down on the wine bottles that Jim had collected from his older brothers or his mother.

Interviewer: Where did you get the bohemian fantasy from?

Margaret: I've got no idea. I think very probably from our boyfriends plus the fact that, we had this idea of considering ourselves intellectuals – part of it was that me and my female friends were all no good at sports. The girls who were interested in sports, there was always this thing about getting a guy in the first fifteen. On principle we would not have gone out with a boy who was in the first fifteen. We all thought and had heard that there was alcohol at some parties the first fifteen went to and we wouldn't have touched any alcohol, apart from communion wine. It was just so straight. If any of us had gone to a party and somebody had opened a bottle of beer we would have gone straight home. We were so virtuous.

For Margaret and her girlfriends, sexual activity consisted of romantic attachments and fantasies of relationships with artistic, bohemian, intellectual men. Indulging in sexual intercourse was a possibility that was never seriously entertained:

I just assumed that nobody was 'having it off' with anyone and really in the group that I moved in I think we were all virgins. I really do . . . . The sorts of girls that weren't virgins, were the ones that went around looking 'knowing', and I didn't know what the hell it was they knew anything about. But I think probably now that those were the ones that weren't virgins, the ones that I used to think looked like they know something that was going on that I didn't. That school was streamed to the end and I was always in the top class. There would be occasional girls in that class that may have been sexually active, they certainly weren't in my friends. We all thought that sex was 'no-no' until you got married. I suppose we all had some kind of semi-religious thing in our upbringing to add to our parents' morality.

Their code of sexual morality protected many of these girls from becoming pregnant, enabling them to pursue their fantasies of intellectual relationships and personal achievement at higher levels of the education system.

Margaret found her intellectual/cultural fantasies validated and extended by the adolescent subculture of the top academic stream. The subjects studied in the school curriculum became part of the everyday currency of her youth culture. This was, however, important not in its own right, but as a means of attracting intellectual men:

When I was in the sixth form I started going out with a guy who I went out with for about five or six years . . . he was sensitive and artistic and Jim and Hamish were best friends and they would lie around with candles and read Eliot to each other. They were quite amazing guys. I just remember reading Eliot ad infinitum in the seventh form – we had to read the complete works. I grew to hate T. S. Eliot. Well, I don't think I ever understood a word of it but I did know that it was a frightfully amazing intellectual thing to understand. These guys couldn't do anything wrong as far as I'm concerned.

In Bourdieu's terms, Margaret's [individual ethos] and her school experience were compatible and continuous, readily convertible to school credentials. Her peer group subculture reinforced this, the value of virginity serving not only her academic ambitions but also her – and her parents' – marital ambitions. As an 'interesting woman' she could attract a 'professional' husband at university.

Tahuri: a cultural outcast

Tahuri was a Maori girl brought up by adoptive parents who were 'working class' in terms of the pakeha [white] world. Both had had unpleasant experiences of schooling. Keenly aware of distinguished scholars in her family history, Tahuri had been taught to read by a relative at the age of 4.[22] She grew up with high academic ambitions, her cultural capital having been internalized from her extended family network. Tahuri was stimulated by some of the teaching she encountered in her primary school career. It was at secondary school that her enculturation as a Maori was viewed as inappropriate and the devaluation of her culture made explicit. In a provincial girls' school, which streamed pupils at least partly on the basis of test results, Tahuri was prevented from taking Maori language:

To get into the Maori language classes you had to be in the General stream, which meant second or third class intellect, certainly not remedial or vocational or technical, but definitely not top stream and I was top stream, and because I was top stream I had to be fed a diet of French and Latin. And there was no way that they were going to let me do Maori, no way at all. My mother actually come up to the school and it was only one of the few times, because she hated the schools, she hated the whole idea of going near schools. She would never go near any of the schools I attended before high school and she actually came up and said that they wanted me to do Maori and the teacher just said, 'There is no way this girl can do Maori, she has to be in the top third form and you should feel very pleased that we are putting her in the top third form because that's where she belongs.'

In order to be 'any good' in the eyes of the school, Tahuri had to deny her Maoriness, which she refused to do. She teamed up with the few other 'outcasts' in the top stream. Part of their resistance was an exaggerated display of sexuality – assuming the trappings of 'tartiness'.[23] As an example of this form of resistance, Tahuri described 'mufti day' at Girls High:

3 Professional A would turn up in little twin sets and pearls, and beautifully cut skirts and neat shoes with discreet heels and they'd be carbon copies of their mothers. You know, with a little bit of lipstick and maybe earrings, and, terribly prissy. Quite fashionable, you know, the sort of East Coast preppy style, that type of dress. And those were 3 Professional A girls. And I'd wear things like black pants and black shirt – in those days they had those things called jerkins, that sort of V-neck sleeveless tunic. When I wore my black pants and black shirt with jerkin I thought I looked real smooth. And I used to Brylcream, oh, coconut oil my hair and get it all like Elvis. And that's how we used to go to school. It was unacceptable. It was totally atrocious. We were just walking catastrophies, us three, we were just not allowed through the door. I mean, it was just so dreadful that we were in that class, degrading its quality like that. Meanwhile, down in 3 Vocational, 3 Reform and 3 Commercial B, there were all the tarts. All the tarts just like us. At Girls High the lower forms were brown. And so there was not only the class-sexuality dimension but there was also the class-sexuality-race. They were brown sluts, bags.

Pakeha [white] women in my study mentioned the stigmatizing of girls in low streams as promiscuous. However, in Tahuri's school, the association of sexual promiscuity with lack of intellect was further exacerbated by racism. Maori girls were concentrated in the lower streams and seen by some of the academic girls as more sexually promiscuous. Tahuri described the headmistress of her provincial girls' school as racist and her account of the practice of 'streaming' suggests strongly that it reflected and reinforced the social class structure of the community.

The women I interviewed described two 'types' of girls: virginal academics, and promiscuous 'deviants' who came predominantly from the lower streams. This double standard served the process of cultural reproduction, in that an unplanned pregnancy would have destroyed an academic girl's professional career, and (bearing in mind that the period studied is the 1960s) an 'illegitimate' child would have jeopardized her chances on the ruling-class marriage market. These attitudes were held and reinforced by the women's parents and by teachers.

Discussion

In this chapter I have attempted to show how a life-history methodology can increase our understanding of what Madeleine MacDonald has called 'the operation of the sexual division of labour in the creation and the nature of cultural capital.'[24] I have shown that within the family the influence of both mothers and fathers must be taken into account, and, especially in the case of Maori women, the influence of other 'significant adults' in the extended family network must not be overlooked. The creation and transmission of cultural capital within the family may be fraught with contradictions – in the case of Sharon, the desire for a 'good education' was maintained despite her parents' deliberate attempts to prevent this. In the case of Margaret, parental educational achievement and ambitions were translated into a family environment which stimulated their daughter to seek academic and professional success. Although 'significant others' in Tahuri's whanau group had stimulated her academic ambitions, her desire to study Maori was treated as deviant by the school – rather than as 'cultural capital' in the eyes of the school administrators.

The case studies described in this chapter suggest strongly that the practice of streaming, at least in the period studied, was a central factor in the process of cultural reproduction. Studying the process of cultural reproduction in the family –school nexus is a complex task revealing many contradictions. For academic girls, professional and marital 'success' (marrying into one's own class level)[25] required at this time delaying sexual gratification – to be successful for most meant to be virginal, or at least to maintain the pretence of virginity. The subcultures constructed by the academic stream girls in my study emphasized virginity, academic success and relationships with boys of the same social class group. Overt displays of sexuality were perceived as deviant and as being more common in the lower streams of the school: to be sexual was to be non-intellectual.

The three women discussed in this chapter have all, ultimately, been successful in terms of the formal education system. Despite the obstacles of ambiguous messages about their sexuality, class and ethnicity, these women had sufficient access to resources within and outside their families to give them the know-how to succeed in the system. As feminists, however, these women have become very critical of their early socialization as females within the family, the school and the wider society. Perhaps (finally), it is the experience of *marginality* – in terms of being working class, black, female or a combination of these – which is radicalizing.[26]

Notes and references

1 Althusser, L., 'Ideology and Ideological State Apparatusses: Notes toward an Investigation', in L. Althusser, *Lenin and Philosophy*, London, Monthly Review Press, 1971.

2 MacDonald, M., 'Cultural reproduction: the pedagogy of sexuality', *Screen Education*, Autumn/Winter 1979–80, pp. 141–53.

3 Plummer, K., *Documents of Life*, London, Allen and Unwin, 1983, p. 3.

4 A woman was considered a feminist if she defined herself as a feminist. I included liberal feminists, radical feminists, lesbians, socialist and anarchist feminists. My definition of 'educator' included one separatist who was working as a community education officer for a feminist social work group; the rest were working, or had worked, within the formal education system. Most had taught at more than one level. In total, three had taught in pre-schools, seven in primary schools, two in secondary schools, seven had either lectured and/or tutored at university level, two had done some part-time teaching in technical institutes, and three in adult education services. Interviews were taped and transcribed. Each woman has been interviewed between two and four times over a two-year period. They live in several different cities.

5 Department of Education, *Report of the Commission on Education in New Zealand* ('Currie Report'), Wellington, Government Printer, 1962, p. 585.

6 A moving account of a collaborative research style is Ann Oakley's paper. 'Interviewing Women: a Contradiction in terms', in H. Roberts (ed.), *Doing Feminist Research*, London, Routledge and Kegan Paul, 1981.

7 Bourdieu, P., 'The School as a Conservative Force: Scholastic and Cultural Inequalities', in R. Dale *et al.* (eds), *Schooling and Capitalism: A Sociological Reader*, London, Routledge and Kegan Paul and the Open University, 1976, p. 110.

8 Bourdieu (see note 7), p. 113.

9 Evidence of this is given by the Department of Education (see note 5) and by R. Harker, 'Streaming and social class', in P. D. K. Ramsay (ed.), *Family and School in New Zealand Society*, Auckland, Pitman, 1975.

10 Latin would rarely have been offered in rural schools. To take Latin, rural children went to boarding schools – either élite private schools or state hostels attached to girls' schools in the larger towns.

11 Frame, Janet, *To the Is-land: An Autobiography, Volume 1*, Auckland, Hutchinson, 1983, p. 170; M. Findlay, *Tooth and Nail: The Story of a Daughter of the Depression*, Wellington, Reed, 1974, p. 23.

12 Willis, P. *Learning To Labour*, London, Saxon House, 1977. In Willis's terms, 'resistance' by working-class youths is unsuccessful – working-class kids get working-class jobs. Tahuri, however, was academically successful.

13 At this time, some of the School Certificate subjects taken by girls in the Commercial streams were not available for University Entrance. To sit UE, they would have had to 'pick up' new subjects for which they did not have the fifth form prerequisite – a difficult undertaking.

14 Taylor, S., *Reproduction and Contradictions in Schooling: the Case of Commercial Studies*, SAANZ Conference Paper, Sydney, August 1982, p. 11.

15 There is no research evidence at hand in this country to support this 'typification' constructed in academic girls' subcultures: both the commercial girls in the study remained virgins while at school. Only one of the academic girls was not a virgin, and she had been molested as a child.

16 Three of the women interviewed had dairy farmer fathers. Five of the women had mothers who at some time had been school-teachers. Information on the incidence of

farmer-fathers and teacher-mothers is given in Department of Education (see note 5), and in P. D. K. Ramsay, *The Vocational Commitment of Student Nurses and Teachers*, D. Phil. Thesis, University of Waikato, Hamilton, 1978.

17 Sharon's views of what constitutes a 'good education' are expressed several times in her interviews. For her, it means the type of teaching received in the top academic streams, which she sees as the knowledge and tastes of the urban educated elite; Shakespeare, classical European music and the languages of continental Europe.

18 An important study of class endogamy among the French peasantry has been written by P. Bourdieu and L. Boltanski, 'Changes in social structure and changes in the demand for education', in Giner and Archer (eds), *Contemporary Europe*, London, Routledge and Kegan Paul, 1978. The framework they present would be a useful one in analysing the drift of young rural women to the cities in the post-war era in New Zealand.

19 Frame, and Findlay give evidence of this (see note 11).

20 Barrington, R. and Gray, A. *The Smith Women*, Wellington, Reed, 1981, p. 23.

21 At the time Sharon sat School Certificate (the mid 1960s), a pass was calculated by the aggregate marks in four subjects; 200 was a pass. So in her second attempt, Sharon scored an aggregate of 207.

22 Both Maori women interviewed had strong female academic role models in their whanau group. Maori and pakeha women frequently mentioned grandmothers as sources of cultural capital. These observations strongly support the contention that sources of cultural capital often lie outside the nuclear family.

23 McRobbie, A., 'Settling accounts with subcultures: a feminist critique', in *Screen Education*, no. 34, 1978, pp. 37–8.

24 MacDonald (see note 2), p. 151.

25 i.e. class endogamy – either upward mobility or simply no 'marrying down'.

26 Bartky, S., 'Towards a phenomenology of feminist consciousness', in M. Vetterling-Braggin (ed.), *Feminism and Philosophy*, Tottowa, Littlefield Adams, 1977.

7 Learning to resist: black women and education

Beverley Bryan, Stella Dadzie and Suzanne Scafe

Black women cannot afford to look at our experience of Britain's education system merely from our perspective as women: this would be to over-simplify the realities we face in the classroom. For black schoolgirls sexism has, it is true, played an insidious role in our lives. It has influenced our already limited career choices and has scarred our already tarnished self-image. But it is *racism* which has determined the schools we can attend and the quality of the education we receive in them. Consequently, this has been the most significant influence on our experience of school and society.

Like our relationship with the police or our treatment by the judicial system, education has been a crucial issue for the black community, for it has highlighted the true nature of our relationship with the state. The education system's success can be measured directly in terms of black children's failure within it. By institutionalizing the prejudices and the undermining assumptions we face in our everyday lives, the schools have kept our children at the very bottom of the ladder of employability and laid the blame on us. The schools' ability to churn out cheap, unskilled factory fodder or 'multi-skilled' YTS trainees may have served the economic needs of this society; but it has not met the aspirations of a community which has always equated education with liberation from poverty.

Education has always been a burning issue for black women. Viewed, in the aftermath of slavery, as virtually the only means for us and our children to escape the burden of poverty and exploitation, it was regarded in the Caribbean as a kind of liberation. Our families made enormous sacrifices to send us to school, even though they could often offer us only the most basic education.

Even when we left the Caribbean, this desire for an education remained with us. On arrival here, however, it was not seen as an issue of immediate concern because permanent settlement in Britain was not something we contemplated. Expecting an early return home to rear and educate our children, we made no demands on the British education system, for whom the isolated black child posed no real challenge or threat.

Our hopes of a swift return, however, were not to be realized. Thus we resigned ourselves to the inevitability of a long stay and began to send for our children. The British education system made no effort to prepare for their arrival. Regarded as a temporary though unavoidable ill born of economic necessity, their growing presence in the schools in the early 1960s was viewed with distasteful complacency. Black children were nothing more than a short-term phenomenon, which would

Source: Extracted from B. Bryan, S. Dadzie and S. Scafe *The Heart of the Race*, London, Virago, 1985.

eventually disappear of its own accord. From the outset, the educationalists with their colonialist superiority regarded black children as a privileged minority, who should be grateful for any education they got.

Consequently, the first black schoolchildren to step into Britain's inner-city classrooms suffered traumas which were largely ignored. Yet for young children who had been uprooted to join mothers they could often barely remember and entire new families of brothers and sisters, the pressures were enormous – quite apart from the need to adapt to a whole new process of schooling.

What the educationalists flippantly dismissed as 'culture shock' was often a far more profound and traumatic experience. In most cases, schools were situated in the worst areas of the inner cities – the only places where housing was available to us – presenting us with a seedy, depressing landscape and a totally unfamiliar environment. This physical hostility was compounded by a barrage of verbal, physical and psychological attacks on our sense of place and identity.

At the beginning of my first playtime at school, one of the more friendly white girls led me into the playground, where all the others crowded around me. Two boys started to call me 'Blackie' and 'golliwog'. This made me very upset. I remember taking my beret off my head and holding it up to my face and saying, 'Look, I'm not Black, this is!' When I told the teacher, she just said, 'Take no notice.' This sounded useless to me. How could I not take any notice? It was so hurtful. And it was the same with my parents, they just told me to ignore it too. I felt really depressed, especially since the name-calling grew steadily worse. Then they started to mock my accent, saying things like, 'What are you saying, golliwog?' and 'Speak English please.' School became a nightmare for me. They poked and pulled at me. 'Is your hair knitted then?' 'Do you live in trees?' When it got too much I ran home, but my parents seemed unable to understand what a torture school had become. 'Just do your work and don't pay anybody any mind' – but I couldn't.

Teachers and pupils alike displayed open curiosity, as they struggled to reconcile the images from a lifetime of racist conditioning with the reality they now saw in front of them.

I remember being constantly asked by the teachers and the children where I came from, what was it like, did I live in a house or a tree, did we wear clothes, did we speak English? You begin to feel so different, you feel uncomfortable, and because you are so young you don't know how to deal with it. The way I dealt with it was I decided I wasn't going to fight it. I gave in to whatever they said. Every day at school, we had to write a diary of what we did at home. I wrote that in Jamaica we lived in trees and ran around with whatever they told us we wore, and I even drew pictures. I think it got to the stage where I wasn't sure what was true anymore, the pictures they were showing me or the memories I had in my head.

This assault on our sense of identity, which we were rarely prepared for, made us vulnerable and isolated, as we struggled to find the language and gestures which could convey our response. It also singled out many black parents as 'troublemakers', when they went into the schools and articulated this response on our behalf.

I remember my early schooldays as being a very unhappy time. People were watching you all the time, and if you did anything it wasn't because you were you, but because you were Black. There was a time when this teacher pulled me up in front of the class and said I was dirty and that she was going to make sure that my neck was cleaned – and she proceeded to do it, with Vim. My father is usually a quiet man, but he went up there with a machete.

When teachers not only failed to challenge the playground taunting, but frequently compounded racialist attitudes through their own ignorance, we were compelled, in many cases, to defend ourselves physically.

My memories of school are of being really laughed at and everyone calling me a golliwog. In my first three years, I was the only Black girl at school, and consequently I had fights with every single girl and some of the boys too, because of their racial taunting. It wasn't until I went to that school that I realized I was Black, as such. All my friends were white. I even wore bows in my hair, like they did. It wasn't until an Australian teacher called me a blackie that I realised. It was a terrible moment.

This cruel rejection of our children was something which black mothers had to respond to. In some cases, hardened by similar daily experiences in the workplace, our response was clearly inadequate. What appeared to the children as a failure to understand the experience was often the bewildered or angry reaction of someone who found her own experiences of racism difficult to articulate. Nevertheless, many of us did find ways of supporting and reassuring our children, as they learnt to cope with the mental bruises.

When I sent my daughter to school, I can remember her coming home one day and asking me why God had made her Black. That really hurt me. I asked her if she didn't like being Black, and she said no, she didn't, because she was the only Black child in her school. I told her God chose to make some of us Black and some of us white, and there's no difference between us. But still she didn't want me to plait her hair, I had to put it in a pony-tail all the time, otherwise she would cry, because all the other kids had their hair flowing down. . . . That made me aware that there was a lot of prejudice in the schools that was affecting the kids deeply.

The hurtful ignorance and implacable hostility of other children was probably the most common experience of the first generation of black children to enter British schools. It is no surprise that we were viewed as oddities, given the colonialist diet on which our peers were still being fed. Our hair, habits, language and customs were seen as the manifestations of savagery, confirmation of our uncivilized past. Even to young children, and at a time when televisions were not a common feature of every working-class home, we represented the foreign hoardes which had been tamed and disciplined under flag and empire. Indeed, it was the attitude of the teachers which did the most lasting damage. They were to interpret black children's disorientation and bewilderment as a sign of stupidity. Their concepts of us as simple-minded, happy folk, lacking in sophistication or sensitivity, became readily accepted definitions. Theories about us, put forward by Jensen in America and endorsed by Eysenck here in the late 1960s, gave such views a spurious credibility by popularizing the idea that race and intelligence are linked in some inherent way. The effect of this process was inevitable. Those of us who had lived in those 'foreign' places either built our own defences or leant to reject the lessons and teachers that presented our lives in such a derogatory way.

Because of such reactions, we came to be labelled 'dull' and 'disruptive'. However, what appeared to teachers to be disinterest or unresponsiveness, was often our only way of responding as children to the negative school environment we had to enter daily. Those of us who had come to England with a joy for learning and a deep-seated respect for the value of education, often found our enthusiasm dampened by the arrogant, insidious assumptions of the school curriculum. In lessons and textbooks we were either ridiculed or ignored. Rarely, if ever, were we acknowledged in a positive way, on equal terms.

I had always liked reading, and could have really enjoyed literature at school. I suppose I liked the strange and different world I found in books, especially the ones about life as it was supposed to have been like in Britain. This couldn't last though, because reading often became a nasty, personal experience. You would be getting deep into a story and suddenly it would hit you – a reference to Black people as savages or something. It was so offensive. And so wounding. Sometimes you would sit in class and wait, all tensed up, for the next derogatory remark to come tripping off the teacher's tongue. Oh yes, it was a 'black' day today, or some kid had 'blackened' the school's reputation. It was there clearly, in black and white, the school's ideology. The curriculum and the culture relies on those racist views.

Children were presented with a world view in which blackness represented everything that was ugly, uncivilized and underdeveloped, and our teachers made little effort to present us or our white classmates with an alternative view. Having been raised on the same basic diet of colonial bigotry themselves, they simply helped to make such negative stereotypes and misconceptions about us more credible. According to them, we 'could not speak English' and needed 'special' classes where our 'broken' version of the language could be drilled out of us. We were quiet *and* volatile. Best of all, we were good at sports – physical, non-thinking activities – an ability which was to be encouraged so that our increasing 'aggression' could be channelled into more productive areas.

In the first form, they found out that I was good at sport. They had the Triple A's Award Scheme and I beat everyone. I became district champion for that year. Then they decided that I could win all the medals for them. But one day, during some special Sports event, I was talking to my friend and missed the race when they were calling me on to the track. It was horrible for me, after that. Because I'd missed the race, my teacher wouldn't have me back in his classes! I decided then and there that I'd had enough of running, but they never stopped trying to coax me back. All I wanted to do was to become an air hostess, but the teachers said I wouldn't be able to do that because I wasn't clever enough. This hadn't seemed to bother them when I was missing classes to train, though. One teacher told me I would never amount to anything and would be better off cleaning the streets . . . so I ended up leaving school without doing any exams. There was no one in school to give me any help and explain things to me, except when it was to do with sport.

Inevitably, the low expectations of teachers affected our performance in school. Our generally poor results in intelligence tests like the 11+ exam seemed to confirm their views. Throughout the 1960s, this test was the greatest arbiter in our future, designed to select and grade the future workforce. Because of its class and cultural bias, we were bound to fail, as were the majority of working-class children. The consequence for us was relegation to the secondary moderns and later to the lowest streams of the comprehensives. The education authorities disregarded the fact that bad schools with poor resources and indifferent teachers had existed in the inner cities long before our arrival and our presence became associated with the lowest educational standards. For most of us coming through that system, we were well on the road to ESN (educationally sub-normal) labels or dismal job prospects.

There were no chances or options offered to me. I would have liked to have stayed on at school, but I left in the fifth year. As far as I can remember, I only saw a Careers Officer once, a few weeks before leaving school. She didn't encourage us or offer any help in getting a decent job. I was fairly good at needlework, and because of this, dressmaking was the only line they were prepared to push me into. They never asked me if I wanted to do anything else. I didn't really want to just leave school and go and do piece-work in a factory, but that was it. Out. It's only when it was too late that I began to realise what had happened.

In spite of all the obstacles, some of us managed to slip through the net. We struggled out of those low streams, from 1c to 2b to 3a. We stayed on in the sixth, despite pressures from all around to leave at 16 and enter the job market. Our parents, anxious that we should escape the menial, low-paid work they had been forced to accept, urged us to seize any educational opportunity which came our way. Our aspirations were usually dismissed as over-ambitiousness by careers officers, who could hardly hide their scepticism when confronted with talk of 'A' levels, college or university for any black pupils. But our earlier experiences of school in the Caribbean undoubtedly influenced our ability to survive in the classroom.

Having had a substantial part of my education back home, I felt grounded in my culture and quite confident about my abilities. I would not allow myself to be swayed by suggestions that we were inferior. Our parents had striven too hard for us in the Caribbean to instil pride and self-respect into us. The church also helped. Not just religious education, although that was there as well, but the teachers who came out of the church. They were often women – very strict but also very sure of themselves. With the family, they fostered an atmosphere of learning, of having certain goals and objectives to fulfil.

Once in England, many of us fought for credibility, adopting the same stubborn determination to make it through the education system, despite the odds. When we found our ambitions frustrated, not through lack of money or too fierce competition this time, but by the teachers and schools themselves, we signed up for evening classes and Further Education courses. Night cleaning, auxiliary nursing and factory work often financed the education which the schools had failed or refused to give us.

The black women of this generation who were able to acquire the skills and qualifications they had set out to gain, did so despite the discrimination and institutionalized racism we encountered in every area of our lives. Where we succeeded, we were projected as examples of the neutrality of the system, as token blacks who had proven the exception to the rule. Although a few did succumb later to the perks which relative success can bring, many black women, recognizing how the system had been organized, went back into the schools as teachers, to wage an often solitary battle against the kind of racism which had made our own struggles necessary.

It was our community's growing readiness to mobilize in support of our children which ensured that our anger or bewilderment as parents could be channelled into a collective response. Probably the most important early initiative was the ESN campaign, which was spearheaded by black parents and teachers. Earlier bussing policies, designed to 'dilute' large concentrations of black low achievement, had been successfully opposed in some areas. The response of the authorities was quietly to transfer large numbers of black children into schools for the 'educationally sub-normal', under the guise of providing 'special' education for them. The by now familiar arguments about 'low IQ', 'broken English' and 'hyperactive behaviour' were once again put forward to justify the disproportionate number of black children who were being classified ESN, some directly on arrival from the West Indies. The whole community, galvanized by Bernard Coard's exposé of 'How the West Indian child is made Educationally Sub-Normal in the British education system' began to challenge these arguments. Foremost among those who opposed ESN schooling were black mothers.

At first I didn't realise what was going on because I really thought they were sending her to a 'special' school. The school sent me a letter telling me they were going to transfer her and that she'd get more attention, they never really spelt out what kind of school it was. But when I went up and visited, the penny dropped. As soon as I saw that most of the other kids there were Black, I knew something was going on. There was a lot of kids there who had nothing wrong with them, and as far as I was concerned my daughter was one of them. I mean, how can you reach ten years of age and still be learning your alphabet? I didn't know what to do, I was so angry. The only thing I could think of at the time was to give her as much extra help with her writing and sums at home as I could. But I went along to this meeting one Sunday and there were a lot of people there with kids in ESN schools who felt the same way. That's how they came to set up the Saturday school, because everyone was saying if the schools wouldn't educate our children, we should do it ourselves. My daughter really got a lot out of those sessions, because it wasn't just about reading and writing. They taught the kids about Black history and showed them that they had nothing to be ashamed of because Black people are as good as anyone else. It took me three years to get her back into the ordinary school, and I really had to fight to get them to accept her back. In the end, she left school with two CSEs because they said she'd missed too much to do any other exams. But after that she went to college, and passed five O levels.

It was our recognition of the need to challenge racist assumptions about the intelligence of our children which gave rise to Saturday and Supplementary Schools up and down the country.

But by the mid 1970s a new generation of black schoolgirls were coming through the system, who were very different to those who had entered school in the 1960s from the Caribbean. A variety of factors had helped to form and mould this new breed. Most had been born or brought up here, and knew no other home. We were not so inclined to regard the schools through the less critical eyes of some of our parents or older brothers and sisters. More importantly, we were able to draw on the legacy of the Black Power era. For most of us, cultural pride was no longer a matter for discussion. We had been raised in an era when blackness had become a source of strength, and militant black response a source of general inspiration. For young black women, the visible signs of this new mood were apparent in the exchange of straightened hair for Afros, and the donning of 'Free Angela Davis' badges and black berets. Many schools were antagonistic towards this outward show of black consciousness and attempted, unsuccessfully, to repress it. As the influence of black nationalism grew, so did the militancy of our response. In state schools, where we were in sufficient number, we took up the demand for Black Studies. Unfortunately, where we succeeded in getting it included in the curriculum, we soon learnt that this new dimension of knowledge was not sufficient in itself to counteract all the other negative forces which prevailed. Taught alongside the geography lesson, which depicted the 'developing' Third World as being totally dependent upon western generosity, and alongside the history lesson which concentrated on glorious white conquest, the value of Black Studies alone was always debatable. When the black community realized that it was being used by some schools as a convenient means of social control, enabling 'non-examinable' black pupils to be pacified and controlled, while white pupils got on with their 'O' levels and CSEs, the demand for Black Studies in schools became less audible.

The teachers have their stereotyped views. They think that if they give you one lesson a week of Reggae, that's enough. That's meant to prove they're not racist. But it doesn't. They're the ones who need Black Studies, not us. It's for them to change their attitudes towards Black people, because I think people are racist in this country but they don't even know it because it's built into their culture and they don't even realise it.

The lessons we learnt from our experiences ensured that we were now prepared to question the attitudes and practices of our teachers in a far more pointed way. Our increased consciousness enabled us to articulate and expose the basis of their thinking and the logical outcome of their assumptions. Above all, we gained the confidence to resist them.

One time we were in the buffet and something or other happened which resulted in everyone of us who was Black having to go and see the Head. My friend Donna wasn't there when it happened, so she went mad when they said she had to go too. She wanted an apology, but they wouldn't apologise. Instead of trying to remember who was there, they just called all the Black girls and never even asked who was there and who wasn't.

We had found the language with which to take on the racism of the school system, and the schools' inevitable response was one of paranoia. Teachers expressed this frequently, by dispersing us if we stood chatting in groups in the playground, because more than one of us was seen as a 'threat'. But increasingly we stood up to them, using the only forms of resistance available to us:

When I went to my last school, I noticed straight away that if they saw a group of Blacks together, they thought it spelt trouble. Typical. Black people together can start a riot. We were type-cast as the troublemakers. They used to get the male teachers to disperse us when we stood together in the corridors, chatting or eating our sweets. Sometimes we even got searched! One time, I was suspended in the fourth year for 'attempting to lead a rebellion'. Me and this white girl were trying to quieten the class down because we had a supply teacher for that lesson and they were all misbehaving. The Head came in and got the wrong end of the stick. The white girl wasn't suspended, though, and the reason they gave my mother was that I was already on report. But the white girl had been truanting for months.

Non-cooperation, disinterest, truancy, strikes and demonstrations were the ongoing response of many black pupils throughout the 1970s to an education which was increasingly seen as irrelevant. While our actions were not always a collective act of conscious resistance, they were nevertheless an expression of our growing disaffection with what the schools – and the society – had to offer us. However hard we studied, the most we could aspire to were a few CSEs, which even at Grade I came nowhere near the value of an 'O' level, as everybody knew. Countless black pupils were shunted into CSE and non-exam classes, because our behaviour or attitudes were considered inappropriate for an 'O' level class. The fact that this behaviour was symptomatic of a deep-rooted dissatisfaction with the education system was neither acknowledged or investigated. Sport continued to be the only subject we were encouraged to excel in. But we knew that while we dissipated our 'aggression' on the track or in the gym, or languished in rows outside the headteacher's office, many of our less rebellious white class-mates were able to pursue their exam classes in relative peace.

The response of the authorities to growing pupil unrest was to continue to lay the blame on us, the children, and our parents rather than admit to the possibility that the schools could be at fault. In individual terms, this resulted in arbitrary and often long-term suspensions, to which many a black mother reacted with bewilderment, anger or bitterness.

It was the black community's angry response to the disproportionately high number of black children who were suspended, which was responsible for the decision of some local education authorities, in the late 1970s, to introduce disruptive units into their schools. These units enabled local education authorities both to hide embarrassing suspension figures from public scrutiny – containing 'the problem' within the education system – and to maintain their liberal façade. They were able to express concern about the recruitment of white schoolchildren to organizations of the extreme right, such as the National Front, and to shed public tears about the low level of black achievement in schools, while doing little to confront their own malpractice. Black mothers played a leading role in the campaign against the 'Sin Bins' and were successful, in some areas, in getting the authorities to reverse their policy of segregating those of us whom they could not educate.

In those areas where relegation to the educational dumping grounds was not challenged, disruptive units and special schools have taken over where ESN schools left off. The same low-level remedial work, social and life skills training and dubious behaviour modification programmes ensure that they provide no meaningful preparation for life, other than for the worst jobs and the dole queues. For black schoolgirls in such units, the experience has often been little more than an exercise in containment and control.

They put me in the disruptive unit when I was in the third year. It was a place called 'the Centre'. We didn't do any work. The teacher said I was to come to the Centre instead of the classes I didn't get on with. I was given a file with my name on it and had to write 'My Personal File' on it. Then she told me to write down anything personal in it. She used to take me into a room once a week and ask me if my parents were beating me, those sorts of questions. I never answered them, because I knew that whatever I said would get twisted around. Most of the time in the unit you played a game called Sorry Lawrence. I thought it was great, at the time. They didn't help any of the children who got behind in their work, though. They treated us as if we were mentally handicapped. There were some ESN people there, too. They let you get away with everything. I used to go in there and she used to say, 'Take your coat off', and I'd say, 'No, it's too chilly'. I gave her hell for two weeks.

The more liberal response to this kind of widespread disaffection was to call for the multi-cultural curriculum to be introduced into schools. For the first time, the grievances which we had been voicing for years began to gain some credibility. A small but significant number of teachers joined forces in organizations like NAME (National Association for Multi-Racial Education) to present a critical analysis of teaching materials and practices in multi-racial schools. However, their emphasis on cultural differences, rather than on the real issue of racism, diffused their initiative. Patties and steel-bands may have lent the school Open Day a multi-cultural atmosphere, but they presented no serious challenge to the numbers of black pupils relegated to non-exam classes in the fourth year. Multi-culturalism enabled many schools to appear to be responding to our needs, while in reality it simply served as another form of subtle social control. How many dub poems, for example, were really introduced into the classroom as a serious exercise in widening critical faculties; how many more as an easy answer to boredom and disobedience? The concerns of a few teachers ultimately made it possible for the liberalism and defeatism of many others to masquerade as care and concern.

There is a kind of racism which you have to be really sensible to realise. For example, you would think that teachers were being really nice to you if they told you they didn't mind whether you came back to the lesson after break. But they didn't mind and they didn't come and check on you because they didn't care. As far as they were concerned, they didn't expect anything of you because you were Black, so it was easier on them if you stayed away from their class.

There can be few more subtle ways of ensuring failure than to surrender all responsibility for guidance. Through this action, teachers effectively allowed almost an entire generation to leave school illiterate, innumerate and with few of the skills necessary for critical thought.

For many black girls leaving school with minimal qualifications, the current prospects appear limited. In areas of high youth unemployment, the only immediate option is the Youth Training Scheme. The racist hierarchy and the narrow sexist bias of such schemes have simply compounded the attitudes which already exist in the schools and careers offices. Low level clerical work, catering and childcare command a lead as the most common YTS courses on offer to black girls, and often the opportunity to attend college on day release is the only redeeming feature of an otherwise unrewarding year. However, thirty-six days on a Welfare Assistants' course cannot hope to compete with an NNEB, and black trainees know this. The black schoolgirls who leave school to enter such exploit-ative non-unionized training schemes frequently find that at the end of the year their long-term employment prospects are no better.

Return to Study and 'Access' courses have gone some way to confront the kinds of difficulties we have faced over the years on traditional courses, by offering us a route into further and higher education which by-passes the more formal stages of progression. Nevertheless, we have had to struggle just as hard to meet the required standards, and the notion that 'positive discrimination' makes things easier for us is a fallacy. Because of the general failure of colleges and adult education to prioritize the needs of women with childcare or domestic responsibilities, equal opportunities policies have fallen far short of their potential to give black women a meaningful opening into training or employment. Quite apart from the adjustments necessary on returning to study after several years, the attitude of white teachers, like their training, has not changed. And childcare still remains our most impeding obstacle, particularly if we are bringing up our children alone:

The reason I decided to do the General Education course was because I couldn't stand it being stuck at home any more. I haven't worked since I had my children and my mind was vegetating. The only time I spoke to anyone, apart from my immediate family and friends, was in Tescos and the only writing I ever did was the shopping list. I was getting so depressed living from hand to mouth on social security.

The course I did had a creche which meant I could leave my children there when I went to classes. None of us who were on that course would have been able to go to college if there hadn't been childcare provided. Out of fifteen of us on the course, twelve of us were Black women and every one of us was there because we wanted to improve our chances of getting a job. When I started, I thought there were things I would never be able to do, like maths, and my idea was to concentrate on the typing and my English. But after about a term, I began to feel a lot more confident about my own abilities, and that made me see the other subjects differently. I realised I didn't have to stop at RSA Typing because there are other things in life that I can do, if I put my mind to it. I suppose this was because I woke up to the fact that it wasn't just me who was in that boat. All the women on that course were struggling to bring up their kids and to make a life for themselves, and I figured we couldn't all be failures. There has to be something wrong with the system, because all of us were facing the same kind of problems.

Probably the most hopeful and lasting result of our struggle to gain access to further education – and one which augurs well for the future – has been the opportunity we have had to re-examine critically our experience of school. Taking part in the education process again, as mature women, has enabled us to gain a far better understanding of the impact our schooling has made on our lives, and its likely impact on our children. Courses which have offered us access to the professions or training in non-traditional vocations such as plumbing and carpentry have had a liberating influence on what many of us felt we could do and achieve. And whatever the level or the eventual goals of such courses, they have highlighted for us the individual and collective intervention which is possible in areas such as education.

It's only since I've been at college that I've been realised what it was all about at school. I didn't know before, but now I do. It makes me feel as if I could go right back to the beginning and start all over again. . . . I never made the connection between learning and having a good job; you get married and have a family. You get this idea from school and from society, even though for most Black girls work always comes into it, whether or not you're married. I think it's outdated to think that way, and I fought it all along. I always felt as if I didn't have the brains because I thought women were stupid before. Now I'm beginning to think very differently.

8   Privileged, schooled and finished: boarding education for girls

Judith Okely

Theoretical and methodological questions

The public school[1] has moulded a large proportion of the dominant male élite in British society, as well as their wives and mothers. It has also had a wider influence and has affected, albeit elusively, the alternative state form of schooling. While we find considerable research into public schools for boys,[2] there is little serious investigation of the girls' schools, nor indeed of the larger topic of gender differentiation in education.[3] It is assumed either that girls' boarding-schools are replicas of those for boys, or that they are of peripheral importance. The male and female institutions are not analysed as parts of one system. In addition to the studies of boys' schools, we have a plethora of autobiographies by men, while little comparable information exists from women, since few achieve the status which calls for an account of themselves.[4]

Statements about the educational achievements of 'the middle class' have tended to conceal their gender bias. Certainly some middle-class girls attend schools, boarding or day, of high academic quality, which encourage independent careers for their pupils. But there are other middle- or upper-class girls who are denied this, and *precisely because of their class*. The development of a distinct class consciousness is seen as more important than scholarship and achievement for them, as are beliefs which maintain the boundaries of their class. The girls are protected for a future marriage contract within an élite whose biological and social reproduction they ensure. They have no economic and political power independent of males such as their fathers, and later their husbands and sons. Born into a privileged and powerful élite, the women learn to live ambitions only vicariously through men.

The girls' school may be, invisibly, a preparation for dependence, while the boys' school is more visibly a preparation for independence and power. Some of the lessons of a girls' boarding-school carry uncertainties, or are inapplicable in later life. There is greater continuity for boys who, for example, are not confronted with the marriage–career dilemma which, for girls, becomes a source of conflict within their identity as female. In the boys' education, self-confidence, the experience of leadership and ambitious expectations are what count. Paradoxically, academic qualifications may not be crucial for public-school boys who, even if they do not progress to university, often move into lucrative and prestigious

Source: Extracted from Ardener, S. (ed.) *Defining Females: The Nature of Women in Society*, London, Croom Helm, 1978.

occupations not made available to their sisters with possibly equal potential. The girls' expectations are circumscribed by marriage.

The ethnographic data for this preliminary inquiry are largely autobiographical, my main informant being myself. Only these resources are explored fully here. In due course they may be synthesized with accounts by other former residents of boarding-schools, including those giving the perspective of the staff, which, of course, will be quite different. Subsequent comparative research will necessarily reveal a diversity of experiences and understanding. Many women will have enjoyed their boarding-schools, especially those who fulfilled the aims of that education. But for some, including myself, it failed to teach its terms. If my sister and I had learnt our lessons correctly, it is unlikely that we should have gone to university. The extent to which my boarding-school is 'typical' of its time, the 1950s, or is similar to any such institution in the 1970s, cannot be examined here. Obviously there will be considerable variations and changes.

I deliberately confront the notion of objectivity in research by starting with the subjective, working from the self outwards. The self – the past self – becomes a thing, an object. Yet this past creates and governs the present and future. Even social anthropologists who usually study other cultures are led back from the other to the self. Indeed Pocock (1973, 1975) has suggested that there is a need to explore the totality of one's 'personal anthropology' and its consequences in order to be able fully to perceive others.[5] This interest in the subjective is no doubt strengthened by my being female and brought up so. Women's language of experience is often distinctly personal, but the general implications are always there to be found. We must therefore explore the abstractions contained in our anecdotes.

A word on the epistemological status of the autobiographical. It is retrospective – unlike a diary which is the record of the present. There will be a loss of memory. Some forgotten experiences may nevertheless affect the narrator unconsciously. The past will have become distorted. Misunderstandings will be revealed later if accounts of events are cross-checked with others who were present at them. But their information will also be skewed. The accuracy of childhood events may, however, be less important than the child's perception of them. They may have important repercussions in later life, some of which may be contrary to the conscious intentions of instructors and parents. The validity of autobiographical material is no different from many presentations by social anthropologists based on data gathered from informants during their fieldwork. The former is merely one account of what is believed to have existed, whereas the latter often include several autobiographical accounts which have been collapsed into one version. I am concerned with what I believed happened. My information is based on nine years as a boarding-school girl in the 1950s and on all the subsequent years of retrospective analysis.

The girls' boarding-school

Boarding academies for ladies existed in the eighteenth century, offering certain 'accomplishments'. But most of the now famous girls' public schools were established at the end of the nineteenth century and later, long after the boys' public schools were founded. Even in the 1920s and 1930s many middle- and upper-class girls, for example Jessica Mitford and her sisters (Mitford, 1977), were kept at home to be taught by governesses, whereas their brothers were sent away to school. My mother had a governess until the age of 16. Her five enjoyable terms at the school I later attended were a release from a somewhat claustrophobic home and gave her a chance to meet other girls. Her brothers went to boarding-school at an early age, but her younger sisters never went to school.

The girls' public boarding-schools may have been depicted as a new freedom and advance in women's education, but there were important class interests. Pauline Marks has noted that in 1898 in England, 70 per cent of girls in secondary education were in private boarding-schools 'often in towns where grammar and high schools had empty places'. The advantage of the schools they attended was their social homogeneity: 'eligibility for marriage and not the content of their daughters' education remained the dominant concern of middle-class parents' (Marks, 1976, p. 189). These observations are relevant to at least one girls' boarding-school in the 1950s.

It is not surprising that the dilemma between a career and marriage scarcely arose in a middle-class and relatively undistinguished boarding-school such as mine. Ideally, marriage was the ultimate vocation. Without records of the stated intentions of my teachers, I reconstruct these from remembered incidents. Some slogans remain: we were 'fortunate to be receiving a good education', and we believed it. Yet if there was academic intent, this was not borne out by the girls' performance, since the majority left after taking a few GCE 'O' levels. Out of a class containing up to thirty-five girls, six or less remained to take sometimes a single 'A' level – an accomplishment which simultaneously prohibited university ambition. There is no memory of the word equality. The pattern after school tended to be a year at a private domestic science or finishing school, preferably in Switzerland, and progress to an exclusive secretarial college. The ideal was to be a débutante, before making a 'good marriage'. Another respectable vocation was nursing, and then only at select London hospitals. Teachers' training was *déclassé*. Whereas work as a private secretary or nurse offered contact with a man of the right social class, teaching did not. Few, if any, of the girls entered occupations comparable to their brothers'.

Scholarly achievements and higher education were, nevertheless, reserved for a few girls,[6] possibly marked as vocational spinsters. These had also to conform to the school's ideas of good conduct. Academic proficiency did not guarantee encouragement.

With 13 'O' levels and while studying for four 'A' levels, I was summoned to the senior mistress. She declared I would be 'selfish to go to University, *even* Aberystwyth', thereby depriving a worthier person of a place. She suggested a career which would make use of my 'A' levels in French and Art – by training as a designer of corsets and lingerie for a famous company in Switzerland.

Separations

The British boarding-school is marked by its forms of separation from urban culture, from other social classes, from family and home, and from the opposite sex. The separation from 'normal' life lasts many years. Although separations exist for both boys and girls, the differing consequences for each sex will become apparent.

Geographical and cultural

Compared to boarding-school boys, it seems that girls are permitted even less contact with the world outside the school grounds. For us, the nearby town was banned, taboo, except for perhaps a termly shopping trip under strict surveillance and with our few shillings handed out on Saturdays. We retained our coppers for Sunday chapel collection. Money found on us on any other days brought the severest punishment. Thus we were withdrawn from commerce, from earning and purchase.

We left the grounds about twice a week in 'crocodile' on set rural routes, skirting the town. Over-15s could go out for 'walks in threes' on certain days. Parents came and 'took us out', perhaps once a term. Written contact from and to the outer world was overseen. Outgoing letters not to parents were placed in unsealed envelopes for checking, incoming mail was examined, steamed open, even confiscated in some cases.

My sister was crazy about Elvis Presley. Her friends paid for her subscription to the Presley fan club. Nothing arrived. Weeks later, the senior mistress summoned her and showed her the pile of Presley literature. My sister was told, 'You are fit only to dance at Hammersmith Palais!' The papers and pictures were destroyed.

Presley, sexually insinuating, was part of that proletarian culture from which we were to be protected. Yet even tamer forces threatened. Except for the *Illustrated London News* and *Punch* in the library, comics and magazines were banned, even *Woman's Own*, which we read secretly in the lavatory, where its torn pages were hung by matron for wrapping our dirty sanitary towels. All personal books had to be checked and signed by staff. Our storage drawers and our mattresses were searched for any offending literature which might have come from that far, urban world. Like the neophytes, the girls were bound together as partners in pain, or we detached ourselves in shared humour, and laughed at our custodians.

Class

Geographical seclusion was matched by our separation from all other social classes in the strange English hierarchy. Parents of middle- or upper middle-class children demonstrate a desire to protect them from any classes below, and from contamination in what were euphemistically called the 'local' schools. Families may see themselves as randomly scattered and without sufficient contact with others of the same class pretensions, thereby risking interclass familiarity. The boarding-school solves the technical problem. Offspring are concentrated with their kind and simultaneously separated from others. That is the meaning of 'exclusive' when applied to these institutions. When the children are home for the holidays, their parents can control their friends and contacts.

Along with our accents went a pooling of prejudices and values, and ways of eating and moving – even our handwriting conformed. When I arrived, aged 9, from my Lincolnshire school, my ornate looped writing had to be unlearnt; it was too proletarian. A distinct set of manners was acquired.

Many years after leaving, I met an old school friend who commented on another former inmate who appeared to have slipped down the class ladder: 'She wrote to me on lined paper. I know when a friendship has to stop.'

We were taught that we could give charity but never receive it, thus defining precisely our class position:

A dormitory mate, whose parents were abroad, asked her relatives to forward a parcel of discarded holiday clothes. Several of us shared out the luxurious dresses, skirts and sweaters. The parcel had aroused the curiosity of the authorities. We were summoned, rebuked for 'accepting charity' and bringing shame on our parents, then ordered to repack and send the items to an East London mission. I managed to conceal a skirt and pair of shoes in the recesses of the games corridor until the end of term.

Family and home

Ironically the 1950s witnessed the popularity of Bowlby's claims that early separation from mothers would produce unstable children. The arguments were extended to schoolchildren of working mothers. The cry went up of 'latch-key' children. It was really directed at working-class mothers. The upper middle classes continued to despatch their children from home, depriving them of affection though guaranteed twenty-four-hour custodial care. In some cases boarding-school has been justified as the solution after divorce or widowhood. The loss of one parent is thereby compounded by separation from the other.

Unlike prison or Borstal, we were there because our parents loved us. Prisoners and Borstal offenders know they are incarcerated in order to suffer for their own misdeeds. Their relatives and parents may lament and oppose their sentences. Even if the parents of a Borstal offender assisted the authorities, it would be apparent that they had failed as parents or rejected their offspring. The trick for us at boarding-school was that we were not ostensibly there as a punishment. We could not take responsibility for what our unconscious might tell us. Parents were wholly in collaboration with our fate. The school song made us declaim: It is well understood/We are here for our good/So our parents/And mistresses say/And I fancy that we/Are inclined to agree,/Though we mean it/A different way.

After each verse, the refrain concluded:

> Your lot's not a bad one at all.
> NOT AT ALL!

The last line was shouted – one of the few occasions when the girls were encouraged, and indeed expected, to raise their voices.

We were orphans but did not know it. Ironic that each child was encouraged to have a collection box in the shape of a house – a Dr Barnardo's home. Here we placed our pennies for the 'real orphans'. 'Family Favourites' on the Sunday radio fascinated us. We unconsciously identified with the messages sent between relatives apart. Our separation meant, indeed, the loss of a personal relationship with any adult. The ratio of staff to child within the school made it technically impossible. Moreover, at least from my experience, the demands of the institution

en the memory of family relationships. For individuals facing the crisis
of a parent or relative few, if any, allowances were made.[7] Misbehav-
from these circumstances was punished. We defied the rules to comfort
n the dormitory at night.

Denied personal access to adults, we were also constrained in rigid peer groups. Friendships, even prolonged encounters, were not permitted between persons of different forms – since they threatened the rigid hierarchy with its ascending privileges and status. Only love could undermine it. Friendships between different ages were deviant and passionate, though rarely expressed in physical terms. For the authorities such relationships were seen as a dangerous emergence of sexuality, and of course a perversion. There were strict regulations also on intimacy between equals. No two girls were ever allowed to be together alone in the bathroom, lavatory or small music rooms. Thus any loving relationship possible was taboo. Two girls were actually expelled, allegedly for mingling their blood from cut wrists and swearing friendship on the Bible.[8]

Gender

Along with the hierarchy of class, another major division of British society is the segregation of the sexes. For girls, separation from boys and men will have meaning and consequences not symmetrical to that of boys in single-sex schools. Compared to the boys, girls are subjected to greater restrictions and less autonomy. Female adolescence, if not childhood, is socially prolonged in such schools, for this is a dangerous time for girls who are sexually mature, but considered too young for a marriage contract. This is especially true of a girl of a wealthy class, since her prospective spouse must be well established in his occupation, and have property, either transmitted or acquired. So the boarding-school offers safe segregation for girls from males of all social classes. Ollerenshaw hints at this:

Some parents and headmistresses feel that there is advantage for some girls in their being withdrawn during the schoolday or at boarding schools for the school term from the emotional turmoil of relationships with boys so that they may develop poise and self confidence (1967, p. 29).

Boys, it will be argued, are likewise segregated from females,[9] and are deprived of heterosexuality. Unlike girls, however, they are not separated from the vision of political power. Indeed, separation from women and the domestic sphere consolidates patriarchy. By contrast, girls in a boarding-school are deprived of both heterosexuality and education for power, our glimpse of which would always be vicarious, would always be through males. Like the disease of haemophilia, as Helen Callaway once said, power can be transmitted through females but is only manifest in males. In schools such as mine, we were separated from those destined to monopolize certain political and economic spheres – those who were to acquire lucrative occupations and earn our living for us. Our own exclusive education, unlike theirs, was not for a career.

The school consisted almost entirely of females – the Head, matrons, teaching and domestic staff – most of whom were resident. The males usually seen within the school grounds can be listed:

the school chaplain;

two non-resident gardeners;

the boiler-man;

two elderly retired male teachers, for German and English 'A' levels, who visited perhaps one day a week;

the part-time tennis coach who appeared in my last two summer terms;

the headmistress's male dachsund.

The majority of girls only directly heard the voice of one male, that of the chaplain. On Sundays we occasionally had a visiting preacher. If we were lucky enough to have a wireless we could hear male voices transmitted from the outer world. Yet men lurked somewhere, unseen. The Board of Governors consisted almost entirely of men – for example, a lord, a Tory MP, JPs and bishops.[10]

Men were directly involved in our most important initiation rite, our confirmation within the established Church of England – giving the right to partake of the body and blood of our male God (which had a peculiar British flavour). The day before the laying on of hands by the Bishop (the supremely visible male authority) we neophytes had to retire, not to the school chapel, but to the local church – where we had to write down all our sins in a notebook which had printed questions on each blank page. One question was 'Have I defiled my body?' I didn't know what this meant. I thought it might be squeezing spots. After filling in our books we then read our sins to the chaplain. We were given absolution and returned to the school to give the notebooks to 'Arold the boiler-man, who committed them to the eternal flames of the school boiler. (In earlier years the girls burned their booklets on the hockey pitch.) Thus the man at the lowest end of the social hierarchy dealt with our impurity. The equally inaccessible Bishop at the top, a member of the House of Lords, gave us purity and access to the sacred – the faith of the majority of the governing élite – while we were veiled in white, as if at a dress rehearsal for our future weddings within that élite.

Famous men, not women, were to be our heroic models. The school was divided into four cosmological 'houses', not represented by buildings but as groups of girls competing for cups in sports, conduct, drama and deportment – but not academic performance. The houses were named Shackleton, Scott, Livingstone and Rhodes, after male explorers and chauvinists of the colonial kind whom we, as Penelope to Ulysses, could never imitate. We could only marry and beget these kind of men and the Bishop's heroes. Aspirations were stimulated which were simultaneously shown to be impossible for women to attain. Our impotence was confirmed. Even our classrooms were named after male, not female, writers: Shakespeare, Cowper, Kingsley (not Brontë, nor Eliot, certainly not Wollstonecraft). The choice of famous men indicates how completely an alternative, potentially revolutionary, female ideology was suppressed.[11]

With no heroines with whom to identify, heroism was always located in the mysterious 'other', from which we were to choose just one man as spouse. The male/female category was not learnt and created by observable opposition, as was possible for those in mixed schools or living at home, but by an absence or omission. There was no way either to become as men, or to find an independent female way. Our lives and potential were presented as those of failed men. We knew and learnt that women were beneath men in that hierarchy in which we ourselves believed. Only a male could confirm us, preach to us. Marriage offered the only release from this multiple separation. Without a husband, we knew we could not maintain our financial hold in the class system, however exclusive our accent and manners. Our privileges were at the mercy of men.

We learnt this also from the teachers. An exclusively female community does not necessarily have feminist aspirations, nor do its custodians provide models of ideal independence. The majority of our teachers were unmarried[12] and, apart from a few proud and self-sufficient ones, they presented themselves as victims of misfortune – so many tales of fiancés killed in the war – perhaps to justify self-confessed failure. They did not teach us to emulate themselves. We recognized our teachers as of a lower social class, some by their accents. In so far as the girls upheld beliefs in their exclusive background, they could not easily identify with women who came from the stigmatized state schools.

Containment and powerlessness

It is sometimes said that girls' boarding-schools are more 'homely' than boys'. Certainly there were feminine touches for us (the rose garden, the floral curtains and coloured bedspreads) and the main building was more a country house than a utilitarian edifice. But within homely or domestic quarters life may still become oppressive. We longed for love and approval from these substitute parents, our custodians, but they were not mothers with relaxed affection and visible femininity. Nor were they like fathers, for we saw how they deferred to male visitors. Girls, in contrast to boys, were addressed by their first names, a practice which states, among other things, that surnames were merely passing premarital stamps of identity. The use of the personal name may not reflect kindness though it speaks of intimacy, which in the boarding-school is not reciprocated between the child named and the adult namer. Some intimacy facilitated greater control. Privacy could be thus invaded. Further research is required into variations between male and female boarding-schools in the extent of control exercised.

The ethnography of the school I describe includes the limitations on the girls' movement in space and time, and on their sounds and speech. Movement *beyond* the school grounds was minimal. Only the five or six prefects could ever go out alone. Control *within* these boundaries was infinitely detailed. The focus on minutiae demanding all our concentration impeded the thought of, reduced the possibility of, bolder action. What counted as crime for girls may seem petty, especially when compared to the misdemeanours of boys. But its very triviality affirmed the pervasiveness of control. For instance, to be 'out of bounds' was almost unimaginable. It rarely occurred, and carried the risk of being expelled. Our triumphs were less dramatic, although meaningful to us – when on a 'walk in three', for example, taking the lift instead of the many steps from the beach, and having the pennies to pay for it. (I still have that lift ticket in my album.)

Just as space, so was time subjected to a changeless grid. An electric bell rang at half-hour intervals, or more often. There was no unorganized time for doing what we wanted or going where we wanted, even at weekends. No way to decide for ourselves the next move. After lessons our prep was supervised: often seventy silent girls sat in one long room. We had no private studies. One of the very few times when the girls were not within sight of an adult was 'after lights out' in the dormitory. The punishment for talking or being found out of bed was therefore the severest. We defied the invasions of our privacy which surveillance implied by hiding in the lavatory or bathroom. I would climb on to the roof at night. A former inmate confessed that she even went for moonlit walks in the grounds. The constraints on space and time were further compounded by the rules imposing silence during the ten or so hours between lights out and the morning bell, also when lining up and entering the dining-room, moving from chapel to 'roll call', indeed in all passages and inevitably in lessons. Not only were our words limited, but at all times sound was abated.[13]

Not being expected to choose, to decide and to make statements, the girls had to exercise extreme self-discipline, especially when they complied with orders which seemed either small-minded or incomprehensible. The notion of 'character' was contrasted favourably by our instructors with 'personality' – a negative trait because it carried the notion of individuality. Leadership of sorts was expected from seniors, not charisma, but the ability to lead others into a conformity to maintain a status quo predetermined by adults.

In contrast, in boys' public schools, seniors and prefects assume dictatorial powers, including the right to inflict corporal punishment, to have 'fags' (junior boys as servants) and to establish rules. They thus acquire near-adult authority before they leave school. Cyril Connolly has compared the position of senior boys at Eton to 'feudal overlords' (1961, pp. 194–5). Lambert describes how, in the 1960s, the boarding pupils at the top of the boy's public-school hierarchies exercised 'more real power over others than sometimes the junior teachers' (1975, p. 241). For girls, obedience rather than authority is emphasized. Present evidence suggests that girls' prefect power is weak compared to that of their male counterparts. Certainly the fagging system is non-existent. Wober found that girls gave low priority to being a prefect (1971, p. 78), and that houses in girls' schools were rarely residential entities 'with separate authority and privilege systems' (1971, p. 116). The vertical social grouping found in boys' schools coincides with the extensive supervision of juniors by seniors. The horizontal social grouping of girls coincides with the reduced authority of seniors over juniors.

The system of punishment plays on the behaviour expected of girls, among whom self-control and self-negation take special forms. From infancy they are made modest, passive and withdrawn compared to boys. The pattern is already set before school, but there it is exploited, reinforced and elaborated. I use again the ethnographic example of my boarding-school. The required behaviour, and that which brought the precious reward of non-interference, included modesty, deference and submission. After a misdeed, part of the punishment was a 'row' from a member of staff and later the house captain. Humility, an apologetic stance, downcast eyes – possibly tears of defeat – were the correct forms. Any appearance of pride or dignity provoked further rebukes. Self-defence was rebuked with 'Don't answer back.' The 'right attitude' was rewarded, in that the girl was permitted to merge into the group. Our 'total institution' had all the elements which Goffman has described as 'stripping' (1968, p. 29), by which he means loss of personal identity. Here we see a closed circuit. The more a girl successfully complied with and internalized modesty, humility and the invisibility of the self, the more devastating the threat of their opposites.

The body: subjugated and unsexed

The concern with demeanour and carriage is one aspect of a total view of the body which reflects the extent of the institution's invasion and the ambivalences of its intentions. Within our school there could be no 'natural' movement which might contradict what the authorities considered correct. 'Bad' ways we had learnt elsewhere had to be changed. We did not merely unconsciously imitate movements and gestures, we were consciously made to sit, stand and move in uniform ways. We were drilled and schooled, not by those in whom we had confidence, but by those who had power over us. Our flesh unscarred, yet our gestures bore their marks.[14] Even when outside the classroom or off the games field, we were to sit, stand and walk erect, chin up, back straight, shoulders well back. At table when not eating, our hands were to rest in our laps. During the afternoon rest period matrons ordered us not to lie on our backs with knees bent. The games mistresses watched girls at meals, at roll call and in chapel, and would award good and bad 'deportment marks', recorded on a chart, and with house cups. If you were consistently upright you won a red felt badge, embroidered with the word 'Deportment'. This, sewn on your tunic, was a sign of both achievement and defeat. Our minds and understanding of the world were to reflect our custodians. With no private space, we could not even hide in our bodies which also had to move in unison with their thoughts.

The authorities observed accurately the language of the body. However much a girl might say the right things, do and act within the rules, and however in order her uniform may be, her general carriage, her minutest gesture could betray a lack of conviction, a failure in conversion. I remember (after yet another term's anxious waiting for promotion) being called to the headmistress who said that I needed to improve my 'attitude' before I could be made a sergeant. I was baffled because I thought I had successfully concealed my unorthodoxy. I had said and done what appeared to me to be in order. But they must have seen through me, just by the way my body spoke. It also had to be tempered. I eventually won my deportment badge, and then soared from sergeant, to sub-prefect, to prefect. But my conformity over-reached itself; the games mistress took me aside and said I was now sitting and walking too stiffly, too rigidly. I was becoming conspicuous again.

As skeletons, we were corrected and straightened, ordered to sit and stand in upright lines. As female flesh and curves, we were concealed by the uniform. Take the traditional gym-slip – a barrel shape with deep pleats designed to hide breasts, waist, hips and buttocks, giving freedom of movement without contour. From the gym-slip of the 1930s, we had graduated to the tunic of thick serge ('hop-sack' we called it), without pleats, but again skilfully flattening the breasts and widening the waist. While my mother's legs had been hidden and desexualized by thick black stockings, we wore thick brown ones, 'regulation shade', and called them 'bullet-proofs'.

In those days before tights, our movements were further constrained lest we expose our suspenders beneath our short tunics. There was no risk of any greater exposure. We had to wear two pairs of knickers – white 'linings' and thick navy blue baggy knickers complete with pocket. For gym we removed our tunics and any girl in linings only was shamed and punished. In summer the navy knickers were replaced by pale blue ones.

A friend still recalls being given a 'disobedience' for doing handstands and, unknown to her, exposing her knickers to a nearby gardener. She was told only to say, 'for handstands' at roll call.

Thus her unmentionable exposure was effectively treated by psychological exposure. For games, our shorts concealed the existence of a split between the thighs. Two deep pleats in front and back made them like a skirt, but one which did not lift and reveal the thighs or buttocks as we ran or jumped. The lower abdomen retained its mystery.

This was the 1950s when the dominant female fashion meant long full skirts. Yet our tunics had to be 'three inches above the knee when kneeling' (note the supplicant pose), even for girls aged 17 years. I have been informed by a girl at another boarding-school in the 1960s, when the mini-skirt symbolized fashionable femininity, that her tunic had to be '*touching* the floor when kneeling'. Thus the girls' schools demand the opposite to the notion of sexuality in the world outside. Our appearance was neutered. Our hair could not touch the backs of our shirt collars; in effect we were given the male 'short back and sides'. The crucial inspection time was the daily march-past at roll call. The dilemma was whether to bend forward and be rebuked for 'poking' the head (and not marching in the male military fashion) or whether to straighten up and risk being summoned for mutilation by the hairdresser. We were caught between conformity to the school, and saving our female sexuality as symbolized by longer hair.

The girls' uniform also had strange male traits: lace-up shoes, striped shirts, blazers, ties and tie pins. Unlike some of the boys' uniforms, ours was discontinuous with the clothes we would wear in adulthood. To us the school tie had no significance for membership of an 'old boy network'. We were caught between a male and female image long after puberty, and denied an identity which asserted the dangerous consciousness of sexuality. Immediately we left school, we had to drop all masculine traits, since a very different appearance was required for marriageability. Sexual ripeness, if only expressed in clothes, burst out. The hated tunics and lace-ups were torn, cut, burnt or flung into the sea.

Conclusion

There are similarities between the girls' boarding-school and that for boys: the separation from urban life, from economic production and members of other social classes, from parents and home, and the separation by gender. For girls, important discontinuities may be found between school and what is realizable in later life. The presentation to girls of models of achievement generally associated with men undervalues any which might be associated with women, and conveys male dominance as inevitable. The girls' school, without corporal punishment, may paradoxically be stricter than that for boys, and allow its pupils less self-determination. Indeed, power may be exercised more completely over girls precisely because it is not visible as physical force. I suggest that in so far as alternatives are not emphasized, the girls are prepared mainly for economic and political dependence within marriage,[15] whether or not this is the intention of the authorities. The differences between the education of boys and girls are important indicators as to how within the same social class each gender is socially defined and culturally reproduced. In this chapter, I have taken as an example a type of education usually regarded as privileged, but the analysis may be relevant to other girls' schools without such pretensions.

Notes

1 The terms 'public' and 'independent' refer to private fee-paying schools in the UK, in contrast to wholly state-maintained schools.

2 See Lambert, 1975, Honey, 1977, and Gathorne-Hardy, 1977.

3 See Blackstone, 1976, p. 199.

4 Wober's *The English Girls' Boarding School* (1971) is a pioneering study but limited in scope. The data are based on only twenty weeks of fieldwork in twenty-three schools, using questionnaires. It is significant that the terms of the original grant for the larger research project by Lambert on boys' schools specifically excluded girls' schools (1975, p. 5). Gathorne-Hardy's research is largely devoted to boys' schools (1977). His two chapters on girls' schools offer some imaginative, although sometimes erratic observations. Recently there has been a revival of interest in the fantasy literature on girls' boarding-schools (Cadogan and Craig, 1976; Freeman, 1976). Angela Brazil, the major pedlar of illusion, never attended such an institution as a participant member. Inevitably crucial aspects of boarding-school experience do not surface.

5 See also Okely, 1975.

6 A girl's academic ambitions will also depend on the extent to which she is encouraged by her parents off-stage.

7 The evening after a 9-year-old girl learnt of her father's death, she was told by the matron not to cry lest she keep the other girls in the dormitory awake.

8 Further research might confirm the impression from the literature and other sources that homosexuality is more explicit in boys' schools (see Gathorne-Hardy, 1977, p. 171). As in other areas, the differences would relate also to early socialization, not merely the effects of schooling.

9 There are, by contrast, more persons of the opposite sex in boys' schools, namely the domestic staff, matrons and masters' wives. But 'boys and staff have learned to relegate women to marginal organizational and largely decorative roles' (Lambert, 1975, p. 116).

10 Wober records that among his sample of girls' schools 'About one-third of the governors were women' (1971, p. 48).

11 In many schools, girls had to sing 'Forty Years On' which was written specifically for boys and included the inappropriate football chorus (Haddon, 1977, pp. 21–2).

12 Even in the late 1960s Wober found that the majority of teachers in the girls' boarding-schools were unmarried (1971, p. 38) and that only a minority had boarded (1971, p. 40). By contrast Lambert records that the majority of staff in boys' public schools were themselves educated in such institutions (1975, p. 54).

13 Wober notes, 'In most cases, no matter at what time one arrived, the schools appeared quiet; girls, if seen, were scurrying about . . . whispering' (1971, p. 293). Gathorne-Hardy, during his visit to Cheltenham Ladies, noted 'a dead silence . . . a silence more

awesome and more indicative of discipline than any bell, 800 girls swished in swift lines down the long, dim, tiled corridors towards the next classroom' (1977, p. 244).
14 See also Foucault (1977, pp. 135–69) for his discussion of 'Docile Bodies'.
15 Since the 1950s the girl's biological virginity may be less important although her social virginity must still be protected. Moreover, greater sexual freedom may not alter a woman's economic and political dependence.

References

Cadogan, M., and Craig, P., *You're a Brick Angela!*, London, Gollancz, 1976.

Connolly, C., *Enemies of Promise*, Harmondsworth, Penguin, 1961.

Foucault, M., *Discipline and Punish*, London, Allen Lane, 1977.

Freeman, G., *The Schoolgirl Ethic: The Life and Work of Angela Brazil.* London, Allen Lane, 1976.

Gathorne-Hardy, J., *The Public School Phenomenon*, London, Hodder and Stoughton, 1977.

Goffman, E., *Asylums*, Harmondsworth, Penguin, 1968.

Honey, J. R. de S., *Tom Brown's Universe*, London, Millington, 1977.

Lambert, R., *The Chance of a Lifetime?*, London, Weidenfeld and Nicolson, 1975.

Marks, P. 'Femininity in the classroom: an account of changing attitudes', in J. Mitchell and A. Oakley, *The Rights and Wrongs of Women*, Harmondsworth, Penguin, 1976.

Mitford, J., *A Fine Old Conflict*, London, Michael Joseph, 1977.

Okely, J., 'The Self and Scientism', *Journal of the Oxford Anthropology Society*, Michaelmas, Oxford, 1975.

Ollerenshaw, K., *The Girls' Schools*, London, Faber and Faber, 1967.

Pocock, D., 'The idea of a personal anthropology', Paper given at the ASA Conference, 1973 (unpublished).

Pocock, D., *Understanding Social Anthropology*, London, Teach Yourself Books, Hodder and Stoughton, 1975.

Wober, M., *English Girls' Boarding Schools*, London, Allen Lane, 1971.

Part Three

Evaluating Texts

9 'The time of your life': the meaning of the school story

Gill Frith

It was at this point, when I was twelve years old, that I took to reading junk books the way some people take to eating junk food. I read long-forgotten authors of books about girls' schools in Switzerland or Paris, as well as Angela Brazil, Noel Streatfield, Pamela Brown and, above all, Enid Blyton. How I envied the schoolgirls of St Clare's or Malory Towers: they belonged to a safe, structured world where rules were rules, good was good, and bad was bad. And in spite of, or perhaps because of, this framework, they all seemed to have such, fun such carefree, girlish fun. My rebellion was only half-consciously directed at my father's choice of reading matter for me, although his disapproving and often angry comments made it clear that he took my behaviour as a personal affront. I wanted to choose for myself, yes, but I also wanted to escape into a world of certainties, which I knew to be unreal while desperately wanting to believe that it might have some reality. I wanted to escape from being at home, from being at school, and quite consciously and openly, from being myself (Sheila MacLeod, *The Art of Starvation*).[1]

The question I want to address in this chapter is, quite simply, why it is that the boarding-school story is now (and has been for the past century) such a popular form of reading for girls. My purpose is to explore the meaning of the school story as a genre, the changes in that meaning since its inception, and its relationship to ideologies of female subjectivity. I shall argue that the pleasure which these stories offer has positive aspects which directly contravene the concept of femininity found in other forms of popular reading available to girls, but that this pleasure contains its own limits and contradictions.

I

Discussion of the girls' school story has been characterized by two forms of unease. The first is an unease about the status of the genre as *literature*, and while this applies to the school story in general, it is particularly true of school stories for girls. While the boys' boarding-school story is now an anachronism, school stories for girls are both widely read and freely available. The most popular examples are still Enid Blyton's *St Clare's* and *Malory Towers* books, written in the 1940s, constantly in print ever since, and currently in Dragon paperback. Stories by

Source: Extracted from Steedman, C., Urwin, C. and Walkerdine, V. (eds), *Language, Gender and Childhood*, Routledge and Kegan Paul, 1985, History Workshop Series.

Angela Brazil, Elinor Brent-Dyer and Antonia Forest are also available in paperback, but it is particularly significant that in the late 1970s an entirely new series in the traditional mould made its appearance: the *Trebizon* books by Anne Digby, now in Granada paperback. Nor is the readership confined to the white middle classes; as a teacher in comprehensive schools, I found that many working-class girls, some of them Asian, read these stories. Recently, with the help of three teachers who distributed questionnaires in their schools, I was able to confirm that this is still true.[2] The readership for these stories falls approximately between the ages of 8 and 12, with some overspill at each end; during this period, a significant number of girls go through a lengthy period of addiction, in which they not only read nothing *but* school stories, but return to the same books over and over again. It is important that this is a matter of choice, sometimes in conscious opposition to the wishes of teachers and parents (although the books may also be 'handed on' from mother to daughter). The books are borrowed from libraries, bought by the girls themselves, passed on from friend to friend. Few teachers will encourage girls to read boarding-school stories; many actively *discourage* them, and at best they are likely to take the liberal view that the addiction should be indulged, in the interests of developing a 'reading habit' until the addict can be weaned off them and directed towards more sophisticated and *realistic* literature, possibly via 'quality' school stories such as Penelope Farmer's *Charlotte Sometimes* and the novels of Mary K. Harris.

The second form of unease, which often coexists with the first, is a question of politics. Quite simply, school stories are embarrassing. Set in that institution which is so clearly a product and reflection of bourgeois capitalism, and a most effective instrument in its perpetuation – the private boarding school – school stories are complacent about class privilege, inherited, wealth and xenophobia. Exclusive, expensive and enclosed, they represent a sealed, rigidly hierarchical world in which 'normality' is white and middle class.

II

I like them because they showed the tricks and scandals children get up to. It wasn't very realistic but I still enjoyed it because I like fantasy stories.   Manjit, aged 12.

The first point I want to emphasize is that the girls who read school stories are aware from the start that they are *fictions*. Almost without exception, the girls in my survey said that they did not believe real boarding schools would be like the schools in the stories, and that they had no desire to go to such a school themselves. Most thought that the teachers and girls in the stories were not at all like the ones they knew. They were drawn to the stories because they were *fun*, because the girls in them were having the time of their lives: they particularly enjoyed the tricks played on teachers (a central feature in Blyton's stories), the jokes, the breaking of bounds, the midnight feasts.

One 10-year-old 'addict' described her reading experience to me in detail. Rachael was a particularly avid reader of these stories, but her account is in many respects typical. She started reading school stories when she was 9, and had been reading them compulsively ever since. Though no one had actively tried to prevent her from reading them, she was aware that they were not particularly approved of by parents or teachers; she herself didn't think that the stories were 'good', she wasn't sure that she even *liked* them, but nevertheless she returned to them almost obsessively. She had re-read each title in the *St Clare's* and *Malory Towers* series about twenty times. She was very conscious that the school stories did not represent 'real life', but she enjoyed them because the girls *did* things, and the things that they did were exciting. Significantly, although she read the stories often, her re-reading was selective; she skipped the bits that did not interest her, and the points she returned to were revealing: the rituals of opening and closure (invariably the 'first day' and 'last day' of term); the points where the order of the school is disrupted, its limits transgressed (the tricks, the sneaking out of the school at night); the rituals which assert the autonomy of the girls within the school (having their own studies and furnishing them). But Rachael's pleasure wasn't confined to the *events* in the stories. She particularly enjoyed the fact that, even on a first reading, she *knew what was going to happen.* She was extremely aware of the ritualistic conventions of the school story narrative: she could identify the recurrent stereotypes (the snob, the sneak, the comically inadequate 'Mamselle', the heroine who succeeds at everything and ends up as Head Girl) and the codes of the narrative itself. For example, she said that often at the outset one of the girls would say what a boring term it was going to be: you would then *know* that exciting things were going to happen, and this would be confirmed by a comment at the end of the chapter. When I looked at the books to verify this, I found that she was quite right.

There are two points of particular significance here. First, part of the pleasure involved in reading school stories rests in the opportunity they offer the young reader to exercise a newly acquired skill: the ability to follow the structure of a narrative, recognize its 'clues', anticipate its development. The very formulaic and predictable nature of the school story, the experience of *knowing what's going to happen*, actively contribute to the enjoyment of the reader, to the feeling of being 'in control' of the reading process. There's a continual interplay between safety and danger, risk and control, in the pleasure which these stories offer. The almost invariable opening gambit of the school story – the first day of term – signifies *both* the movement out of the safe, normal, humdrum world of the family into the exciting, varied, turbulent world of the fantasized 'school', *and* the movement from the uncontrollable world of reality to the predictable, clearly defined world of fiction. The school story firmly addresses itself to the reader *as* fiction, demanding only that she share the desires it expresses, and its fictionality is quite transparent. For example, the moral code of the school story is apparently quite simple, but when you look closely it becomes clear that many of its 'codes' are in fact devices, subject to adaptation according to the demands of the narrative. The pervasive taboo against 'sneaking' is useful because it keeps the teachers *in the dark*, leaving action, responsibility, procedure and control in the hands of the girls, but this apparently inflexible taboo may be ignored when the narrative demands that the teachers be involved in the action. There is a similarly fine distinction between 'lying' and bending, or concealing, the truth, between 'cheekiness' and 'rudeness', 'naughtiness' and 'disobedience', 'loyalty' and 'blind devotion'. What matters, in fact, is not *what is done*, but *who does it*: whether the character concerned has the reader's sympathy, or the reverse. There's an interesting, if characteristically repellent, variation on this in Blyton's school stories, in her representation of 'foreign' or 'exotic' girls, like Carlotta (half-gipsy) in the *Malory Towers* series and Claudine (French) in one of the most popular stories, *Claudine at St Clare's*. Their consistently mischievous and subversive behaviour is simultaneously *celebrated* in the sense that it provides much of the 'fun' of the story, and *undercut* by being represented as a distressing result of origin, of ignorance of the 'English code of honour'. Carlotta and Claudine often dare to say and do what the other girls *want* to say and do; unlike 'bad' English girls, they are neither expelled nor fully tamed, but their actions are not imitable because you can't *choose* to be a 'foreigner'. The contradiction between the illusion of a rigid structure and inflexible morality, and the anarchy which actually reigns, is central to the appeal of these stories.

Her recognition of the stories' status as fictions allows the reader to read selectively, to suspend involvement or judgement where necessary. This seems to me the only way of understanding how Asian girls can enjoy these stories, and also important in explaining their appeal to white working-class girls, but there is a further point to be made in relation to the question of class. I would suggest, tentatively, that children of this age, perhaps especially girls, perceive class less as a specific distinction based on occupation and income than as a distinction between 'ordinary people' and 'snobs' (and perhaps 'rough people'). It is precisely this distinction which the school stories endorse: a pervasive stereotype is that of the 'snob' who boasts about her wealth, 'steals' other people's writing in order to impress her rich parents, or the girl who *pretends* to be wealthier than she really is, and steals or lies in order to maintain the deception. While the snob is sometimes represented as 'nouveau-riche', this is by no means *always* the case. Paradoxically, the effect of locating the novels within a sealed, self-sufficient class institution is to *efface* the question of class. While 'rough people' may lurk outside its walls, within the school to be in the same *form* is to be in the same *class*; to be part of the group is all that matters, and acceptance is represented as meritocratic, based both on 'proving yourself' as an individual and on sharing the 'common-sense' values of the group. While the scholarship girl from a poor home is often *rewarded* with an unexpected inheritance and/or the return of a 'dead' father who proves to be a 'gentleman', the stories nevertheless preserve the fiction that income doesn't *matter*, that to be poor but honest is better than to be rich and 'spoilt'. The stories address the reader, then, as part of a unitary group in which 'girlhood' is the significant factor, and it is of course in its configuration of girlhood that the appeal of the school story really lies.

III

The significant point here is that the school story presents a picture of what it is possible for a girl to be and to do which stands in absolute contradistinction to the configuration of 'femininity' which is to be found in other forms of popular fiction addressed specifically to women and girls. With the wealth of recent work on images of women in women's magazines, romantic novels, children's fiction and advertising, we are now familiar with the dominant models of femininity which work to define women in relation and in contrast to men, to confirm that woman's 'natural' base is the home, the family, the domestic.[3] Angela McRobbie's illuminating analysis of *Jackie* provides a particularly relevant example, since many of the older girls in my survey read it regularly.[4] A few read *Jackie* and school stories simultaneously, although some read the stories in conscious opposition to such magazines: 'Mostly for my age are love stories about really sickly sweet girls who never get greasy hair. And boys who are really good-looking and popular' – Lisa, aged 12, a school story 'addict'. Thirteen-year-old Kuldip's fiercely dissenting comment illustrates the other side of the argument, the 'scandal' of the school story: 'I didn't enjoy the books because it shows or gives a bad reputation for us girls. Especially the naughty parts it just shows us girls up. That's what I hate in these girls books. . . . I like to read girl magazines like *Jackie*.' This was an unusually severe criticism, but by the age of 13, most had 'moved on' from the school story to *Jackie*, *Tammy* and pop magazines like *Smash Hits*. A brief summary of Angela McRobbie's analysis will help to illustrate the difference between *Jackie* and the school story.

McRobbie argues that although the world portrayed in *Jackie* stories is an oddly empty one, populated by rootless young people in search of love, both stories and features nevertheless confirm the narrowness of women's role and prefigure the girl's future isolation in the home. Male and female roles are clearly separate and distinct. Boys *do*, girls simply *are*; a boy may be 'rough' and still irresistible, but to be a girl is to abide by the law, to *wait* passively, to be chosen, taken, loved, rescued. To be female is also to be isolated. Women are united by their femininity but divided by jealousy and sexual competitiveness; friends, even best friends, are not to be trusted, and the romantic relationship is the only relationship which matters and can provide fulfilment. Romance, fashion, beauty and pop stars provide the limits of a girl's concern; her personal life is a continual source of *problems*, but the problems can only be solved individually, in isolation, by compromise or acceptance. While she will almost certainly fail to meet the exacting standards men demand, she must 'work' continually, secretly, in the privacy of the home, to measure up: to disguise the faults in her appearance, to create the illusion of natural beauty, to fashion and re-fashion herself into the image which will secure her man.

The representation of 'girlhood' in the school story stands in almost total opposition to this ideology. In a world of girls, to be female is *normal*, and not a *problem*. To be assertive, physically active, daring, ambitious, is not a source of tension. In the absence of boys, girls 'break bounds', have adventures, transgress rules, catch spies. There is no taboo on public speech: in innumerable school stories, girls hold and address a tense, packed meeting. The ructures and rewards of romance are replaced by the ructures and rewards of friendship, and pop stars by idealized Head Girls. 'Pretence' and 'pretension' are questionable; mysteries are unravelled, codes broken, secret passages explored, disguises penetrated. 'Tricks' played on teachers replace 'tricks' of make-up; in place of diets, there are midnight feasts. Away from the family, girls are free; domestic tasks are invisibly performed. Clothes and appearances are of little significance in the unchanging world of the school, and to be beautiful is not an advantage. The exceptionally pretty and 'feminine' girl is represented as weak, frail, easily led, often vain. The heroine, on the other hand, is often 'lovable' for the very qualities which *Jackie* represses: she is often wilful, outspoken, impulsive, loyal to her friends. While the 'best friend' is the crucial relationship, *the group* is equally important: what matters is to be in the team, in the play, sharing a dormitory with friends. 'The group' itself has almost unlimited licence. The institutions within the school – clubs, teams, magazines – are initiated, organized and controlled by the girls themselves, sometimes by girls as young as 12. While the teachers are the ultimate arbiters, their presence is discreet and not infallible: the stock figure of 'Mamselle' represents the teacher whose power can be subverted, who is easily duped and teased. Other teachers smile secretly at the 'naughtiness' of the girls. The prefects, by contrast, have astonishing powers and influence; a 'bent' prefect can create havoc.

While some of these characteristics appear also in other forms of story popular among girls (pony books, stories of ballet or tennis 'stars'), the particular appeal of the school story is that it depends on no specialized interest or skill. Despite her ubiquitous success, the heroine is represented as 'ordinary' rather than exceptional; when she scores the crucial goal, writes the prize-winning poem, or saves the Head Girl from drowning, it is simply a reward for her energy and determination. It is a fantasy accessible to any girl who dreams of vindication, independence, freedom from constraint; a fantasy which combines the dream of autonomy and control with the freedom to be irresponsible within 'safe' limits.

The question that presents itself, then, is not so much why girls *read* school stories, as why they should be willing to give them up. How is it that girls relinquish the excitement and solidarity of the school story for the passivity and isolation of *Jackie* and the Mills & Boon romance? I want to suggest that while the school story *does* represent a subversive challenge to conventional representations of femininity, it *also* contains an implicit negation of that subversiveness, for the freedom it celebrates has clearly defined, and insuperable, limits.

IV

If we see ideologies of femininity in terms of a unitary, if overdetermined, progression towards passivity, domesticity and a reproductive role, then the representation of femininity within the school story clearly stands as an expression of resistance and subversion. The school story *makes sense*, however, in the context of an ideology which is just as pervasive and perhaps more insidious, since it embraces and normalizes the contradictions in women's experience. The school story 'fits' into a configuration of female subjectivity which perceives it not as a smooth progression towards an unchanging goal, but as essentially and naturally fragmented: flexible, chameleon, infinitely adaptable and continuously adjustable. Within these terms, it is woman's task (and her desire) to create something orderly and smooth out of the unpromising and resistant material which is her physical and emotional self; to 'fashion' herself anew at the appropriate moment. Like Alice in Wonderland, if the house is too small or too large, she must change her size to fit it.

It was precisely this understanding of female subjectivity that the girls in my survey recognized when they said that they had 'grown out of' the school story. The reasons why they had enjoyed the stories were often still vivid in their memories, but they accepted that it was time to move on, to refashion themselves, to put aside childish desires. This is not to say that this process is necessarily smooth or easy, or even complete. Thus Violent Trefusis, recalling herself as a precocious and sophisticated upper-class schoolgirl at the turn of the century, remembers:

The clock has been put back twelve years: I am fourteen, romantic, pedantic, mystery-loving. I haven't got over my stay in Florence: I allude to Verrochio, Dontatello, Cimabue. I am deep in Majorie Bowen – but not too old to surreptitiously enjoy L. T. Meade (letter to Vita Sackville-West, August 1920).[5]

The testimony of 13-year-old Rebecca in 1983 gives a more immediate insight into a similar conjuncture, all the more eloquent because barely articulated:

They are sometimes funny but never boring. . . . I like the sports matches. They are exciting. Also on one book I have recently read 'Claudine at St Clares'. I liked it when she fell into the pool. Really I enjoy the whole book because I found that I never got bored with the stories. [And in tiny, cramped handwriting] But now I have stopped reading them as I have grown out of them.

This is not simply a question of succumbing to social pressure, for the temporal limits of the school story are defined by the stories themselves: they clearly locate the fun and licence they celebrate as a *stage*. In those stories which form a series, as the original girls grow older new little ones are introduced who now form the focus of the stories, who do the things their elders once did, in which the seniors take a vicarious pleasure while pretending to disapprove. The slang which the girls talk is a language which defines them as a group, which 'belongs' to them and is passed on from one generation to the next, used in resistance to the 'authorities' – but it is a language which has no currency beyond the schoolgirl world. Blyton's emphasis on 'naughtiness' clearly identifies such behaviour with childhood, only legitimate within the scope of 'the school'.

It is not simply a question of representing childhood as a 'golden age'. Sheila MacLeod's account of her girlhood reading of school stories, with which I began this essay, suggests a further point which is central to the appeal of these stories. The quotation is taken from MacLeod's analysis of anorexia nervosa, *The Art of Starvation*, in which she argues from her own experience that the anorexic is not motivated by the desire to be slim or sexually attractive, nor yet by an aversion to sexuality. Her refusal to eat is, rather, a bid for autonomy: a response to contradictory messages about the female body which leads her to believe that by starving herself, and thus delaying the physical effects of puberty, she is able to avoid growing up, to resist 'the burden of womanhood' and achieve control over her own identity. The logic would be impeccable, were it not that its ultimate conclusion is death.

In describing her own youthful addiction to the school story, Sheila MacLeod is not drawing any *literal* connection between anorexia nervosa and the boarding-school story, and it is certainly not my intention to do so here. Implicit in her account, though, is the relationship between the school story and the illusion of control which she so persuasively identifies as a central feature of anorexia, and I would argue that there is a further connection. For the crucial 'trick' of the school story is that, though set in 'a world of girls', it in fact evades the question of gender: the heroines occupy a position apparently somewhere *between* 'the masculine' and 'the feminine'. This is not exactly to say that they are 'androgynous'. When I asked Rachael to explain how the girls in the stories were different from the girls she knew, she began by saying, 'They're half girls and half boys', but then corrected herself: 'They're not like boys, they're *girls*, but they do things like boys.' The heroines in contemporary school stories are not so much 'like girls' or 'like boys' as *ungendered*: whereas the occasional tomboy will have an uncompromisingly boyish nickname like Bill or Tim, the central characters often have names or nicknames which can't precisely be identified in terms of gender: Nicky, Darrell, Aldred, Lawrie, Tish, and so on. The 'tom-boy' and the weak feminine girl represent the oddities, the extreme limits: the average girl, the heroine, is suspended somewhere between the two.

This is particularly interesting because, while the present *readership* of the stories falls roughly between the ages of 8 and 12, the *characters* in the stories, including the most recent ones, are significantly older. Generally, the central characters in the stories are in the second to fourth year at secondary school: in other words, the age of puberty. Yet the onset of puberty, its physical effects, are nowhere in evidence. In Anne Digby's *Summer Term at Trebizon*, second-year Rebecca has a difficult term. Her life is dominated by three problems, all, as the narrative emphasizes, beginning with M: Maths, her worst subject, Max, the new male maths teacher, and her name, Mason, which is the source of complicated difficulties. The disruptive effects of Max's Maleness within the all-female school are explored, but the other significant M – Menstruation – is entirely absent. That there should be no direct reference to menstruation or sexuality isn't surprising. The point is that the heroines remain as slender, as fleet-footed, as physically unaware of themselves, as they were as children. Bodies are not a problem; plump girls are extremely difficult for the school story to incorporate, and tend to be suspect. The physical and emotional changes which preoccupy girls of this age, and which signal their unequivocal entry into a female identity, are simply evaporated.

It seems to me that this fact is central to the appeal of the school story. The girls who read these stories are at an age when to be female is not obviously 'a problem'. At school, they are competing on equal terms with boys, are often more successful – yet they are constantly receiving cultural messages which make it clear that this will not always be the case. It's significant that a favourite 'trick' involves playing with time – turning the clock forwards or back. The stories hold out the impossible, Canute-like fantasy of a future in which the waves of time can be held back, a fantasy which cannot survive the material arrival of puberty. The gymslip, hallmark of the school story, is appropriate only for the slender, prepubescent body; the *St Trinians* films, designed for a voyeuristic adult audience, drew on the incongruity of the bosomy, physically mature female form bursting out of its gymslip. When breasts develop, menstruation arrives, and bodies become a source of secrecy and difficulty, the schoolgirl reader can no longer place herself within the school story; she is obliged to move on to the next stage, to a more unambiguously 'female' identity. Like anorexia, the school story represents a dream of control, an illusion of power, which contains its own termination, its own inevitable failure.

V

It is important to recognize that this has not always been the case. The school story as it exists at present is not simply an 'anachronism': it is a hybrid and deeply contradictory form which has retained some of the impetus of an earlier age while constantly evolving in response to new concepts of education and its relationship to women's role. If we are to understand the nature of the school story's current appeal, we need also to understand the ways in which it has departed from an initially feminist impetus, so I shall outline the major changes before discussing their implications.

School stories became established as a popular genre during the 1880s and 1890s. Many of the conventions still prevalent appear in the early stories: the ivyclad mansion behind high walls, the wilful and impulsive heroine, the stolen poem, the inadequate Mademoiselle, the central importance of friendships. The real precursor of the modern story, though, is to be found in the 'college' stories pioneered by L. T. Meade:[6] here we find the scholarship girl, the institution with its own codes, traditions and language, the emphasis on a new-found freedom, and a loving and elaborate portrayal of the girls' rooms which anticipates the later stress on 'dormitories' and 'studies'. These stories became popular during a period of intensive expansion in schools and colleges for women, a time when women's education, specially higher education, was an extremely contentious and widely debated subject.[7] The higher education debate is especially significant, not because it provided access to university life for a handful of women, nor simply because it provided a means of access to professions from which women had previously been excluded, but because it involved a re-definition of women's role and of the concept of 'woman' itself. [This concept] presented an obvious challenge to [the] ideology which confined middle-class women, at least, to the home and to the domestic role. The 'college' takes on a symbolic significance in stories for girls (clearly related to the exceptional numbers of single women in this period) through which the writers directly counter current arguments against the changes in women's education and celebrate an understanding of women's role as, within clearly defined limits, *plural*: narrative devices, especially the friendships, distinguish between the shy, poor, industrious scholarship girl who is destined for *work* and the romantically fascinating, wealthy, wilful girl who is destined for *marriage*, but equally validate each through the closeness of their relationship. Two of the most popular early writers of the school and college stories, Sarah Doudney and L. T. Meade, were both members of the progressive and fervently feminist women's club, the Pioneer, to which many leading feminist writers also belonged.[8]

The early stories, then, were clearly feminist in their impulse, though it is a feminism specifically of its period, a feminism which emphasizes social purity, women's moral superiority, the importance of self-sacrifice and religious devotion.[9] In these early novels there is a persistent *celebration* of women's newly found access to knowledge, in which the young women perceive themselves as pioneers with an obligation to pass on their knowledge; the pleasure of learning for its own sake is always balanced by an emphasis on its *usefulness*, on the necessary relationship between the knowledge acquired in the college and its currency in the outside world, and the college stories often show their young heroines moving on to settlement work in the East End of London. The intensely romantic friendships which characterize these novels are closely linked with the joys of learning, and also depend on a secure concept of gender difference, of 'womanliness' perceived as a state so absolute that once achieved it is secure, and which can only be achieved by and through the models presented by other women. There are many idealized teachers who have consciously *chosen* to abjure marriage in order to devote themselves and their lives to the education of girls, and for whom their pupils feel a strongly romantic affection, such as Miss Thornhill in Sarah Doudney's *When We Were Girls Together*:

That mouth always seemed to Jennet the loveliest that she had ever seen; the smile that haunted the full, red lips was indescribably dreamy and sweet. To her, Una Thornhill, with her deep blue eyes and creamy skin, had the looks of an enchantress, and 'The

Enchantress' was the name by which she called her in thought, little guessing that by this very name Miss Thornhill had been really known in other days. . . . The peculiar charm of eyes and smile which had 'enchanted' many world-worn men and women, now won the hearts of the most impressionable schoolgirls, and achieved more conquests over stubborn wills than Miss Sand could ever boast of having gained.[10]

L. T. Meade's *The Girls of Merton College*, clearly inspired by Girton, shows such a relationship from the teacher's point of view. Jocelyn Silence, the college principal, is (remarkably but symbolically) the first girl to have been born into the 'House of Silence' for a couple of hundred years. Noble-looking, with soldierly bearing and 'eyes like the softest brown velvet', she has been inspired by Dorothea Beale to devote her life to the education of girls. The chapter which describes her first meeting with Katherine, the brilliant scholarship girl heroine, is highly emotional and ritualistic:

Miss Silence felt a sort of tingling coming down to the very tips of her fingers as she considered what this girl might do for the college, for the life there, for women generally. She trembled with pure pleasure at the thought of seeing her.[11]

Katherine's role as acolyte is underscored when she receives a ceremonial kiss and serves her 'Head Mistress' with tea: 'I am hungry', says Miss Silence, 'be sure you serve me well.'

The school story continued to have an appeal for a younger, more 'bohemian' generation of feminist writers, like Evelyn Sharp, member of the 'Yellow Book' circle, socialist, and, later, militant suffragette.[12] Sharp's very funny story, *The Making of A Schoolgirl* (1897), presents itself as a debunking of the 'priggishness' of earlier stories, but in fact employs many of the familiar conventions: romantic friendships, idolized teachers and dizzy enjoyment of learning.

The shift which took place early in this century can be most clearly seen in a novel written for adults, Clemence Dane's *Regiment of Women*, which created a considerable stir when it was published in 1915. Set in a girls' high school, the novel traces the destructive effect of Clare, a cool, highly competent and ruthlessly ambitious teacher, on two younger women. One, the motherless schoolgirl Louise, becomes infatuated with Clare; when her affection is not returned, she becomes unbalanced through overwork and overstrain, and finally kills herself. Louise's passion for Clare is represented as 'innocent' though excessive, and Clare herself represses all emotion, but the novel nevertheless has an extremely strong atmosphere of 'unhealthiness', and that unhealthiness is firmly located in the hothouse, highly charged atmosphere of the single-sex girls' school. Clare is *dangerous* because she usurps the place of the mother and exploits her position of power; cold, 'warped', sterile, she provides an 'unnatural' role-model in her choice of career over marriage and motherhood. Now, Clemence Dane was later a regular contributor to the feminist journal *Time and Tide*, a member of the Six Point Group, and moved in 'sapphic' circles in the 1920s;[13] her novel is not simply the product of anti-lesbian, anti-feminist propaganda. I would suggest that it's indicative of a shift in progressive and feminist thought of the period, which perceived the distinction between marriage and work as oppressive for women, and which, in arguing for a recognition of women's sexuality, was dubious about the model presented by the 'spinster' teacher.[14] The single-sex school and college no longer stood as an unambiguous symbol of advancement for women; the form is increasingly taken over by writers who are either ambivalent about feminism or actively opposed to it. The school story increasingly turns in on itself, and there is a shift of emphasis from the school as a source of *knowledge* to the school as a source of *fun*. Teachers are not idealized 'role-models', but remote one-dimensional figures, 'frozen' in time and place; lesson-time is play-time. Whereas the early stories saw the time of education as an 'oasis' which was both rewarding in itself and crucially *related* to life afterwards, the twentieth century increasingly represents the school as a *refuge* from the real world, an *escape* from knowledge.

There is a marked shift also in the representation of friendship. Relationships between the girls in the stories become steadily less passionate, but perhaps because schoolgirl attachments were exempted from early studies of lesbianism and perceived as a 'normal' phase, the change is gradual.[15] It is directly resisted by Angela Brazil, who continues to represent her schoolgirls as 'in love' and 'at white-hot heat'.[16] The influence of the boys' public school may be a more significant factor in the emergence of a new pattern, exemplified by the Anti-Soppist Society formed by the girls in Dorita Fairlie Bruce's 'Dimsie' stories of the 1920s; the rules of this society forbid its members to give flowers to teachers or seniors, to sleep with a senior's hair ribbon under her pillow, or to kiss anyone at all during the term 'unless absolutely obliged to'.[17] In the modern school story, friendship between girls of the same age remains extremely *important*, but as a matter of comradely loyalty, based on shared interests and characteristics. They are no longer romantic love affairs, crucial elements in the girl's moral and intellectual development, or a means of defining her future role in society; they are static mirrors which find their most perfect expression in the popularity of the 'twin'. What remains is the schoolgirl 'crush' on an older girl, still a significant feature in Antonia Forest's stories in the 1940s and 1950s, and residually in more recent stories.[18] This romantic attachment finds expression as a courtly and chivalric devotion, especially in protecting the older girl from the machinations of less scrupulous prefects. The importance of this is that it firmly locates the crush as a 'phase'; the older girl has already passed *through* this phase, so it can't be reciprocated and must rest at heroine-worship from a distance.

These changes are important because they are both drastic and incomplete; the result is a form which can be simultaneously reactionary and subversive. The stories retain a residue of their original feminist impetus, in that they offer a positive and active identity for girls, an emphasis on comradeship and shared female identification, but the changes I've identified work to narrow the period in which such an identity is practicable to an increasingly limited 'stage'. Whereas the early stories expressed a broad concept of girlhood which extended from 10 to 20 and appear to have appealed to a similarly broad readership, the modern school stories locate the ending of girlhood at puberty. The 'time of your life' is getting shorter.

Equally significant, though, is the way in which the school story has become divorced from 'real life'. The early stories were 'fantasies', in that they described a dream which could only be realized by a small number of readers, but it was a dream which was related to feminist aims, which saw access to knowledge as access to power, and the experience of school or college as a crucial preparation for the public and private life of the 'New Woman'. In the modern story, the school behind its walls is neither microcosm nor formative experience, but another place, suspended in time, complete in itself.

VI

The popularity of the school story demands that we confront the questions of 'realism' and 'relevance', for it is precisely *because* the school story has had an increasingly tangential relationship to 'real life' that it continues to have an appeal for young readers. Some of the girls in my survey explained the discrepancy between the stories and their own experience by suggesting that the novels were set in the past, 'in the fifties', but most showed a more sophisticated awareness of the relationship between literature and life, and of the difference between 'realism' and 'reflection'. Many emphasized *both* that the stories were 'true-to-life' and 'realistic', *and* that the schools, the girls and the teachers in the stories were unlike the ones they knew in life. These points are not as incompatible as they may seem. The girls who enjoyed school stories were not seeking an experience which mirrored their own: Rachael, for example, thought that the stories in Blyton's *Naughtiest Girl* series (set in a mixed school, with younger characters) were 'better' than the boarding-school stories because they were more like her own life – but she didn't *enjoy* them as much, and rarely re-read them. Similarly, other school story 'addicts' enjoyed the *Grange Hill* television programmes, which are set in a mixed comprehensive school, but had no desire to read the books which are based on the series.

Girls read school stories during the complicated period of transition from the 'motherly' world of the primary school to the bigger, more anonymous, more competitive world of the secondary school, and on the edge of the transition from 'girlhood' to 'womanhood'. The messages they are receiving in 'real life' – from home, school and the media – are often contradictory. Girls may be simultaneously urged to compete, to pass exams, to aim for the world of work, and to define themselves in terms of the domestic role; to see their power as located within the family, while accepting a subordinate position within that family; to see their sexuality as a source of power which must also be 'passive' and 'innocent'.

The school story takes the familiar pieces of the jigsaw – family, gender, school, friends, lessons, rules – and puts them together in a different way, making a picture which is more brightly coloured, more sharply defined, less complex than its real-life original. In its re-assemblage of lived experience, the school story also re-assembles the ideologies which inform those experiences, offering the possibility of a positive female identity not bound by the material or 'the possible'. Central to the school story, for example, is the fantasy of escape from the family, yet many of the girls who particularly enjoyed school stories commented that they would not like to go to boarding school themselves because they could not bear to leave their families, would hate the feeling that they were being 'pushed out'. It's not that they were deceiving themselves; the simultaneous desire to be within the comfort and the secure identity offered by the family, and to escape the constraints of that same identity, is a real contradiction which can only be resolved on the level of fantasy. Located in an impossible time – the age of puberty in which puberty never happens – and an impossible place – the fantastic dream of a school which has no relationship with the world beyond it – the school story offers its young reader the possibility of resolving the contradictions in her life without ever needing to confront them directly.

The difficulty here is not so much that this resolution is 'ideological', nor yet that it expresses contradictory desires, for it is in the nature of fiction to do so. It is, rather, that the school story is most 'relevant' when it seems most 'unreal'. The 'time of her life' which the schoolgirl heroine enjoys, the time of puberty-and-not-puberty, can never be realized by the reader; asked to recognize that the stories cannot be *good* because they are not *realistic*, she may come to accept that the desires they allow her to express – for fun, freedom, friendship and a life unconstrained by gender difference – are also 'unreal'. As the schoolgirl reader 'moves on' to the alternative fantasies offered by romantic fiction, by *Jackie* and *Smash Hits*, female subjectivity itself becomes identified with pleasure deferred, with an endless succession of impossible dreams.

Notes and references

1 Sheila MacLeod, *The Art of Starvation*, 1981, p. 42.
2 The questionnaire was distributed in July 1983 to a first-year class in a mixed comprehensive school, a second-year class in a single-sex comprehensive, and a small random sampling of girls in a mixed primary school. All three schools were in predominantly working-class catchment areas. It is not my purpose here to present a sociological analysis of girls' reading, and the sample is clearly too small to be definitive, but some further detail may be of interest to future researchers.

In the first-year class, four girls out of fifteen came into the category of 'addict' (i.e. those who had read all of the *St Clare*'s and *Malory Towers* series at least twice, and in some cases five or more times, and who had also read school stories by authors other than Enid Blyton). This seems an exceptionally high number, and was in striking contrast to the second-year class, only one of whom approached the 'addict' classification, although many had read several school stories and were clearly familiar with the genre. However, the second-year girls were noticeably more distanced from and critical of the school story – all, including the ex-'addict', emphasized that they had now 'grown out of' these stories – and it does seem possible that they had already censored their own memories of their reading.

There were few Afro-Caribbean girls in the three schools in the survey, and none in my sample, so I am not able to comment on whether the school story also has an appeal for Afro-Caribbean girls.

Quotations in the text are taken verbatim from the girls' answers to the questionnaires, but spelling has been 'normalized'.

3 See for example Janice Winship, 'A woman's world: *Woman* – an ideology of femininity', in Women's Studies Group, *Women Take Issue*, 1978 pp. 133–54, Judith Williamson, *Decoding Advertisements*, 1978, and Cammilla Nightingale, 'Sex roles in children's literature', in Sandra Allen *et al.*, *Conditions of Illusion*, 1974, pp. 141–53.

4 Angela McRobbie, *Jackie: An Ideology of Adolescent Femininity*, 1978.

5 Violet Trefusis to Vita Sackville-West, 23 August 1920. Reproduced in Philippe Jullian and John Phillips, *Violet Trefusis: Life and Letters*, 1976.

6 See for example L. T. Meade, *A Sweet Girl Graduate*, 1891, *The Girls of St Wode*'s, 1898, and *The Girls of Merton College*, 1911, and also Alice Stronach, *A Newnham Friendship*, 1901, and Mrs G. De Horne Vaizey, *A College Girl*, 1913. There is a brief discussion of these novels by John Schellenberger in 'Fiction and the first women students', *New University Quarterly*, autumn 1982, pp. 352–8. The extremely popular and prolific L. T. Meade (1854–1914) wrote over 250 novels, mostly for young readers. Her school stories include also *A World of Girls*, 1886, and *Betty, A Schoolgirl*, 1894. [For an analysis of Meade's work and others such as Angela Brazil and Dorita Fairlie Bruce, see M. Cadogan and P. Craig, *You're a Brick, Angela! A new look at girls' fiction from 1839–1975*, 1976, and J. S. Bratton, *The Impact of Victorian Children's Fiction*, 1981.]

7 For fuller details see Joan Burstyn, *Victorian Education and the Ideal of Womanhood*, 1980.

8 Mona Caird, Sarah Grand, Menie Muriel Dowie and Lady Florence Dixie were all members of the Pioneer Club in the 1890s. Sarah Doudney (1843–1926) was a popular and well-respected writer of stories for girls. Her school stories include *Monksbury College*, 1872, and *When We Were Girls Together*, the latter serialized in 1885 in *The Girl's Own Paper*, to which Doudney was a frequent contributor.

9 For fuller details see Constance Rover, *Love, Morals and the Feminists*, 1970, chapters 6–9, and Olive Banks, *Faces of Feminism*, 1981, especially chapter 6.

10 Sarah Doudney, *When We Were Girls Together*, 1886, pp. 161–2.

11 L. T. Meade, *The Girls of Merton College*, 1911, p. 45.

12 See Evelyn Sharp's autobiography, *Unfinished Adventure*, 1933.

13 See *Time and Tide*, the feminist journal founded by Lady Rhonnda in 1920. For Dane's friendship with Violet Trefusis, see Victoria Glendinning, *Vita: The Life of V. Sackville-West*, 1983, p. 110, and Julian and Phillips, *Violet Trefusis*, p. 193. Lillian Faderman speculates that Dane may herself have been lesbian, but sees *Regiment of Women* as the product of internalized lesbian self-hatred. (See Lillian Faderman, *Surpassing the Love of Men*, pp. 341–3 and 392.)

14 The journal *The Freewoman*, 1911–12, published several articles on this theme; see also Dora Russell, *Hypatia*, 1925, and Clemence Dane's own *The Women's Side*, 1926.

15 See for example Havelock Ellis, 'Appendix B. The School-Friendships of Girls', in *Sexual Inversion: Studies in the Psychology of Sex*, vol. 2, 1897, revised edn 1928, and Sigmund Freud, *Dora*, p. 95 (first English translation 1925).

16 Passionate friendships are pervasive in Brazil's stories, but see for example *A Patriotic Schoolgirl*, 1918, and *Loyal to the School*, 1921.

17 Dorita Fairlie Bruce, *Dimsie Moves Up*, pp. 39–40.

18 See for example Antonia Forest, *Autumn Term*, 1948. There is a faint echo of the 'crush' in Anne Digby's *Summer Term at Trebizon*, 1979, but it is emphasized that Pippa's relationship with Rebecca is like that of an 'older sister'.

Bibliography

Allen, S., Sanders, L. and Wallis, J. (1974), *Conditions of Illusion; Papers from the Women's Movement*, Leeds, Feminist Books.

Banks, O. (1981), *Faces of Feminism*, Oxford, Martin Robertson.

Blyton, E. (1941), the 'St Clare's' series, *The Twins at St Clare's*, London, Methuen.

Blyton, E. (1942), the 'St Clare's' series, *The O'Sullivan Twins*, London, Methuen.

Blyton, E. (1943), the 'St Clare's' series, *Summer Term at St Clare's*, London, Methuen.

Blyton, E. (1944a), the 'St Clare's' series, *Second Form at St Clare's*, London, Methuen.

Blyton, E. (1944b), the 'St Clare's' series, *Claudine at St Clare's*, London, Methuen.

Blyton, E. (1945), the 'St Clare's' series, *Fifth Former at St Clare's*, London, Methuen.

Blyton, E. (1946), the 'Malory Towers' series, *First Term at Malory Towers*, London, Methuen.

Blyton, E. (1947), the 'Malory Towers' series, *Second Form at Malory Towers*, London, Methuen.

Blyton, E. (1948), the 'Malory Towers' series, *Third Year at Malory Towers*, London, Methuen.

Blyton, E. (1949), the 'Malory Towers' series, *Upper Fourth at Malory Towers*, London, Methuen.

Blyton, E. (1950), the 'Malory Towers' series, *In the Fifth at Malory Towers*, London, Methuen.

Blyton, E. (1951), the 'Malory Towers' series, *Last Term at Malory Towers*, London, Methuen.

Bratton, J. S. (1981), *The Impact of Victorian Children's Fiction*, London, Croom Helm.

Brazil, A. (1918), *A Patriotic Schoolgirl*, London, Blackie.

Brazil, A. (1921), *Loyal to the School*, London, Blackie.

Brazil, A. (1925), *My Own Schooldays*, London, Blackie.

Bruce, D. F. (1921), *Dimsie Moves Up*, London, Oxford University Press.

Burstyn, J. (1980), *Victorian Education and the Ideal of Womanhood*, London, Croom Helm.

Cadogan, M. and Craig, P. (1976), *You're a Brick Angela!: A New Look at Girls' Fiction from 1839 to 1975*, London, Gollancz.

Dane, C. (1917), *Regiment of Women*, London, Heinemann.

Dane, C. (1926), *The Women's Side*, London, Herbert Jenkins.

Digby, A. (1978), *First Term at Trebizon*, London, Granada, 1980.

Digby, A. (1979), *Second Term at Trebizon*, London, Granada, 1980.

Digby, A. (1979), *Summer Term at Trebizon*, London, Granada, 1980.

Doudney, Sarah (1878), *Monksbury College: A Tale of Schoolgirl Life*, London, Sunday School Union.

Doudney, Sarah (1886), *When We Were Girls Together*, London, Hodder.

Ellis, Havelock (1879), *Sexual Inversion: Studies in the Psychology of Sex*, vol. 2, London, Macmillan; revised edn, Philadelphia, Davis, 1928.

Faderman, Lillian (1981), *Surpassing the Love of Men: Romantic Friendships and Love Between Women from the Renaissance to the Present*, London, Junction Books.

Farmer, Penelope (1969), *Charlotte Sometimes*, Harmondsworth, Penguin, 1972.

Forest, Antonia (1948), *Autumn Term*, Harmondsworth, Penguin, 1977.

Freud, S. (1977), *Case Histories 1: Dora and Little Hans*, Pelican Freud Libraries, vol. 8, Harmondsworth, Penguin.

Glendinning, Victoria (1983), *Vita: The Life of V. Sackville-West*, London, Weidenfeld & Nicolson.

Harris, Mary K. (1963), *Penny's Way*, Harmondsworth, Penguin, 1979.

MacLeod, Sheila (1981), *The Art of Starvation*, London, Virago.

McRobbie, Angela (1978), *Jackie: An Ideology of Adolescent Femininity*, Birmingham, Centre for Contemporary Cultural Studies, Occasional Paper.

Meade, L. T. (1886), *A World of Girls*, London, Cassell.

Meade, L. T. (1891), *A Sweet Girl Graduate*, London, Cassell.

Meade, L. T. (1894), *Betty, A Schoolgirl*, London, Chambers.

Meade, L. T. (1898), *The Girls of St Wode's*, London, Chambers.

Meade, L. T. (1911), *The Girls of Merton College*, London, Chambers.

Rover, Constance (1970), *Love, Morals and the Feminists*, London, Routledge & Kegan Paul.

Russell, Dora (1925), *Hypatia, or, Woman and Knowledge*, London, Kegan Paul.

Sharp, Evelyn (1897), *The Making of a School Girl*, London, Marshall & Russell.

Sharp, Evelyn (1933), *Unfinished Adventure*, London, John Lane.

Stranach, Alice (1901), *A Newnham Friendship*, London, Blackie.

Vaizey, Mrs G. De Horne (1913), *A College Girl*, London, Religious Tracts Society.

Williamson, Judith (1978), *Decoding Advertisements*, London, Marion Boyars.

Women's Studies Group (1978), *Women Take Issue: Aspects of women's subordination*, Birmingham, Centre for Contemporary Cultural Studies, and London, Hutchinson.

10 Racial bias in children's literature

Olivia Foster-Carter

Introduction

There are few British literary texts with West Indian, let alone black British, characters. I chose in my research to use my experience as someone categorized in Britain as 'Afro-Caribbean' to explore biased images of Africa and Africans. What follows are the 'fruits of my labour'.

It proved impossible to examine racial bias without also considering gender and class biases. All three are interrelated and for some women form a triple oppression. It will be their identity, or categorization, as black, possibly working-class, women which will determine their analyses. Without a recognition of this, black women's work will remain invisible.

Biased images of black people have long been seen in the UK. In Charles II's time, writers described Africa as a country of terrifying monsters and its people as hellish savages who killed their prisoners with poisoned arrows and ate them (McCullough, 1962). Much Elizabethan literature was dependent on stereotypes that the audiences would understand; thus black moors (or blackamoors) were portrayed as ignorant, ravenous and brutish.

Today, race tends to have a place in the media which reinforces the stereotypes of black people as the symbols or embodiments of a problem (Hartmann and Husband, 1974). Bias is reinforced at the subconscious level by the very language that is used. Black is associated with evil (black list, black sheep); criminality (blackmail, black maria) and negative imagery, such as the verb to denigrate, or the phrase 'nigger in the woodpile' (Dixon, 1979).

Some twentieth-century authors, such as Olive Schreiner, Evelyn Waugh, Doris Lessing or Alan Paton, are humanitarian and egalitarian (Jablow and Hammond, 1977, p. 105). In their literature, Africa is described as varied, changing and complex, and inhabited by people no more or less civilized than anyone else. However, organizations such as the World Council of Churches, Teachers against Racism Group or the National Association for Multi-Racial Education have shown that racism informs many books – even some which were written for a multiracial society (Broderick, 1973; Dixon, 1979; Dorfman, 1983; Hill, 1975; Stinton, 1979).

Comics are problematic because they are so widely read. They rarely give the impression that black people living in the UK are equal to whites. The few non-white characters who do appear are usually portrayed as criminal, savage, treacherous, stupid, exotic, childlike or subordinate (Dummett, 1973; Johnson, 1966; Laishley, 1972).

Source: Sage Race Relations Abstracts, Institute of Race Relations, Sage 9 (4), pp. 1–11.

Even textbooks have gross stereotypes, distinctions and omissions. Geography books tend to show Africa as undeveloped. They describe quaint, traditional ways of life which are implicitly inferior to western ways. In my own research on these textbooks and their effect on school children in Yorkshire, one 10-year-old child, describing agricultural systems, stated: 'We use tractors, Africans use sticks' (Foster-Carter, 1981). Poverty is attributed to a shortage of western technology and expertise.

Similarly, many modern history textbooks are carelessly and inadequately revised (Procter, 1975). They have poor illustrations and often portray black people as childlike, lazy and happy in a white-dominated world (Glendinning, 1977; McLaurin, 1971).

Racial bias is either overt, in words or illustrations, or covert, in selected facts and implied relationships. This review examines those authors who have attempted to dissect children's literary texts to discover their implicit meanings and the mechanisms in operation behind them. It focuses mainly on the historical and materialistic perspective, tracing many of the most pernicious stereotypes and images to the period of slavery and imperialism. The review demonstrates how Europeans' ethnocentric definitions determine the way that they perceive Africans. It also shows how science, myth, literature and ideology serve to reinforce images which distinguish the European self from others.

Cultural xenophobia

In the early nineteenth century, many people believed that the European explorers were uninfluenced by a mundane concern for money. They travelled to Africa merely to map unknown territory, to introduce the blessings of Christianity, or bring about the benefits of just government (Jablow and Hammond, 1977, pp. 28, 53; Kiernan, 1972).

This image is often reproduced in literature – European heroes are portrayed as voyaging to the frontiers of the continent in order to perform mighty deeds (Conrad, 1912; Johns, 1969; Lofting, 1922, 1923, 1924; Haggard, 1953, 1968). They travel around the world bearing the 'white man's burden' (a phrase invented and exemplified by Kipling). They reinforce the myth that great men can transform the world single-handed.

The early visitors to Africa contributed to the emergence of racial bias. They arrived in other lands with preconceived ideas, influenced by the collective representations of European society which were propagated in fiction and scholarship. On their return, they disseminated a distorted picture of primitive life. It is not surprising that they were ethnocentric; they admitted only one valid way of life and judged others less positively than they judged themselves. Exotic aspects of other cultures were exaggerated and distorted, giving the impression that other people were what Europeans were not. This gave life to their accounts of their journey.

The significance of customs within a culture was ignored. For example, in India, early explorers and missionaries were horrified by *suttee*, or the practice of burning a wife on her husband's funeral pyre. In China, they found foot-binding abhorrent (Kiernan, 1972). In Africa, polygamy was seen as a sorry substitute for marriage. The early explorers to Africa were also critical of the practice of killing slaves at a great man's funeral so that they could attend him in the next world (McFarlan, 1946, pp. 2–3).

Travellers to Africa were attracted by tales of widespread cannibalism (Jablow and Hammond, 1977, p. 94), and this has long remained a literary theme (Ahlberg, 1975; Ballantyne, 1858; Dahl, 1967; Haggard, 1953). In the *Story of Tarzan of the Apes*, cannibalism is described as a hereditary characteristic of inferior races. Tarzan's natural instincts prevent him from transgressing a 'world wide law' (Burroughs, 1912).

The quantity of clothing worn by a people, or the complexity of their language, were frequently used to determine the degree of advancement of a culture or an individual. Sontag characterizes the early anthropologists and missionaries to Africa as far from objective; they were often 'stoney-eyed spinsters . . . bent on redeeming the savages of their follies . . . and making them into civilised Christians . . . [determined] to cover the bosoms of the women and put pants on the men' (Sontag, 1970, p. 190). Victorian morality is passed on to Tarzan through his blood. Thus, as a youth, he has 'a great desire to cover his nakedness with clothes'. As a man, he instinctively bows to the European lady, Jane (Burroughs, 1912, p. 64).

Christianity was equated with civilization and had to be the only respectable religion (Jablow and Hammond 1977, p. 49). While Europeans were 'religious', Africans were merely 'superstitious'. This meant that their beliefs were irrational, out of the ordinary, or simple 'pagan error' (Curtin, 1965, p. 23). The assumption was that primitive people were in awe of natural and supernatural phenomena, and attributed spirits to inanimate things, such as eclipses (Street, 1975, pp. 54, 61). Haggard (1885) and Burroughs (1912) reproduce this image of the primitive mind as being at a pre-logical stage of development. Even anthropologists such as Frazer (1890) described black people's attempts to understand the universe as childlike and their beliefs as debased.

Witchdoctors had a particularly poor image. They were portrayed as an arm of government and the power behind the throne. As tyrants, they exploited the naïve superstitions of the gullible natives (Street, 1975, p. 138). They were often described as dressed in cowtails, entrails and hideous paraphernalia – Rider Haggard's Gagool, in *King Solomon's Mines*, is one vivid example. Tarzan so abhors witchdoctors that he locks one in a lion's cage as bait (Burroughs, 1919). Burroughs also suggests that 'all forms and ceremonies of modern church and state' developed from the rites of apes ('our hairy forebears'), and not from African people. The novels simply translate the conflicts of the day into dramatic form.

Africa was described as a continent of continually warring tribes with ineffectual leaders (Ballantyne, 1858; Haggard, 1887; Street, 1975, p. 134; Wallace, 1911). It is implied that African chiefs and kings were responsible for the slave trade, as is made clear in *Doctor Dolittle's Post Office*. King Koko is a comic buffoon, but also a money-grabbing slave trader. The expansion of a small-scale trade in slaves and war criminals because of overseas demand is ignored.

These negative images of the African people and their customs are summed up by Baker: 'There is neither gratitude, love, nor self-denial, no idea of duty, no religion, but covetousness, ingratitude, selfishness and cruelty. All are thieves, idle, envious, and ready to plunder and enslave their weaker neighbours' (Jablow and Hammond, 1977, p. 64).

Noble savages in a dark continent

Two themes run constantly through the literature on Africa. Baker's image (above) is of a 'Dark Continent' and its inhabitants (a label that was first given to Africa by Stanley). As a world of bestial savages, it was described as a wild, dangerous jungle containing such horrors as crocodiles, fatal diseases and steaming heat. The misery that the Europeans suffered in the conquest of Africa was projected on to the continent itself (Jablow and Hammond, 1977, p. 137).

The people were portrayed as stupid, dishonest, degraded and treacherous. The very word savage, once meaning wild and uncultivated, came to imply gullible, howling barbarians, or cannibals, who were judged as ugly, using Eurocentric ideas of beauty (Jablow and Hammond, 1977, p. 63; Street, 1975, p. 55). The distorted, ignoble side of savage life was stressed in this imagery.

This had much to do with the fact that many Europeans regarded Africa as they did woman – something to be conquered (Jablow and Hammond, 1977). It is a theme of many of Haggard's novels (1885, 1887, 1905), where European explorers seek a treasure in Africa's interior. This idea is clearly expressed by Thompson: '. . . Imagine . . . some lovely damsel, or great treasure deep hidden in the interior, surrounded by a land teeming with horrors and guarded by the foul monsters of disease, darkness and savagery' (Thompson, 1895, p. 201).

The other thread to the European image of Africa and Africans is of the noble savages and their world. Theirs is a good, primitive land, something of a paradise or Garden of Eden. The image arose because there were those who doubted the value of civilization, and the materialist vulgarity and indulgences of advanced modern life. This view was expressed in Rousseau's (1753) essay on inequality. These Europeans longed to return to the simplicity of nature and, in their view, Africa was undefiled in comparison with a repressive, destructive Europe.

This image was stressed in the writing of the Abolitionists (McCullough, 1962, p. 61). They often so enobled the Africans as to make them almost superhuman. Kain, for example, describes 'uncorrupted men of nature endowed with virtuous courage, nobility and sentiment, dwelling in a . . . grand, though terrible, [land] abounding in scenes of awe and inspiring beauty, and filled with a profusion of tropical fruits in life that was carefree and unrestrained. Africa was indeed a terrestrial paradise' (1936). This is the Africa that Tarzan and Jane inhabit during their African romance (Burroughs, 1912).

Historical and materialist explanations of bias

Neither of these images of Africa or the Africans is very positive. Both could be used to justify slavery and imperialism. In the first, Europeans were portrayed as necessary to bring the enlightenment of civilization to this 'dark' land. They perceived themselves as natural colonizers, saving the world from the barbarians.

The term noble savage was used to denote the inferiority of happy, simple children, barely able to control their natural desires (Husband, 1975; Jablow and

Hammond, 1977, pp. 69, 92; Street, 1975, pp. 8, 73). It perpetuates the myth that while black people develop physically, their mental growth stops at an early age. This is clear when a comparison is made with images of Europeans, who are shown as mature, complex people of self-controlled, virtuous character, with rational, logical minds.

This stereotype of the happy children of nature controlled by Europeans crops up repeatedly in literature. In Brunhoff's *Babar the Elephant* (1972), Babar signifies the baby from Africa and is contrasted with the old lady from Europe. Its message is that backward, undeveloped countries and people should imitate advanced, 'grown-up' countries and people, and invite foreigners to assist them (Dorfman, 1983, p. 40).

In these ways, threatening figures from the enemy race are tamed or destroyed. In literature – and other media – noble savages tend to be the loyal assistants of Europeans: Dolittle's cook and bodyguard, Prince Bumpo, Robinson Crusoe's Man Friday, James Fennimore Cooper's Indian Chingakook, the Lone Ranger's Tonto, the Star War's black beast, Darth Vadar, are all examples. In some cases they are noble followers prepared to give their lives for Europeans. Haggard's Umslopogas dies in heroic defence of Quartermain's friends. In *The Cay* (T. Taylor, 1969), the black man is an ignorant, subservient inferior who adds to colonialist mythology by sacrificing his life to save the white boy (Dixon, 1979, p. 115; Schwartz, 1979).

Whole groups of Africans are described in literature as having been created merely to serve their European masters. Tarzan becomes lord of the jungle because of his superior brain (Burroughs, 1912). *Pippi Longstocking* (1948) by Astrid Lingdren, 1978, has been proclaimed for its anti-sexist main character. However, the black characters are pitiful ignoramuses, smiling, singing, dancing and incompetent (Reeder, in Stinton, 1979, p. 114). They worship Pippi's shipwrecked father and make him their chief.

Similarly, in early editions of *Charlie and the Chocolate Factory* (Dahl, 1967) the Oompa Loompas were laughing, singing, childlike pygmies, perpetual servants of white bosses (Bouchard, in Stinton, 1979, p. 43). In more than one of Haggard's novels (1887, 1905), a white queen rules over childlike, black subjects. Haggard writes: 'It is a depressing conclusion but, in all essentials, the savage and the child of civilisation are identical' (1887, p. 4).

A popularized version of Darwin's polygenist model from *Origin of the Species* was congruent with the prevailing mood in the periods of imperialism and slavery – it gave chauvinism an air of scientific respectability. The model implied that the conquered races were not just different, but innately inferior; they were at lower points on the same progressive scale. Each race was given a place in a Eurocentric hierarchy, thus providing a tailor-made explanation for the black person's place in nature and society. The notion of 'survival of the fittest' was used to justify the colonization of people regarded as less fit. It implied that inalienably superior qualities had brought Europeans to the top, and not better weaponry (Jablow and Hammond, 1977, p. 90; Jordan, 1969, p. 228; Street, 1975, pp. 30, 56).

Writers referred to contemporary academic theories: black people were categorized as inferior and closer to nature. Writers classified them as on a level with orang-utangs. The Bannerman books, such as *Little Black Sambo*, like the American *Epaminondas* stories (Broderick, 1973), lend support to these unfounded, but damaging, theories that black people are inherently less intelligent (Kuya, 1972).

Humour is sometimes used to make points similar to those listed above, or to express what would be unacceptable in another context (Hartmann and Husband, 1974). In Lofting's Doctor Dolittle tales, all black characters are depicted as quaint, comic and childlike, with simple customs and funny-sounding names (like King Koko, who is called Coconut, Chief Nyam, Nyam or King Kakaboochi). Even the animals feel superior to them (Suhl, 1979, pp. 6, 23).

The same idea is reinforced in the Tarzan novels, where the 'apeman' goes through a rapid transition from ape to nineteenth-century European, from child-like thought to mature reflection (Burroughs, 1912). This gives the impression of a hierarchy of human races, as well as of human species (Street, 1975, p. 88). The images of animals, such as talking, anthropoid apes, are more positive than those of the 'still more hideous human beasts' (Burroughs, 1919). Similarly, in the prizewinning book *Sounder* (W. Armstrong, 1969), the dog is given a name, but the black family remains anonymous.

These images of black people as subhuman were used to justify their exploitation and enslavement by a 'higher race'. Class superiority was translated into racial superiority. But racial ideology was still allied to the interests of the dominant group, which manipulated racial imagery, as it had class imagery, to maintain a privileged position in Europe and the Third World. The message was that those degraded people with inferior minds had to be controlled – if necessary, by force (Jablow and Hammond, 1977, p. 189).

The stereotypical slave loafed around in the sun, and had to be taught the value of work, chiefly by being forced to do it. Black people were described as less susceptible to heat and pain than Europeans (Lofting, 1922, p. 40). They were shown as being happier in slavery than in the barbarous land from which they were taken – they were carefree, shackled in body, but spared the heavy load of thought and doubt. Resistance was rarely shown. For example, *The Slave Dancer*, by Paula Fox, received the Newbery Award in 1974, but presents an inaccurate picture of slavery and portrays the slaves themselves as completely passive (Schwartz, 1979).

The scientific theories were embodied in fictitious characters and this planted them more firmly in the popular mind than abstract debate could do (Street, 1975, p. 74). Both fed off each other in a dialectical process.

Children's literature often fosters racial attitudes while having the appearance of innocence and charm (Hill, in Stinton, 1979, p. 35). Some, like the Bannerman books, or Lofting's adventures, were understandable products of their time, but are unacceptable in contemporary Britain. There is no such excuse for books like *Sounder*, *The Clay*, or *The Slave Dancer*, which were in fact written for a multiracial society.

Western books are available and widely read throughout the Third World. Searle (1972) suggests that this could lead children to become divorced from their roots. Much literature serves as the fulfilment of the dominant countries' colonial dream (Dorfman, 1983; Richardson, 1966; Searle, 1972). The Babar books, for example, reinforce the myth of noble savages living in a providential natural environment. The élite of the African elephants attain a level comparable to that of the highest humans, Frenchmen in a tropical world, but the mass of elephants and African people remain unchanged. The message is that it is enough for Europeans to maintain economic, technical and cultural dominance – there is no need to exercise political or military control (Dorfman, 1983, p. 40).

Dorfman writes that below the surface of much European literature there lurks, unconsciously, a whole theory of development. 'Even before they can read, the child has come into contact with an implicit history that justifies and rationalises a situation in which some countries have everything and other countries have almost nothing.' The plundering, exploitation and underdevelopment, and the misery inherent in the relationship between the two worlds is never mentioned.

Kiernan writes, in relation to this: 'Whenever the European community depended on the permanent subjugation of the African, it had the strongest inducements to believe that they were inferior by nature and grateful to their betters' (Kiernan, 1972, p. 239). The presuppositions of much of this literature seem distorted to modern readers because they are based on the dubious ideas of nineteenth-century scientists and explorers who were influenced by the ideology of slavery and imperialism (Street, 1975, p. 128).

To summarize, the Victorian imperialists saw themselves as agents of a fundamentally good civilization; the basic message of this period was that Africa could become a paradise under European influence. Myth, religion and science were used to justify imperialism and slavery. The image of Africa that was created did not correspond with reality, but was simply the opposite to that of Europe: Africa is the continent of 'dark negation' (Kiernan, 1971); it is the negative reflection, or dark shadow, of the British self-image (Jablow and Hammond, 1977). Thus some of the images used to contrast Europe and Africa are: light/darkness, civilization/savagery, good/evil.

The theme of a terrestrial paradise is strong but, taken with the image of the 'dark continent' or 'white man's grave', it implies that danger lurks behind the beauty of the tropics. Europeans can create oases, and bring the ruling powers of the conscience to the dark areas of the world (Street, 1975, p. 84). However, the light serves only to intensify the surrounding darkness.

The African people are given images opposite to those that Europeans have of themselves. In some imagery, they are childlike, noble savages, but elsewhere they are portrayed as barbarous savages, the negation of all human decency. When whole races are stereotyped, there are often contradictions. However, both the happy 'children of nature' and the savages, with their bestial forms of humanity, were controlled by inadequate leaders or political and religious tyrants. This paved the way for European imperialists and missionaries to bring the ruling powers of conscience to an undeveloped world.

What is described in literature and ideology is not Africa or black people, but the Europeans' reaction to them. This idea has been expounded by Marxists and psychoanalysts, who claim that Europeans are ethnocentric and project on to others the characteristics that they deny in themselves. Thus they exaggerate and distort differences (Engels, 1970; Freud, 1953; Tajfel, 1981).

Kiernan (1972) questions whether the loss of Empire has freed Europeans to find a clearer picture of themselves and to form a new relationship with their neighbours, 'recollecting in tranquility its adventures across the seven seas'. Kiernan is perhaps too optimistic. Exploitation and oppression, and the ideology that accompanies them, have continued with the crossing of racial boundaries and the intermingling of races involved in the migration of Europeans to the Third World and of black people to Europe. And imperialist relationships have persisted in a less formal way.

Outright racism is not respectable in the UK, partly because modern science has exposed the fallacies of scientific racism (Kamin, 1977). However, bias in language, comics, literature and school textbooks continues in more subtle ways. Social stereotypes are historically specific; the dominant group never stops working to distinguish itself from others, and from the masses. Today, black people are frequently portrayed as living in 'urban jungles of dirt and crime'. New, working-class stereotypes of black people are being created.

Authors who have addressed these problems have suggested that publishers, parents and teachers should instigate change by selecting and distributing non-racist or anti-racist material (Kuya, 1972). There are two main ways of looking at black experience, exemplified by Ezra Jack Keats, who stresses that all humans are the same under the skin, or John Steptoe, whose books are a celebration of ethnic difference.

Some authors in this area would not deny children current images of reality, but would teach them to be aware of disguised interests (Dorfman, 1983). For example, are races equal? Are white heroes attempting to gain victories over stereotypical black victims? Are differences between countries and people distorted and exaggerated?

Zimet (1976) believes that authors should not only reflect the existing, socially constructed reality, but should also portray life both as it actually is and as they would like it to be. It seems trivial to talk of the need for a raising of consciousness and for more unbiased literature in a context of prejudice and discrimination at other levels. However, raising the social and historical consciousness of the young may ultimately lead to the social change that is essential in a multiracial society. Transformation may come about through minorities' efforts to redefine themselves and their own world.

References

Broderick, D., 1973, *Images of the Black in Children's Fiction*, New York, Bowker, 1973.

Curtin, P., *The Image of Africa*, Macmillan, 1965.

Dixon, R., *Catching them Young*, vols. I and II, London, Pluto Press, 1979.

Dorfman, A., *The Empire's Old Clothes*, London, Pluto Press, 1983.

Dummett, A., *A Portrait of English Racism*, Harmondsworth, Penguin, 1973.

Elkins, J., *Books for the Multi-Racial Classroom*, Birmingham, Birmingham Library Association, 1971.

Engels, F., *The Origin of the Family, Private Property and the State*, International Publishers, 1970.

Foster-Carter, O. *et al.*, *Feasibility Study of Books for a Multi-Racial Society*, British National Bibliography, 1981.

Frazer, J. G., *The Golden Bough*, Macmillan, 1963.

Freud, S., 'Civilisation and its discontents', in *Complete Works*, London, Hogarth Press, 1953.

Glendinning, F., 'Racial stereotypes in history textbooks', *Race Today*, **3** (2), 1971, pp. 52–4.

Hartmann, P. and Husband, C., *Racism and the Mass Media*, London, Davis Poynter, 1974.

Hill, J., *Books for Children. The Homelands of Immigrants*, IRR, 1975.

Hoch, P., *White Hero, Black Beast*, London, Pluto Press, 1979.

Husband, C. (ed.), *White Media, Black Britain*, London, Arrow Books, 1975.

Jablow, H. and Hammond, D., *The Myth of Africa*, New York, Library of the Social Sciences, 1977.

Johnson, N., 'What do children learn from war comics?', *New Society*, 7 July 1966.

Jordan, W., *The White Man's Burden* New York, Oxford University Press, 1974.

Kain, R., 'English literature of the abolition', *Philogical Quarterly*, vol. XV, April 1936, p. 103.

Kiernan, V., *The Myth of Africa*, New York, Library of the Social Sciences, 1972.

Kovel, J., *White Racism, A Psychohistory*, London, Allen Lane, 1974.

Kuya, D. (Teachers Against Racism Group), 'Little Black Sambo', *The Times*, May 1972, p. 15.

Laishley, J., 'Can comics form the multiracial society?' *Times Educational Supplement*, 24 November 1972.

Leeson, R., *Children's Books and Class Society*, Children's Rights Workshop, 1977.

Malinowski, B., *The Sexual Life of Savages*, London, Routledge, 1929.

McCullough, V., *The Negro in English Literature*, New York, Arthur Stockwell, 1962.

Mead, M., *Male and Female*, New York, Dell, 1968.

Millett, K., *Sexual Politics*, New York, Avon, 1970.

Procter, C., *Racist Textbooks*, London, NUS Publications, 1975.

Richardson, P., 'Teach your baby to rule', *New Society*, 10 March 1966, pp. 25–6.

Searle, C., *The Foresaken Lover*, Harmondsworth, Penguin, 1972.

Sontag, S., 'Claude Lévi-Strauss, the anthropologist as hero', 1970.

Stanley, H., *In Darkest Africa*, New York, 1890.

Stember, C., *Sexual Racism*, New York, Elsevier, 1976.

Street, B., *The Savage in Literature*, London, Routledge and Kegan Paul, 1975.

Thomson, *Through Masai Land*, London, Sampson Low, 1895.

World Council of Churches, *Racism in Children's School Textbooks*, 1979.

Zimet, S., *Print and Prejudice*, London, Hodder and Stoughton, 1976.

Examples of children's fiction

Ahlberg, A., (1975), *Here are the Brick Street Boys*, Collins.

Ballantyne, R. M. (1858), *Coral Island*, London, Nelson.

Brunhoff, J. (1931), *Babar's Childhood*, London, Methuen, reprinted 1972.

Brunhoff, J. (1934), *Babar and the Old Lady*, London, Methuen, reprinted 1972.

Brunhoff, J. (1935), *Babar's Balloon Trip*, London, Methuen, reprinted 1972.

Burroughs, E. R. (1912), *The Story of Tarzan of the Apes*, Ballantyne, reprinted 1975.

Burroughs, E. R. (1919), *Jungle Tales of Tarzan*, Ballantyne, reprinted 1976.

Conrad, J. (1912), *A Smile of Fortune*, London, Dent.

Dahl, R. (1967), *Charlie and the Chocolate Factory*, London, Allen and Unwin.

Haggard, H. R. (1885), *King Solomon's Mines*, Harmondsworth, Penguin Books, reprinted 1968.

11 'Mind that you do as you are told': reading books for Board School girls, 1870–1902

Anna Davin

In England, state interest in working-class education was established in the middle decades of the nineteenth century, starting with the first grants-in-aid to existing schools ('voluntary' ones run by religious authorities); developing its own system of inspection and partial control administered by a specialized bureaucracy; and consolidated by Forster's Education Act in 1870, which permitted increase of the existing network and also the setting up of a complementary system of 'Board Schools' under local non-denominational administration, both kinds to be funded (one partly, the other entirely) by a combination of local rate and government grants. These developments were justified at the time, and have been discussed since by historians, in social, political and economic terms.

Ruling-class fear of the working class in nineteenth-century England was expressed not only through apprehension of sedition or violence, and repression of working-class militancy, but also through attacks on the working-class way of life, or their 'morals'. The family (in its bourgeois form – male breadwinner, dependent housekeeping wife and dependent children) was an essential stabilizing force in the bourgeois ideology, and the source of harmony and civilization. The explanation of disharmony and malfunction in society must lie in the failure of the family, and the antidote to class conflict was of course to re-establish 'morality' through the family.

In an article called 'Educational policy and social control in early Victorian England' Richard Johnson (1970) suggests that education was to become a panacea expected to resolve every problem of industrial society. The education of the poor, he argues, was essentially a question of control. His analysis, based particularly on the writings of school inspectors in the 1840s, suggests that the school was to replace the deficient family, at least as far as education was concerned, and in the inculcation of morals and discipline. I would argue also that a further aim of schooling was to impose on working-class children the bourgeois view of family functions and responsibilities. Education was to form a new generation of parents (and especially mothers) whose children would not be wild, but dependent and amenable, accepting not only the obvious disciplines of school and work but also the less visible constraints of life at the bottom of the heap. Education was to establish (or as they believed to re-establish) the family as a stabilizing force.

The following material is based on part of my work on girls' experience of school under the London School Board. The source I have used in this chapter to explore the ideological content of education is the range of reading textbooks

Source: Extracted from *Feminist Review*, no. 3, 1979, pp. 89–98.

approved for use under the Board. They are a slightly dubious source in that they were mostly patchworks of extracts from an eclectic variety of authors, often going back to the early nineteenth century or to La Fontaine and even Aesop. But certain themes emerge in them with great consistency and seem worth consideration, though always with the proviso that we can only show that this was what the children were given to read, not how much of it they believed or remembered or internalized. Effects are always more complicated than intentions because of continual interactions between the instigators and institutions of change, and the recipients who themselves are actors and not objects. But this is a larger question than can be dealt with here.

On the whole, board schools served the poorer end of the working class, though the intake and status of the individual school might vary a great deal. According to calculations by Charles Booth in the late 1880s we can suppose that 60 per cent of board school pupils came from families struggling or failing to make ends meet on £1 a week or less.

The establishment of board schools, as Spalding pointed out in 1900, was a spur to writers and publishers, encouraging them 'to devote intelligence and capital to the production of . . . primers' (Spalding, 1900, p. 90). Reading textbooks were required to be distinct from other textbooks or manuals, though in the higher standards they could have a geographical or a historical emphasis (Parliamentary Papers, 1884 lxi, p. 5). But although the demand was a new one, the readers were often distinctly old-fashioned. The usual format was the anthology, and often it would include stories based on Aesop, poems from the early nineteenth century (for example, by Mrs Barbauld, Sara Coleridge, and the Taylor sisters), and didactic dialogues or stories reminiscent of Maria Edgeworth.

[One] particular series specialized in morals about the importance of contentedness in work: 'Don't count your chickens before they are hatched'; 'All men to their trades'; 'Hard work no misery'; 'The idle man is seldom a happy man'; 'Work to have, to give, and for the happiness there is in work'; and so on. The stories preach content, cheerfulness and perseverance. In one story, 'Rich and Poor, or the Discontented Haymaker Reproved', a couple are haymaking when a rich and beautiful lady rides past. The wife is envious, but the husband says:

God knows what is good for all his creatures. Don't let us murmur, Peggy dear, for if many seem to be better off than we are, it is still quite certain that we are better off than many more. . . . While I have hands to labour, a good tidy wife to make home comfortable, and dear little children to divert me with their prattle, I am not going to fret because perhaps others have something else that I never feel to want (Howard and Conley II, 1873).

Shortly after this admirable declaration the rich lady is thrown from her horse and brought insensible to their humble (but tidy) house. ('Peggy took pride in the thought that she could provide a nice clean pair of sheets and pillow cases.') The lady dies, so Peggy resolves 'to feel more kindly towards the rich, who, she now saw, were no more free from great sorrows than were the poor' (Howard and Conley II, 1873). Like other stories in these books, this one is set in a static, hierarchical world, where fulfilment and content come through keeping one's place and doing one's duty. For a woman this involves listening to one's husband as well as to class superiors, being 'a good tidy wife' and keeping the house clean and comfortable, as well as being generally industrious and content. Other virtues recommended in the readers included patience, humility, modesty, obedience, unselfishness, punctuality, tidiness and so on. They warn that 'little girls ought to know that it is during childhood that good or bad habits are formed', and set out to make quite clear which habits are to be considered good. 'Don't be envious'. 'To do our duty well in one situation is the best proof we shall discharge it properly in another' is illustrated in a book for Standard IV girls by a story in which a girl who is lazy at home imagines herself in the grand situation of housemaid at the Hall (Bilton IV (Girls), 1870), and again and again girls who are tidy and diligent at home are rewarded with good places in service.

Neatness in dress is constantly urged, and rewarded; its significance being presumably that it shows the values of tidiness and industry have been internalized. A writer on 'Waste' deplores girls who do not mend their clothes, failing 'to put in that stitch in time which saves not nine but nine hundred', for 'Such children lose all sense of respectability, and do not care what they look like.' A poor frock is not shameful 'if it is clean, and well mended, and patched' (Grant V, 1871, p. 16). Alice's mother worries about her carelessness: 'You ought soon to get a place, but who will take a girl in rags like you?', and she is shocked when Alice says 'Oh I will mend up my things if I go after a place; but till then, mother, do not tease me so.' Nor can Alice escape by saying there are many girls worse than her, for although 'Patty Fell has not a hat or a shawl, and only rags for clothes', the mother points out

Poor Patty has no mother, and will soon, I fear, go to the workhouse. They will make her neat and clean there, but you have a good home and a good father to work for you, and need not go about in rags and dirt, and what is more you shall not . . . you shall have nothing to eat today until you have made your frock fit to be seen, and have found your bootlaces (Grant V, 1871, p. 45).

Carefulness would be rewarded: the writer on 'Waste' told how a girl who had only one frock but washed and mended it every Saturday and was always neat and clean, was helped to an excellent situation as nursery maid, 'and you may see her on Sundays going to church in a nice tweed dress, and a cloth jacket, looking as creditable as any tradesman's daughter in the place' (Grant V, 1871, p. 16). But discretion is important – the girl who is in a position to buy herself clothes must ask herself 'Am I going to buy what is most suitable for my station in life . . . best and most durable for the work I have to perform?' (Bilton IV, 1867 'On Dress'), and there is of course no doubt as to the answer.

Perseverance is often advocated: stories about spiders are frequent, especially that of Bruce and the spider. But resistance is not advised. Another recurring tale is that of the oak which is torn apart in a storm, while the reeds, which being 'frail and weak', have bent to the rough blast instead of standing up against it, once it was over could 'rear our heads once more to meet the bright sunshine that greets us with a smile' (Marshall and Laurie II, 1870, p. 69). ''Twere better sure, than break, to be like me, and bend' (Marshall and Laurie V, 1872, pp. 48–9). Work is endlessly recommended:

. . . Most children look forward with pleasure to the time when they will become workers, and earn money for themselves, which will certainly be a very pleasant thing . . . a life of labour is much pleasanter than a life of idleness. No one can be happy without something to do . . . while people are at work they are doing three good things: they are getting a living, exercising their minds, and keeping themselves strong and healthy. . . . What a good thing it is that God has so made us, that what is necessary for us to do, is pleasant and healthful too; that doing our duty is a pleasure and a gain (Jarrold IV, 1871, pp. 23–4).

But it is made clear that woman's work will be in the home, her own or someone else's. Mothers are almost always shown doing some kind of house or kitchen work, except in the animal fables where the point is to show how wise, devoted, and even fierce they are in the care of their young. A series called 'Universal Readers' is particularly rich in these: a wise old mother rook teaches her young not to be alarmed by geese; a hen, who 'when she has little ones . . . cares for them first, as a good mother always does', attacks the fox who tries to carry off a chick; another hen refuses to go for a walk with the cock because she's sitting on her eggs – 'My little chicks will soon be hatched,/I'll think about it then.' A brave cat drives off the hawk which has grabbed her kitten: 'If you had been there, you might have heard her purr with joy at having saved her young one from the wild bird.' There maternal solicitude at least assures safety, but when rescue is impossible the mother's selfless love even runs to self-immolation. In a poem about a stork's nest threatened by fire the last verse adjures the reader:

> Think not maternal love can tire;
> That nest will be her funeral pyre.
> More closely still she spreads her wings
> Above those feeble trembling things;
> And since their lives she cannot save,
> She shares with them one common grave.   (Marshall and Laurie II, 1875–7, p. 14.)

Sometimes too the mother is not all-powerful in the defence of her little ones and has to call in the father, as in the story of the lamb caught in thorns: the ewe after vain attempts to disentangle him summons the ram, who with his big horns at once effects a release (London School Series, Infant Reader, 1878).

Females other than mothers are presented as weaker, sillier, quieter than males. Pets, especially birds, cats and little motherless creatures brought in by the gardener, always belong to girls; and it is girls who compassionately try to stop naughty boys from teasing or hurting animals, butterflies, birds and so on. Personification from the animal or vegetable world follows the same pattern: in one story the maple tree, vain but deciduous, is female, the holly, modest, cheerful and evergreen, is male (Nelson III, 1984). In another, a lesson on the industrious bee, describing the work and organization of the hive, a silly snail which blunders into the hive and disrupts their work is female (Marshall and Laurie II, 1870, p. 17). (This last is a particularly gratuitous identification, since snails are in fact hermaphrodite.) Girls do less:

You should have seen Harry and his sister Ellen at the launching of their little ship. . . . Harry had been at work for three or four days, forming the hull of a vessel out of a piece of deal, and fitting it up like a ship. Ellen supplied the cloth for the sails, as well as the thread for the rigging. It had three masts; and when finished it was as pretty a little ship as you could expect a boy to make. . . .

That day Harry was a Captain Cook or a Columbus in his own opinion, and his sister . . . could not too highly estimate her brother's cleverness . . . (Marshall and Laurie II, 1875–7, p. 105).

Boys are more likely to be naughty, and their naughtiness springs from exuberance or adventurousness – they are wild and rough. Girls' naughtiness is tamer and less positive – they are lazy and untidy, or inquisitive (rather than exploratory), or a bit self-willed, or they think too much of showy clothes, and not enough of solid worth. But beside boys they are good; the docile, contented, industrious example of modesty and restraint. Out in the woods Mary, being 'of a contented mind', picks such flowers as she sees, while Henry, 'more difficult to satisfy' ends up with none but those she gives him (Howard and Conley I, 1872). Or the boy is determined to get a flower which is hard to reach, his sister begs him not to, he persists, slips, and is stung by a nettle. (Their father then draws the moral (Bilton III, 1869).)

Boys and girls alike are exhorted to industry, but the girls' work is always service, in their own family or for an employer.

> We who have to earn our bread,
>   We must all endeavour,
> Strive against our laziness,
>   Try to grow more clever.
>
> Elder sisters, you may work,
>   Work and help your mothers,
> Darn the stockings, mend the shirts,
>   Father's things, and brother's.
>
> Younger boys, and you may work,
>   If you are but willing
> Thro' the week in many ways
>   You may earn your shilling,   (Jarrold II, 1871, p. 58.)

Boys could remember men like Richard Arkwright, George Stephenson, or Sir Joseph Paxton, who 'from being very poor, rose to be rich and celebrated', even though they must not expect so much themselves, since such instances were 'very rare'. (Besides, 'There is more happiness to be had by remaining in the station of life to which it has pleased God to call you, living in comfort and respectability, than in quitting it to associate with those with whom you cannot feel on an equality.' (Grant V, 1871, p. 43).) But the perspective offered to girls did not even offer such unattainable peaks, it was entirely domestic.

Amongst girls . . . great mistakes are made by their longing to 'better themselves', as they say. And in one sense it is quite right that they should have such a wish. But first let them be sure that it is bettering themselves to change merely for higher wages, or to go into a higher family. When the girl who is only fitted for housework thinks that because she has been well educated at school, she ought to be a lady's maid, when the lady's maids wish to be governesses, depend upon it they are not getting on in life . . . (Grant V, 1871, p. 45).

If boys were honest and diligent, and loyal to their masters (one lesson on 'Work and Wages' explains why strikes are bad and why socialism wouldn't work), there was 'no reason why some . . . should not some day become masters' (Grant V, 1871); but for girls the ultimate aspiration was either a good place, and the trust and respect of their mistress, or a good husband, who equally would value their thrift and industry. In the meantime they must learn at home to acquire the necessary domestic skills and virtues.

It is interesting that few of the stories are about school situations: home and the family loom much larger. The family as presented (even in the animal world) almost always has a breadwinning father and a housekeeping mother. Occasionally, however, reality impinges, and it is admitted that mothers (especially widowed ones) may have to go out to work.

Household management . . . is, or may be, your business any day. Do not many of your mothers go out to work, leaving you to manage the house, and the baby as well? Are not your mothers ill sometimes, and in bed, and unable to see to anything downstairs? Some of you have had the misfortune of losing your mothers, and have to mind the house and keep things comfortable for your father . . . (Grant V, 1871, p. 60).

Such contingencies merely reinforce the overriding importance of the girl's domestic role, which in one story is even put before achievement at school. The 'best scholar in the class', full of self-confidence in her scholastic prowess, looks down on her humble quiet sister, who is no good at school. But when their mother falls ill, the older sister has to stay at home to look after her, and learns that she is useless as housewife or nurse, whereas her sister is a marvel of unobtrusive efficiency. Her father is quite firm about which kind of knowledge is more to be valued: 'school could not be the right place for Alice if it made her so useless at home', and he told her to learn by her mother, who all her life had 'thought nothing of herself, only to do her duty by God and man'. Alice learnt her lesson, and the mother

recovered at last to find her eldest daughter a different person, humble and thoughtful, and affectionate, and though not neglecting her home lessons, always making much more effort to do her home duties (Grant V, 1871, pp. 25–31).

It is clearly out of the question to assess the impact of these books, to decide how far the assumptions and prescriptions of their writers influenced the children who laboured through them. But it is worth noticing that their tendency, both through the behaviour they advocated – unselfishness, compassion, devotion to housewifely industry and family duty – and through the situations which they presented as natural to women, was to direct girls towards an exclusively domestic role, even at the expense of school.

References

Bilton, Charles, *Bilton's Reading Books* London, Longman, 1867–70.
Howard, F. and Conley, R. M., *New Code Reader and Speller*, London, Longman, 1872–3.
Johnson, Richard, 'Educational policy and social control in early Victorian England'
   Past and Present, no. 49, 1970.
Jarrold, *New Code Reading Books*, London, Jarrold and Sons, 1871.

London School Series, London, Lockwood, 1878 (not in British Museum catalogue, but shelved there at 12203.ccc.26. I owe this reference to Eileen Allwall).

Marshall, J. and Laurie, J. S., *Technical Series of Reading Books*, London, Marshall, 1870–2.

Marshall, J. and Laurie, J. S., *Universal Readers*, London, Marshall, 1875–7.

Nelson, *Royal Crown Readers*, London, Nelson, 1894.

Parliamentary Papers 1884 lxi, Revised Instructions to Her Majesty's Inspectors.

Grant, A. R., *School Managers' Series of Reading Books*, London, Weale, 1871.

Spalding, T. A., *The Work of the London School Board*, London, 1900.

12   Sex roles in reading schemes

Glenys Lobban

The major premise underlying the current debate about class and race bias in reading schemes is that the content of the schemes influences children's attitudes to the world and to themselves. Reading schemes are presumed to be particularly influential because they are usually the child's first introduction to the written word and they are presented within a context of authority, the classroom, and most children read them. They are hence presumed to convey official approval of attitudes the child will have already learned in the pre-school years from parents, the media and other persons in the society. Current knowledge suggests that children's books and particularly their first readers do influence children's attitudes. They do this by presenting models like themselves for the children to identify with and emulate. In addition they present an official view of the real world and 'proper' attitudes.

It is now generally agreed that reading schemes such as the *Ladybird* scheme, which show a white middle-class world peopled with daddies in suits, and mummies in frilly aprons, who take tea on the lawns in front of their detached houses, are likely to be irrelevant and harmful for urban working-class and black children. They do not provide them with models like themselves, they implicitly, if not explicitly, denigrate these children's culture and imply that what is real and proper is also white and middle class. If this argument is accepted for race and class bias in reading schemes then it must equally apply to another type of inequality within our society, namely sexual inequality.

Ours is a patriarchal society where females are economically and legally discriminated against, where males control all the major social institutions, and where two distinct sex roles, the 'feminine'-passive and the 'masculine'-active, exist. As nobody has proved any genetic difference between females and males other than those related to reproduction, we must conclude that the sex differences in temperament, interests, abilities and goals, are the results of socialization. If we assume that despite class and race discrimination in our society, reading schemes should not mirror this and denigrate these groups, then we should also demand that such schemes do not mirror male-dominated sex roles and denigrate females.

This chapter will describe a preliminary study on sex-role content in readers. The sex-role content of six popular British reading schemes was coded. I chose two schemes published before 1960 (*Janet and John* and *Happy Venture*), two published in the 1960s (*Ready to Read* and *Ladybird*), and two schemes published in the 1970s,

Source: Extracted from *Forum – for the discussion of new trends in education*, Spring 1974, vol. 16, no. 2, pp. 57–60.

(*Nipper* and *Breakthrough to Literacy*) which are designed specifically for urban children. I coded the content of 225 stories in all. 179 of these had people as their central characters and I listed the toys and pets, activities and adult roles these showed for each sex and both the sexes. Table 12.1 gives a summary of these results. It lists the toys and pets, activities and adult roles for each and both of the sexes that figured in three or more of the six reading schemes. In all cases single sex activities are those which figured as single sex in five of the schemes and in some of the readers in the remaining scheme.

A glance at Table 12.1 shows that the schemes rigidly divided the sphere of people's activity into two compartments, 'masculine' and 'feminine' with very few common characteristics. The number of 'masculine' options exceeded the number

Table 12.1   *The sex roles that occurred in three or more of the six schemes coded*

The sex for which the role was prescribed	The content of the children's roles				
	Toys and pets	Activities	Taking the lead in both sex activities	Learning a new skill	The adult roles presented
Girls only	1 Doll 2 Skipping rope 3 Doll's pram	1 Preparing the tea 2 Playing with dolls 3 Taking care of younger siblings	1 Hopping 2 Shopping with parents 3 Skipping	1 Taking care of younger siblings	1 Mother 2 Aunt 3 Grandmother
Boys only	1 Car 2 Train 3 Aeroplane 4 Boat 5 Football	1 Playing with cars 2 Playing with trains 3 Playing football 4 Lifting or pulling heavy objects 5 Playing cricket 6 Watching adult males in occupational roles 7 Heavy gardening	1 Going exploring alone 2 Climbing trees 3 Building things 4 Taking care of pets 5 Sailing boats 6 Flying kites 7 Washing and polishing Dad's car	1 Taking care of pets 2 Making/ Building 3 Saving/ Rescuing people or pets 4 Playing sports	1 Father 2 Uncle 3 Grandfather 4 Postman 5 Farmer 6 Fisherman 7 Shop or business owner 8 Policeman 9 Builder 10 Bus driver 11 Bus conductor 12 Train driver 13 Railway porter
Both sexes	1 Book 2 Ball 3 Paints 4 Bucket and spade 5 Dog 6 Cat 7 Shop	1 Playing with pets 2 Writing 3 Reading 4 Going to the seaside 5 Going on a family outing	—	—	1 Teacher 2 Shop assistant

of 'feminine' ones in every category and they tended to be more active and instrumental and to relate more to the outside world and the outdoors than the 'feminine' options which revolved almost entirely around domestic roles. Only thirty-five of the 179 stories I coded had heroines, while seventy-one had heroes. The heroines were seldom being successful in non-'feminine' spheres, while the heroes were frequently brave and adventurous. In the *Nipper* scheme, for example, a heroine who ran away got lost, caught the wrong tube and found herself back home and gave up, whereas boys who went off on their own frequently found adventure. In the remaining seventy-three stories there were female and male central characters but it was almost always a boy who took the lead in all non-domestic activities and let the girl help or watch. In the *Janet and John* scheme, for example, while both children had dogs, Janet's was a puppy while John had a big dog. Boys were more frequently responsible for the care of the pets, and owned larger versions of a common toy such as a boat, and usually did better at common activities; e.g., the boy reached the top of the tree while sister sat on a lower branch. In the classroom situation both sexes were equally good at reading and writing, but they were frequently shown with toys or apparatus conventionally appropriate to their sex. Frequently in situations where the children participated equally, their parents played out conventional roles. When both sexes made or built anything the boy usually did so more or excelled and Dad was the instructor unless they were learning to make cakes. Mum was never shown teaching them to build anything or to play sport.

It is illuminating to contrast the female and male worlds the schemes showed. The female world was almost entirely oriented around domestic activity and childcare. The message that the schemes conveyed was that a woman's place is in the home and that little girls should spend their time learning 'feminine' skills such as cooking and childcare. It is significant that the only new skill learned by girls in three or more of the schemes was taking care of a younger sibling. The adult models available were all situated in the home and shown doing domestic activity. The *Nipper* scheme was the only one which showed working mothers and this was for a minority of the mothers shown. The fact is that the majority of women in Britain are in paid employment outside the home and many of them are neither shop assistants nor teachers (the only both-sex jobs in the schemes). This makes the schemes' relegation of women to the home even more invidious. The only two girls' activities that allowed physical activity were skipping and hopping. Neither of these develop group co-operation nor the varied motor skills that the range of boys' activities and games offered.

The male world the schemes described did not include toys or activities that allowed expressive or nurturant behaviour. Boys' toys and activities were such as to allow the learning of independence and a variety of instrumental and motor skills. The boys' world was oriented outside the home and their toys and their adult models suggested a variety of future occupational goals. Boys, unlike girls, spent time watching adult males, who weren't relatives, performing their occupational roles. The idea that it was the boys who would have jobs was often explicitly stated. While girls were told they'd be like Mum or voiced such ideas, the boys expressed the desire to be train-drivers and the like. In only one of the *Nipper* readers was a jobless father shown, and this dad was just temporarily out of work, while virtually all mums were jobless permanently. Thus, while the scope of adult male roles was somewhat limited, the schemes clearly conveyed the idea that it was males who had jobs, and who were responsible for the maintenance of all aspects of the 'real' world except for childcare and cooking.

The schemes also showed the interaction within the family in rigidly traditional terms. *Nipper* was the only scheme which showed female single-parent families and none of the schemes showed male single-parent units. None of the schemes showed Dad doing housework or cooking anything other than a cup of tea. (The one exception was in *Ready to Read* when Mum was in hospital having a baby.) Dad was always the one who drove 'his' car (only one reader in one scheme showed a woman driver), his authority was ultimate and he usually initiated and directed all family activities. All the schemes abounded in pictures of Dad reading the paper or watching television, while Mum bustled about preparing and serving food, and washing up, often with the help of daughter. Once again, as in the case of female employment, the schemes' version of the family was even more rigidly traditional than current practice. Many British women drive cars and do handiwork, and in many homes cooking and cleaning are tasks which are shared by the family, but none of this was reflected in the schemes.

In summary the reading schemes showed a 'real' world peopled by women and girls who were almost solely involved with domestic activity and whom the adventurous and innovative males might occasionally allow into their world (the rest of human activity and achievement) in a helpmate capacity. The world they depicted was not only sexist, it was more sexist than present reality, and in many ways totally foreign to the majority of children, who do have working mums, and at least some experience of cross sex activities.

The question that now arises concerns the impact of these readers on the attitudes of girls and boys to themselves and the world. If, as research suggests, characters like themselves suggest new modes of behaviour for children and define what they should do and want, then the models of their own sex available to the readers could only serve to reinforce the patriarchal sex roles the children have already learned. The policy in primary schools is for all the pupils to do traditionally one sex activities like cooking and metalwork. The content of the reading schemes is opposite to this policy, and might well neutralize these non-sextyped experiences, or convince the children that experiences in school are unrelated to the 'real' world outside. The schemes, like the rest of children's and adults' literature (see Millett, 1970), concentrate on the exploits of males. The girls who read them have already been schooled to believe, as our society does, that males are superior to females and better at everything other than domestic work, and the stories in the schemes cannot but reinforce the damage that our society does to girls' self-esteem. The total lack of female characters who are successful in non-'feminine' activities and jobs and who are independent, ensures that girls with these aspirations will receive no encouragement. In the same way, boys who feel the need to express gentleness and nurturance will find no male models to emulate. In short, these schemes in no way question the correctness of a society which deprives both sexes of full expression of their capabilities, and, in fact, they endorse a set of sex roles that are even more rigid than our present role division.

Notes and references

Reading schemes used:

Breakthrough to Literacy, D. Mackay, B. Thompson and P. Schuaub, London, Longmans, for the Schools Council, 1970.
Happy Venture Reader, F. J. Schonell and I. Sarjeant, London, Oliver & Boyd, 1958.
Janet and John, M. O'Donnell and R. Munro, Herts, James Nisbet & Co, 1950.
Ladybird Key Words Reading Scheme, W. Murray, Loughborough, Wills & Hepworth Ltd, 1964.
Nipper, London, Macmillan Ltd, 1968.
Ready to Read, M. Simpson, London, Methuen, 1964.

References cited in text

Millett, K., *Sexual Politics*. New York, Doubleday and Co. Inc., 1970.

13   Girls and boys in primary maths books

Jean Northam

As evidence has mounted on the differential achievement of girls and boys in mathematics and science surprisingly there has not been the widespread concern with the portrayal of sex roles in maths books that was shown in relation to reading materials. The report of the National Child Development Study (Davie, 1972), for example, indicates that by the age of 7, boys are marginally ahead of girls in certain mathematical skills. Whereas the report draws attention to the part reading materials may play in the slower progress of boys in reading, no such suggestion is made in relation to girls and maths. Indeed, the problem arithmetic test included in the appendix to the book suggests that the researchers were not conscious that such a possibility might exist. Out of ten problems in the test, five mention people, namely Peter, a man, John, four boys and a boy.

Maths books do not usually present information about the social world in the coherent, narrative way that usually occurs in reading books. There is no story line, little characterization, and experiences are explored for their mathematical properties rather than their intrinsic interest. However, children's test books are often lavishly illustrated and glimpses of social life are found in the problems and in the explanations of mathematical processes. There are notes for teachers which convey information about the assumptions authors make about children and childhood, and in schemes for younger children there may be guidelines on assessment and records of progress. The selection of areas of experience defined as mathematically interesting and relevant gives clues to underlying attitudes and values. When the style and content of the pictorial and written material in the books are analysed, it is possible to detect a particular view of the social world which forms a 'hidden curriculum' in the teaching of maths.

The books discussed in this chapter were not chosen as 'worst offenders' in their portrayal of girls and boys. They were selected from schemes known to teachers taking a maths diploma course, and cover a variety of styles and approaches. For younger children in nursery and early infant classes, the *Early Mathematics Experiences* (EME) (Schools Council, 1978) and Nuffield *Mathematics – the First Three Years* (1970) were studied. Both series are addressed to teachers rather than children. *Mathematics!*, books 1a, 1b, 2a, 3a were included as books addressed to children in infant and first schools (Golding, 1971). The years 8–11 are covered by *Maths Adventure*, books 2, 3, 4 (Stanfield, 1973), and *Discovering Mathematics*, book 2 (Shaw and Wright, 1975) takes the study into the lower secondary or upper middle school years. Thus different publishers, styles of presentation and approaches to maths teaching were represented.

Souce: Extracted from *Education*, **10** (1), Spring 1982, pp. 11–14.

Women dominate the child's world in the infant teachers' books. Though unnamed children are invariably 'he', the teacher and the parent are 'she'. The Nuffield book describes the world of the under-5 as with mother at home; fathers are rarely mentioned. The contents of mother's handbag form a set (lipstick, pen, purse, diary with pencil, nail scissors, powder compact), mother's necklace is an early object of interest, and she unpacks the shopping, takes the child to buy new clothes and does the cooking. EME chooses the word 'parent' for these early experiences but for the most part defines the under-5 as a pupil in a nursery or infant class. Mathematical experiences are rooted in the provision for play that is made by teachers. The stereotyped picture of family roles is reinforced in both series by the presentation of the 'typical' family, consisting of father, mother, brother, sister and baby in descending order of height. In the book on the Home Corner, the EME team make this reservation: 'Usually, we assume that dad will be the tallest, mum the next and so on, but of course this may not be so and unless we know the family there may be little point in exploring the idea.' It is relevant to consider how far the model corresponds to the experience of most children in a number of respects besides that of relative height. Maths books tend to confine themselves to this model, however, throughout the primary age range.

There is little differentiation in the presentation of children engaged in play with basic materials and in sorting activities. In EME illustrations often show mopheaded trousered figures who could be either male or female. The dominant characteristic of children in all the infant books is not their gender but a particular kind of dependence. They are chubby, doll-like and expressionless apart from a vague smile. They sometimes lack sense organs such as noses, mouths and fingers, yet the clothes are carefully elaborated and decorated, the hair curled, beribboned, plaited or appealingly tousled. The arms and legs may lack joints, the feet are stiff and stubby. The child is presented as a passive receiver of adult attention, staring round-eyed out of the picture, physically and psychologically incapable of self-initiated action.

Two considerations underline the significance of the concept of childhood implicit in the three infant schemes studied. The first is the marked difference between the portrayal of children and women and that of men, which will be considered later. The second is the close correspondence between this concept and that implicit in some of the items in EME's suggested methods of recording.

In the EME guidelines we find the following items of behaviour used as criteria for assessment of developmental progress: 'helps with activities', 'keeps himself occupied', 'puts on own shoes', 'talks freely to strangers', 'understands simple instructions quickly' and 'draws writing patterns'. These items are not necessarily and directly related to the development of skills and abilities but may well be viewed as outcomes of adult/child relationships. The picture is one of the compliant, conforming child whose behaviour does not delay or baffle or challenge or trouble the teacher. It is a pattern which conforms to a female rather than male stereotype of behaviour and, if it accurately reflects teachers' expectations of pupils, seems designed to reinforce the kind of teacher-approved behaviour in girls which is likely to impede the development of self-assertion and initiative. Certainly, evidence from other sources suggests that infant teachers rate girls' behaviour more highly, on the whole, than boys' (King, 1978) and this would not be surprising if their criteria resemble those suggested by EME.

As the analysis of books for older children shows, the concept of the pupil in infant books is at odds with the definition of the pupil-mathematician. What is particularly interesting is that it is also at odds with the descriptions of children given in the teacher's notes in the infant books. Nuffield, for example says: '. . . children must be set free to make their own discoveries and think for themselves'. A similar message is expressed in EME: 'The same learning experience goes on as they explore the whole gamut of toys, books, music and physical activity, gaining experience in the way materials must be manipulated.'

The active, exploring, discovering child of the teachers' introductory notes is similar to the pupil-mathematician in *Maths Adventure*, but may not emerge with too favourable a rating on drawing writing patterns, putting on shoes, or talking freely to strangers: any relationship between the two styles of behaviour would appear to be coincidental. It seems significant that Nuffield and EME are written for teachers, and therefore it must be concluded that the style of presentation is intended to appeal to them rather than the children.

Two further considerations related to infant maths are suggested by the examination of the *Mathematics!* series. These books are addressed to children, and are therefore, especially in the early books, more abundantly illustrated. One of the first sets the children are invited to make is that of girls and of boys. This suggestion is also made in the other infant books, but here the implications of this division become more clearly apparent. In order to distinguish clearly between the two sets, differences are emphasized. Dress, demeanour and sex-typical behaviour must be sharply contrasted so that the notion of 'set' is clarified. Thus we find no mopheaded, trousered boy/girl figures in the sets. All the girls are in dresses and have elaborate hairstyles; four out of five of them are standing gazing into space. The boys' hair is cropped short and out of seven boys, five are on the move. This example, taken from book 1b, further reinforces the differences by adding the instructions: 'Draw a chair for each girl', 'Draw a drum for each boy.'

The visual material contains a number of adult figures, cowboys, soldiers, sportsmen, clowns, pedestrians and tractor drivers; they are tall, short, fat, thin, they climb ladders, they mend roofs, and they are almost all men. Two examples only depict women. Mr and Mrs Smith are seen walking to church and two female heads are seen in relation to three hair ribbons. The men are highly individualized in the ways described and also in terms of facial expression and characteristics. Whereas the women appear bland, expressionless, and lacking in individuality, the men have ages, personalities, distinguishing features, occupations, tasks and intentions. Men are not depicted staring vacantly out of the picture, in sharp contrast to the portrayal of women and children.

Women disappear almost completely from the junior books studied. There are more than forty references to men, six to women. *Maths Adventure* adopts something approaching a narrative style, in that six major characters are followed throughout the series. These are Gary, Clarence, Joe, Jill, Ann and eccentric Uncle Harry. The initial impression on glancing through the book is that sex-role differences are somewhat diffused by the characterizations and by situations in which all the children are involved in the same or similar activities. In order to see whether this impression would bear closer examination, the vocabulary was analysed. Sentences which begin 'Gary noticed . . .' or 'Jill invented . . .' suggest particular skills; they imply in the first example, an ability to identify problems and in the second initiative and inventiveness. 'Ann recorded this way' suggests an elaboration of a process already learned. Instances of behaviour were categorized in the following ways:

a   identification, setting and solving of problems;
b   taught, explained processes to others;
c   made something, displayed a skill;
d   planned, initiated, invented;
e   performed, played tricks, boasted;
f   competed;
g   repeated or elaborated upon a process already learned;
h   co-operated, shared, helped, complied;
i   corrected another's behaviour; e.g. 'Calm down', said Ann.

In Table 13.1, examples which involve both boys and girls have been omitted.

Table 13.1

	a Problems	*b* Teach	*c* Skills	*d* Initiate	*e* Perform	*f* Compete	*g* Repeat	*h* Co-op	*i* Correct
Boys	27	35	9	11	12	7	8	6	3
Girls	10	10	2	3	0	2	19	12	13

The initial impression, that girls are featured in proportion to their membership of the group, is substantially supported by this closer analysis. The roles they play in the group, however, are strikingly different from the boys'. They are featured as less likely to be involved in the identification, setting and solving of problems, less skilful and competitive, less likely to teach maths skills to others, and to display less initiative and inventiveness. Significantly, they are never shown performing in a play or boasting or playing jokes, activities which appear to be associated with self-assertiveness in the boys. They are efficient record keepers, they practise and modify already learned mathematical skills, develop themes suggested by others and set standards of behaviour. The girls continue to conform to the standards described in the EME books, while the boys develop interests and skills specifically related to discovery and exploration.

There are a number of less subtle examples of sex typing:

Jill and Ann made machines which frightened even the boys.

(Ann said) 'I am a fair damsel and when I drop this handkerchief you must fight for me'.

'Don't you know, Jill', said Joe, 'he is crazy about you'. Clarence blushed.

Food, pets and toys continue to feature prominently in problems, but the context is the peer group and outdoor life rather than the family at home. Maths in the junior books moves away from the domestic sphere and takes to the sportsfield, the battleground and worlds of business, space travel and machines where no women are to be found. In *Discovering Mathematics*, not only are women under-represented but girls have also disappeared from the content of problems and illustrations. In the forty-four pictures with human figures, twenty-nine are of males only, three of females only. Out of 109 figures, sixty-eight are men, twenty-one women, fourteen boys and six girls. The women are almost without exception confined to sitting in cars and buses driven by men, watching men at work or being rescued by a fireman. The men are using telescopes, making calculations, building houses, mending roads, they are shop-keepers, cricketers, skin divers, soldiers and waiters. One picture shows a male chef on television demonstrating cake baking and being copied by four women.

A similar picture emerges from an examination of the problems, in which boys are mentioned twenty-three times, men eighteen times, girls seven times, and women once. The impression that maths is and inevitably must be concerned with masculine activities is reinforced by descriptions of the mathematical prowess of people in history, illustrated by pictures of men and punctuated with references to famous mathematicians, Hipparcus, Napier, Pythagoras, Pascal. There are occasions when maths is distanced from childishness, 'softness' and the subjective content of situations by humour and by author's comments. A sentence opposite a picture of Goldilocks and the three bears reads: 'No! The picture opposite has not got into this book by mistake.'

There is a clear tendency in the books studied to define mathematics as the province of males, and especially adult males. The fact that the social world is presented in fragments, through illustrations and problems, does not necessarily diminish its significance. Individual examples of behaviour, briefly and starkly presented, accumulate as one works through the books into highly stereotyped images of males and females with little of the blurring and elaboration that may occur in a longer narrative. The impact of such images is unlikely to be reduced merely because the social content is intended to be secondary to the mathematical.

Adult women are largely absent from these books, and by the age of 13 girls have joined them in near-oblivion. There is an interesting parallel between the decline in girls' involvement in maths between 7 and 16 years of age, and the gradual disappearance of girls from maths books over the same period. It suggests that ameliorative action could profitably be focused on the values and assumptions which form the hidden curriculum of maths books and possibly that of teaching and learning in the classroom.

References

Davie, R., Butler, N., Goldstein, H., *From Birth to Seven*, Harlow, Longman/National Children's Bureau, 1972.

Golding, E. W., *et al.*, *Mathematics!* (1a, 1b, 2a, 3a), Aylesbury, Ginn, 1971.

King, R., *All Things Bright and Beautiful?*, Chichester, John Wiley, 1978.

Nuffield/CEDO, *Mathematics – the First Three Years*, Edinburgh, Chambers and Murray, 1970.

Schools Councils, *Early Mathematical Experiences*, London, Addison Wesley, 1978.

Shaw, H. A. and Wright, F. E., *Discovering Mathematics*, (2) 3rd edn., London, Edward Arnold, 1975.

Stanfield, J., *Maths Adventure* (2, 3, 4), London, Evans Bros, 1973.

Part Four

Investigating Gender Dynamics

14   Gender differences in pupil–teacher interaction in workshops and laboratories

Gay J. Randall

Introduction

One suggested contributory factor in girls' reluctance to choose the physical sciences and technological subjects is their experience of practical work. Already disadvantaged by a relative lack of out of school experience of 'tinkering' activities such as mending bicycles or playing with construction toys (Kelly *et al.*, 1981; Lie and Brynhi, 1983), it has been suggested that they also experience different forms of pupil–teacher and pupil–pupil interaction than do boys, and that this tends to discourage them from practical work and to undermine their self-confidence. A number of incidents which illustrate this have been reported (Samuel, 1981; Harding and Randall, 1983; Lensinck, 1983; Whyte, 1983, etc.), although incidents illustrating boys' experience of Home Economics or Textiles are less frequently reported.

The evidence so far

A certain amount of evidence has already been presented for sex differences in teacher–pupil interaction for pupils of various ages and in various school subjects. Boys are described as more active in the classroom than girls; they both initiate more and receive more teacher-initiated contacts, they are asked more questions and contribute more to classroom discussion, they receive both more praise and more criticism than girls, and are more likely to call out or make unsolicited comments, etc. (Brophy and Good, 1974; Elliot, 1974; Stanworth, 1983; Spender, 1982; Crossman, 1984; French and French, 1984; Staberg, 1985, and others).

It is all too easy for those of a feminist inclination to accept the above claims uncritically as 'proven' and as true in all classroom situations, but some caution should be exercised. Stanworth's work, for instance, which is sometimes used as evidence for these claims, is based on interviews with pupils and teachers. While it certainly shows that the girls she interviewed believed claims such as some of the above to be true (does this contradict Spender's work which found girls to be unconscious of discrimination against them?) it does not show them to be 'objectively' true. It can of course be argued that pupils' perceptions of reality are of more importance than 'objective reality', but this should be made clear when quoting such work.

Work which is merely qualitative is also insufficient for the present purpose. Although the in-depth illumination of classroom processes which can be provided

Source: Commissioned.

by good ethnographic studies is often invaluable, it is necessary to give quantitative evidence for claims phrased in terms of 'more' and 'less' in a field as emotive and sometimes controversial as that of gender differences. In particular, the sceptical reader is likely to doubt whether incidents described are in fact 'typical' and also whether only incidents representing a particular point of view have been described (or even noticed by the observer) to the exclusion of those opposing that view. The investigator triangulation technique described by Whyte (1983) in the observations of pupil practical work she describes is effective in dispelling the former criticism but the latter criticism cannot be dispelled so readily. An ethnographic study which also includes some quantification, as in the case of French and French, would be more acceptable to the sceptic, although in this particular case their admission that the lesson described was chosen because it best represented the patterns they had noticed in a larger study could be problematic.

Of the quantitative observational work on gender differences, perhaps the best publicized is that of Spender, but the lack of detail in her description of the fieldwork makes it difficult to evaluate her conclusions. Thus when Delamont (1984, p. 331) compares Spender's writings with those of other classroom researchers she goes so far as to suggest that:

It is perfectly possible that Spender's claims are true, but it is definitely true that her data are inadequate, her methods left so unspecific that her work could not be replicated, and that sex equality is not advanced by such polemical and unsubstantiated claims.

Brophy and Good have produced a review which is more scholarly, but this is no longer particularly recent and most of the studies they quote, which are mainly American, were designed to find out whether boys were disadvantaged by the feminine school environment in the elementary grades. Their finding that boys are more salient in the classroom in a number of ways (including, for example, response opportunities and teacher praise as well as teacher criticism) is particularly noteworthy as it is in the context of investigating discrimination against boys. It is, however, open to question how much similarity there is between classroom interaction in American elementary schools and in British secondary schools, and also whether there is likely to have been any change in the intervening years. A later American review by Bossert (1982) in fact finds that there is conflicting evidence on the nature and extent of gender differences in classroom interaction, and suggests that this might be explained by differences between subjects and between types of instructional activity.

Thus, in order to give any substance to claims about gender differences in workshops and laboratories, we are left with observational studies carried out in British science and technology lessons and which have at least a quantitative element, such as those described by Crossman and by Whyte. Other kinds of work can give supportive evidence but cannot be regarded as conclusive. Crossman in fact finds a number of sex differences similar to those mentioned earlier, although she finds differences between Physics and Biology lessons in this respect, while Whyte shows that it is possible for teachers to achieve numerical equality in the 'formal' parts of lessons if they try to do so. In both cases, however, the quantitative results were mainly or entirely obtained during 'formal' lessons or parts of lessons, and in fact many existing observation schedules are unsuitable for pupil practical work.

Characteristics of pupil practical work

There are a number of ways in which pupil practical sessions differ from the more formal sessions. In formal sessions (including teacher demonstrations) the class is taught as a whole and the focus of attention is usually the teacher. During practical work pupils work either individually or in small groups and the focus of attention is usually local; thus there are a number of foci of attention within the room. Both pupils and teacher are more mobile during practical work, and pupil–pupil talk is at least permitted, if not encouraged, in contrast to the 'formal' situation. This, together with noise made by equipment, ensures a higher level of background noise, particularly in workshops. Most teacher–pupil interactions are private rather than public which, with the background noise, often means that they are inaudible by those not fairly close to the teacher (this can make it difficult for an observer who does not wish to follow the teacher intrusively closely). There is more opportunity for pupils to initiate contact and define the topic during practical work; in the formal situation the teacher usually defines the topic and most teacher–pupil contacts are teacher-initiated, often in response to a teacher question.

Practical classes in technology (and also in textiles) have two other distinctive features. Projects usually last for a number of lessons so that during any one lesson different pupils are at different stages. Thus they may need to recall and use for the first time techniques which were demonstrated one or more weeks previously. In addition neatness, a quality often associated with girls but considered intellectually irrelevant, is an integral part of skill in working with wood, metal or other materials.

The present study

From the above arguments it is clear that gender differences can only be assumed in interaction during pupil practical work if there is evidence from studies carried out during pupil practical work. Thus the present study aims to provide some quantitative evidence in just these situations to complement the existing quali-tative evidence. Only teacher–pupil interactions were recorded (rather more class-room time would have been needed to record pupil–pupil interactions adequately as well) but the system used allowed for as many categories of pupil communi-cation as teacher communication. (Many existing observation schedules are very teacher centred, which may be of use when discussing different teaching styles but is less useful when distinguishing between the classroom experience of different pupils.) Pupils were distinguished as individuals rather than treated as homo-geneous subgroups labelled 'girls' and 'boys'. This was in response to a pilot study finding that one particularly disruptive pupil (of either sex) could engage in a disproportionate quantity of pupil–teacher interaction, thus distorting any aggregate by sex; such a finding was echoed by French and French (1984).

Distinguishing pupils as individuals also enables comparisons between pupils' classroom experiences and any attitude changes or expressed opinions.

Problems of audibility and the rapid pace of pupil–teacher interaction were overcome by tape recording lessons with the aid of a radio-microphone worn by the teacher after an initial period of several weeks familiarization with the class. This allowed the observer to concentrate on recording the identities of participants as well as certain non-verbal interactions and complete the coding at leisure; even these limited field notes were not always easy to make when change of participant was particularly rapid.

In order to allow some comparison between subjects it was decided to observe the same pupils in several practical subjects. This of course limited the number of classes that could be observed, so the study is perhaps best described as a quantified case study. Like all case studies, its results only have general application to the extent that the classes observed may be considered representative, but within the study it is possible to give suitable evidence for claims that certain things may happen more to boys than to girls or vice versa. However, a number of small-scale studies can be as acceptable as one large-scale study in providing evidence.

The sample

The group described here was a mixed second year group in an 11–18 comprehensive school, and was observed in science, CDT and art lessons, although only CDT lessons are described here (the other school observed was experimenting with single sex groupings in this subject as a means of encouraging girls). Most of the work observed during the year was in wood although some work with plastics was also done. The teacher, who was the head of CDT, the headteacher and the LEA were all strongly committed to equal opportunities for girls, and projects were chosen which were likely to be of interest to both sexes. The observer's subjective impression was that there was very little sex-stereotyping in the way the CDT lessons were conducted.

An initial opinion questionnaire, with questions about liking for, interest in, difficulty of, self-perceived ability in, and possibility of choice or use of each subject, showed no overall sex differences for CDT except for use in a hobby. Over the period of observation, however, nearly all the girls deteriorated in their attitudes to the subject as evidenced by their less favourable answers to most of the questions whereas boys gave both more and less favourable answers on the final questionnaire. Even so about half the girls rated CDT among the top half of subjects in order of preference on both initial and final questionnaires.

The two lessons chosen for initial analysis were consecutive lessons chosen at random from the good recordings (some were of poor quality because of equipment malfunction). They were recorded towards the end of the period of observation. Of the nineteen pupils (ten girls and nine boys) in the group, all except two of the girls were present at the first of these lessons and thirteen (six girls and seven boys) were present at the second lesson. One of the boys who was absent for the second lesson was often disruptive in school (although not particularly so in this subject) and so spent a lot of lesson time in a withdrawal unit. One of the girls often failed to attend school and so was absent for both lessons while another girl was in school on both days but only attended the first lesson. This girl often missed CDT lessons (and also admitted to missing lessons in a number of other subjects); when asked why, she said that although she liked the teacher she found the subject 'boring'.

Results – initial demonstration

Another lesson in a different room was usually observed immediately before the CDT lesson, so it was often not possible to set up the equipment and hand the radio-microphone to the teacher until the end of the initial demonstration. Subjective impressions were that boys were as active or slightly more so than girls at these times. In the first of the lessons described here it was in fact possible to record part of the initial demonstration, and during this time three girls and three boys volunteered answers to questions, while a further girl answered a question directed specifically at her. One of the three boys also volunteered a statement in anticipation of a question, and was praised for this. When holding up a piece of work as an example the teacher often chose something by a girl (not necessarily one from the same group).

Pupil positions during the initial demonstrations of these two lessons are shown in Figure 14.1. In both cases it can be seen that there were only boys directly in front of the teacher (in the second lesson some had been able to seat themselves on the workbench), while the girls stood in a peripheral position or seated themselves on a bench some distance behind the teacher. Most CDT lessons had an initial 'formal' demonstration and some (but not the two described here) had further such demonstrations during the course of the lesson. Of the seventeen such demonstrations observed with this group, boys occupied the more central positions eight times, girls five times (three of which were during the same lesson in the early part of the observation) and on four occasions there was no clear

Figure 14.1

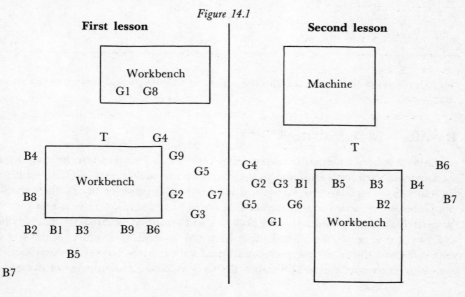

Table 14.1   *Pupil–teacher interaction: girls*

	G1	G2	G3	G4	G5	G6	G7	G8	G9
Total time with	1'06"	0'52"	0'46"	0'34"	0'19"	—	0'23"	1'31"	1'04"
teacher	7'27"	4'03"	3'26"	5'03"	2'55"	0'45"	—	—	—
Teacher-initiated	3	0	0	1	1	—	0	2	2
contacts	0	2	1	2	5	0	—	—	—
Pupil-initiated	2	4	4	3	0	—	3	2	1
contacts	10	8	8	10	3	1	—	—	—
Pupil interrupts	0	1	2	0	0	—	0	0	0
	5	3	4	5	0	0	—	—	—
Pupil unsuccessfully tries to initiate	1	2	1	0	0	—	2	0	0
contacts	4	6	3	3	0	0	—	—	—

Table 14.2   *Pupil-teacher interaction: boys*

	B1	B2	B3	B4	B5	B6	B7	B8	B9
Total time with	0'45"	1'19"	0'55"	0'00"	1'00"	0'09"	0'45"	1'05"	0'28"
teacher	0'35"	0'51"	1'53"	1'08"	0'46"	0'31"	0'52"	—	—
Teacher-initiated	1	2	1	1	3	0	0	1	2
contacts	0	1	1	1	3	0	2	—	—
Pupil-initiated	3	3	3	0	1	5	1	6	0
contacts	4	3	1	3	3	3	2	—	—
Pupil interrupts	0	0	1	0	0	5	0	2	0
	0	0	4	1	0	0	0	—	—
Pupil unsuccessfully tries to initiate	1	0	0	0	0	3	0	0	0
contact	0	3	2	0	0	1	0	—	—

difference. Thus there was a tendency for boys to occupy the 'action zone' more than girls.

Results – practical work

The analysis here covers the main part of each of the lessons from the end of the initial demonstrations until the pupils were told to clear away. (The quality of interaction changes at this stage, and interactions become so brief and frequent as objects are returned to the teacher that it is difficult to make an accurate record of participants' identities; in addition the teacher often wanted to remove the radio-microphone at this point so that he could take off his overall.) Tables 14.1 and 14.2 show the total time each pupil spent with the teacher during each lesson, and how each contact was initiated if this was clear. If contact was renewed immediately after an interruption a new initiator is not recorded. Thus the actual number of pupil–teacher contacts recorded is higher than might appear from the tables (girls 106, boys 74). In each category the first row of figures refers to the first lesson and the second row to the second lesson.

It can be seen from the tables that overall, girls had more contacts with the teacher than boys did and that girls' contacts were longer. Girls also interrupted more and made more unsuccessful attempts to initiate contact, and these tendencies were most apparent in the second lesson, which had a longer practical period. In the first lesson the practical period was curtailed by the teacher because most pupils had not completed the homework, which was an essential piece of design. The average total contact time for girls was 49s in the first lesson and 3m 45s in the second lesson; for boys it was 43s in the first lesson and 56s in the second lesson. The average length of contact was 12s in the first lesson for girls and 19s in the second lesson, while for boys it was 11s in the first lesson and 10s in the second lesson. The boy who had the largest number of pupil–teacher contacts in the first lesson had been absent for several lessons and thus had not yet started the project.

The nature of all interactions was coded although a detailed analysis is not included here; the numbers in many categories are as yet rather small and will have more meaning when it is possible to produce an aggregate over a larger number of CDT lessons. Girls, however, asked more questions about work (11 in the first lesson and 25 in the second lesson) than boys (who asked 7 in the first lesson and 9 in the second lesson). Most of these questions were of the 'what do I do now' type. On four occasions in the second lesson girls mentioned difficulty, danger or easiness as a reason for wanting to do or not to do something, whereas boys did not mention this at all.

The teacher mentioned each pupil by name at least once (this is important to pupils – Stanworth, 1983) but he made momentary mistakes with two of the boys. While in the second lesson the teacher gave 'hands-on' help to girls five times and to boys only twice, in the first lesson he gave such help equally to both sexes. In addition there was one occasion on which he held the work while a boy (B3) did something that the teacher had done for most of the other pupils. During pilot studies it had seemed that teachers were more likely to give 'hands-on' help to girls while merely showing boys what to do or giving them verbal instructions. If this were to be the case it could be conjectured that it might lead to greater dependence on the part of girls, but the results so far do not give particularly good support to such a conjecture.

A number of comments about individuals can be made with respect to the tables opposite. For example, there was only one girl in the second lesson who did not have a longer total contact time than all of the boys; she was the pupil named by the teacher as best in the group. The teacher praised her ability to work independently – 'once she gets started she's away'. In contrast the boy named by the teacher as second best in the class (B3) had a relatively long total contact time in each of the two lessons. This boy shows 'hard work' and 'keenness'. He had a tendency to suggest what he might do next, e.g. 'Shall I . . .' or 'I'll do it'.

Also notable are two pupils who showed a negative attitude to CDT on their questionnaires. A boy, B5, had no verbal interaction noticeable on the tape for the period in question during the second lesson, which is why the time given for him is zero (there was one non-verbal incident). He was, however, the only one to have completed his homework and brought it to the lesson. There was also a girl, G5, who had less contact time with the teacher in both lessons than most of the other girls; the contacts she did have were more likely to be teacher-initiated.

Two more comments can be made about these lessons. As suggested earlier, it can be seen that most contacts are pupil-initiated during the practical work. The overall percentage of teacher-initiated contacts is similar for both boys and girls, being about 30 per cent and 25 per cent respectively. In addition, the analysis of the tapes showed that the pace of teacher–pupil interaction could be extremely brisk. At many times during these lessons the teacher was carrying out different conversations with three or four pupils and sometimes as many as six in the space of a minute, with two or more of these conversations often being simultaneous.

Discussion and conclusions

Although gender differences in classroom interaction have received a certain amount of publicity in recent years, many people, including a number of science and technology teachers, are unconvinced and this will, of course, act as a barrier to change. Studies based on the assumption that gender stereotyping is transmitted in the classroom and aiming to illuminate the processes by which this occurs are of interest to those sharing that assumption but will not easily convince those who do not share that assumption. In particular, if it is to be claimed that girls and boys experience practical work in the sciences and technological subjects differently and that this contributes to girls' reluctance to choose these subjects, the evidence quoted must be relevant and must include quantitative as well as qualitative evidence if claims using words such as 'more' and 'less' are made.

The present study is aiming to meet some of these requirements by providing quantitative evidence from within practical classes. Although firm conclusions cannot be drawn until more evidence is available (and, it is hoped, more studies of a similar nature have been carried out) the results so far highlight the differences between pupil practical work and the more formal lessons or parts of lessons. In practical sessions the usual ratio of teacher- to pupil-initiated contacts is reversed, and it would also appear that girls can have a higher profile in the lesson than boys. Although it might be suggested that the teacher had been particularly successful in eliminating sex stereotyping from his workshop, the boys' positioning for demonstrations could be an indication that his success was not total. There are at least two other possible reasons, however, for this finding, which was also noted in one or two lessons in the pilot study but is at variance with the classroom research which is usually quoted. They are first, that girls who do not have the confidence to engage in public interaction might prefer to speak to a teacher privately or second, that girls are less independent in this subject than boys (this would explain the number of 'what do I do next' type questions).

Several writers (e.g. Fennema, 1983; Licht and Dweck, 1983; Beyer *et al.*, 1985) have suggested that girls have less self-confidence than do boys and that this could be a factor in subject choice. The above results so far could be explained in these terms, and so could the impressions gained from a fairly sex-stereotyped class in another school, in which it appeared that the boys had a higher profile during practical work. Lack of self-confidence can be manifested either in dependence, in which one does not trust oneself to do the right thing without guidance at every step, or in a reluctance to have too much contact with a teacher, who might perhaps notice or have already noticed one's inadequacies. The nature of classroom interaction is more important than its overall quantity in investigating such a possibility and it is hoped that analysis of further lessons may give some illumination.

Many teachers who are unhappy at the suggestion that they may contribute to the sex-stereotyping of their pupils like to feel that they treat all their pupils as individuals regardless of sex. When pupils enter the classroom, laboratory or workshop they have already been subjected to years of socialization into their sex roles, and all that is needed to reinforce this is just to accept it. Accepting it, however, is what can very easily happen when the teacher attempts to treat pupils as individuals, particularly in a situation in which most contacts are pupil-initiated. The teacher who is aware of stereotyping that could be reinforced in his or her classroom, however, is in a position to intervene by changing his or her responses so that potentially harmful stereotypes and patterns of interaction are not reinforced. For example, if a lack of self-confidence is suspected in some pupils (e.g. girls) the teacher would look for ways to build up their self-confidence rather than accepting their dependence on him or her. The pace of classroom interaction is, however, too fast for very much thought 'on the spot', so the teacher will have to take time outside the classroom to decide how best to react. It is hoped that the developing research into practical classes will be of help in this respect.

References

Beyer, K., Blegaa, S. and Vedelsby, M., 'Girls' self-confidence seems crucial to their success in physics education', Oslo, Second GASAT Conference, 1985.

Bossert, S. T., 'Understanding sex differences in children's classroom experience' in Doyle, W. and Good, T. L. (eds), *Focus on teaching*, Chicago, Chicago University Press, 1982.

Brophy, J. and Good, T., *Teacher – student relationships: causes and consequences*, Holt, Rinehart and Winston, 1974.

Crossman, F. M., 'Girl-talk – teacher/pupil interaction', paper presented Girls – Friendly Schooling Conference, Manchester Polytechnic, 11–14 September 1984.

Delamont, S., 'Sex roles and schooling or "see Janet suffer, see John suffer too" ' *Journal of Adolescence* **7**, 1984, pp. 329–35.

Elliot, J., 'Sex role constraints on freedom of discussion: a neglected reality of the classroom', *The New Era* **55**, 1974, p. 6.

Fennema, E., 'Success in mathematics' in Marland, M. (ed.), *Sex differentiation and schooling*, London, Heinemann, 1983.

French, J. and French, P., 'Gender imbalances in the primary classroom: an interactional account', *Educational Research* **26**, 1984, p. 2.

Harding, J. and Randall, G., 'Why classroom interaction studies?', Oslo, Second GASAT Conference, 1983.

Kelly, A., Smail, B. and Whyte, J., *Initial GIST survey: results and implications*, Manchester, Girls into Science and Technology, 1981.

Lensink, M., 'Girls, physics and technology in the Netherlands, the MENT project', Oslo, Second GASAT Conference, 1983.

Licht, B. G. and Dweck, C. S., 'Sex differences in achievement orientations: consequences for academic choices and attainments', in Marland, M. (ed.), *Sex differentiation and schooling*, London, Heinemann, 1983.

Neill, S. R. St J., 'Should systematic observers investigate participants' views?', *Research Intelligence* **19**, 1985, pp. 6–7.

Samuel, J., 'Feminism and science teaching: some classroom observations', in Kelly, A. (ed.), *The Missing Half*, Manchester, Manchester University Press, 1981.

Spender, D., *Invisible Women: the schooling scandal*, London, Writers and Readers Publishing Cooperative, 1982.

Staberg, E-M., 'Girls in science lessons', Oslo, Second GASAT Conference, 1985.

Stanworth, M., *Gender and schooling: a study of sexual divisions in the classroom*, London, Hutchinson, 1983.

Whyte, J., 'Non-sexist teachers: evaluating what teachers can do to help girls opt in to Science and Technology', Oslo, Second GASAT Conference, 1983.

15 The relations between teachers and Afro-Caribbean pupils: observing multiracial classrooms

Cecile Wright

The aim of this chapter is to discuss life in the multiracial classroom and to suggest how this contributes to the formal outcomes of schooling for black children/young people, that is, their attainment at 16+ in public examinations.[1]

The research described here was concerned with studying school life of black children, particularly those of Afro-Caribbean origin, and included the document-ation of their personal experiences of school and the classroom, institutional processes and outcomes, and comparing the academic attainment of these pupils with their school and classroom experiences.

To achieve this end, an intensive ethnographic and statistical survey of two multiracial comprehensive schools in the Midlands was undertaken from autumn 1982 until 1984. A cohort of Afro-Caribbean girls and boys from the two schools were studied over their fourth and fifth year of schooling. These pupils were observed in the classroom (approximately 900 hours of classroom observation was undertaken for both schools), as well as around the school; that is, in the corridor, the playground and elsewhere. Observations, particularly in the classroom, were recorded through the use of field notes and a tape-recorder. Essential to the understanding of the classroom and school life observed were the participants' (teacher and pupils) respective perceptions of their situation. The participants' perceptions were thus acquired through the use of informal and loosely structured interviews. In addition to the qualitative techniques used in the study, question-naires were used, and the assessment data accumulated on each pupil over the entire period of time that they had been at the school was analysed and docu-mented. Also a careful study was undertaken of schools' assessment and disci-plinary procedures.

In this chapter the observed classroom relations between the white teachers and the Afro-Caribbean pupils at both schools are considered. The outcomes of social relations between teachers and their Afro-Caribbean male and female pupils are then assessed.

Classroom relations

Observations of multiracial classroom relations at the Midland schools indicated that for the Afro-Caribbean pupils, more than for white and Asian pupils, class-room life was generally characterized by frequent antagonism and conflict between

Source: Commissioned. The chapter is based on the findings of an investigation of school processes, undertaken by a Social Science Research Council (recently renamed the Economic Social Research Council) student linked to a Department of Education and Science funded project.

them and their teachers. Classroom interaction *vis-à-vis* the teacher and the Afro-Caribbean pupil often took the form of either enforcing the teacher's authority and/or expressing criticism. Also there were a few teachers who, in their interaction with these pupils, persistently made disparaging remarks regarding the Afro-Caribbean pupil's ethnicity and physical characteristics. This was observed to cause these pupils great consternation and distress in the classroom.

Observations suggest that the teachers' attitudes and expectations played a significant role in influencing the nature of interactions which exist between them and their Afro-Caribbean pupils in the classroom. Field notes and the dialogue from two of the lessons observed, presented below, serve to illustrate this point. Further it will be seen later in the chapter that the classroom incident documented below from one of the two lessons (by Mr Gray) is referred to by the Afro-Caribbean pupils in their conversations, suggesting that such classroom experiences can become firmly fixed in the pupil's consciousness and obviously exert some influence on their perception of schooling.

Metalwork CSE (Mr Gray)

This metalwork class was comprised of two Asian boys, five Afro-Caribbean boys and fourteen white boys. The teacher's relationship with most of the pupils was a fairly amenable one, but his relationship with most of the Afro-Caribbean boys was observed to be characterized by high degrees of antagonism. Central to the nature of the relationship between the teacher and the Afro-Caribbean boys was the teacher's classroom management style used for enforcing discipline and learning. In general, the methods used by the teacher were those of taunting, name-calling and verbal sparring with the pupils. This management style when applied to the Afro-Caribbean boys (unlike other pupil categories) was used in such a manner that the pupils were inevitably forced into highly significant face-winning, face-retaining and face-losing contests between themselves and the teacher.

Furthermore, the Afro-Caribbean boys considered the teacher's overt lack of respect for their colour as being central to his treatment of them. The following exchanges between the teacher and some of the Afro-Caribbean boys, serve to illustrate this point.

The teacher was talking to the class. Whilst he wrote on the blackboard, a group of four white boys sat talking to each other in an ordinary tone of voice. The teacher, being annoyed by the noise level in the room, threw a piece of chalk at an Afro-Caribbean boy who was not being particularly noisy.

Teacher (Shouted): Pay attention. (To an Asian boy) Could you get me that piece of chalk.

Peter (Afro-Caribbean boy): Why don't you use black chalk?

Teacher (Turning to the researcher): Did you hear that? Then I would be accused of being a racist. Take this for example, I was down at Lower School, I had a black girl in my class. She did something or another. I said to her, if you're not careful I'll send you back to the chocolate factory. She went home and told her parents. Her dad came up to school, and decided to take the matter to the Commission for Racial Equality. It was only said in good fun, nothing malicious.

Keith (Afro-Caribbean) (aggressively): How do we know that it's a joke. In my opinion that was a disrespectful thing to say.

Teacher (raising his voice and pointing his finger at Keith): If I wanted to say something maliciously racist, I wouldn't have to make a joke about it. I'd say it. I've often had a joke with you, haven't I?

Keith (angrily): Those so-called jokes, were no joke, you were being cheeky. I went home and told my mum and she said that if you say it again she would come and sort you out. As for that girl, if it was my father, he wouldn't just take you to the CRE, he would also give you a good thump. My father says that a teacher should set a good example for the children, by respecting each one, whether them black or white. He says that any teacher who makes comments like that in front of a class, shouldn't be in school that's why he said to us if a teacher ever speaks to us like that he would come up to school and sort him out.

Harry (Afro-Caribbean): If it was me that you said that to, I wouldn't go home and tell my parents, I would just tell you about your colour.

Keith: Teachers shouldn't make racist jokes.

Keith was eventually sent out of the class to see the Headmaster for being insolent.

In a formal conversation with the teacher after the lesson when we talked about the classroom events, it became clear from the teacher's comments, that he recognized that a poor relationship existed between him and most of the Afro-Caribbean boys. The nature of this he attributed largely to the pupils' low ability and their attitudes. As the teacher stated:

It is very difficult to teach pupils like Keith Thomas, Steven Hutton and Calvin Fern, who are really remedials. These pupils and other black pupils have this thing about their colour, this chip on their shoulder about being black. They have accused me of being racist. I must admit that I can be racist at times, but I'm not aware of being racist towards them. To an educated person like yourself [referring to the researcher] you don't use the issue of race to explain everything; however, to these black children of no or low ability, they use this as an explanation almost all the time.

English Language – CSE class (Miss Simms)

This class of middle ability band pupils was taught English Language as a form group. The group comprised three Asian girls, six Asian boys, one Afro-Caribbean boy, six Afro-Caribbean girls, one Chinese boy, three white girls and eight white boys. There was generally a noisy start to most lessons, and it often took the teacher several attempts to secure silence. Once silence had been achieved, however, the pupils usually settled down to work and appeared to show a degree of involvement in the task they were given to do. The teacher's relationship with the class and in particular with some of the Afro-Caribbean girls was often a strained one.

Teacher: I really dislike this group, they are the worst group I have in terms of behaviour and motivation. The problem is, a certain group of pupils, they make things very difficult. I'm referring to the group of four West Indian girls who sit together. I suppose it's something to do with group dynamics. On their own they are reasonable. This group of girls are always in trouble with other teachers and their parents have constantly to be brought in.

In addition to perceiving the Afro-Caribbean girls as a threat to her classroom management skills, the teacher also held the Afro-Caribbean girls directly responsible for what she considered to be her inability to establish conducive learning conditions. As she stated:

If this group of Afro-Caribbean girls were not in the class, I feel I'd be able to do a much more effective teaching job with the others. . . .

Such deduction on the part of the teacher, it may be assumed, cannot be conducive to enhancing a good teacher–pupil relationship. Indeed, observations show the classroom relations between most of the Afro-Caribbean girls in this class and the teacher to be based on frequent open confrontations, which generally took a similar form as illustrated in the following classroom incident:

The teacher was already in the classroom when the pupils arrived for the lesson. The pupils arrived five minutes later than normal because they had been to assembly.

Miss Simms: Sit down quietly 4L. (The teacher stood at her desk waiting for the pupils to settle down.) Will you all settle down quickly, I've waited long enough. On the board is a comprehension question taken from last year's CSE English Language paper. I would like you to work through this question, work in your English folder. I will collect your work for marking at the end of the lesson. Now please get on quietly.

The pupils worked in silence. The turning of pages and a pupil tapping a pen on a desk are the only sounds. The teacher is sitting at her desk at the front of the room marking a pile of books. The silence continues for ten minutes; then a chair scrapes as an Asian girl leans forward to talk to the white girl sitting in front; four other pupils begin to talk. There is low level noise in the classroom.

Miss Simms (looks up from her marking and barks at the whole class):   Right, quiet please get on with your work.

The silence resumes, and is then broken by an Asian girl talking aloud to a Afro-Caribbean boy.

Kulwinder (Asian girl):   Hey, Vincent, when will we be having our maths exam?

Other pupils begin talking among themselves. The teacher looks up from her marking as a result of the increasing classroom noise. She looks to the back of the classroom where four Afro-Caribbean girls sit, talking among themselves.

Miss Simms (in a raised voice):   Will you four girls stop talking and get on with your work.

Barbara (Afro-Caribbean):   We are working, we're just talking about the question.

Jean (Afro-Caribbean):   It's not only us talking. What about her (pointing to Kulwinder) shouting, why do you always pick on us?

While the teacher was talking to the Afro-Caribbean girls, three white boys sat playing with a pocket computer game, which the girls had noticed.

Miss Simms: Whenever I look up you're always talking.

Barbara: That's 'cause you only see us, everybody else is talking. Look at them (pointing to the boys playing with the computer game) they're not even working. (Turning to the other Afro-Caribbean girls and talking in a loud whisper) Damn facety.

The Afro-Caribbeans burst into laughter at Barbara's comment to them.

Miss Simms (shrilled):   Barbara and Jean will you leave the room.

The girls left the room, closing the door loudly behind them.

Miss Simms (to the class):   Will the rest of you settle down now, and get on with your work. I'll be gone for just a few minutes.

The teacher leaves the room.

In an interview with the teacher after the lesson, she had this to say about the two Afro-Caribbean girls and the incident which had led her to send them out of the lesson:

Miss Simms: Well I'd say perhaps I have more problems with them than most in the class, perhaps they are the ones whom I'm usually driven to send to Mrs Crane [Deputy Headmistress for discipline] I'll put up with so much but they're inclined to become very rude sometimes, which others wouldn't do. They know their limits but those two frequently go over them. It's difficult because I've tried having them sitting separately which doesn't seem to improve things because then they just become very resentful and will try then to kind of communicate across the room, which is almost worse than this business here. As I've said before they're quite good workers, when they get down to it they enjoy the actual work and they usually get good marks. Their work is generally handed in on time and nicely presented. As I've said, I've sent them out quite frequently and I know lots of other teachers have the same problems. I'm not sure what the solution is. I believe things are being done with them.

Q: What happened when you sent Barbara and Jean out of the lesson and you followed them out?

Miss Simms: I sent them down to Mrs Crane. I told them to take a note and just wait outside her room. They got into so much trouble last term, she [the Deputy Headmistress] threatened to bring their parents up. I don't know if it actually got to that. I never know quite what to expect, what sort of mood they will be in, they are either in a bad mood or a good mood. Yes I can't tell really, and I find it difficult because I resent having to jolly them along which I do slightly. Because if I just home in on them straight away at the beginning of the lesson and normally they do start their chattering and things right away. Well I try to put up with so much. They react, they just resent it, if I do tell them off. But then I mean they do accept it. In the past when I've sent them off to Mrs Crane, and after perhaps a blazing row, or having brought her up here [to the classroom], and we have had a big confrontation and I expect them to be quite cool for weeks afterwards, or really rude. And they haven't been at all. . . . Really I have no reason to believe that they would not come in as charming as anything next lesson, or they'll be troublesome, it just depends on them more than me.

When analysed, the teacher's conversation provides insight not only into possible factors underlying the incident described above which transpired between her and the Afro-Caribbean girls, but also an indication of the criteria used for judging the girls as 'unteachable'.

First, the teacher considered the Afro-Caribbean girls' behaviour in class to be generally unpredictable, as her own comments suggest. She therefore invariably expected the girls to be 'troublesome' in class, and as a consequence she also expected to be engaged in frequent confrontation with them. Furthermore, this teacher appeared to use the experiences of other teachers with the girls to both support and explain her expectations and judgement of them. As a result of her expectations she was inclined to treat any conciliatory act on the part of the girls towards her, following a confrontation, with a degree of suspicion, as being out of character, and subsequently dismissed.

Second, the teacher considered the girls to be academically able and co-operative in their attitude to work, and this was borne out by observations. Yet from her behaviour towards the pupils it appears that these features received only secondary consideration from the teacher, compared to the pupils alleged 'troublesome' classroom behaviour.

Pupils' perspectives

Conversations undertaken with the Afro-Caribbean girls and boys in both schools, in an attempt to ascertain their perspectives on classroom life and their adaptation to their perceived experiences, suggest that these pupils often wonder whether there is anything more to classroom activity for them than insults, criticisms and directives.

A discussion with a group of Afro-Caribbean girls in which they talked vividly of their experience of some teachers supported this claim:

Barbara: The teachers here, them annoy you, too much.

Q: In what ways do they annoy you?

Barbara: They irate you in the lesson, so you can't get to work.

Group: Yeah

Barbara: One day Mr Beresford gave the class a piece of work to do, I type fairly fast and so I finished first. I took the piece of work to Mr Beresford and told him I'd finished the work, he said that 'I wasn't the only person in the class and he had to see other children before me'. I asked a question on the work and he gave me a funny answer saying, 'I should know by using a typists' intuition'. I told him I wouldn't be able to know, if we were told to do straightforward copying; with that he threw the piece of paper at me. I was angry, so I threw it back at him. . . .

In the third year, I did sewing with Mrs Lewis, we got on well until one day, she kept telling me off for talking loud, then she accused me of saying 'How now brown cow' and sent me down to Mrs Crane, [Deputy Headmistress for discipline]. She insisted that I did call it Mrs Lewis, even though I kept telling her I didn't know what it meant and that I didn't even know a verse like that existed. I got sent out of the lesson for the rest of that year, which was about four and five months. . . .

I was thrown out of sewing by Mrs Lewis, out of French for some reason I can't remember why, out of art, for a misunderstanding with the teacher about wiping glue off some scissors, out of office practice about three times for about a period of two to three weeks each time. . . . I've been in trouble all my school life, I think the girl who I used to hang around with gave the teachers the impression I wasn't worth the bother. I feel some teachers are prejudiced.

Vera: Yeah, I agree with her, take the cookery teacher.

Susan: For example in cookery, there were some knives and forks gone missing, right, and Mrs Bryan goes 'Where's the knives and forks?' looking at us lot [the Afro-Caribbean pupils in the class].

Vera: Yeah, all the blacks.

Sonia: Seriously right, in the past most coloured children that has left school they've all said she's prejudiced.

Jean: She's told some kids to go back to their own country.

Sonia: Seriously right, if you go to another white teacher or somebody, and tell them that they're being prejudiced against you, they'll make out it's not, that it's another reason.

Jean: When Mrs Bryan told Julie to go back to her own country, she went and told Mrs Crane [the Deputy Headmistress], Mrs Crane said that Mrs Bryan was depressed because her husband was dying.

Sonia: So why take it out on the black people – then she's told black people to do many things, she's even called them monkey.

Sandra: As for that Mrs Crane I can't explain my feelings about the woman. Because Mrs Bryan, right she just prejudiced, she comes up to me in the cookery lesson, tell me to clean out the dustbin, and I was so vexed I started to cry, I was so vexed by it. I didn't come to school for two weeks.

Sonia: You see the thing is right, they can get away with saying anything to your face, there isn't anything you can do about it.

Jean: In geography, this teacher dashed a book at me, and I dashed it back, and I got into trouble for it.

(Group roared with laughter.)

Vera: Most of the things that the teacher says, right, they say things that annoy you they know that you're going to answer them back, so they can get you into trouble. Take Mrs Bryan she'll walk around with a towel, and if you look at someone and smile and she thinks you're talking, she flash water in your face or she'll slap you over the head, but I've just told her that if she boxes me I'll have to hit her back. Because she's got no right to walk round doing that. If you answer her back in any way, then she'll send you down to Mrs Crane then you're in trouble.

Susan: Mrs Crane is prejudiced herself because, I mean, she said to Karen that she is only getting bad because she hangs around with too many black people. It's not as if (shouting in anger) as she says, black people are going to change you to bad.

Vera: Some teachers are all right but others, you can tell that they're prejudiced by the things they do. Every time Mrs Bryan is cooking, even if she's doing say, a boiled egg or something like that, any little simple thing you can think of, coloured people and Asian people have to cook it different . . . 'Oh, well the coloured people and Asian people always cook their things different. . . .'

Jean (with disdain): Is that what she says?

Vera: Yeah, she's really facety you know, that's why I don't get on with her, and when I was telling me mum, me mum was going mad because she must think that we're some aliens, or something . . . . If the teachers have no respect for you, there's no way I'm going to respect them.

Mr Newson [new Headmaster] all he does now is go straight on to the teachers' side and then the next minute that pupil is suspended, for doing something really daft . . . look at Jane [Afro-Caribbean girl] she got up in the classroom, and she was walking to the door and Mr Webb said to her 'Where are you going?' She said, 'I'm not going nowhere'. 'Well,' he said to her, 'well sit down then.' Jane was walking back slow, right, and he just went behind her and pushed her and told her to go and sit down. So Jane turned around and pushed him back. She said 'Listen you're not my dad so don't push me around' and he goes get out and go to Mrs Crane. Mrs Crane, sent her to Miss Roberts [at the time the Head of school, who suspended Jane. Vera is claiming that the suspension decision was upheld by the Headmistress's predecessor – the new Headmaster]. And Miss Roberts suspended her, Miss Roberts left and just left it at a dead-end like that. They didn't say nothing to Jane's mum, they didn't say nothing to Jane. All they said to Jane was that she can't come back to the school until further notice, and up till now its been eleven weeks, she haven't been back to school. And it was about two weeks ago she had a Governors' meeting and that's when they told her that she can't come back to school. So you're made to miss out on your education for reasons like that.

Q: Would you say that the Afro-Caribbean boys have the same experience with the teachers as yourselves?

Vera: The boys I know don't get the same treatment because most of the lads are quicker to box the teachers – dem than the girls, you see.

Group: Yeah.

Similarly, a group of eight Afro-Caribbean boys were asked about their classroom experience. They responded as follows:

Mullings: The teachers here are too facety, they don't give you a chance.

Michael: For example Hill [Anglo Afro-Caribbean boy] who was expelled.

Paul (Williams):   That just prejudice, he never did nothing wrong.

Michael: He never done nothin much you know. He's half-caste, but he was more to the coloured people dem.

Q: Why was he expelled?

Michael: What it is I think, he got suspended three times and he was on report, kept getting bad grade, they just put him in front of the Governors. Yet a big skinhead [white boy] boy right, he go in front of the Governors three times already, right, they expelled him. He came back, and dem let him back in a de school yesterday.

Paul: Teachers look down on you, Mr Parks, Mr Gordon, Mr Henry, Mr Gray and some others. I can remember the time I was in metalwork, Mr Gray keep saying to me 'Why you've a tan? Why have you got a tan?' I say 'Well I've been like this all me life.' He say, 'Well you should go back to the chocolate factory, and be remade', or something like that, [with anger] that's not nice at all.

Michael: One day I was in there [in the classroom] so I don't know what happened between him and Errol, he came up to me and say, 'Why Paul, Errol and Delroy is always giving us hassle' and all that. So I said, 'Oh well, you know how Paul and Delroy are, they won't take anything off you lot in'it. If anything, them like to stick up for them rights.' So he said to me, 'You know I like running a joke, Michael.'

Keith: Mr Gray, right, he says its a complete joke what he says to black kids, he said one day he was at lower school and he came [the classroom] and said to this girl, this coloured girl was a bit upset, so he said to her 'What's wrong with you' and he said, 'I'll have to send you back to Cadbury's to let them wipe the smile on your face' and the girl went home and told her father. And her father took her to the Race Relations Board, and he says [Mr Gray] he's to go to court.

Michael: One day I was in there [in the classroom] I don't know what him and Errol had but Errol called him a 'mother fucker', what happened between him and you?

Errol: We were messing about right, he said something about black people. So I called him a mother fucker, he looked at me.

Michael: He said, him going to dash you out of the school in'it?

Errol: He could have but he didn't.

Michael: It's like once the man [referring to the teacher] come in the class, and ask me in front of the class, why me coffee coloured, he say, 'How come Wallace dark, and Kennedy black and Kevin a bit browner? How come you that, you a half-breed.' Me say, 'No man, me no look like me half-breed.' Me say, 'Just like some a una white like a chalk and another couple a una got blond hair, some have black hair, me no come ask wha that'. . . . That's how he is, he just come around, crack him few sarcastic jokes about black kids.

Paul: But they're not nice at all. They're not nice. The jokes aren't nice. The jokes are disrespectful.

Keith: They're not jokes man.

Errol: You can't call them jokes. When he cracks a joke or whatever he does in front of the class, he just turn round and laugh. You get him and the class laughing at you.

Keith: What he is doing is running you down. He's just bringing you down like dirt. Nobody is bring me down [said with anger]. Everytime I'm chuck out of [subject] completely man, because every time in [subject] he always keep calling me something about me colour and I answer back.

Errol: The teachers are forever picking on the black boys.

Michael: Like me now, them no too bother with me because them think, say me a half-breed, you know. Half the teachers in the school think say me a half-breed so they don't too bother me. Just lately they find out, say me black, so they've started bothering me. Like the half-caste kids them they used to left me alone.

Keith: They don't give half-caste kids no hassle, no hassle whatsoever. However, if the half-caste kids act black, they pick on them, hassle man.

Errol: And the Asians.

Group: Yeah.

Q: Are you all also saying that the Asian pupils are not treated in the same way by some teachers, as you suggest, the Afro-Caribbean pupils are treated?

Keith: Because with the Asians, right, Asians just keep themselves to themselves, like we now, we just want equality with the white people. Asians don't speak their minds, they keep it all in because they are afraid.

Michael: They get fling around, they won't say nothing about it.

Keith: Because of that Asians are better off than black pupils that's all I can say.

Paul: Yeah, Asians aren't the ones what go around causing trouble with the teachers.

Q: Are you all saying then, that the Afro-Caribbean or black children, as you put it go around causing trouble?

Group (defensively): No, No.

Keith: No, the thing that we want right, we want equality just like the white people, we want equal rights.

Paul: I'm not saying that we cause trouble, but I'm just saying the teachers think black boys are always going round causing trouble. That's what they think . . . .

Keith: Teachers look down on you.

The Afro-Caribbean boys were asked to explain further how the nature of the relationship which they considered existed between some teachers and themselves affected their behaviour towards these teachers. Using their analysis the pupils felt that they were forced into a stimulus–response situation, as the dialogues which follow demonstrate:

Paul: The school don't respect black pupils. We are treated badly, we are forever hassled. . . . I can remember the time I was in [subject], Mr X keep saying to me 'Why you've got a tan?' – I say, 'Well I was born like this.' He say, 'Well you should go back to the chocolate factory and be remade' or something like that. To me that wasn't a nice thing to say.

Kevin: We are treated unfairly, because we are black. They look after their flesh not ours.

Michael: They look after fe them white people-dem, you know what I mean, but we get dash at the back all the time.

Q: You have all said that you feel that you are treated unfairly in the school. How do you feel this makes you behave?

Delroy: Bad.

Q: When you say 'bad' what exactly do you mean by this?

Paul: It means that we turn around and make trouble for them.

Delroy: Yeah, we try to get our own back on them. We behave ignorantly towards them, and when the teachers talk to us and tell us to do something we don't do it, because we just think about how they treated us.

Paul: Like when you walk down the corridor, and a teacher stops you, you just ignore him. When they stop you for no reason you just irated.

Q: How about you, Errol?

Errol: I try to keep out of trouble the best I can. If they cause trouble with me I cause trouble with them it's as simple as that. If you are a troublemaker, right, and you're pretty intelligent, they still keep you down. Look what they've done to Delroy, he's pretty intelligent, yet they keep him down, no wonder he causes trouble. Because I want to get on I try to keep out of trouble.

Michael: I'm going to the Cayman Islands to live with my parents when I leave
school. . . . I don't want my children to go through the same experience I've been
through in these schools.

Gender, race and classroom interaction

In their conversations the Afro-Caribbean girls and boys voiced the same
complaints and dissatisfaction regarding their teachers' attitudes and behaviour
towards them in the classroom. Certain similarities were observed in the ways in
which the girls and boys responded to their teachers' treatment of them. For
instance, they were both prepared to openly confront and challenge the teacher
and engage in hostile exchanges in which they subjected the teacher to a barrage
of Jamaican patois. There was no doubt that in this situation a number of teachers
felt threatened by the use of a dialect they could not understand and the teachers'
anxiety served only to compound their adverse attitudes and behaviour towards
those pupils who used patois.

However, certain marked differences were also observed among Afro-Caribbean
pupils in their response to their classroom experience. For example the girls at
one and the same time appeared apparently disaffected from schooling yet were
committed to aspects of it. They were generally hardworking in class and
expressed a commitment to acquiring good qualifications. Their commitment was
such that they were prepared to behave in a conciliatory manner towards a
teacher following a previously heated classroom confrontation with that teacher.
The Afro-Caribbean girls' approach to school was constantly a source of bewilderment to the teachers. By contrast the boys, although committed to education,
lacked motivation and worked inconsistently in the classroom. They displayed
increasingly hostile attitudes towards their teachers and their school experiences
in general. They formed an all Afro-Caribbean subcultural group which moved
around the school at break-time baiting the teachers. The boys in their behaviour
entered into a self-fulfilling prophesy, which further appeared to justify the
teachers' expectations of them. The following comment from an Afro-Caribbean
pupil, regarding his experience of some teachers, epitomizes the boys' response
to their classroom experience.

When you know that they [teachers] are sort of negative and they don't really talk to
you as a person, you know that they're not really bothered about what happens to you
whether you pass an exam or not and you think to yourself, well they're not really
bothered about what you do, so that means you don't really think of it in terms of, oh
well, he is really taking pride in me or her and really want me to do well, it goes beyond
just teaching me, it's something personal as well . . . I suppose it makes me behave
bad, they pick you out, on your colour. . . . They tend to say, oh well, he's black, so it's
to be expected, they're bound to do that, so when they give you that kind of attitude,
you think, oh well, blow them, if that's what they think, why not act like it.

The observations supported by the pupil's own views suggest that classroom
experiences of both the Afro-Caribbean girls and boys were not altogether
dissimilar. In the classroom both received a disproportionately large amount of
the teacher's attention, even though the attention received was generally negative
or in the words of the pupils a case of being 'picked on'. Such observations appear

to run contrary to our understanding of gender and classroom life, according to studies in this area (e.g. Davies and Meighan, 1975; Spender and Sarah, 1980; Stanworth, 1983). Girls were generally found on the margins of classroom encounters, receiving little attention from teachers, whereas teachers were generally portrayed as more attentive to boys, involving them more in classroom activities. Indeed, Davies and Meighan (1975) in their study comment that the girls complained about receiving less attention in class. In contrast, as we saw above, the Afro-Caribbean girls (and the boys) complained about too much attention from their teachers.

Clearly, the observation that Afro-Caribbean girls and boys experience *similar* classroom interaction with their teachers would suggest that studies on gender and classroom interaction which have failed to give some consideration to the participants' race (or ethnicity) as an important variable run the risk of either projecting too simplistic or distorted a picture of classroom dynamics. Certainly, it can be speculated from the evidence above that gender variables may operate quite differently in the multiracial classroom from an all-white classroom.

Another way in which race was observed to supersede gender was in the area of friendship groups. Studies of friendship patterns (e.g. Ball, 1981) in mixed secondary schools, generally found a segregation of the sexes; that is, a process of polarization and differentiation where pupils typically form single sex friendship cliques. This, however, was not the picture observed for the Afro-Caribbean girls and boys. A considerable amount of interaction took place between these pupils both inside and outside the classroom – a relationship which seemingly arose out of their common experience of schooling as black pupils.

The outcomes

As indicated so far, the relationship between teachers and Afro-Caribbean pupils within the two schools was often antagonistic. There is evidence to suggest that the nature of this pupil–teacher relationship may precipitate certain sanctions taken by the school against these pupils. The ultimate sanction is that of removing the pupil from the school. Figures on the suspension and expulsion for the year group studied for both schools show a higher proportion of suspension and expulsion among the Afro-Caribbean pupils, even though they represented the smallest ethnic group. For one school, over half of the pupils suspended or expelled from the school from this year group were Afro-Caribbean. In addition to this it was found that none of these pupils expelled from the school in the fourth year were offered alternative education provision. These pupils were thus totally deprived of formal education.

Another means by which the Afro-Caribbean pupils were also found to be denied educational opportunities as a consequence of the adverse relationship between them and their teachers stemmed from their teachers' faulty assessment of their abilities and achievements. Evidence suggests that in their assessment of the Afro-Caribbean pupils the teachers allowed themselves to be influenced more by behaviour rather than cognitive criteria. That is, the assessment given would be most likely to reflect the teachers' subjective involvement with the complex behavioural aspects of classroom relations. This, in turn, led to a situation where

Afro-Caribbean pupils, more so than any other pupil group, were likely to be placed in ability bands and examination sets well below their actual academic ability. This suggests that in their assessment of the Afro-Caribbean pupils' ability the teachers were less able to exercise professional judgement. This claim is clearly demonstrated in Table 15.1, which shows the allocation of pupils to examination sets for one school.

Table 15.1   *School B: individual pupils and allocation to exam sets*

Pupil		Subject marks (out of 100)				Set placement (0 = GCE 'C' level)			
		English	Maths	French	Physics	English	Maths	French	Physics
Afro-	A	73	44	58	—	CSE	CSE	CSE	—
Carib.	B	62	63	60	59	CSE	CSE	CSE	CSE
	C	64	45	56	72	CSE	CSE	—	CSE
	D	68	37	82	—	CSE	CSE	CSE	—
Asian	E	51	77	—	55	0	0	—	0
	F	60	56	58	—	0	0	0	—
	G	61	62	55½	—	0	0	0	—
	H	54	55	—	40	0	0	—	0
White	I	61	62	—	62	0	0	—	0
	J	52	57	55	—	0	0	0	—
	K	75	82	77½	72	0	0	0	0
	L	54	75	64	72	0	0	0	0

The scores in the table represents the pupils' third-year examination marks. At this school pupils are allocated to an 'O' level or CSE course at the beginning of their fourth year on the basis of their performance in the third-year examination. An analysis of the allocation of Afro-Caribbean, Asian and white pupils clearly shows that a higher proportion of Afro-Caribbeans appear to be allocated to examination sets below their ability than is the case for the other two pupil groups (i.e. Afro-Caribbean pupil 'D' attained 82 per cent in French yet was allocated to a CSE set). The apparent misplacement of the Afro-Caribbean pupils on the basis of their ability, demonstrated in Table 15.1, would strongly suggest that within this school overt discriminatory practices were operating against the Afro-Caribbean pupils. This suggestion is supported by the comment of one of the teachers, who had this to say about pupil 'D' in a CSE examination set:

This pupil has been on the fringe of trouble all year, her attitude to the teachers is not at all good, she can be a nuisance in class.

It is obvious from this teacher's statement and from the allocation figures that, in some teachers' eyes, ability is a positive quality only if it is shown by a white and possibly an Asian pupil.

An analysis of the overall attainment in the public examinations at 16 for all the pupils in the cohort studied for both schools shows that the proportion of Afro-Caribbean pupils entered for 'O' levels, and who gained 'O' level passes, was dramatically lower than for the Asian and white pupils. The attainment of the Afro-Caribbean pupils is particularly poignant when it is realized that for one of the schools, the Afro-Caribbean pupils entered the school at 11+ with a reading age averaging slightly above the whole intake for their year.

The evidence presented here suggests that explanations for the relatively poor educational attainment documented for Afro-Caribbean pupils over the last decade can be sought in such factors as teacher–pupil interaction, and teacher attitudes and expectations coupled with school practices such as the processes of selection and grading of black pupils. Afro-Caribbean pupils, it seems, are not assessed in terms of their actual abilities but rather by teachers' subjective judgements. The following comment by a senior teacher from one of the schools serves to support this conclusion:

This school is a low ability school because of its catchment area, which consists of a low social class and a high immigrant population. More fundamentally, it is the high proportion of immigrants in this school which is responsible for the lowering of standards.

References

Ball, S., *Beachside Comprehensive*, Cambridge, Cambridge University Press, 1981.
Davies, L. and Meighan R., 'A review of schooling and sex roles, with particular reference to the experience of girls in secondary schools', *Educational Review* **27**, 3 June 1975.
Spender, D. and Sarah. E. (eds), *Learning to Lose*, London, The Women's Press, 1980.
Stanworth, M., *Gender and Schooling – a study of sexual divisions in the classroom*, London, Hutchinson in association with the Explorations in Feminism Collective, 1983.

16   Groping towards sexism: boys' sex talk

Julian Wood

The chance to gather the information on which this chapter is based came from an individual research project that I did in a school 'sin bin'. The centre was a small on-site unit for 'disruptives' in a London, coeducational, secondary school. It may well be that there were specific features of the institution that helped to facilitate the behaviour described, and so I will sketch in the salient features of the place. It was set up, mainly on the initiative of the head, essentially to remove 'problem' children from the school and re-educate them into a position where they could once more 'benefit from what the school had to offer' (as well as re-introducing into them the habit of attendance). The staff (one male head of centre, one male assistant teacher and one female assistant teacher) saw their brief as more pastoral than academic. They wanted to help the kids *individually* to over-come what the staff defined as a rejection of adults and the adult world. The curriculum consisted mostly of basic maths and English with some craftwork and lots of recreation time. The centre was quite like the school it served except that some of the more rigid controls on movement, posture and language had been relaxed in order to avoid excessive conflict. Nevertheless, there was a constant struggle by the staff to stop the older kids using the centre as what the staff termed a 'day-time youth club'. It was important for the overall work of the centre, and especially for the elusive goal of re-integration, that the kids should be subject to definite, if not authoritarian, adult restraint.

The centre took kids from 12 up to the school-leaving age (no one would stay on as a sixth former) and usually they took the same lessons together. It is a feature of such centres that the numbers attending fluctuate, with lots of kids coming and leaving, around a core group. Although the average stay was two to three years this is not a very useful statistic because the long-term kids, who usually became informal leaders, could be there for their whole secondary careers.

One of the most important dimensions along which the state of the centre could be measured was the overall balance of power between the genders. In terms of friendship groups, particularly outside school, and in terms of unspoken under-standings, the boys related primarily to the boys and the girls to the girls. For convenience I shall write *as if* the boys formed one cultural grouping and the girls formed another. However, this stresses the cultural separateness of the genders in a way which does oversimplify lived relations. What needs to be captured here is a series of *moods* present in the centre about relations between the genders. For example, there would be certain periods when the girls would become more united

Source: Extracted from A. McRobbie and M. Nava (eds), *Gender and Generation*, London, Macmillan, 1984.

and acquire more collective confidence, they would complain that the boys were getting most of the attention, choice of lessons and so on. In these periods great emphasis would be put, by both genders, on the real, and imagined, social separateness of the genders. This contrasted sharply with times of inter-gender harmony when the more confident girls would join in with the boys on practical jokes ('wind ups') on the staff, sit close to the boys in lessons and so on. Times of inter-gender conflict were worrying to the centre staff not just because there was more likelihood of rows and even pitched battles occurring, but because trouble with the main school and more 'disruption' generally were associated with such periods. Sometimes it seemed the kids could only fluctuate between a strained rebelliousness and a listless quiescence.

It was the issue of sexual attraction and sexual 'awakening' (as ideology would have it) that provided the axis for one of the centre's most interesting periods as far as inter-gender relations were concerned. There had often been a flirtatious tinge to relations between the genders: on school trips for example. In this particular period there was an apparent upsurge in (for the want of a better term) 'sexiness' in the centre. This produced some new forms of behaviour culminating in fairly boisterous groping sessions, as I shall describe later. It was from this phase, too, that most of the quotations from the kids were taken.

The groping sessions were, as it turned out, the last manifestation of the sexy period, for after that time the protagonists were dispersed for various reasons. The girls who were most involved either went back to the main school or became defined as 'too old' for the centre and went on to another centre. The boys were left without any girls to 'practise' their sexist attitudes on.

In the next section I want to consider some of the attitudes and practices of the boys (and in less detail, the girls) that I argue are characteristic of their general class culture as well as of their age and location.

Some features of sexist sexual practice

The most common simple kind of sexist practice was a sort of feeding off the sight of the girls and of adult women teachers or visitors to the centre. Any slight revelation of flesh (a T-shirt, a skirt) focused the boy's attention on parts of the girls' bodies. In fact many hours must have been spent day-dreaming about the girls' bodies because at times a boy would come out with an unprompted sexist utterance to the air such as 'tits'! At other times the boys would giggle and grin and nudge each other about a particular posture of one of the girls. At this point it is very important to note what elements of redress were available to the girls. They were obviously not as weak as they were depicted by the boys, in fact they were often stronger. Not only did they have a strong group sense, at times some of them were stronger physically than the boys. If sexism was one of the dominant modes of the centre it was resisted by the girls. The boys had to be careful that their sexist remarks were not seen to be personally insulting a stronger girl face to face. Here Tim, a leading centre joker, is talking to the air, extolling the virtues of parts of women's bodies. He is misconstrued by Lorraine (she thinks he is talking about her) who, being larger and stronger, can give him a sharp rebuke.

Tim: . . . I like them with great big tits with great big nipples!

Lorraine (aggressively): *What?*

Tim: I, er . . .

Lorraine: Just shut up, O.K. Tim?

Tim: Alright humpy.

I think the utterance is received as offensive by Lorraine really because she thinks it is about her rather than as part of any general attempt to correct Tim's sexism. However, the remark is only quashed by the implicit threat of violence to Tim. As patriarchy so often finally rests on male violence there is a certain piquancy to this reversal.

One of the specific features of men's sexism is the dissecting approach that is taken to women's objectified bodies.[1] This came out in the centre boys in numerous ways, for example, Tim's selection of parts of the body, and was a crucial element in their assessments of girls. It was externalized most frequently in sexist slang; the part of the language capable of holding the most sexist male meanings. This use of slang is common to the broader class culture to which the boys belonged; it involves a detailed cataloguing of the female body in alternative terms, a literal naming of parts whose use when 'skilfully' applied did seem to hold a certain power. Perhaps part of its appeal was that it seemed to impart to the user a tenuous sense of control. But, if this fierce objectification in slang is a displaced attempt to control (and re-control each time?) the object that it was labelling, then it also showed tell-tale signs of that fixation which is part of an alienated view of the female body.

The following extracts were taken from a conversation between two boys about which girls they fancied. This was also, incidentally, at the time at which the boys were trying in the most heavy-handed fashion to obtain sexual contact with the girls.

Jake: I reckon Helen's got a nice face, she's good looking but her body, man! If she was slim . . . like her sister . . . she used to be really ugly didn't she, really fat? But now she's really slim, 'aint half nice now, she's got a nice body now . . . . Lorraine, though, she's big. She ain't got a nice personality, too much mouth. She thinks she can rule everybody just because she's big.

The conversation passes on to assessing the younger sister of one of the girls in the centre. Jake urges Don to consider fancying her:

Don: What's the sister like?

Jake: Lovely! Ginger hair, ginger minge [minge = pubic hair].

Don demurs, indicating he is not attracted.

Jake: Oh my good God! Don't worry, you don't fuck the face! She's got a nice body.

Obviously this discussion, very typical of the sort the boys would have together to pass the time, is laden with sexist assumptions. However, I do not think one can fully understand it only in those terms without knowledge of the specific relationships involved. Helen is being dismissed in as kindly a way as the boys are capable of, because she is liked. Her friendly physicality and lack of resistance to the boys' dominating ways secure her the label of a 'nice personality'. Perhaps if she slimmed down they would do her the big favour of fancying her! Lorraine on the other hand is not going to suffer the boys' put-downs to secure some dubious camaraderie (as her reprimand to Tim showed) and she has the physical strength to take an independent line. Therefore, perhaps what is most unfair about the boys' assessment of 'personality' is the way it is not only traded off against looks but is considered 'not nice' if it indicates a more-than-usual independence from male standards.

Early in the same conversation the boys had referred to Lorraine as 'a dog'. This judgemental term (specifically on a girl's *looks*) is a very common term within the sexist mode. Sometimes it seems that all women who are not dogs ('dog rough' in the full phrase) are automatically 'tasty' or fanciable. Of course it is absurd even by sexist standards that 'dog' and 'tasty' should be a sort of binary opposition. However, in that absurdity may lie the secret of the power of the category. It relies for its power on the simplicity with which it attempts to sort out the whole female gender and, perhaps, *the emotions of the speaker*. How character-istic that is in fact of so much of the lack of subtlety of male sexism. If vacillation is imputed to women, then unwavering over-sureness may perhaps be, by negative implication, very male.

As I have noted, the various abstracted parts of a girl are traded off against each other by the boys. A 'good body' beneath an ugly 'boat' may rescue the lucky subject! In this mode all girls are 'worth one' (i.e. worth having sex with) but this brings with it certain internal contradictions. Not least, the speaker must try to be a tireless Tarzan with the ability and looks to 'pull' any girl. Of course (and this is a *relief* to the boys) actual inter-gender encounters are much more *negotiated* and *real*, however one-sided. This must be allowed for too; any attempt to actualize attraction or act out fantasy may be rebutted which is why we have the classic sour grapes ploy. It is amazing how little discouragement from the girl is required to turn a 'tasty bird' into 'a bit of a dog anyway'.

'Unfeminine' girls – the case of Eve

The arrival of Eve during the time that the boys were trying more successfully to occupy a sexist masculine space, prompted some very interesting aspects of their ideology to come to light. Particularly, she brought a practical questioning of the vital, insecurity-producing area of the division between the sexes. Eve was 15 at the time; she was short and physically very strong. She also had, as she put it, 'a bad temper on me'. Within ideological definitions she was plain-looking rather than the received idea of 'sexy'. The boys labelled her 'a dog' but also, making fantasies out of what was currently happening, imputed to her an instinc-tive craving for sex. Perhaps at the back of this labelling was the pervasive projection from the boys that *all* girls want sex, without necessarily knowing it themselves. More than that, there was the unspoken notion that 'bad looks' or a shy personality prevent some girls from getting their fair share. Thus 'dogs' are constructed as being especially 'horny' because they cannot find any boy to have sex with them. (Gay sex was merely disgusting to the boys within their sexist mode.)

This of course also constructs the girl as passive, for she has to wait for a boy to condescend to seek her out. There was another belief, apparently deeply embedded in the boys at the time, that 'sexy' girls are 'right whores', but what exactly that last phrase signifies seems to be flexible. By a strange process of ideological addition Eve seemed to be lumbered with both labels. As I hope will be clear, this chapter is especially concerned with the complexities of the process of the imposition of sexist labels. Not least of the questions that Eve's case raises is that of the relationship of her 'plain' looks to the violence of the boys' stereotyping.[2]

Within a month of coming to the centre Eve had demonstrated her actual physical strength (and willingness to use it) by having a fight with one of the more peripheral male members of the centre. She inflicted a cut eye before the fight was broken up. The boys were especially disgusted with the boy participant for the weakness his poor showing implied for the rest of them. Whether they could have done any better against Eve at full strength was a question they were all, secretly, glad not to have had put to the test. An interesting reaction to female strength came up soon after in a less fraught situation. While the kids were playing Chinese arm-wrestling Eve beat all but the two strongest boys. As she strained and pulled one boy exclaimed: 'Look at those fucking muscles, man! It's not human, she's a fucking caveman not a human!'

I have chosen only the most crystallized example of what I take to be a generalized ideological notion about the proper division between the sexes. I take it to be a popular belief (in this country at least) that there are particular male attributes – of which muscular strength is only the most 'natural' – and that women who exhibit too much of these qualities can be said to be going against their natural state or damaging their femininity in some way; they are considered 'butch'.

The sequence of invasion

In this section I want to discuss what I call the sequence. I think the tendency to act out this sequence did reproduce itself, especially in the boys. This idea is itself located within the empirically-based assumption that men still do make most of the sexual advances in the early stages of heterosexual sexual encounters.

[The] invasion of female bodies, on male terms, cuts across class and is finally grounded in the male dominant aspects of the social order. Power and ideology are the indispensable 'supports' of the lived relations described. Things like the sequence act as an unspoken common ground beneath the level of immediate consciousness, but not removed from, or completely controlling, that consciousness.

It seems that, in initiating sexual contact, the boys operate a sequence from the least 'serious' regions of the body to the most 'serious'. That is, in petting, they would usually start by trying to get to a girl's breast before 'going below'. There is a sequence for forms of behaviour as well: that is to say, kissing is less serious than petting and petting is less serious than heavy petting. Of course, specific conditions may override this, such as the time available or the visibility of participants. I am assuming that most serious sexual activity still takes place in private (e.g. a room) or in semi-private (e.g. a party or a darkened public place).

The following short extract points towards the ideological uses of the sequence. The boys try to use it to grade and label girls. There is another way in which this labelling can be secured. If the girl does take some power and initiative away from the boy (especially in relation to the sequence) then she may be fixed in male views – by means of smirking and gossip – as congenitally licentious.

While walking along with two of the centre boys I asked about a particular girl who had just left the centre. Alan, the eldest boy (he was 16), volunteered this:

Q: Do you remember Tina?

Alan: Yeah! She's a right whore!

Rob: What did you get?

Alan: On the [school trip] man, I got fucking tits, a wank, everything!

A good deal about certain sexist assumptions can be told from this throw-away remark. Most obviously it attempts to signal to other males how competent this male is by getting so far down the sequence. Also, importantly, it indexes the girl's putative promiscuity as a shaping aspect of her whole personality. It is one of the oldest and commonest variants of the double standard, in which the girl is blamed for what she has done and for what is a 'virtue' in men. Looked at logically it is all very strange. If Tina is a 'right whore' what does that make Alan – a right client? But, of course, we are not dealing with logic or equitable views of the world, but with power-based distortions. Tina is, like Eve, forever the possessor of a hard-to-control unfeminine lust. Moreover, in the tone of voice there is real contempt, as if to say that this girl is really stupid for allowing herself to be had.

Sexist fantasizing revisited – plans for a rape

Partly because of the tradition within which I was working, I went, time and time again, for the male and the spectacular in my ethnography. Perhaps I imagined it to actually equal youth culture. The aspect of this that I have had to be most critical of, in this attempt to represent my material, is my effective identification with the boys. This becomes crucial in sections like the following. Having, semi-consciously, engineered conversations about sex, I withdrew from active participation in them. I did not attempt to explain my ideas about sexism. I made only a limited attempt to redress the balance by getting close to the recipients of the boys' sexism, and this only because the following conversation, and the whole period that spawned it, were so extraordinary to me (not to the kids) that I was *forced* to find out at least something about the girls. First let us return to the period in which the conversation took place – the period when Eve was first referred to the centre. What is being discussed by Don and Jake below, is a plan to get Eve back to Jake's flat so that they can force her to have sex with

them both. Had it occurred it would have been a gang rape. However, the
hallmark of this conversation (*as a conversion*) is its utter unreality. As much as
anything, this demonstrates how the two genders (as presently constructed) can
not only start from different premises but seem to be in different worlds. I do *not*
say this to excuse the intent of Don and Jake in the rest of their dealings with
Eve but to convey a quality which may have been lost in transcription.

Jake: ... we get out at quarter past two and go to collect my sister at three. Forty-five
minutes, that'll do. Get her on the bed, tie her up, say 'sit down you prat! you can
scream as much as you like but you aint getting out of here till we've fucked you' ...
have you got the bottle [courage] to fuck her?

Don: I've got the bottle anytime.

Jake: ... 'not going to tell her that we're going to fuck her, I'm just going to say, 'do
you want to come up the house after?' ... I'll say, 'come up the house listen to some
records'. I ain't going to say, 'I'm going to fuck you'. If she says, 'yeah', I'll say,
'alright then, just come up on your own', I'll say, 'have you got any money?' She'll
say, 'yeah'. We'll get on a bus, get to my house, go in the pub, get the key from mum.

Don: Be quick in the pub.

Jake: ... No, wait, this is dodgy ... if me dad comes home ... so if he comes in while
you're there don't worry, just get off her, don't fucking be fucking away while he's
there. Whoever's not doing it, right, at the same time keep watch, and anything you
hear just jump off of her and pull her knickers up.

The whole of this transcript may (rightly) shock radical sensibilities, but, in terms
of insight into the boys, it is important to understand how they relate to this sort
of conversation. For them, though it is 'daring', nothing untoward has been
broached and they pass on to discussing particular boys in the main school,
leaving this 'fiction hanging in the air. They did not try to pursue this idea in
real life (leaving aside the bundles). The 'function' of this talk for the boys is
titillative. Conversation being less constrained than practice, they can play with
Eve's body here in a way which they cannot in real life. Of course some might
argue that the unreality of the conversation is not a credit to the boys, who are
still culpable in intent, but is a function of the constraint of the real world, as I
have noted. Certainly, it is an open and challenging question as to what type of
self-delusions and distortions of the social world are likely from carrying around
this sort of ideological baggage in one's head.

The bundles – from sex talk to sex practice

The bundles were a particular craze that swept the centre for about two months.
For the boys they were a chance to practise sexist sexual practices. Attempts at
flirting had always been around in more or less submerged ways (e.g. Alan and
Tina) but the bundles were definitely something extra which crystallized certain
aspects of the boys' sexism. They started when new girls came into the centre
and changed the balance of numbers between the sexes. The actual bundles would
start when there were about four boys and girls sitting in the small back room.
The staff were overstretched at this time and had to break their rule of continuous

cover when they were called to the main school for ten minutes or so. At these unguarded moments certain kids who were not liked would be told to stay out of the back room by those who were going to have the bundles. This could be very humiliating if you were eligible by the criterion of age. Sometimes the lights would be turned out before the bundles began, and the room, which had painted-in windows, would be thrown into half-darkness. Amid whoops and giggles the kids would pile on top of each other and have bundles. They would never last very long (luckily for the girls) and could be stopped either when they all 'packed up' laughing, or became exhausted, or were disturbed by the sound of approaching staff or pupils. The other more usual way for the bundles to end was for a girl to apply the only veto the situation allowed and to protest vigorously that the boys were being too heavy-handed or too rough.

The bundles were used by the boys to find out how the girls reacted to their pressure – they were games of invasion; though feminists might reasonably object that invasion cannot, other than very euphemistically, be described as a game. Even if they started on a nominally equal basis – a fair swap – they soon became more and more, by the boys' actions, just crude attempts at touching up. The boys simply could not draw the line, but always wanted to push it further and further. Every physical closeness afforded by the bundles became a chance for attempted sexiness which further encouraged them in their notions of female complicity, and, out of that, came the rape fantasy, and so on. If the girls thought the bundles were a bit of a laugh it was an absolute hallmark of the boys' developing sexism that they completely lost sight of the girls' feelings in the matter and, once on a runaway train of their own exclusively male meanings, pushed for more and more. If they had succeeded in touching a girl's breast, they would go for her crotch.

It was as if they wanted the girls to loan them their bodies on *male terms*. There was no question in this context of any relation to sharing time or pleasures outside the situation (unlike courting, where personalities are more properly on the agenda). Interestingly one of the boys had been out with one of the girls for a week but in the bundles that might as well have never happened. In going out together relations are a little more contractual, if not mutual, but here people of different genders who like each other, or have some things in common, are just in competing camps. The bundles did not seem to be about the production of actual physical pleasure, as in petting for example. For the boys (and for the observer) the other part of the pleasure is in the electric atmosphere generated. Again, the licence for this pleasure was simply the presence of the girls themselves, all other considerations being collapsed into what could physically be got away with. The boys were very rough. Partly to cover themselves from a straight rebuff and partly through ineptitude, the boys transferred the bundles into their own problematic – the problematic of roughness. The girls knew that it was this that represented the most immediate danger. The girls too wanted 'kicks', physical closeness, excitement, some exertion, with perhaps a few careless touchings, but they did not want to be suffocated or crushed!

Once again Eve is the key figure. In an informal interview with her I tried to draw her on the fact that the boys seemed to be more active in defining the situation. Not surprisingly she was extremely suspicious. She blocked me for most of the interview. She blocked me not just as an older person and as a man but specifically as myself. After all I had been silent observer at many of the bundles and I had not lifted a finger to help her. She denied that the bundles were a sexual thing for her, and insisted that they were just 'messing about'.

Q: So that is how it looked to you . . . . It always seems to me, that it is the boys that want to touch the girls. Why didn't you or Mary touch them, or did you?

Eve: No. We was messing about, right? I said, 'Mary, come on let's jump them, right, for a laugh'. She said, 'Don't! They'll turn round and rape you, if I was you I'd forget it.' So she turns round to him [Ewan]. We jumped him, right? And they got hold of Mary – not me right, *Mary* – and I got out the room.

In setting the record straight, Eve's account, though mildly contradictory, outlines a justified fear of the boys' physicality; not so much their lust (elsewhere she said they were too young to rape) as their heavy-handed use of force. However, we should not forget that the girls kept on lining themselves up with those same boys in that same specific situation. At no time did the girls say they were going in for anything other than a 'laugh' but that phrase can cover a multitude of meanings in their class culture. I am not trying to say the girls were two-faced, or that they were in any significant detail as the boys constructed them, but I do want to raise the issue of their continued re-entry into that room, albeit against their better judgement. The girls presumably hoped each time that they could maximize their 'laughs' and minimize or neutralize the worst aspects. So far so good, but *both* sexes seem partly constrained to repeat a sequence shot through with elements of distortion, rip off and oppression.

The other important factor in the bundles was the attitude of the centre staff. They knew about the craze, though not in detail (that is to say how far the boys were trying to push it) but they considered the whole thing in terms of the *individuals* involved in it. This common-sensical approach seemed to be based on the idea of free sellers at the sexual market place. My own analogy of invasion was countered by the empiricist argument that the girls had entered the room of their own volition. There were many other ideological distortions that intersected the staff's assessment. First, there was the idea that sex and sex-related activities are private (even though the boys were not hindered by such considerations). Second, and more specifically, they had no special liking for Eve because she was 'uncouth' and, perhaps by association, potentially promiscuous.[3] Lastly, they seemed to operate with the very common notion of adolescence as a problem period when sex is bound to raise its head. This is what I called the ideology of emergence, an empiricist construction on the apparent greater sexiness of lads when they reach their teens. Within this I think there is the idea that a person's sexuality is an innately formed miniature primed by nature to explode in the hot climate of adolescence. There is also the idea here that boys and girls (especially boys) are prey to their own sexuality[4] but if you do not interfere the phase will be self-correcting. In terms of the centre bundles, the only way the staff felt they could intervene was under the rubric of procedures to prevent 'disruption' or the contravening of public propriety. How different would the staff's attitude have been if it was two stronger boys trying to touch up a weaker boy?

Conclusion

I have looked at boys' sex talk when there are just males together and I have tried to emphasize the dominating and disrespectful attitudes to women that develop in such exchanges. I have also tried to show that such talk is often very near to taking off into what I have called, *in a qualified way*, fantasy or part-fantasy. I have also tried to make a number of distinctions in what might otherwise be the monolithic concept of sexism. Most obviously I have argued that different aspects of sexism (imputing lust and inconsistency to women, feeding off the sight of 'alien' bodies and so on) are empirically observable as related to specific, actual situations. Last, but not least, I have tried to emphasize that while sexism comes out on aggregate as the general domination of men over women (grounded in patriarchy) it is individually discontinuous and, on the male side seen here, experientially insecure.

Notes

1 Advertising, one of the most pervasive forms of representation in our culture, constantly dissects women and uses 'significant' parts of them in its attempts to 'glamorize' products and manipulate consumption. The extent to which this prompts, or reinforces, the boys' sexism is still undecided. That question certainly begs others about ideology and cultural production that are beyond the scope of this chapter. However, at the very least, such representations have a background saturation effect. Certainly, advertising usually heavily emphasizes and celebrates stereotypical views of gender roles. For an interesting further discussion of stereotypes see T. E. Perkins (1979).

2 It was most commonly at this point in the chapter that, I think, feminist friends who read it regretted the absence of a properly political anger. I accept that the case of Eve *is* upsetting. Some people felt that she was being made powerless in the situation solely on the basis of her face, and that the boys imagined that they could do what they liked with her without even having to pretend to be friendly. I accept also that I have found it difficult to raise these sorts of issues clearly enough. I still believe, however, that it would be tactically and analytically incorrect to assume that the boys *could* totally 'scrap' Eve (in the sense of refuse to relate to). Though the boys' attitudes are seriously warped in relation to Eve, there is a subtle interplay of repulsion *and* attraction. That attraction is 'sexist' too and is not held up here as the opposite of rejecting stereotypes. However, if one does not also recognize that the boys wanted to contact Eve, then an important element of contradiction has been lost.

3 For interesting work on the ideological associating of active and 'delinquent' girls with promiscuity by the courts see Shacklady-Smith's article in Smart and Smart (eds), *Women, Sexuality and Social Control* (1978).

4 Foucault, paradoxically always best on ideologies, has written very well on the 'speaking sex' and the biologistic notion of sex drive as implied by theories of repression. See Foucault (1978 edn) especially pp. 3–35.

References

Foucault, M., *The History of Sexuality*, vol. 1, London, Allen Lane, 1979.

Perkins, T. E., 'Rethinking stereotypes', in Barrett, M. *et al.* (eds), *Ideology & Cultural Productive*, London, Croom Helm, 1979.

Shacklady Smith, L., 'Sexist assumptions and female delinquency: an empirical investigation', in Smart, C. and Smart, B. (eds), *Women, Sexuality & Social Control*, London, Routledge and Kegan Paul, 1978.

Willis, P., 'Shop-floor culture, masculinity and the wage form', in J. Clarke *et al.* (eds) *Working Class Culture*, London, Hutchinson, 1979.

17   Girls on the margins: a study of gender divisions in the classroom

Michelle Stanworth

What follows is an attempt to shed some light on the practices of pupils and especially of teachers which actively reproduce a hierarchical system of gender divisions in and through the classroom. The research[1] draws upon detailed individual interviews with teachers, and with a sample of their male and female pupils, in seven 'A' level classes. The objective was not to produce a description of events in the classroom as they might appear to an impartial observer, but rather to capture the quality of classroom life as currently experienced by pupils themselves. How, I wished to know, do girls and boys make sense of their educational experience? What effect does this have for their own self-image, and for their views of their own and the other sex? The design of the sample and the structure of the interviews made it possible to trace connections or inconsistencies between, on the one hand, teachers' attitudes towards pupils of either sex, and, on the other, the character of classroom life as reported by the pupils themselves.

I chose to focus on 'A' level classes in the humanities department of a college of further education with a large sixth form intake partly because of the absence, in this setting, of more obvious forms of gender differentiation: in this department, all classes are coeducational; academic and extracurricular activities are technically open to all pupils, male or female; type of dress can be freely chosen; there are relatively few regulations concerning conduct, and certainly none to my knowledge that differentiate between girls and boys; the proportions of female pupils and female staff are much higher than in, say, the maths and science department; and the girls are, in terms of academic performance, as successful as the boys. In short, one would expect that if any mixed educational establishment would avoid the marginalization of girls – the definition of female pupils as 'second-rate citizens' – it might happen in a relatively liberal setting such as this. As the research proceeded, however, it became apparent that fairly subtle aspects of classroom encounters continued to regenerate a sexual hierarchy of worth, in which men emerged as the 'naturally' dominant sex.

The significance of gender in teachers' views of their pupils

Teachers carry in their heads an impressive range of information about individual pupils for whom they are responsible; this is true at least of the teachers I know, and certainly of the teachers interviewed in this study. But is it the case that the

Source: Extracted from *Gender and Schooling: A study of sexual divisions in the classroom* (1983 edn), London, Hutchinson in association with the Explorations in Feminism Collective.

male/female distinction acts as a fundamental anchor point for the way teachers categorize their pupils?

A special procedure was used to investigate the possibility that teachers would be more sensitive to similarities between pupils of the same sex, than to characteristics which girls and boys may have in common. Each teacher was presented with a number of coed triads (a set of cards bearing the names of two boys and one girl, or two girls and one boy) and invited to pair the two pupils who were, in some educationally relevant way, most alike. A calculation was made of the number of occasions on which teachers paired the two pupils of the same sex. Overall, there was only a moderate tendency for teachers to confine their comparisons to pupils of the same sex. There were, however, marked differences between the choices made by female teachers and those made by men. Of the coed triads considered by female teachers, only 39 per cent were sorted into same-sex pairs. Male teachers, by contrast, selected same-sex pairs in 80 per cent of the cases.

There might be several ways of explaining this finding. First, it might be suggested that male teachers consider gender itself to be evidence of, or explanation for, different educational skills. Such attitudes are not unknown among the teachers interviewed, as the following comment suggests; the remark is, however, atypical of teachers' statements, and was made by a woman rather than a man.

Female teacher: On the other hand, Nick, being a boy, he's rather slapdash. The girls write more diligent essays.

Another explanation for same-sex pairings might be that, perhaps because of different upbringings, girls are more likely to resemble their female classmates than their male ones, in ways that are significant within an educational context; and that, therefore, the pairing of girls with girls, and boys with boys, merely reflects teachers' perceptions of the 'actual' characteristics of their pupils. This suggestion must be rejected, because it cannot account for the different patterns of choice between male and female teachers. If girls are radically different from boys in the classroom, how is it that male teachers paired pupils of the same sex twice as frequently as female teachers?

The most adequate explanation of the findings is that male teachers tend, far more than their female colleagues, to view the sexes whom they teach in mixed classes as relatively discrete groups. If male teachers are particularly attuned to dissimilarity between the sexes, this orientation may, in turn, be translated into actions which have the effect of further polarizing girls and boys in classes which they teach. In sum, the pairings made by male teachers may reflect both their own way of looking at the world (through a framework which emphasizes male/female dissimilarity), and behavioural differences between girls and boys which the men's own attitudes may help to create.

Initial impressions of pupils

In the early weeks of the academic year, teachers are faced with the arduous task of getting to know not just one, but several, groups of pupils; it is not surprising that it takes a while for the name and face of every pupil to be clearly linked in teachers' minds. What is remarkable is that the pupils who were mentioned by teachers as being difficult to place were, without exception, girls.

Interviewer:　What were your first impressions of Emma?

Male teacher:　Nothing really. I can only remember first impressions of a few who stood out right away; Adrian of course; and Philip; and David Levick; and Marion, too, because among the girls she was the earliest to say something in class. In fact, it was quite a time before I could tell some of the girls apart.

Interviewer:　Who was that?

Teacher:　Well, Angie, and her friends Leonore and Helen. They seemed rather silent at first, and they were friends, I think, and there was no way – that's how it seemed at the time – of telling one from the other. In fact, they are very different in appearance, I can see that now. One's fair and one's dark, for a start. But at the beginning they were just three quiet girls.

As the quotation suggests, the anonymity of girls is due in part to their reticence. The girl who is mentioned as speaking out early is instantly 'fixed' by her teacher; she has, among the girls, a sort of rarity value. However, this cannot entirely explain the greater readiness with which teachers identify boys, for the few male pupils who were reported by their teachers to be exceptionally quiet in class were, nevertheless, clearly remembered. Teachers' slowness at identifying girls has strong implications for the comfort and involvement of female pupils for, as we shall see later on, pupils take it as a sign of approval if teachers know their names right away.

Looking to the future

Teachers were asked to predict what each of their pupils might be doing two years, and five years, from the time of the interview. Boys – even those in danger of failing their examinations – were seen in jobs involving considerable responsibility and authority, the most frequent predictions being for civil service or management careers. One boy, for example, of whom his teacher had earlier said – 'His essays are bald, childlike and undeveloped; his statements are simple and naïve' – was expected to rise to head office:

Female teacher:　I suspect he might be quite good at summing things up. I don't know quite whether local government or civil service, but I can't just see him pushing paper around. I can see him writing reports on things. Perhaps an information officer, or sales planning, or something like that; something in head office.

Marriage cropped up in teachers' predictions of boys' future only once, in the case of a pupil who was academically very weak, but in whom his teachers recognized exceptional personal qualities; they described him as having 'a warm streak, almost Mediterranean', and 'the gift of communication' (a reference to his sympathetic manner in face-to-face encounters, for he was reported not to speak in class). He alone among the boys is defined more in terms of his personality than his ability, and it may be no accident that he is the *only* boy for whom the future anticipated by his teachers includes marriage and parenthood.

Male teacher:　I wonder if he's the kind of boy who will marry fairly young, once he's sure of his sexual self as it were.

Female teacher:　I see him having a frightfully happy girlfriend who's terribly fond of him.

So long as she's not ambitious, I think they'll be very happy. He would be a super father. I think children would adore having him for a father, though I'm not immediately sure what he'd be doing to support his family.

By contrast, the occupations suggested for girls seldom ranged beyond the stereotype of secretary, nurse or teacher. These predictions do not match either the girls' academic standing or their own aspirations. For instance, the girl who is envisaged as a secretary in the following quotation is thought to be fully capable of getting a university degree, and is herself considering a career in law.

Female teacher: I can imagine her being a very competent, if somewhat detached, secretary. She looks neat and tidy, her work's neat and tidy, she's perfectly prompt at arriving. And she moves around with an air of knowing what she's doing. She doesn't drift.

Interviewer: Why would she be a *detached* secretary?

Teacher: I can't imagine her falling for her boss at all! or getting in a flap.

Interviewer: What about in five years' time?

Teacher: Well, I can see her having a family, and having them jolly well organized. They'll get up at the right time and go to school at the right time, wearing the right clothes. Meals will be ready when her husband gets home. She'll handle it jolly well.

Remarks such as this indicate an implicit assumption that girls' capacities for efficiency and initiative will be channelled into nurturant or subordinate occupations (and, of course, into childcare and housework) rather than into other, less traditional, spheres.

Marriage and parenthood figure prominently in teachers' visions of the futures of their *female* pupils: teachers volunteered that two-thirds of the girls would be married in the near future. The prediction of marriage was applied not only to girls whose academic record was unremarkable, as here –

Male teacher: She is the sort of girl who might up and get married all of a sudden, and kick over the traces.

Interviewer: You mean she might abandon her 'A' levels?

Teacher: I'm not saying she would, but I wouldn't be surprised.

Interviewer: What do you imagine her doing in five years' time?

Teacher: Definitely married.

– but also to girls who were considered to have outstanding academic capacity.

Male teacher: Well, I'd be surprised if she wasn't married.

Interviewer: Is she the sort of person you would expect to marry young?

Teacher: Well, not necessarily marry young, but let's see . . . 16, 17, 18, 19 years old . . . somewhere along the line, certainly. I can't see what she'd be doing apart from that.

In only one instance when teachers anticipated the future was the possibility of early marriage viewed regretfully, as a potential interruption to a girl's development:

Male teacher: I should like to see her doing some kind of higher education, and I wonder whether something in the HND line might be more suitable than a degree course.

Interviewer: Because it's slightly more practical?

Teacher: Yes. This is pure supposition, but it does seem to me that there is a practical vein in her. She successfully holds down a job in one of the chain stores. I can see her making a very great success of management, retail management, because I would have thought she would be very skilled at dealing with people. And though she's a little unsure of herself still, there is a vein of sureness in her. She wouldn't be taken aback by awkward situations, for instance.

Interviewer: What about in five years' time?

Teacher: Quite possibly early marriage, which I think would be a pity. Not because I'm against the institution of marriage, but because I think that an early marriage would prevent her from fully realizing her potential.

Apart from the reaction to marriage, the preceding quotation is atypical of teachers' comments about their female pupils in other respects. First, it is the only prediction in which a management post was suggested for a girl. Second, the fact that a possible career was specified by a male teacher is itself unusual; in two-thirds of male teachers' discussions of female pupils, the girl could not be envisaged in any occupation once her education was complete. In some cases, it is almost as if the working lives of women are a mystery to men:

Male teacher: She would be competent enough to do a course at a university or polytechnic, though not necessarily the most academic course.

Interviewer: What sort of a course might suit her then?

Teacher: I can't say. I don't really know about jobs for girls.

Male teacher: She will probably go on to further or higher education. You'd know better than I what a young girl with an independent sort of mind might be doing in five years' time!

The type of futures teachers anticipate for girls seem to be related to classroom interaction in two important ways. First, teachers' views of 'women's work', and their emphasis upon the centrality of family in women's lives, are likely to make high achievement at 'A' level seem less urgent for girls than for boys. To the extent that teachers underestimate the ambitions of their female pupils, they will be reluctant to make girls prime candidates for attention in the classroom. Second – and more pertinent to this study – it seems likely that the current dynamic of classroom interaction does nothing to undermine stereotypical views of appropriate spheres for women and men. The reports gathered here from both teachers and pupils indicate that (whatever girls may be like outside) they are in the classroom quieter, more diffident and less openly competitive than their male classmates. No matter how conscientious and capable female pupils are, they are perceived by their teachers to lack the authoritative manner and the assertiveness which many teachers seem to believe to be prerequisites of 'masculine' occupations.

This interpretation seems to be the best way of accounting for a curious anomaly in the teachers' predictions. One girl who is ranked as the top performer in both her main subjects, and who wants a career in the diplomatic service, is envisaged by her teacher as the 'personal assistant to somebody rather important'. In contrast, the girl with the poorest academic record is one of only two girls to be suggested for a job that is not in the traditional feminine mould. The comments made about these two pupils are reproduced below; they indicate that teachers attach a great significance to assertiveness in classroom situations.

Interviewer: And can you think ahead to five years' time, what Clare might be doing in five years' time?

Female teacher: I could possibly see her as a kind of committee type person. She's not a forceful public speaker, you see. She says something rather quietly, and it's absolutely right. The people next to her take it in, but it doesn't have any impact if you see what I mean. I can imagine her as the personal assistant to somebody rather important, dealing with things very competently, and arranging things very competently, and giving ideas backwards and forwards, and dealing with individual callers face to face. She's good at face to face things, or in small groups, rather than in large groups.

Interviewer: What about Alison in five years' time?

Female teacher: She could have a professional job of some sort, I think. I can imagine her in publicity or almost anything. She's got a strong presence, and she definitely makes an impression. She's pretty downright and forthright and forthcoming in her opinions. In fact, she is a very good stimulus in the group, though she does make some of the pupils feel a bit antagonistic.

It is, apparently, only when a girl's behaviour in class sharply contradicts the retiring feminine stereotype (a contradiction that may produce antagonism from classmates), that teachers are likely to imagine her in a career at odds with highly traditional expectations.

Pupils' interpretation of teachers

Although pupils were not questioned about discipline in the classroom, many ventured criticisms of teachers for being, in their view, insufficiently authoritarian.

Male pupil: He's too nervous, I think, to put them down. They could be joking, they could be laughing, they could be doing anything and he would just pretend nothing was happening. He doesn't seem to know how to get angry. It's the only thing I've got against him.

Female pupil: Well, I don't know about Mrs Stephens. She seems very nervous. She sort of patters on, all the time. She is always trying to seek approval, wants very much for the class to approve of her. We don't know what to do. It makes you feel embarrassed for her.

Interviewer: How do you mean, she tries to seek approval?

Pupil: She just seems to want us to approve of her. For example, she never tells you you're wrong, she just says, 'Well, perhaps' or something like that. I wish she would be more . . . um, authoritarian.

Comments like this, bemoaning a lack of firmness in particular teachers, were directed at men as often as at women; and yet the pupils still seemed to hold the general preconception that men are the more effective disciplinarians. Many expressed a conviction that male teachers in general tolerate 'less mucking around', and that pupils respond more readily to a rebuke or command when it comes from a man.

Female pupil: I think men probably have a securer. . . . They know how to handle a class better, and you pay more attention to them. I think. I mean if someone sort of starts mucking around, they will say so, won't they? Miss Austin is quite competent, but I've had quite a few women teachers and they will let the class go. I think men can handle the class better.

Male pupil: A man would take a much stronger line. I always used to prefer women teachers to men because you could sidetrack them.

Female pupil: Some people might be more threatened by a male teacher.

Interviewer: Some girls, do you mean?

Pupil: Yes, and even boys I think. Because if a male teacher yells at you for not doing your work or not getting it in on time, I think it produces a harsher effect. I don't think it should be like that, but that's society, isn't it?

Male pupil: Women may find it harder to get the attention of the group, and try to compensate by being more friendly, almost trying to win friends.

Although these issues cannot be resolved in the present study, one can speculate about the possible implications of pupils' preconceptions for classroom interaction. Do pupils commonly interpret the friendliness of female teachers as an attempt to compensate for lack of power? Or, for example, are pupils likely to be more submissive with male teachers, thereby confirming their expectations of masculine authority?

When asked to indicate which of all their current teachers are most successful on twelve different aspects of teaching performance, the teachers who were most often named, by girls as well as boys, were men. But both groups of pupils tended to designate at least successful those teachers of the other sex from themselves. The reports of boys are very decisive; there is among boys a strong consensus that male teachers are best, and female teachers worst. Girls, on the other hand, divided both their positive and negative choices much more evenly between the men and the women who taught them. It was as if boys took a more united line than girls on their preference for male teachers and their rejection of teachers of the other sex.

Pupils' preference for male teachers is most marked with respect to the academic or pedagogic side of the teacher's role. Both boys and girls are inclined to name male teachers as the ones who know their subject best; are most successful at getting their subject across; are most likely to give sound advice about higher education and careers; and are, all in all, most competent. Boys and girls tend to agree, furthermore, that they get more work done in classes taught by men, and that male teachers come closer to dealing fairly with all the pupils in their classes; however, the meaning which pupils give to these two latter categories deserves to be looked at more closely.

In the first place, 'getting lots of work done' is usually regarded as synonymous with note-taking:

Male pupil: Mr Salisbury. We take reams of notes in his class.

Male pupil: We write the whole time!

Female pupil: It must be Mr Jensen first; we are always taking notes in his class.

Second, pupils' comments when asked which teacher came closest to 'dealing fairly with all pupils' seemed to equate 'fairness' with a failure to acknowledge the individuality of pupils:

Female pupil: I'll put Mr Belton first, because he hardly ever sees us, so he doesn't know anyone well.

Male pupil: He talks to the class as a whole, never to individuals. As if everybody was the same.

Female pupil: I suppose who's most objective is somebody who doesn't know us very well, who can't tell us apart.

These comments should serve as a warning against the pitfalls of trying to measure teacher objectivity or impartiality by means of a straightforward question; when not pinned down to a single question, pupils' judgements of teachers' fairness, are in fact much more complex.

If male teachers are more favourably perceived on academic dimensions, pupils prefer teachers of their own sex when they are evaluating the interpersonal side of the teacher's role. That is, girls are inclined to name female teachers as the ones who are more helpful; understand them best; and can most readily be consulted about personal problems. Girls report, furthermore, that they get on best with female teachers and that they have more fun in classes taught by women. Boys, on the other hand, are more likely to nominate male teachers as the ones who are most successful on all these interpersonal dimensions.

Experiences of classroom interaction

Sections of the pupils' interviews were designed to elicit a picture of classroom life as seen through the eyes of the pupils. Each was asked a series of questions of the type: 'Which of these pupils does the teacher pay most attention to?' In pupils' experience, it is boys who stand out vividly in classroom interaction. Despite the fact that there are almost twice as many girls as boys in the seven classes, boys' names appeared nearly two and one-half times as often as girls.

Boys are, according to the pupils' reports, four times more likely than girls to join in discussion, or to offer comments in class. They are twice as likely to demand help or attention from the teacher, and twice as likely to be seen as 'model pupils'.

More importantly, it seems to pupils that boys receive the lion's share of teacher's attention and regard. Boys are, on pupils' accounts:

Slightly more likely to be the pupils for whom teachers display most concern.
Twice as likely to be asked questions by teachers.

Twice as likely to be regarded by teachers as highly conscientious.
Twice as likely to be those with whom teachers get on best.
Three times more likely to be praised by teachers (and slightly more likely to be criticized).
Three times more likely to be the pupils whom teachers appear to enjoy teaching.
Five times more likely to be the ones to whom teachers pay most attention.

Looking at each of the seven classes separately, boys far exceed girls as the more prominent participants in classroom encounters in every class but one. They retain their advantage over girls (although it is slightly less pronounced) in classes taught by women, as well as those taught by men. The preponderance of boys over girls on each of these dimensions is no less marked in the reports provided by female pupils than in those provided by males – except that girls give a slight edge to classmates of their own sex when nominating model pupils, those for whom the teacher shows most concern, and those who are most frequently criticized. The implication is that *both* male and female pupils experience the classroom as a place where boys are the focus of activity and attention – particularly in the forms of interaction which are initiated by the teacher – while girls are placed on the margins of classroom life.

While discussing classroom interaction and their relationships with teachers, nearly all the pupils mentioned instances in which male teachers were, in their eyes, substantially more sympathetic or more attentive to the boys than to the girls.

Interviewer: What is Mr Fletcher's opinion of you, as far as you can tell?

Female pupil: I don't know. Because my opinion of him changed quite a lot over the year. At first I thought he was quite good, quite friendly. . . . Then I really noticed that he had some favourites, and he kind of despised, which is what I feel he does, some of the people.

Interviewer: Who does he despise, do you think, in this group?

Pupil: Well, there's some girls at the back who don't say anything or don't talk, and he doesn't seem to encourage them to say anything, he just ignores them.

Interviewer: And is it those girls that you think he despises? It's quite a strong word, isn't it?

Pupil: Yes. Well, perhaps not despise. Perhaps he just looks down on them a bit, I don't know. It's just the kind of feeling you get if you're in that class.

Interviewer: That he doesn't have much respect for them?

Pupil: Yes.

Interviewer: Would he be like that with anybody quiet, do you think, or is it especially with girls.

Pupil: I don't know. It's probably because there's quite a few girls in our group, that it shows like that.

Interviewer: And who are his favourites then?

Pupil: Well there's a couple of boys who are quite sporty and he kind of jokes with them, and he lets them go off from class to play their rugby, and various things like that. And there's two boys he seems to talk to quite often outside class, and things like that.

Interviewer: Who does Mr Hurd most often direct questions to in this group?

Male pupil: I think he asks Arthur and Phil. he seems to ask all the boys a lot actually.

Interviewer: Why is that? Why does he ask all the boys?

Pupil: I don't know. Perhaps it's because they always have something to say.

Interviewer: And the girls are more likely to be quiet?

Pupil: Yes. I guess so.

Interviewer: Which of these pupils does Mrs Hertford get on best with?

Male pupil: I think Mrs Hertford does get on well with . . . . Well, she gets on better with the boys on the whole, both these teachers do. Mr York would lean towards George and Simon and Ken. Although he's very broadminded, he'd lean towards the boys in the class. But it's not an absolutely firm division – he'll listen to Martha too, sometimes.

Boys and girls report the same actions by their teachers, but the interpretations they give to these actions can be very different. The two passages which follow (in response to the only question in the two hour pupil interviews which explicitly refers to gender), illustrate starkly how a teacher's actions can be insulting to girls, but regarded by boys as a trivial matter. Although they share the same classrooms, the experience of classroom life is clearly not the same for girls and boys.

Interviewer: Does it make any difference, do you think, that Mr Macmillan is a man and Mrs Wilson is a woman?

Female pupil: I suppose so, because you think he's a bit of a twit, at least I do. Whereas Mrs Wilson, I suppose I relate to her more because she's a woman.

Interviewer: And do you think she feels the same way, that it's easier for her to relate to girls?

Pupil: Possibly. . . . No, I think it's equal actually, the way she relates to boys and girls. But take somebody like Mr Macmillan, he tends to relate better to the boys actually. When he's talking about military history or something like that he says, 'I know you ladies won't like this' or something.

Interviewer: I see what you mean. You might feel a little bit as if you'd been excluded from that discussion.

Interviewer: Does it make any difference, do you think, that Mr Macmillan is a man and Mrs Wilson is a woman?

Male pupil: Possibly, yes, I suppose the men sort of tend to . . . be a bit chauvinist, I suppose you could put it, but they do that as a joke really. Particularly Mr Macmillan. He tends to jokingly separate the two teams really. If it's a sort of social rights issue, he'll ask for the point of view of both sexes. Or he'll tease the girls that they won't understand something, say like military history. But he doesn't really concentrate on it.

Whatever the causes of what pupils take to be discriminatory behaviour on the part of their teachers – and the causes are undoubtedly complex – the consequences for pupils' views of themselves must be given serious consideration. Small tokens of individual attention are important clues that pupils go by when deciding whether they are looked on with favour by their teachers. Because boys are given prominence by both male and female teachers in classroom activity, they have a far greater chance of feeling valued. Girls, on the other hand, who are less often singled out for attention in class, tend to assume (despite their good marks) that teachers hold them in low esteem. The girl who described herself as a 'wallpaper person' was by no means the only one to react in this way to apparent indifference from teachers.

It is not only the self-images of *individual* pupils which are shaped by this process. The classroom is one of the few highly structured environments where adolescent girls and boys encounter one another on a regular basis, as comparative strangers.

The faceless bunch: gender divisions in coeducation

The experiences boys and girls have in mixed classes contribute to their evolving views about their own, and the other, sex. When boys are more outspoken and manifestly confident – and especially when teachers take more notice of boys – pupils tend to see this as evidence that boys in general are more capable, and more highly valued, than girls.

Interviewer: Which of these pupils gets asked questions most often by the teacher?

Female pupil: Well, Terence does. And Johnny. And Mr Howard asks Rob a lot of questions as well.

Interviewer: And which pupils join in discussions or make comments most often?

Pupil: Rob says a lot, and Julian, and Paul, and Johnny too. They all make a lot of noise, all those boys. That's why I think they're more intelligent than us.

The down-grading of girls in their own eyes and those of their male classmates is confirmed by other parts of the interviews. Both teachers and pupils ranked the members of each class according to their success in the subject. Before comparing the rank orders made by teachers with those constructed by pupils, the following hypotheses were set out: first, that girls would know where they stood in relation to other girls, but would place boys higher in the rank order than teachers had done; second, that boys would give an accurate account of the rank order of boys, but would assign girls a lower position than teachers had done; and third, that the net effect of pupils' 'errors' would be an overestimation of the academic standing of boys, and an underestimation of that of girls.

The results support these predictions to a striking degree. In the nineteen of twenty-four where pupils' rankings were different from those of their teachers, all of the girls underestimated their rank; all but one of the boys overestimated theirs. Furthermore, two-thirds of these errors involve only classmates of the other sex – that is, girls down-grading themselves relative to boys, boys up-grading themselves relative to girls.

These data on pupil rankings, combined with the comments of the pupils themselves, strongly support the contention that the prominence of boys in classroom interaction plays an active part in the regeneration of a sexual hierarchy, in which boys are the indisputably dominant partners. Girls appear to boys – and more importantly, to themselves – as less capable than they 'really' are.

The devaluation of girls which is the typical consequence of interaction in these classrooms can be, on occasion, undermined. In the first place, when girls are forthcoming in class, boys appear to take them more seriously than before. The pupil in the following quotation, for example, spoke well of only one girl – Audrey – during the entire interview:

Male pupil: Audrey, hmm. Well, I'd like to classify myself as a better person than her, but she takes a more active part in the history class. She speaks out a lot, even though the statements are a bit, well. . . . She is certainly well read, there's no denying that.

Second, when pupils do have access to the marks awarded to classmates of the other sex (something which rarely happens), they are able to challenge the supposed relationship between outspokenness and ability:

Interviewer: Which of these people are least like model pupils?

Male pupil: Really these people here [pointing to a group of six girls]. They don't say much, they don't contribute . . . . On the other hand, I think a lot goes unsaid. Take, for example, Sandra, this girl here. She says very little, but I'm told on very good authority that she gets the best marks in the class. We might have lots of budding A. J. P. Taylors among those girls, but I guess I wouldn't really know about it, because I only really know George and Stan and Sebastian.

In the course of interviews, girls were more aware of their male classmates, and more circumspect in comments about them, than boys were about girls. Girls, for example, recognized the names of all their current classmates, male or female, but most boys had difficulty placing some of the girls. Some boys acknowledged female classmates only in ways that indicated the low opinion in which those girls were held.

Male pupil (sorting cards bearing classmates' names, points to several names):   A bunch of cackling girls, all of them.

Interviewer: The ones that you just recognized, do you mean?

Pupil: Yes. They sit at the back of the class and might as well be sucking lollipops all day.

Interviewer: Do they speak out in class?

Pupil: Yeah, but it's usually pretty mundane.

Interviewer: Who speaks the least out of this class?

Pupil: This faceless bunch.

Interviewer: Ah – the reason they're faceless is, presumably, because they don't speak out?

Pupil: Yeah. Also, they sit behind me, so. And also because they're stupid.

Male pupil (looking at card):   Hah, hah! Maggie!

Interviewer: Why 'hah hah'?

Pupil: Because me and Martin were after young Maggie for weeks at the beginning of the year.

Interviewer: With any success?

Pupil: No. She said we were too outspoken. No, I think I'll rank myself above her.

Pupils were invited to name the classmates who most influenced them, those whom they would most wish to be like, and those with whom they compared themselves in terms of academic performance. There was a strong tendency for girls to name only girls, and boys to name only boys, in answer to these questions. On the rare occasions when boys mentioned girls among the people they would most wish to be like, they were quick to draw attention to girls' shortcomings:

Male pupil: Well, I'm very much like these three [boys] and those other three girls. But I don't think the girls have got any ambition. It would have to be a step up for me!

Boys' remarks indicated, as well, a reluctance to acknowledge girls as equals.

[One] pupil, sorting out the cards of those pupils who were better than him in History, remarked:

Male pupil: I'll put him in as well. Funny, actually, it's all boys in that pile.

Interviewer: Strange, isn't it?

Pupil: It's hard to imagine a girl that's better than me.

Interviewer: Can you imagine? Is it unusual?

Pupil: Yes, I can if I try maybe, but it *is* unusual. Rosemary – well, I don't know if she is better at History than me, but she is probably better at other subjects like English than me. I was at the same school as her for five years, so I know that.

Interviewer: So you can imagine a girl who's better than you.

Pupil: Yes, I can, but not in History.

Interviewer: Do you think History is more a man's subject, then, in a way?

Pupil: Probably, there's lots of wars in History. That's basically what it's about, why one country's greater than another. And as a rule, girls aren't so good at it.

If this young man had seen the marks of the girls in his History class, he would have discovered that, as his teacher reported, there were several girls who were performing more capably than him. But cross-sex comparison of marks is rare among these pupils, and this boy's insulation from comparison with his female classmates enables him to maintain his conviction of their inferior capacity for History.

Girls as well as boys seem wary of comparing themselves in a positive way with members of the other sex. However, as Jenny Shaw has argued,[2] boys in mixed classes may emphasize their masculinity by seeking to be as *unlike* girls as possible – in other words, by taking girls as a negative reference group. Certainly this seems to be the case in the present study. In reply to the question, 'Who would you least wish to be like?', all of the boys named girls (and only girls). It must be emphasized that the characteristic of female pupils most vehemently rejected by boys is the apparent marginality of girls in classroom encounters. The term 'faceless', used time and again by boys (but by none of the girls) to describe their female classmates, seems to sum up the boys' feeling that silence robs girls of any claim to individual identity and respect.

Interviewer: Who would you least wish to be like?

Male pupil: I don't know, let's see . . . [sorting through cards with names of classmates] . . . Oh, one of the faceless bunch I suppose. They seem so anonymous. Probably one of the gaggling girls, let's pick one. Linda, she's ugly. Yes, Linda.

Interviewer: Is that because she's ugly?

Pupil: No, but she just seems to be immature, she doesn't contribute much to the class. She stands for everything I dislike.

It appears that the quietness of girls makes them an easy target for boys' disdain. Boys see this as a sign that girls are academically weak; they also ascribe to girls other traits, such as lack of ambition or of commitment, on the basis of their reticence in class.

Interviewer: Who does the teacher think is most conscientious in this group?

Male pupil: Well, he thinks these two are very conscientious, Mark and Ben. And these two, Stella and Eileen, they are as well. They will try and get their essays in on time, and they will work and make an effort, they read the books and so forth. They don't only work, they go to the same discos as Mark and Ben. But the boys, you see, they very much want to get on in the education system.

Interviewer: Do you mean that the girls are less ambitious than Mark and Ben?

Pupil: No, perhaps not. Well, they may end up in university, but . . . well, actually, I can't really imagine where the girls will end up. You can't really imagine that they want to *be* anything. Whereas the boys, they definitely want to get to university and to get good jobs – they make that clear.

Male pupil: I don't really know these three well, but I think I'd put them all in the same bracket, they're typical girls.

Interviewer: What's a typical girl, then?

Pupil: Well, maybe they've all got the same attitude, like they don't want to be here, but they are doing 'A' levels, so they might as well do some of the work. They would rather do 'A' levels, I guess, than go out and get a job.

Interviewer: Because you said 'typical girls', do you think that's the case more often with girls than with boys?

Pupil: No. What I meant was, they are all the same. They all sit down in the back corner, and they don't say much out loud, you hardly know they are there . . . . You can't really say 'typical girls' anyway these days, because you'll get your head bitten off.

Although boys constitute their female classmates as a negative reference group, girls do not reciprocate. When asked whom they would least wish to be like, it is not boys, but other girls whom girls reject. All but one of the female pupils named girls (and only girls) as the persons they would least wish to be like. The reasons they gave suggested that they were not simply adopting the standards of the boys, and disowning those members of their sex who were held by boys in contempt; on the contrary, many of the girls who were rejected by female classmates were more than ordinarily outspoken, and were condemned for 'speaking out too aggressively' or 'hogging the limelight'.

Summary

In undertaking this research, I chose to focus not on achievement *per se* — not, that is, on the sexual distribution of knowledge and qualifications — but rather on the subtle ways in which classroom encounters bring to life and sustain sexual divisions. Part of that learning involves the regeneration of a gender hierarchy, in which those qualities and attributes that are associated with males are also the ones that are valued; becoming a woman means, all too often, learning to accept second place.

The central concern of the study has been then with the way in which, in pupils' experience, girls are placed on the margins of classroom encounters, and with the consequences this has for pupils' evolving images of the worth and capability of the sexes.

Pupils in these classes rarely pass their marks, or evaluations made of them by teachers, on to members of the other sex, and so they draw upon their experience of classroom interaction when judging the performance of the other sex. Since the sexual distribution of interaction appears decisively weighted in favour of boys, classroom encounters contribute to the devaluation of girls in their own eyes and those of their male classmates. All pupils have a clear idea of the rank order of their own sex in academic performance, but in the vast majority of cases, girls downgrade themselves relative to boys, and boys upgrade themselves in comparison to girls. Although the girls in this study are judged by their teachers to be as capable as the boys, girls' marginalization in the classroom, and teachers' apparently lesser attentiveness to them, contribute to pupils' views that boys are the more dominant, and capable, sex. Classroom interaction — the way in which pupils and teachers relate to each other — does not merely transmit beliefs about the superiority of one sex over the other, but actively serves to give such beliefs a concrete foundation in personal experience.

Notes

1 For those who wish to have further details of the research techniques and design, copies of the dissertation in which the research is fully written up, entitled *Gender and the Classroom; a study of male and female views of classroom*, available from the libraries of the University of Essex and the Institute of Education, London.

2 See, for instance, J. Shaw, 'Sexual divisions in the classroom', mimeo, University of Essex, 1977.

18   Young women and the transition from school to un/employment: a cultural analysis

Christine Griffin

In January 1979 I began work on a three-year study of the transition from school to the labour market for young working-class women in Birmingham. Analyses of the empirical 'results' of this project are available elsewhere (see Griffin, 1982; 1985), but this paper focuses on the methodological side of the research. I used mainly qualitative methods to develop an ethnographic cultural analysis of the young women's experiences. This paper looks at the potential advantages – and limitations – of such an analysis for research concerning gender relations and women's position in particular.

The young women and work project

The first stage of the project involved visits to six Birmingham schools of varying size, student intake, organization and academic reputation. I visited mixed and single-sex (girls') schools; Roman Catholic, Church of England and non-denominational; as well as independent schools and those that had been grammar and secondary modern schools before the shift to comprehensive education in 1974. As the sole research worker, I interviewed headteachers, careers officers, careers and form teachers as well as 180 school students. The latter included middle- and working-class girls; fourth, fifth and sixth formers; Asian, Afro-Caribbean and white students; and some boys. I talked to more 'academic' sixth formers who hoped to move on to university or college; fifth formers taking CSEs or 'O' levels who were unsure whether to stay on or leave at 16; and 'non-academic' students taking few or no exams who were determined to leave school as soon as possible.

The second stage of the project was a longitudinal follow-up of twenty-five young white working-class fifth formers with few or no academic qualifications into their first eighteen to twenty-four months in the labour market. This involved a series of informal interviews in coffee bars, pubs and in the young women's homes; with their families and friends (mainly mothers, sisters and girlfriends); and ten workplace case studies. The latter covered 'women's jobs' in offices and factories, and 'men's work' in engineering, as well as interviews with unemployed young women. I talked to young women's employers, supervisors, co-workers, careers officers and Youth Opportunities Programme (YOP's) tutors.

The process of 'selecting' young women for the second follow-up stage was far from one-sided. It depended on the active co-operation of the participants, combined with the need to limit the breadth of the research in line with the time

Source: Extracted from R. G. Burgess (ed.), *Field Methods in the Study of Education*, Barcombe Falmer, 1985.

and resources available.[1] I had little difficulty in talking to female relatives and friends (usually in the kitchen, which was very much a female space), but the young women's fathers and elder brothers (if they lived with the family) proved to be the most elusive and unforthcoming, showing a wary interest in my presence.

I visited each school at least three times, and my first visit involved an informal chat with the head. This gave her/him a chance to 'vet' me before bringing in the careers or form teacher who would be organizing my visits. The first introduction to students would set the tone for subsequent interviews, so I asked teachers to describe me as: 'Chris Griffin who is doing a project about girls at school and at work.'

I was never introduced to students in front of a whole class, but set up my tape-recorder in a separate room. I could then introduce myself to students on my own terms, setting an informal atmosphere from the start, usually by laughing and smiling and adopting an informal conversational tone. I made it clear that I was not connected with the school or the Careers Service, and that the interviews would be treated in complete confidence, before asking the students' permission to tape their words.

Qualitative and quantitative methods

Before discussing my use of qualitative and quantitative methods in this project, I want to clarify the differential status of these methods in social science research. At the most basic level, qualitative and quantitative methods are sets of different research *techniques*, each with their own potential advantages and limitations. These various techniques can be (and often are) employed simultaneously in a given study, but they can take on a different status depending on the overall research approach or epistemology.

Broadly speaking, quantitative techniques involve codifying (i.e., quantifying) phenomena, using questionnaires, social surveys or structured interviews, for example. Such techniques allow social scientists to carry out large-scale comparative analyses like the government census. Qualitative techniques involve more open-ended, 'free response' questions based on informal, loosely-structured interviews, observation, or diaries. They are fairly time-consuming and often used in smaller-scale case study based research concerned with subjective experience and social meanings. Although both sets of techniques have their own advantages and limitations, western social science has come to favour quantitative research as the main source of 'hard' and 'rigorous' data.

Williams (1979) has argued that quantitative techniques have dominated social science research since their use in conjunction with a logical positivist philosophy during the development of industrial capitalism. This positivist philosophy advocates the search for universal laws through the use of natural scientific methods. 'Facts' are assumed to exist external to the researcher, waiting to be discovered. The researcher is seen as an objective, apolitical and value-free being, who works at a necessary distance from the 'object' of study.

The Young Women and Work project employed both quantitative and qualitative techniques, but not in a positivist context. It was relatively unusual in the use of mainly qualitative methods, which were based on interviews and systematic observation. Most of the interviews were taped, or recorded in as much detail as possible in fieldnote form. They were loosely structured around a series of key topics and questions to allow for a degree of flexibility.[2]

Both individual and group interviews in schools centred on these topics, with sufficient space for me to follow up particular areas, for example, if students had a grievance against a given teacher or the school. This also allowed students to discuss issues amongst themselves. This often happened during questions about their future status in family life and the labour market, managing the demands of marriage and/or motherhood, or surviving as independent single women. Some of these discussions became extremely heated, since the whole area was fraught with contradictions and confusion for many of the young women.

In another case, a group of Afro-Caribbean fifth formers began to discuss a series of recent confrontations with the police outside the school. Such conversations always occurred towards the end of the interviews, when the students had relaxed a little and developed a degree of trust in my promise of total confidentiality. These discussions did not always fall within my list of pre-set topics, and I could amend this list as the research progressed. As a white woman in her late twenties with a highly academic education, I could hardly predict all of the main concerns of young white and black working-class women. The use of qualitative methods meant that the research did not have to rely on my preconceptions, nor on material from comparable studies, of which there were very few.

In all research studies where people are the 'subjects', their views of the research worker(s) and of the research itself will affect their responses and behaviour. It is just as impossible to eradicate these influences as it is to remove the researcher's assumptions about the participants. Rather than deny, ignore or minimize these effects, I have tried to recognize and understand them as a part of the research analysis (see Willis, 1980). Young women often turned my questions around, asking how I had felt on leaving school, how I had found my first job and so on. During the later stages of the research, young women used their continuing contact with me to find out about ex-schoolfriends with whom they had lost touch since leaving school. A positivist approach might treat these questions as irrelevant or unwanted intrusions, or as potential sources of 'data contamination', but I saw them as part of the reciprocal nature of the research process.

The project involved systematic observation as well as informal interviews. This was most important in the workplace case studies where it was often too loud or too busy to talk, and where relevant episodes could not always be recorded on tape. I did not use true participant observation, since I could not have worked alongside young women on typewriters, data processors or sewing machines in the more skilled jobs.[3] Quite apart from the disruption which this would have caused, I would have been doing unpaid work in a situation of rapidly rising youth unemployment. Participant observation does have the advantage of allowing researchers to share some of the participants' experiences, and to 'blend in' to their lives to a limited extent (see Willis, 1979), but it was inappropriate in this case.

I used the non-participant 'fly-on-the-wall' technique to observe the pattern of the working day in various workplaces, either sitting in a corner or walking around the office or factory floor. My presence was explained as 'seeing what X's job involves' for the project on 'young women leaving school to start their first full-time jobs'. Once the initial novelty had worn off and everyone knew who I was, pressure of work usually meant that I was more or less ignored. Several managers and employees remarked that they had soon forgotten about my presence.

While the project relied primarily on qualitative techniques, I did use some quantitative analysis and research materials. The responses of the 180 school students to specific questions about domestic work, part-time jobs and family structures were collated in quantitative form and subjected to fairly basic statistical analysis. This information was used to put the qualitative work in a wider national political context, since this material was the primary focus of the ethnographic cultural analysis.

Ethnographic cultural analysis

Most of the school interviews were recorded on tape and transcribed later. I kept comprehensive field notes throughout the fieldwork, even after taped interviews in case of equipment failure (a wise precaution as it turned out). These field notes were all dated, giving details of place, context and who was present, as well as dialogue, including my own contributions, and relevant events and episodes.

However comprehensive these field notes were, a degree of selectivity was inevitable, particularly when whole working days were spent 'in the field' in offices or factories. In these cases I recorded those incidents which I judged to be relevant, surprising, or those which seemed to illustrate commonly-occurring themes. I also included my own initial interpretations of the events, and more subjective reactions, such as 'felt at ease' or 'terrified'.

Following the tape transcription, I went through all of the fieldnotes and transcripts to categorize the material according to a series of topic headings.

This initial categorization generated more interpretative ideas towards the development of a theoretical framework, all of which were recorded at the time, however vague and seemingly incomprehensible. Since this process began in the second year of the study, such initial analysis could be acted upon and incorporated into the continuing fieldwork. For example, leisure played an important part in the young women's lives in and outside the school and the workplace, and particularly in relation to pressures to be heterosexual and 'get a man' (Griffin *et al.*, 1980). As the research progressed I was able to focus more on young women's leisure time and on the various social meanings of 'leisure' as compared to waged work and unpaid housework and childcare (Griffin, 1982a; 1982b).

This is one example of what has been called 'theoretical sampling' (see Glaser and Strauss, 1967; Willis, 1980), in which theory is developed throughout the fieldwork via the continual interaction between research 'in the field' and the generation of a theoretical framework. In this way theoretical analysis was not a discrete event which took place outside the 'field' when the work was written up, but was an integral part of the research process.

I have tried to balance the simultaneous pressures of 'making the strange familiar and the familiar strange'; to maintain my responsiveness to new insights, my capacity to 'be surprised', and my willingness to examine and 'see beyond' my own preconceptions. All research workers bring their own set of expectations and assumptions to a project, and I am no exception. Willis (1980) has not been alone in arguing that the positivist promise of 'objective' and 'value-free' research is illusory. It is important to recognize and examine (as far as possible) one's own expectations from the outset, in what Willis has called a 'theoretical confession'.

As a woman concerned with young women's experiences, there were certain areas of shared knowledge which helped me to establish an informal rapport with female participants, such as laughing at how 'stupid and useless' boys and men could be, or at the contents of some romantic novels and magazines. While this shared knowledge was an advantage, it could also hinder the examination of my own 'common-sense' assumptions. Although I did have a degree of shared experience in common with the female students, this was limited by differences in class, age, race and social context which could not be discounted.

I employed qualitative techniques to provide an ethnographic account of the young women's lives using a form of cultural analysis. Ethnography has its origins in social anthropology, in studies based on qualitative participant observation techniques which have tended to be overly descriptive. Much of this research has involved white academics, and produced patronizing studies of supposedly 'primitive' black communities in parts of Africa and Asia.

Cultural analysis developed out of this somewhat suspect tradition via the National Deviancy conferences in North America and Britain, and the more recent studies of youth subcultures (see Hall *et al.*, 1980). This brought ethnography out of its relatively descriptive mode, defining culture as 'the shared principles of life, characteristic of particular classes, groups or social milieux. Cultures are produced as groups make sense of their social existence in the course of everyday experience' (Education Group, CCCS, 1981, p. 27).

Cultural studies in Britain has developed a form of ethnographic cultural analysis based on qualitative methods, which concentrates on specific cultural processes 'as they are lived'. This has aimed to move beyond the youth subcultures studies which have focused on descriptive accounts of particular 'gangs' or styles, to develop analyses of broader processes such as the transition from school to the labour market (see Willis, 1977; Hebdige, 1979). Unfortunately, such cultural analyses have tended to retain the subcultural emphasis on the experiences of young white working-class men (see McRobbie, 1980 for a feminist critique of this work).

Cultural analysis provides a means of understanding individual experience in a group context. We are both determined by and potential determinants of social forces. People are neither passive reflections of stereotyped images and ideas, nor acquiescent victims of oppressive social conditions. Conversely, we are not all active 'social agents', able to make 'free choices' and rise above the most harrowing social conditions through sheer effort, willpower or 'individual resourcefulness' (see Griffin *et al.*, 1980 for a critique of this approach). Qualitative cultural analysis tries to maintain that tension between the individual as active social agent, the product of a given 'life history', capable of making positive decisions and choices, and the individual as influenced by specific social structures and ideologies. The stress on the cultural as it ties the individual to the group is the key to holding on to both sides of this particular relationship.

When I used this form of cultural analysis, I was aware that it had been developed to explain the experiences of mainly white and working-class men, as had the very concept of 'culture'. I also knew that other women working on girls' and women's schooling had expressed serious reservations about the potential value of cultural analysis. Walden and Walkerdine (1982) and Davies (1979) have questioned the relevance of concepts such as 'culture' and 'identity' to an understanding of female experience. The former have identified specific 'discursive practices' in a Foucauldian analysis of mathematics education for girls. Davies has preferred a form of interactional analysis which looks for the various 'social scripts' associated with given roles and social positions. McRobbie has worked within the cultural studies framework, maintaining a feminist critique and developing her own analysis of a white working-class 'culture of femininity' (see McRobbie, 1978).

My own approach falls between Davies's analysis and McRobbie's cultural framework. I also felt the pressure to fit young women's experiences into the dominant cultural paradigm, and to identify 'feminine' cultural forms. At first I too searched for female equivalents to Willis's 'lads' and 'earoles', striving to identify female pro- and anti-school cultures, and the cultural links between school and the world of full-time employment (see Willis, 1977). I tried in vain to fit the young women's experiences into this 'gang of lads' format, but their lives were far too complex.

I found no neat link between young women's attitudes to school, their status as 'good girls' or 'trouble-makers', their expectations about full-time employment, and their eventual positions in the labour market. Berni, for example, defined herself and her four girlfriends as 'mad', and teachers referred to them as 'trouble-makers'. They all detested the 'swots' and 'pets' who hoped to leave school and get office jobs. Berni's first priority was to leave school as soon as was legally possible: 'any job will do'. She ended up with two CSEs and a job as an office junior, spending her leisure time as a 'weekend punk'.[4]

My difficulties with this form of cultural analysis did not arise because Paul Willis's arguments were misguided: they simply did not apply to these young women's lives (see Davies, 1979). The latter did not go around in large groups or 'gangs' with fairly static memberships and recognizable styles or identities. Their 'culture' was based on close, sometimes intense, friendships which were continually shifting, usually involving three or four, perhaps only two, young women. Although the structure of these groups differed from that of their male counterparts, they still operated with some 'shared principles of life' (e.g., the importance of 'having a laugh'). So I did not abandon cultural analysis altogether, but tried to use it without tying the notion of culture to a 'gang of lads' model. Like Lynn Davies, I saw young women as able to adopt a range of different (though limited) strategies in a given situation, which would have varying social meanings and implications depending on the young women's position.

So a female student might use a sullen, uncooperative stare to undermine a teacher's authority, but because girls receive less attention than boys in school, this form of silent resistance could work against them (see Griffin, 1982a; Spender, 1980). When they adopted more vocal and visible forms of resistance, young women tended to be written off by teachers (and male students) as a 'bunch of giggling girls' (see Stanworth, 1981). The dominant images of female deviance in school centred not on aggressive 'macho' disruption, but on uncontrolled sexuality (Griffin, 1982b).

Qualitative cultural analysis and feminist research

I was forced to recognize the political implications of the research from the outset. While Paul Willis admitted that he had never been asked 'why only boys?', teachers, employers, young people and some (male) researchers often asked me why I was talking mainly to young women. Exclusively male studies pass without comment, accepted as perfectly normal, whereas my work was seen as unusual from the start. I was frequently assumed to be a feminist, simply because I was a woman interested in young women's lives.

I was careful to present a suitably 'feminine' appearance (no monkey boots or dyed pink hair), and I never mentioned feminism because of the overwhelmingly negative media representations of 'women's lib'. Despite my precautions, one headmaster of a small mixed comprehensive took me aside to inform me exactly why 'this equal opportunities thing is a waste of time'. The headmistress of a large girls' comprehensive made similar assumptions about the 'political' nature of the research, but her 'little talk' was more supportive. She told me of the barriers to women's promotion in teaching, and her opinion of the project: 'Girls have such a low self-image, and so do women teachers, I'm all in favour of your study.' Like so many of the women I talked to, she prefaced her more 'controversial' (i.e., feminist) statements with the disclaimer, 'I'm not a women's libber but'.

Since I could hardly avoid the gender-related political implications of the research, my ideas about methodology were influenced in part by the developing debates about feminist research in and outside of the women's liberation movement (e.g., Eichler, 1980; McRobbie, 1982; Stanley and Wise, 1983).

Feminist academics have objected to the sexist language used in many studies which either ignore or marginalize women, and judge them according to a norm of male experience. Social science has been criticized for its emphasis on rational objectivity, its rigid hierarchical structure, and the individualistic methods of generating and sharing knowledge (Spender, 1980; Roberts, 1981). Feminists have not been alone in criticizing social science on these terms, but they have focused on the way that this has denied and distorted women's experiences, presenting a specific 'male' view of the world.

Many older people (I include myself and other feminists and researchers here), and especially those who make decisions about young people's lives, see young working-class women as 'silly giggling girls', 'jailbait' or future 'supermums'. Social science research has kept these young women silent and invisible (on anything other than male terms), and done little to challenge or transform these assumptions (McRobbie, 1980). Qualitative cultural analysis has the potential to move beyond these preconceptions, with its stress on 'knowing the internal dynamics of the situation as experienced by the participants' (Willis, 1980).

While qualitative methods and cultural analysis have particular advantages for research concerning women's lives, they are not the *only* appropriate methods in this respect. Quantitative research can provide valuable insights into women's – and men's – positions. These different methods should be used with an awareness of their relative strengths and weaknesses, in the context of an approach that recognizes the political implications of 'doing research'.

Notes

1 Although I interviewed young Asian and Afro-Caribbean women (and some young men) in schools and workplaces, I followed young white women into the labour market. As a white woman, I decided that it would be more appropriate for me to look at white racism (both my own and that of white participants), as it structured the lives of young white and black women. The recent 'ethnic minority' studies have constructed black cultures and black people as a problem, and I wanted to turn this around and focus on a more obvious source of racist 'inequalities': white people and white cultures.
2 These topics included students' experiences of school, teachers, friendship groups, expectations of full-time waged work, unemployment, present and future family life, domestic work, leisure, part-time jobs, etc. I did not use a pre-set interview schedule or sit with a list of questions in front of me, but I did operate with a predetermined (and memorized) set of key questions.
3 Most young working-class men move into jobs which fall into a fairly clear hierarchy based on differential skill levels. Young women's jobs have no equivalent structure, since where their work is skilled (e.g., typing, shorthand, sewing), this is seldom reflected in the pay, promotion prospects or on-the-job training provision (see Griffin, 1985).
4 This was in 1979 and 1980. Everyone mentioned in this paper is referred to by a pseudonym.

References

Davies, L., 'Deadlier than the male? Girls' conformity and deviance in school', in Barton, L., and Meighan, R. (eds), *Schools, Pupils and Deviance*, Driffield, Nafferton, 1979.

Education Group, CCCS (eds), *Unpopular Education: Schooling and Social Democracy in England since 1944*, London, Hutchinson, 1981.

Eichler, M., *The Double Standard: A Feminist Critique of Feminist Social Science*, London, Croom Helm, 1980.

Glaser, B. and Strauss, A. L., *The Discovery of Grounded Theory*, Chicago, Aldine, 1967.

Griffin, C., 'Cultures of femininity: Romance revisited', stencilled paper, CCCS, Birmingham University, 1982a.

Griffin, C., 'The good, the bad and the ugly: Images of young women in the labour market', stencilled paper, CCCS, Birmingham University, 1982b.

Griffin, C., *Typical Girls? The Transition from School to Un/employment for Young Working Class Women*, London, Routledge and Kegan Paul, 1985.

Griffin, C. et al., 'Women and leisure', paper presented at 'Leisure and social control' conference, CCCS, Birmingham, 1980; also in Hargreaves, J. (ed.), *Sport, Culture and Ideology*, London, Routledge and Kegan Paul, 1982.

Hebdige, D., *Subcultures: The Meaning of Style*, London, Methuen, 1979.

McRobbie, A., 'Working class girls and the culture of femininity', in Women's Studies Group, CCCS, *Women Take Issue*, London, Hutchinson, 1978.

McRobbie, A., 'Settling accounts with subcultures', *Screen Education*, **34**, 1980, pp. 37–49.

McRobbie, A., 'The politics of feminist research: Between talk, text and action', *Feminist Review*, **12**, 1982, pp. 46–57.

Roberts, H. (ed.), *Doing Feminist Research*, London, Routledge and Kegan Paul, 1981.

Spender, D., *Man Made Language*, London, Routledge and Kegan Paul, 1980.

Stanley, L. and Wise, S., *Breaking Out: Feminist Consciousness and Feminist Research*, London, Routledge and Kegan Paul, 1983.

Walden, R. and Walkerdine, V., 'Girls and mathematics: The early years', University of London Institute of Education, Bedford Way Papers no. 8, 1982.

Williams, R., *Politics and Letters: Interviews with New Left Review*, London, New Left Books, 1979.

Willis, P., *Learning to Labour: How Working Class Kids Get Working Class Jobs*, Farnborough, Saxon House, 1977.

Willis, P., 'Shop floor culture, masculinity and the wage form', in Clarke, J., *et al.* (eds) *Working Class Culture*, London, Hutchinson, 1979.

Willis, P., 'Notes on method', in Hall, S. *et al.* (eds). *Culture, Media, Language*, London, Hutchinson, 1980.

19 Talking about school: the experiences of young lesbians and gay men

Lorraine Trenchard and Hugh Warren

Schools need to deal sensitively and appropriately with such issues as contraception, sexually transmitted diseases, homosexuality and abortion. (*Health Education from 5 to 16*, Department of Education and Science Report, 1986)

Sexuality, and especially homosexuality and lesbianism, has always been a delicate and controversial topic as far as educational institutions have been concerned. In schools sexuality generally has been under-researched, and there has been little examination of the experiences of young lesbians and gay men within these institutions. The issue has been neglected despite the fact that the school years are often the critical years for young people coping with a growing sexual awareness; sometimes an awareness of being homosexual.

Dealing with the issue of homosexuality or lesbianism in a sensitive and appropriate way is made all the more difficult for teachers because of the paucity of relevant literature, be that general or research material. However, teachers may be constrained in how they might themselves research the issue because of factors such as the law about the age of consent for male homosexuals (21 years), the problems of pupils 'coming out' and saying that they are homosexual, and the problems of labelling and harassment which might follow this. Gaining trust within an environment which these young people will have experienced as hostile and threatening, and overcoming the power-based nature of staff–pupil relationships may make such research extremely difficult. How could pupils be convinced of the protection of confidentiality in an environment where the pressures not to be identified as lesbian or gay are enormous? Given all of these factors, would the number of pupils willing to take part in such research be large enough for any statistically useful findings?

These are some of the questions which were considered when we explored the feasibility of conducting such research within the context of a single school, or with a group of young pupils who had 'come out' and were interviewed within the school setting. The research project set up by the London Gay Teenage Group took school experiences as one of its major themes (a separate booklet was produced on its findings; see Warren, 1984). Our sample was not contacted through formal education institutions – schools and further/higher education – but rather through leisure clubs, support groups (particularly developed in London) and through a media campaign to find young lesbians and gay men under 21 years old, who lived in London.

The advantages of this approach were that young people were self-identified and

Source: Commissioned.

volunteered their contribution. The anonymity and confidentiality we guaranteed using survey methods meant that we were likely to obtain accounts about young gay and lesbian experiences in school from a broader and more representative sample. Many of our respondents, had they been asked for information in school, would not have felt able to articulate their feelings because they had not yet identified them or come to terms with them. The choice of filling in the questionnaire gave individuals the chance to be positive about their sexuality. Also the range of respondents' experiences meant that we could learn about different educational institutions (e.g. mixed and single sex schools, public and comprehensive schools, schools in different areas).

The research had to be exploratory due to the lack of pre-existing research. It could, therefore, only give indications of where the problems lay for young lesbians and gay men. School was only one aspect of these young people's lives which we investigated (we also looked at experiences within the family, other educational institutions, accommodation, social life, sex and relationships, employment and so on). As our initial research required considerable amounts of information about a variety of facets of these young people's lives, we opted for a questionnaire. Time and financial limitations, and the problem of access to respondents made a survey the best choice of method. The information collected was later supplemented by interviews, including interviews with gay teachers.

The questionnaire we used consisted mainly of multiple choice questions, but about one-quarter of the questions were open-ended. This allowed respondents to raise their own issues or comment in more detail about their experiences. The results of this research were summarized and published as a 168 page report titled *Something to tell you* (Trenchard and Warren, 1984). On the strength of this report the research project was funded for a further year (by the Greater London Council). During the second year we were able to examine specific areas in more detail; one of these areas was school.

The experiences of the gay and lesbian young people we surveyed were dramatic. Our sample of 416 respondents consisted of two-thirds male, predominantly white (88 per cent), and almost half (45 per cent) self-defined working-class young people. They were, on the whole, surprisingly positive or open about their sexuality: 93 per cent had told someone that they were lesbian or gay; 70 per cent had told at least one member of their family; 57 per cent defined themselves as 'completely lesbian or gay'; 84 per cent had had sex with someone of the same sex and 59 per cent had currently or in the past a 'long-term homosexual lover'. This positive attitude towards their sexuality was surprising because of the harsh treatment and reaction which they had already faced in response to their sexuality: one in five of the sample reported having been beaten up because they were lesbian or gay; six in ten had been verbally abused for the same reason. Also, as a consequence of their sexuality, one in seven had been sent to a psychiatrist, one in ten had been thrown out of home, one in ten had been sent to the doctor, one in five had experienced contact with the police. Perhaps the most frightening figure was that one in five of these young people had attempted suicide because they were lesbian or gay.

The lives of these lesbians and gay men, and their experience of youth had already been shaped by their sexuality and by other peoples' responses to it.

Schools, in particular, had played a significant role in shaping these experiences. For many, it was crucial whether educational institutions offered any support or information to buffer the effect of negative responses to gay or lesbian pupils inside schools and in their lives in general.

School experiences

The majority of the young people in the survey (60 per cent) reported that within their schools the topic of homosexuality or lesbianism had *never* been mentioned in any lesson at all. Furthermore, 80 per cent of the people who said that the topic *had* been mentioned said it was in a way that was not helpful to them. Thus less than one in ten said that homosexuality or lesbianism had been talked about at their school in a way that they found personally helpful. The distribution of subjects in which respondents said that homosexuality had been raised is shown in Table 19.1.

Table 19.1 *School subjects in which homosexuality or lesbianism was mentioned*

Subject	Frequency	Percentage of survey population
English	44	11.0%
Religious education	43	10.0%
Biology	36	8.7%
Sociology	19	4.6%
General studies	12	2.9%
Social studies	12	2.9%
Sex education	11	2.6%
Art	4	1.0%
Life studies	2	0.5%
Psychology	1	0.2%
Other	14	3.4%

While the incidence of discussion about homosexuality or lesbianism was generally low, perhaps the most surprising figure here is that only one in forty said that homosexuality or lesbianism had been mentioned in sex education lessons.

When at school sex education did not touch at all upon gays. There were leaflets and books available on social problems, drugs, abortion, contraceptives, VD, but *nothing* for gays (Male, 20).

I do not remember homosexuality/lesbianism coming up at all in sex education (in my school in the first year) or in discussions on relationships/world issues (in fourth and fifth year RE lessons) (Female, 17).

School sex education said it was perverted, that if your glands over-secrete then you're gay. Young men at a discussion group.

Moreover, we found that schools were failing to provide any recognition of, or information about, homosexuality or lesbianism: for instance, only forty-seven respondents (11 per cent) said that their school library stocked books on the subject, and less than half of these people said that the books that were stocked were helpful. 'The only book it was mentioned in was the Bible' (Female, 19).

Table 19.2 *Problems at school*

Problem	Female freq. + %	Male freq. + %	Overall frequency + %
Isolation/nothing in common with classmates	10 (27%)	28 (24%)	38 (25%)
Verbal abuse	3 (7.7%)	29 (25%)	32 (21%)
Teasing	5 (13%)	15 (13%)	20 (13%)
Beaten up	1 (2.6%)	18 (16%)	19 (12%)
Ostracised	4 (10%)	7 (6.1%)	11 (7.1%)
Pressure to conform	6 (15%)	5 (4.3%)	11 (7.1%)
Other	10 (26%)	13 (11%)	23 (15%)
Total	39 (100%)	115 (100%)	154 (100%)

Note: The total figure, 154, is smaller than the total number of people who said that they had problems because ten respondents did not specify what sort of problems they had.

For nearly half the sample school life had created even more difficulties because of their homosexuality or lesbianism. Not surprisingly a wide variety of problems were described, but there were common problems among those responding. These are shown in Table 19.2. In an environment where homosexuality and lesbianism is rarely even formally acknowledged it is inevitable that young homosexuals, as well as those who are questioning their sexuality, will feel very isolated.

I found that at school I didn't know what gay was, and I felt very alone. When I did eventually get to know what the feeling I had was I was frightened because those who were gay or supposed to look like they were, were picked on. Jokes about gays were very frequent and people were very hostile about gay people, or they took it as a joke (Male, 20).

[I had problems at school as a lesbian because] I wasn't interested in the social life. I was considered boring because I didn't want to go to parties. I wasn't able to talk about girlfriends (Female, 17).

Alienation – everybody seemed to be straight (Male, 20).

It was an all boys' school and they all talked of getting their girlfriends after school, you didn't (Male, 18).

Feelings of insecurity and paranoia that people knew (Male, 20).

The hostility directed at homosexuality and lesbianism in schools is not some form of paranoia in the minds of pupils who are homosexual or lesbian, or feel that they might be: it is very real. Mark Baker (1984), writes in his thesis 'Gays in Education':

It soon became clear to me that the pupils of [a South London Comprehensive] School (especially, but not exclusively, the boys) use the usual terms of abuse associated with gays regularly. Gay abuse is to be found from the first year upward. Not in a specifically sexual sense, although that meaning comes into the abuse as the pupils become more sexually aware, but in a generally negative sense. Anyone who might be a bit slow, or dim, or weak, or ugly, or poorly dressed is liable to be called a poof or queer, etc. So whatever a gay person might really be, these pupils soon learn that is something definitely not to be.

Furthermore, the evidence suggested that this sort of hostility and abuse was usually effectively condoned by staff who did nothing to challenge it, as well as by local education authorities who appeared not to consider these issues serious enough to warrant any action or statement of policy.

What the survey also revealed was that young people were in fact constantly exposed to uninformed and derogatory images of homosexuality and lesbianism through the media, playground talk and anti-homosexual/anti-lesbian jokes. All of these images defined homosexuality and lesbianism as something immoral, unhealthy and unpleasant. Yet at the same time the topic was rarely, if ever, discussed formally in the curriculum or in the classroom. It was this contradiction in how and when homosexuality was discussed that was especially confusing for those young people who felt that they were lesbian or gay.

I found it very difficult at school, mainly because, being surrounded by male classmates who all had girlfriends, I often felt there must be something wrong with me. It might have helped me if we were told simply that not everyone's sexuality is the same (Male, 20).

I was unable to cope with the fact that I felt/saw things differently from everyone else (Male, 20).

I was emotionally confused. The atmosphere was very straight and I had no useful help in coming to terms with my sexuality (Male, 18).

It was also evident that this state of anxiety and stress about such a fundamental and important aspect of an individual as their sexuality and their perception of that sexuality, was likely to have negative effects on their whole life. In school it affected not only the quality of their relationships with other pupils and staff, but also their academic performance.

I had difficulty concentrating on school matters because I didn't understand myself. There needs to be an acknowledgement that teenagers can make decisions about their sexuality at an early age (Female, 20).

Furthermore, such a restrictive environment about sexuality was regarded as not only detrimental to lesbian and gay pupils and those questioning their sexuality. The values implicit in the unchallenged use of anti-lesbian and anti-gay abuse, the neglect of homosexuality in the curriculum, and the lack of any information, support or positive role-models for those questioning their sexuality, all help to create an environment where *all* pupils feel that they have to live up to artificial and very narrowly defined gender-roles and sexualities. As an example, consider Mark Baker's observations at the same South London comprehensive school:

A boy or girl coming to their sexual identity in a school such as this, in which the pressure to be 'normal' is immense, will reject or suppress if they can those aspects of themselves which might bring into doubt their 'normality'. Thus we have the unpleasant spectacle of third, fourth, fifth or whatever year boys being, or trying to be swaggeringly, aggressively, manly. The emphasis is on strength, manliness, macho male chauvinism. Similarly girls have a restrictive model of femininity to live up to.

These restrictive models of sexual identity have a damaging impact on the emotional and sexual health of everyone, and on all human relations. The very negative impression of homosexuality compounded by ignorance is particularly harmful to those coming to see themselves as such, so for them it is important that positive images and ideas be available. But so too for all pupils if we want them to develop into stable, well developed people, confident in themselves and free from the need to denigrate others.

It is also important to bear in mind that *all* young lesbian or gay pupils in schools, whether or not anyone else knows that they are lesbian or gay, are exposed to these pressures and to misinformation about their sexuality. They are all likely to experience the resultant feelings of despair, loneliness, guilt and isolation. Too often staff feel able to mentally assure themselves that there are no 'homosexual problems' in their school as they witness 'queer-bashing'.

Given this background it is remarkable that any young person at school could have the strength and courage to tell anyone that they are lesbian or gay, yet many of our survey population had done so. Just over half of the respondents said that they had told some of their friends that they were lesbian or gay, and a third said that their teachers knew. While these individuals may have been able to enjoy the support of close friends, and perhaps even sympathetic teachers, they were also vulnerable to further pressures and prejudices, often of a less subtle, and more immediate and physical nature. Schoolfriends and teachers are exposed to the same misinformation and prejudices, and so cannot be guaranteed to react favourably.

No one talked to me for a year, I nearly got beaten up and all the girls thought I'd jump them (Female, 17).

Many of our survey population, especially the young men (see Table 19.2), were subjected to verbal and/or physical abuse.

People, especially the boys, kept saying: 'Poof, gay, black bastard'. The usual uneducated names (Male, 19).

I went to an all boys' school and found myself attracted to them. When other boys became aware of this they used to tease me, call me names, etc., I got beaten up once and was frightened to tell the teachers in case it happened again (Male, 19).

Bullying, victimization (Male, 17).

Abuse, both verbal, mental and physical. School sent me to a psychiatrist after I had attempted suicide as a result of said abuse (Male, 20).

Staff may be unaware of this abuse, or unaware of its motivation. Even if staff are aware of this sort of abuse they may be unsure how to tackle it. One young man at a discussion group told us:

They called me 'queer' because I never played football and hung around with girls. I got beaten up and had my face slashed. The teachers didn't know how to deal with it. I had to leave school because of the threats.

Ignorance and insensitivity may also affect a teacher's response:

The Head of Sixth Form, who warned that I might get expelled, enquired if I had been dropped on my head as a baby (Male, 18).

I told my teacher who sent me to psychiatrist (Male, 19).

School referred me to a psychoanalyst or psychiatrist on the pretext of 'being worried about my work'! (Female, 20).

This description of life for young lesbians and gay men in schools is bleak. From such accounts it appears that school *is* pretty bleak for a number of young lesbians and gay men. Yet the survey also identified a range of strategies that can be adopted, often of a very simple and immediate nature, that can help ease the pressures on these young people.

The implications of the research

Evaluating the research project and the reports three years later has revealed that it provided two important resources: an anthology of the experiences of young lesbians and gay men; and statistical evidence about them and their lives. The findings have been useful for raising issues of homosexuality and heterosexism, for example in the adoption of equal opportunities policies which include consideration of lesbian and gay pupils. They have been a useful campaigning resource, and they have provided groundwork for other projects concerning lesbians and gay men in schools (for example, the ILEA Relationships and Sexuality Project). On a broader level, the material has provided some insight into the lives and experiences of young lesbians and gay men.

Teachers may take up these issues by considering alternative strategies for investigating the extent, nature and power of heterosexism and heterosexist attitudes in schools. Systematic examination of teaching resources for heterosexist assumptions and for the presentation of positive lesbian/gay images respectively is one possibility. Surveys of attitudes towards sexuality among staff, pupils and even parents may also be valuable in providing a context for any anti-heterosexist strategies/policies a school might adopt. Once adopted it may be useful to monitor the effectiveness of any such policy or strategy, which in turn presents opportunities for carrying out ongoing longitudinal research within a school.

Issues of sexuality, and homosexuality specifically, have a relevance to a whole range of subjects and areas besides relationships and sex education (though of course homosexuality and lesbianism could always be discussed in any part of the curriculum dealing with these). Lesbians and gay men have a literature, a history and a sociology. These could be dealt with in relevant subject areas, just as the separate history, literature and politics of, say, the Afro-Caribbean community in this country could be discussed. Young lesbians and gay men often have a very different view of society that results from their oppression, and the hostility shown towards their sexuality. This means that they may be able to present a different perspective that may be important and valuable in, for example, lessons looking at sex-role stereotyping and sexism.

There are opportunities to raise the issue of homosexuality throughout the curriculum, in places where at first sight sexuality may appear totally irrelevant, such as a maths or physics lesson. This is quite obvious when the extensive reference to heterosexual lifestyles throughout the curriculum is considered – maths examples that begin 'Mr and Mrs Wilson take out a mortgage of £20,000 . . .', physics examples that begin 'Mr Smith is driving his children to school . . .', design problems like 'Mr Walters is fitting a new kitchen, his wife has specified . . .'. This sort of reference to exclusively heterosexual lifestyles occurs throughout the curriculum and serves to reinforce further the idea of conventional heterosexuality as the only natural and viable option for a young person. This bias can easily be countered if examples of lesbians and gay men were used as illustrations of any particular idea or concept.

There are a number of issues which further research could address. Our research, for example, pre-dated public awareness of AIDS. The attention the media has given the syndrome, its effect on the psychological well-being and the lifestyles of gay men, and the repercussions for lesbians, would obviously have been one area we would have looked at. (This area, sadly, also raises the question of lesbian and gay bereavement, a topic more usually associated with older groups.) The experiences of other age groups was outside our brief, but it would certainly have been interesting to explore these; the effect of the change in the law (the 1967 Sexual Offences Act) and the influence of the Gay Liberation Front in the 1970s. How similar were the experiences of those who were young and gay a decade ago, or a generation ago?

Although our results differentiated between men and women, we had little opportunity to fully explore the implications of these. We might have asked for example how different the experiences of lesbians are compared with their gay male peers? What different influences do sexism and sex-role stereotypes have on young lesbians and young gay men? Does heterosexism affect the sexes differently, especially in the way in which it inhibits a positive self-image?

Many of the same questions could be asked about the experiences of young black and ethnic minority lesbians and gay men: further research is needed to investigate the influence of racism upon these young people. Also what effect do different cultural and religious perspectives have on young lesbian and gay men growing up in a wide variety of environments? The larger research question is, of course, how do issues of gender, race, class and sexual orientation interweave and shape young peoples' lives?

What the survey has achieved is to put the experience of lesbian and gay young people on the agenda in schools and in local education authorities. It is hoped that it has also opened the door on yet another level of the reality of schooling, one which most analysts have so far failed to tackle or even identify.

Note

We would like to thank the Lesbian and Gay Teenage Group (formerly the London Gay Teenage Group) for permission to use material from *Talking about School*.

References

Baker, M., 'Gays in Education', PGCE thesis, University of London, Institute of Education, 1984, unpublished.

Inner London Education Authority, *Relationships and Sexuality Project*, co-ordinator Liz
  Dibb, ILEA TV and Publishing Centre, Thackeray Road, London SW8 3TB.

ILEA Learning Resources Branch, *Positive Images: a resource guide for teaching about
  homosexuality* (including lesbian and gay literature for use by teachers and librarians
  in secondary and Further Education colleges).

Trenchard, L., *Talking about Young Lesbians*, London, London Gay Teenage Group, 1984.

Trenchard, L. and Warren, H., *'Something to tell you': the experiences and needs of young
  lesbians and gay men in London*, London, London Gay Teenage Group, 1984.

Trenchard, L. and Warren, H., *Talking about Youth Work*, London, London Gay Teenage
  Group, 1984.

Warren H., *Talking about School*, London, London Gay Teenage Group, 1984.

Part Five

Researching Teachers: Teachers Researching

20 Traditionalists and trendies: teachers' attitudes to educational issues

*Alison Kelly, with Angela Baldry, Elizabeth Bolton,
Suzanne Edwards, Jo Emery, Charmian Levin, Simon Smith
and Malcolm Wills*

Introduction

Teachers are the bearers of educational change. As Hurn (1978) has demonstrated, opposition from teachers limits the impact of many new ideas in schools; but equally when change does take place it is teachers who implement the innovations. [In this study] we wanted to update and extend our knowledge of teachers' attitudes and the way these varied between different groups.

Pratt *et al.* (1983) have recently completed a detailed analysis of teachers' attitudes on the single issue of sex equality, and found both sex and subject-specialism differences. Women teachers were more emphatic about equality of the sexes than men; English and humanities teachers strongly endorsed equal opportunities, while maths and physical science teachers expressed the most doubts. In our study we wanted to explore teachers' opinions on a range of current issues (including sex equality) and see if we could detect similar patterns.

Data

The data on which this report is based was collected as part of an undergraduate course in Survey Methods. Using random number tables seventy secondary schools in England and Wales were selected from the list of local authority schools in *The Education Authorities Directory and Annual, 1983.* We were interested in six main curriculum areas within the school, namely maths, science, craft, English, modern languages and humanities. Taking each of these in turn, letters containing ten copies of our questionnaire were sent to a Head of Department at each school, with a request to distribute them to members of the department. If the department had less than ten staff members (as most did) Heads were asked to distribute the remaining questionnaires to other teachers in the school. In this way we drew a semi-random sample of 700 teachers from across the country.

An additional sample of 200 teachers was drawn by sending the same letter to the Head of Science and Head of Technical Craft at the ten schools involved with the Girls into Science and Technology (GIST) project [an action research project which attempted to improve girls' attitudes to and achievements in physical science and technology (see Whyte, 1985)]. The letter stated that they were part

Source: Extracted from *British Educational Research Journal*, **II**, no. 2, 1985, pp. 19–104.

of a national study and did not mention GIST. However, it is possible that some teachers in these schools recognized the signature as that of one of the directors of the GIST project.

The final response rate was 43 per cent (47 per cent from the GIST schools and 41 per cent from other schools). This is certainly not as high as we would have liked, but given the indirect manner of distribution and the common complaint of teachers about the number of forms they have to fill in, it is quite encouraging.

The questionnaire consisted principally of a list of thirty-seven statements about education to which teachers were asked to indicate their agreement or disagreement on a five-point scale. Respondents were also asked to give their sex, age group, the type of school in which they worked, main and subsidiary subjects taught, years teaching experience and qualifications. In addition schools were classified on the basis of their addresses into region of the country and size of town served.

The questionnaire invited teachers to comment on any of the issues raised, and many of them did so. A lot of red ink was expended in correcting and improving on the wording of the questions, and many teachers qualified their answers to specific questions, told us about the latest research or apologized for not having read it. In addition several respondents outlined their philosophy of education. For example a history teacher told us that, 'my basic structural view would be that nurture is the basis of character (ideology and culture) and that class is the predominant influence in educational attainment measured by the examination system'.

Results

Teachers' responses to the thirty-seven attitude items are shown in Table 20.1. The replies were scored from 5 for strongly agree to 1 for strongly disagree; means and standard deviations were then computed. The results show that there is considerable unanimity amongst teachers on many of the issues. A majority of teachers strongly disagreed with items such as no. 26, 'boys need more education than girls' and no. 6 'men are better teachers than women'. They also disagreed that 'examinations are the most important part of education' (no. 3) and 'children from ethnic minorities are less academic' (no. 34). Teachers agreed that 'practical subjects are as important as academic subjects' (no. 19), 'parents should be held responsible for the behaviour of their children' (no. 27) and 'it is important to find ways of encouraging girls to study physical science' (no. 20). Most teachers also thought that education led to greater equality of opportunity (no. 4) but that it should not be a political issue (no. 5) – although several commented that education is inevitably political. On some items, such as 'inner city schools are rewarding to teach in' (no. 15) and 'racially mixed are more difficult to teach than white groups' (no. 12) many teachers ringed 'unsure' and commented that they had no experience of these conditions on which to base their opinions.

However, there were some issues on which opinion was sharply divided. The most pronounced of these (with the largest standard deviation) was no. 18, 'all remaining grammar schools should be abolished', closely followed by no. 9, 'corporal punishment should be available in all schools'. Opinion was also divided

Table 20.1 *Teachers' responses to the attitude items*

	Strongly agree (%)	Agree (%)	Unsure (%)	Disagree (%)	Strongly disagree (%)	Mean	s.d.	N
1 I am satisfied with my present school	13	48	16	20	3	3.5	1.0	366
2 Only people with a sense of vocation should teach	28	38	15	16	3	3.7	1.1	372
3 Examinations are the most important part of education (T)	1	6	9	55	29	1.9	0.8	370
4 Education leads to greater equality of opportunity	14	42	17	21	6	3.4	1.1	368
5 Education should not be a political issue (T)	49	23	7	12	8	3.9	1.3	368
6 Men are better teachers than women (S)	1	3	12	30	55	1.6	0.8	367
7 Coeducational schools produce better balanced children than single-sex schools	22	38	26	12	2	3.7	1.0	370
8 Parents should have freedom of choice concerning the school their children attend (T)	23	48	18	8	2	3.8	1.0	365
9 Corporal punishment should be available in all schools (T)	17	33	12	19	18	3.1	1.4	369
10 Very little is learnt in unstructured lessons (T)	8	38	15	32	7	3.1	1.1	367
11 Pupils should be involved in planning the curriculum	2	25	24	39	10	2.7	1.0	367
12 Racially mixed are more difficult to teach than white groups (T)	4	13	41	32	10	2.7	1.0	358
13 Free expression in the classroom should be encouraged (Y)	7	43	21	27	2	3.3	1.0	365
14 Girls are naturally better than boys at art-based subjects (S)	1	5	19	51	25	2.1	0.8	370
15 Inner city schools are rewarding to teach in (T−)	5	18	52	20	5	3.0	0.9	352
16 A-level education is too specialized (T−)	9	31	19	35	6	3.0	1.1	367
17 Mixed-ability groups hold clever children back (T)	22	34	14	23	7	3.4	1.2	369

Table 20.1 *(Cont.)*

	Strongly agree (%)	Agree (%)	Unsure (%)	Disagree (%)	Strongly disagree (%)	Mean	s.d.	N
18 All remaining grammar schools should be abolished (T−)	23	18	11	28	20	3.0	1.5	373
19 Practical subjects are as important as academic subjects (Y)	44	49	3	3	0	4.4	0.7	367
20 It is important to find ways of encouraging girls to study physical science (Y)	34	50	11	5	0	4.1	0.8	370
21 Children from deprived backgrounds can do well if they have special attention (Y)	22	58	16	4	1	4.0	0.8	367
22 Teachers often allow boys to dominate in mixed classes (F)	7	30	21	35	6	3.0	1.1	367
23 The major function of school is to teach social values (Y)	3	23	21	45	8	2.7	1.0	366
24 Boys have a naturally better grasp of science and maths than girls (S)	1	11	23	41	24	2.3	1.0	368
25 Girls can cope with figures as well as boys (S)	28	51	14	5	1	4.0	0.9	368
26 Boys need education more than girls (S)	1	2	4	34	58	1.5	0.8	366
27 Parents should be held responsible for their children (T)	45	43	8	2	1	4.3	0.8	368
28 Pupils should be encouraged to pursue any subject in which they show promise (Y)	42	50	5	3	0	4.3	0.7	371
29 Girls should be encouraged to learn office skills	1	19	21	41	17	2.5	1.0	369
30 School uniform is necessary to maintain discipline (T)	6	26	19	30	18	2.7	1.2	369
31 Teachers should use new developments as much as possible (Y)	17	49	22	12	0	3.7	0.9	369
32 Science is less popular with girls because they receive less encouragement (F)	8	31	26	29	6	3.1	1.1	368

Table 20.1 *(Cont.)*

	Strongly agree (%)	Agree (%)	Unsure (%)	Disagree (%)	Strongly disagree (%)	Mean	s.d.	N
33 All secondary school leavers should have acquired basic computing skills (Y)	14	50	18	16	2	3.6	1.0	368
34 Children from ethnic minorities are less academic (T)	1	5	23	39	32	2.1	0.9	363
35 Pupils should think about their career when choosing subjects (T)	13	60	12	12	3	3.7	0.9	369
36 Most subjects are best taught in mixed-ability groups (T–)	6	13	18	39	23	2.4	1.2	369
37 Lessons are geared to boy's interests rather than girls (F)	2	12	19	51	16	2.3	0.9	368

Notes: (T) TRAD., (S) SEXEQ., (F) FEM., (Y) TRENDY – item reversed before inclusion in scale.

on the question of mixed-ability teaching (nos 17 and 36) and the efficacy of school uniform for maintaining discipline (no. 30). These results suggest that arguments for comprehensive schooling and mixed-ability grouping have still not been completely accepted by the teaching profession.

The responses to individual items can yield many fascinating insights. However, to paint an overall picture of teachers' orientations it is more useful to group the items into scales measuring underlying traits. In this study factor analysis revealed four main dimensions to teachers' attitudes. By far the most pronounced was a general measure of traditionalism (TRAD.) associated with an endorsement of academic values, strict discipline and differentiation among children. The second dimension was equality between the sexes (SEXEQ.) which showed itself in a rejection of the idea that males and females were different in their needs or capabilities. The third factor, feminism (FEM.), was concerned with recognition of the ways in which differentiation between the sexes *does* occur. Finally TRENDY measured teachers' enthusiasm for new ideas in areas as diverse as free expression in the classroom, encouraging girls in science and acquiring basic computing skills. The fact that two of the four scales are concerned with gender-related issues reflects the weighting of questionnaire items in this direction. If there had been an equal number of items concerned with ethnicity, for example, this would probably have emerged as a factor.

The items which go to make up each scale are shown in Table 20.1 and the scale statistics are in Table 20.2. Only teachers who replied to all the items on a scale have a score for that scale. The minimum possible score on each scale is 1 and the maximum 5, with a neutral point of 3.00. TRAD. has 16 items and a high reliability. The mean is slightly on the traditional side of neutral. SEXEQ. has a very high mean, showing that most teachers strongly endorse equality of

Table 20.2   *Scale statistics for the measures of teachers' attitudes*

	No. of items	∞	Mean	s.d.	N
TRAD.	16	.83	3.18	0.59	328
SEXEQ.	5	.76	4.11	0.60	356
FEM.	3	.63	2.78	0.80	365
TRENDY	8	.57	3.74	0.42	345

the sexes. Its reliability is satisfactory. FEM. has a lower reliability, but this is not surprising given that it consists of only three items. Its mean is below the neutral point, showing that most teachers do not think that schooling favours boys. However, FEM. has a larger standard deviation than the other scales, suggesting that there is less agreement among teachers on this issue. The fourth measure, TRENDY, has an unacceptably low reliability for a scale of eight items. This scale also has a less conceptual clarity than the others, consisting as it does of a heterogeneous collection of items. Accordingly it was omitted from subsequent analyses.

Teachers' characteristics

It is clear from [the data] that male and female teachers did not differ in traditionalism. However, there was a marked tendency for women to be more emphatic than men in their statements about equality between the sexes. Women were also more likely than men to endorse a feminist analysis of the present situation. Turning to age differences there was a definite trend for older teachers to be more traditional in their attitudes and less committed to equality between the sexes (although it must be remembered that the over 55 group consisted of only eleven respondents). The age differences were much less marked on FEM. There was a similar pattern with length of teaching experience. Not surprisingly this variable was closely related to age. However, age turned out to be a slightly better predictor for all three scales, and it is used in preference to years spent teaching throughout this report. Graduate teachers appeared to be somewhat less traditional and more feminist than non-graduates.

Some of the most interesting differences emerged when the scale scores were examined in relation to the subject specialism of the teachers. [The statistics show] that the craft teachers, in both technical and domestic areas, were the most traditional. They were followed by maths and science teachers. Modern language and English teachers were much less traditional while the humanities teachers were the most innovatory. This group included history, geography, social studies, religion and economics teachers. This pattern was almost exactly reversed for FEM. The small group of domestic craft teachers emerged as least feminist, followed by the technical craft, science and maths teachers. Humanities and English teachers were the most likely to espouse a feminist approach with modern language teachers scoring slightly above average. The pattern of scores on SEXEQ. was less clear cut. Physics, technical craft and modern language teachers had relatively low scores, with biology, domestic craft and humanities teachers scoring relatively high.

The vast majority of the respondents taught in comprehensive schools and their score is, by definition, close to the mean. The numbers from other types of school are small but it is noticeable that grammar school teachers seemed more traditional and less sure about sexual equality than other teachers, whereas the reverse was true for teachers in secondary modern and miscellaneous other types of school. The number of teachers from single-sex schools was tiny, and no significant relationships were found between this factor and any of the scales.

When the data was analysed by region of the country and size of town from which the teachers came, some interesting patterns emerged, although these were not particularly pronounced. Teachers from the rural areas of Wales, East Anglia and the south-west were considerably more traditional than other teachers, whereas teachers from Greater London were more innovatory. Similarly teachers from large cities were less traditional than those from smaller towns. The variations on SEXEQ. could have arisen by chance, but it is noticeable that teachers from London scored significantly higher than any other group on FEM. It is tempting to attribute this to strong feminist influence on the equal opportunities policy adopted by ILEA.

These factors do not operate independently. In fact the four individual characteristics – sex, age, graduate status and subject taught – were quite strongly interrelated. All the technical craft teachers in the sample were men, and men also predominated among the physical science teachers. Conversely all the domestic craft teachers were women, as were the majority of English and modern language teachers. Humanities, maths and biology teachers were more evenly balanced by sex. Technical and domestic craft teachers were much less likely to be graduates than were teachers of other subjects, and older teachers were also less likely to be graduates. Women teachers were over-represented in the youngest age group and under-represented in the two oldest age groups. However, there were no significant relationships between age and subject taught or sex and qualification. Grammar schools were much more likely than other types of school to be single sex, and they also tended to employ more graduates, more males and more older teachers. There was a strong tendency for boys' schools to employ male teachers and girls' schools females. There was also a strong relationship between region of the country and town size, with teachers from the North, Wales, East Anglia and the south-east being mainly from small or tiny towns and the other regions being mainly represented by large or medium-sized conurbations. Region and town size were also related to sex and subject specialism of the teachers partly due to the over-representation of craft teachers in the north-west because of the GIST sample.

Analysis of variance was employed to examine the four factors of sex, age, graduate status and subject taught simultaneously. Thus older teachers tended to be more traditional whatever subject they taught and irrespective of whether they were male or female, graduate or non-graduate; humanities teachers were more feminist than other teachers of the same age, sex and graduate status. The most notable change is that subject taught was no longer significantly related to SEXEQ. when allowance was made for sex, age and qualification. In particular technical craft teachers were no less in favour of equality between the sexes than men of a similar age teaching other subjects.

Type of school and whether it was single sex or mixed were also combined in an analysis of variance, allowing for sex, age and graduate status of the teachers. The results show that neither of these variables was significantly related to teacher's attitudes when allowance was made for other factors. However, the numbers of teachers not in coeducational comprehensive schools was so small that no firm conclusions can be drawn.

Finally region and size of town were examined together. When this was done the effect of size of town declined quite sharply, but region still had a marked – if barely significant – relationship to teachers' attitudes. In particular London teachers were noticeably less traditional and more feminist than teachers in other large cities such as Birmingham or Manchester. These results were hardly affected when the GIST schools (containing mainly teachers of science and craft in a large town in the north-west) were omitted from the analysis.

Discussion

This study has both confirmed and extended our knowledge of teachers' attitudes. It shows that while the profession is united on many issues, some of the most basic changes of the past twenty years (the abolition of grammar schools and the spread of mixed-ability teaching) are still controversial. In some ways these could be seen as administrative changes which can be introduced irrespective of the opinions of the classroom teachers. But as numerous studies (e.g. Ford, 1969; Ball, 1981) have shown, administrative changes do not *necessarily* alter what goes on within the classrooms. Teachers who remain unconvinced of their value can and do find ways of coping with the new situation so as to minimize the effects of change. This survey showed that the majority of teachers were less than wholeheartedly in favour of mixed-ability teaching and completely comprehensive education, and their views have probably limited the effects of the innovations.

When the items were combined into scales, we found that older teachers, teachers of science and craft subjects and those in rural areas were the most in favour of traditional practices.

Turning to the issue of equality of the sexes we found that older teachers were less convinced than younger teachers and men were less emphatic than women. However, the overall level of agreement was high. The vast majority of teachers disagreed with statements like 'boys need education more than girls' and 'men are better teachers than women'. Although this was not explored in such depth, teachers also seemed to be convinced proponents of racial equality and they overwhelmingly rejected the suggestion that 'children from ethnic minorities are less academic'. However, their belief in sexual equality seemed to blind teachers to the many inequalities that exist in schools. Researchers like Delamont (1980), Spender and Sarah (1980) and Whyld (1983) have documented the ways in which girls are disadvantaged in secondary schools. But most teachers remain either unconvinced or unaware of this work. Science teachers, especially the all-female domestic science staff, were more sceptical than arts teachers.

Pratt *et al.* (1983), found a similar contradiction in teachers' attitudes. They concluded that,

Most teachers were committed to equal opportunities in principle, though they showed decreasing enthusiasm for practical implementation of the principle. Their views were to an extent associated with their sex, but more strongly with subject, with teachers of traditionally stereotyped subjects such as physical science and crafts often holding strongly stereotyped views.

Pratt *et al.* did not build their items into scales measuring the different aspects of attitudes to sex equality. This is an unfortunate omission since we found that there was virtually no relationship between endorsing equality of the sexes (SEXEQ.) and accepting a feminist analysis of current educational practice (FEM.). Nor did they examine the subject differences after controlling for other variables such as sex, age and graduate status. This makes it difficult to compare their results with ours. However, it is noticeable that, when controlled for other variables, we did *not* find that subject taught was strongly related to SEXEQ., although it *was* related to FEM. In particular teachers of science and technical crafts did not score particularly low on SEXEQ., although their FEM. scores were below average. Conversely the sex of the teacher seemed to affect attitudes to equality of the sexes more than it affected perceptions of male domination in class.

The policy implications of these findings are interesting. The idea that girls and boys are basically equal and should have the same opportunities in education seems to be well accepted by teachers. But the idea that there are informal barriers to equal opportunities or that the present system is biased towards boys, is still highly contentious.

The effect that positive action can have can be seen by comparing the FEM. scores of London teachers to those of their colleagues in other parts of the country. ILEA has a strong anti-sexist policy which involves school committees and discussions of feminist issues. GIST teachers have been involved in similar discussions. This does not seem to have affected attitudes to sex equality, which are generally favourable within the teaching profession, and where there is perhaps little room for improvement. But it does appear to have made these teachers more aware of the classroom interactions which disadvantage girls. And this is surely crucial in effecting any lasting alteration.

Conclusion

One of our respondents commented that, 'this questionnaire is far too vague and simplistic for your results to be meaningful', and several others expressed similar views. Clearly many of this highly educated and articulate group felt constrained by the form of the questionnaire. As one said, 'I don't like these type of question-naires. They force you to make unreal decisions. The questions cannot take account of all opinions and therefore are biased. Results cannot be truly accurate. Written sentence answers are much better.' While it is undoubtedly true that written sentences (or indeed interviews) are better than closed questions at reflecting the views of any one individual, it does not follow that they are better for studying the teaching profession as a whole. The more they have to write the fewer people reply; what they do write is difficult to analyse. Despite the inadequacies of this questionnaire – compiled by students with little more than

common-sense knowledge of educational issues or item construction – some fascinating trends have emerged. Another teacher suggested that the questionnaire
was, 'clearly designed to divide the respondents into reactionary/over 35/male/
white on the other hand and trendy/under 35/female on the other', and in some
ways he was right. Teachers' views did divide along these lines. Although individual men and women, old and young, physics and English teachers may have
similar views, on average they disagree. This study aimed to map out the average
teacher's attitude (on the grounds that this affects the average pupil's experience
of education) and for this the closed questionnaire is most effective. It is of course
quite valid for any individual teacher or pupil, to say, 'that's not how it is for
me'. But the task of mapping individual experiences belongs to the biographer.
We hope that many more will recognize the picture of the statistical average
which we have presented here. And we hope that reformers and policy makers
in education will find it useful to know what teachers think about various issues
and where they may expect to find support for or opposition to their innovations.

References

Ball, *Beachside Comprehensive*, London, Cambridge University Press, 1981.

Delamont, S., *Sex Roles and the School*, London, Methuen, 1980.

Ford, J., *Social Class and the Comprehensive School*, Henley, Routledge and Kegan Paul,
1969.

Hurn, C., *The Limits and Possibilities of Schooling*, London, Allyn and Bacon, 1978.

Pratt, J., Seale, C. and Bloomfield, J., *Option Choice: a question of equal opportunity*, Slough,
NFER/Nelson, 1984; or *Curricular Differences in Secondary Schools: a report for the equal
opportunities commission*, May 1983.

Spender, D. and Sarah, E. (eds), *Learning to Lose*, London, The Women's Press, 1980.

Whyld, J. (ed.), *Sexism in the Secondary Curriculum*, London, Harper and Row, 1983.

Whyte, J., *Getting the GIST*, Henley, Routledge and Kegan Paul, 1985.

21 Anti-sexist action research in school: the Girls and Occupational Choice Project

Lynne A. Chisholm and Janet Holland

Introduction

In the tradition of action research the Girls and Occupational Choice (GAOC) project was designed to investigate a social phenomenon while simultaneously attempting to change the situation. This chapter gives an account of the project as anti-sexist educational action research, describing the nature of collaboration in schools to produce anti-sexist curricula, and considering some of the methodological issues arising from this form of action research.[1]

This kind of project has a number of advantages for both teachers and researchers which are not so readily available to research studies which remain distanced from practice or curriculum development as an isolated activity. The *simultaneous* inquiry into gender specific occupational choice and into methods of introducing change, using the curriculum as a focus, provides access to the processes of schooling as a complex, differentiated phenomenon. It is only when the different aspects of those processes are seen in relation to each other that we can move towards a deeper understanding of what schooling means, in this case especially for girls.

Linking the study of schoolgirls with curriculum development created an arena in which the concerns of teachers and researchers could be combined in ways which were both theoretically and practically productive. We could discover more about how existing curricula deliver messages about gender roles, and at the same time use the idea of 'hidden messages' as a theme within the project's curriculum units to deconstruct those messages with the pupils themselves. We could look at the ways teaching styles and methods interact with curriculum content to promote or subvert anti-sexist aims, and simultaneously explore the possibilities of alternatives. In considering girls' experiences of schooling, we could take account of teachers' constructions of their pupils along gender-specific dimensions. In the same way, teachers could make use of researchers' constructions in addition to their own in the process of developing professional understanding and making judgements about their own and their pupils' actions. The experience of developing anti-sexist curricula necessitated a measure of critical self-analysis, which in turn could be reflected back into pedagogic practice. This last may not necessarily have been what all the teachers with whom we worked expected at the outset, but it became one of the most rewarding aspects of their involvement with the project.

Source: Commissioned.

Project design and methods

The GAOC project had two interrelated strands. First, a pure (as opposed to applied) research component, which consisted of an investigation of the processes which girls of 11–16 go through in coming to decisions about their future work. Theory and data in this area are limited, and we saw this part of the study as generating both. The target group was working-class girls, but boys were included for comparative purposes. The research techniques specific to this part of the study were a series of questionnaires and recurrent interviews over a period of three years.

Second, the action research component, which involved working in close collaboration with teachers on the development of curriculum-focused intervention strategies designed to attack sex stereotypical occupational choice for *both* sexes, but centred on girls, and directed towards first and third year pupils in three London schools. This aspect of the study necessitated long periods of immersion in schools in interaction with teachers and pupils, developing, transmitting and evaluating tailor-made curriculum units, and using a wide range of research techniques. The proposal for curriculum development came from the research team, and so was not a grassroots initiative, but was premised upon close collaboration with teachers.

At this level, the project involved school-based curriculum innovation and change in which strategies specific to the particular school context could be devised and implemented using the resources of existing institutions and supported by the research team. For us it had seemed clear that this could only take place on the basis of collaborative work with volunteer teachers committed to the project's aims. This precludes the notion of ideological neutrality on the part of the teacher, and on the contrary, we hoped that commitment to positive action for girls would form a basis for solidarity and partnership in the teacher/researcher teams. We saw our role as facilitative and working in equal partnership with teachers, envisaging that this, in conjunction with the hoped for shared political commitment, would ease the potential tensions typically found in relations between researchers and teachers (e.g. Shipman, 1975; Freeman, 1986).

The project as a whole has assembled research data dealing with occupational aspirations, expectations and perceptions of the labour market for approximately 1000 girls and boys aged 11–16 in four state comprehensives (three coeducational and one single sex girls' school), all predominantly working class. We worked with children in the first, third and fifth years in these schools over a period of three years. A partially overlapping but largely different and smaller number of children took part in the curriculum development aspect of the project's work. This has ranged from 100 children in the first year of the project, to roughly 250 in the third year. Initially we worked with one girls' and one mixed comprehensive school; did pure research only in a third (mixed) school; and used a fourth school as a control, to provide basic information on job aspirations and destinations.[2] The research is still in progress, in that we have yet to analyse all the material systematically;[3] we have been primarily engaged so far in the curriculum development work and its dissemination.

We saw the action research as consisting of two related processes: first, the process of development of the curriculum units; and second, the process the children went through during the implementation of these units. Over time, a third, unintended, process assumed equal importance; the process of consciousness-raising for teachers, which had both positive and negative outcomes.

The curriculum development process

A working party of volunteer teachers was set up in each school and met weekly for a term to discuss the characteristics and problems of the school and pupils, and what the teachers considered it important to cover in the curriculum units. In each of the two schools in which the intervention took place in the first year of the project, the working party developed a scheme outlining the aims of the curriculum unit in that school context, the issues which thus needed to be addressed, and the lesson content which would be required. Figure 21.1 gives the scheme developed for one school. The teachers planned and taught the lessons, the researchers provided materials and an extensive back-up programme of visitors, visits, videos and other activities. Figure 21.2 gives the teacher/researcher division of labour. Both the content and style of curriculum development varied in the different school contexts. Some teachers wanted a very specific programme with detailed lessons plans; others wanted to be able to construct their own lessons from a resource bank of materials and ideas which we were to provide (see for example Worksheet 1).

The resulting teaching programmes were slotted into schools' curricula in a variety of ways: for example in a regular slot each week, as part of the pastoral programme, or social education; as the programme for one particular department for a set period; or inserted into the timetable of particular teachers who were working with us and were able to provide the time. The departments to which we gravitated were English or humanities. Careers programmes in which we might have expected to find a home are not generally provided in schools for the age groups with which we worked. In fact, teachers frequently objected to the introduction of issues relating to work with such young children, but for us it was crucial to reach the girls prior to option choice at 14. At this point they typically drop those subjects which could potentially lead to a wider range of occupational possibilities; patterns of option choice are still radically gender differentiated (see Pratt *et al.*, 1984).

Curriculum intervention was not for us an end in itself, but a means to an end: that of changing the children's attitudes and perceptions relating to gender divisions and stereotyping, their level of information in crucial areas to do with women's work, and indeed, ultimately, their occupational choices. We had objectives, and the efficacy of the content and transmission of the curriculum units which were developed could be measured in these terms.[4] But equally if not more important for evaluation has been detailed feedback from the teachers on all aspects of the curriculum development process; we observed more than 80 per cent of the lessons in the second year of the project. During the course of the action research itself such observations formed the basis for discussions with teachers in which we compared our perceptions of and responses to a particular session within the teaching programme. We thus were able to adapt activities

Figure 21.1 Scheme for curriculum unit School B

Identified problem	Goals	Methods
1A Severely depressed labour market 1B Class and gender related restriction of occupational horizons	1 Raise awareness of significance of skills and training 2 Identify the promising 'spaces' for women in contrast to the dangers of traditional choices 3 Disconnect occupational horizons from gender and class	1.1 Explain the significance of scientific/ technical based jobs and skills, at all levels for the future 1.2 Illustrate from patterns of women's employment how currently opportunities are not being optimized 1.3 Introduce low visibility occupations 1.4 Promote traditional male-dominated occupations within class-related horizons as suitable/promising for women 1.5 Propose that choosing occupations more strategically can secure greater stability for future family by optimizing both sexes' chances, but especially women's given existing patterns, i.e. families have more to gain relatively by improving women's situation
2A Lack of confidence and low self-esteem: both sexes 2B Fatalism and passivity: both sexes	1 Locate sources of problem and build from there 2 Encourage effective use of *existing* opportunities	2.1 Explore gender and class correlates of esteem 2.2 Point up positive aspects of working-class and female cultures and traditions 2.3 Provide positive role models e.g. community activists, members of self-help groups 2.4 Introduce strategies for achieving change

3 Persistence of very entrenched traditional sex-role attitudes, behaviour	1 Offer attractive and plausible alternatives	3.1 Explore sex-roles through
		  – option choice patterns
		  – own experiences in family/ community (e.g. the domestic division of labour)
		3.2 Provide positive role-models (e.g. house-husbands, single parents, etc.)
		3.3 Demonstrate advantages to both sexes of alternatives
		3.4 Explain that paid employment is the major route to economic independence and security for women as it is for men

Figure 21.2   Teacher/researcher division of labour

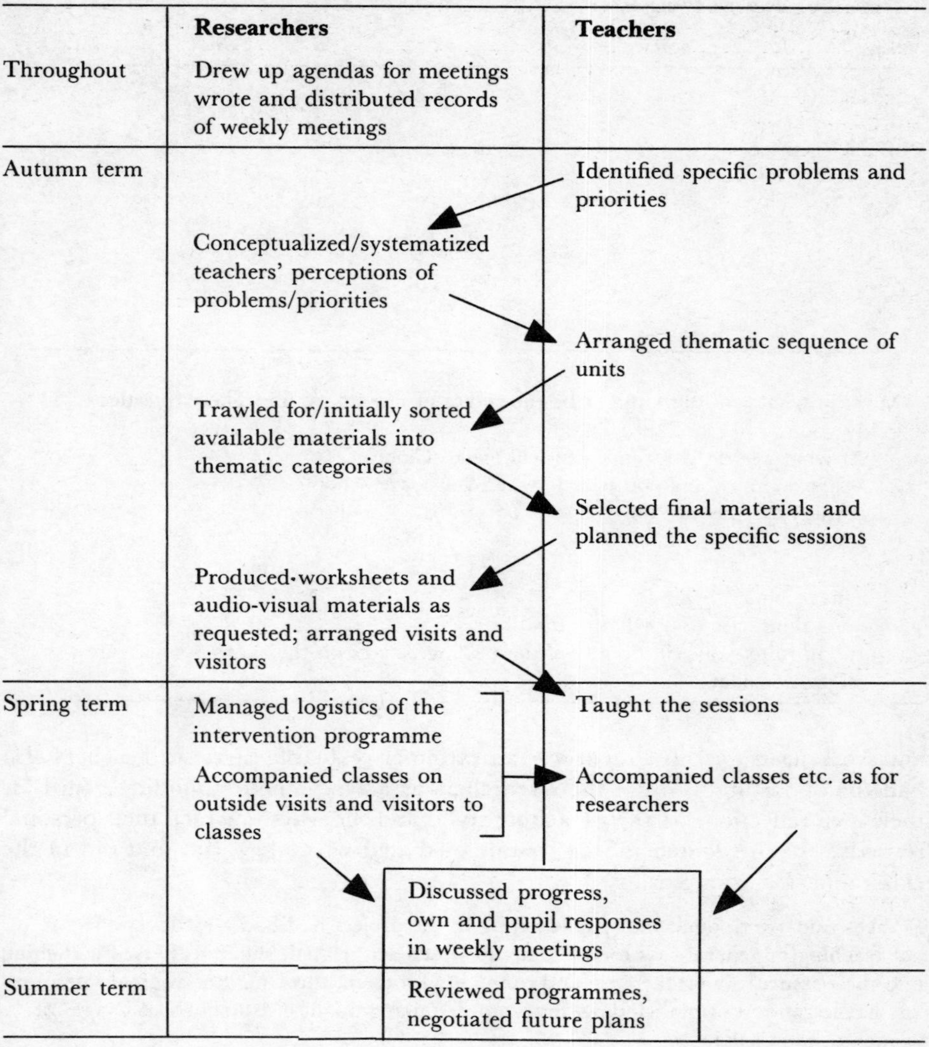

	Researchers	**Teachers**
Throughout	Drew up agendas for meetings wrote and distributed records of weekly meetings	
Autumn term		Identified specific problems and priorities
	Conceptualized/systematized teachers' perceptions of problems/priorities	
		Arranged thematic sequence of units
	Trawled for/initially sorted available materials into thematic categories	
		Selected final materials and planned the specific sessions
	Produced worksheets and audio-visual materials as requested; arranged visits and visitors	
Spring term	Managed logistics of the intervention programme	Taught the sessions
	Accompanied classes on outside visits and visitors to classes	Accompanied classes etc. as for researchers
	Discussed progress, own and pupil responses in weekly meetings	
Summer term	Reviewed programmes, negotiated future plans	

Worksheet 1

How long is a working life?

Age	10	20	30	40	50	60	70

Mark in what you think might be the stages of *your* future life. These questions will guide you.

1   At what age do you think you will leave school?
2   What do you think you will do when you leave school?
   a study, further training
   b work
   c marry
   d have children
   e anything else. Say what that will be.
   If you think you will do any of these things, mark on the chart at what age you might do them.

and worksheets for subsequent use, an extremely valuable exercise. Teachers also had the opportunity to use the researchers as a sympathetic sounding board for their own reflections on their teaching styles and the ways in which their personal responses to the content of the lessons mediated what they said and did in the classroom, for example:

Frances said she'd found that participating in the project had had a spillover effect into her teaching in general – as topics come up which are related, she finds herself launching into these issues, taking them up and running with them, throwing her original intentions for that lesson out of the window, for example talking about censorship and images of women in the media.

Content of the curriculum units

The two main themes which emerged in all curriculum units developed through the project were sex roles and stereotypes, and what work means in people's lives.[5] Three principles underlay the work on stereotypes and sex roles with the pupils: first, to use their own experience – the school is a good starting point; second, to take care that in exposing stereotypes to scrutiny they are not reinforced – again limitations to and alternatives for stereotypical behaviour and beliefs can be found in the pupils' own experience, but a range of other sources of counter-examples were also used; and third, to avoid devaluing both the traditional areas of women's work and concerns in the family, and *positive* aspects of gender stereotypes, which inevitably form part of the self-identity of the pupils. Uncovering hidden messages about sex-roles in all forms of media proved a useful exercise in this context. One first-year teacher obtained reading books from the pupils' former primary school to use in this way. The children were initially excited and engaged by the familiarity of the material but during the course of the lesson were able to change perspective on these books from their past. As the teacher put it 'They were interested in what was going on, they caught on to the idea that there's more than one level in the book, and that was a genuine discovery for them. One girl made a mental leap beyond that: "*You* are trying to give us a hidden message".'

To describe 'what we did in the classroom' solely in terms of the substantive content would be misleading, for it implies neglect of what is at least as important in anti-sexist curriculum development: critical reflection upon teaching methods and classroom practices. A number of issues are involved here. First, the need to use alternative and more varied methods than the traditional ones of 'chalk and talk' and teacher-directed question and answer sessions. These methods are compatible with a classroom environment characterized by authoritarianism and hierarchy, and favour patterns of interaction founded on competition and reaction. Other types of teaching method – small group discussions, role play etc. – are certainly attractive to teachers and used widely, but they demand a recasting of the structure and dynamics of the teaching–learning context which is both challenging and on occasion threatening. For some teachers such a recasting can cast doubt on their acquired professional perceptions of the self and the teaching act. There is reason to suppose, however, that such teaching methods are more in accord with exploiting the positive aspects of female perspectives and interaction patterns. They are an important part of bringing girls in from the periphery of the classroom.

Second, new curriculum content, a wider range of methods and learning to reflect critically do not guarantee that what happens in the classroom is a perfect example of the anti-sexist curriculum in action. This is partly because of the complexity of the task at hand, but equally because essentially the curriculum in action is only a momentary snapshot of an endless filming process. Nevertheless the project field notes show very clearly just how important the issues are, as indicated in the following two extracts:

Daniel obviously needs a lot of feedback, he is worried about his own teaching and his own sexism. He's enthusiastic about the programme but he thinks it needs reworking, he wants us to have a long meeting. . . . In all the lessons I've observed [during group tasks] I go round and talk to the children, so I'm not totally aware of what Daniel is doing . . . he [feels he pays] more attention to the boys and that he should try to balance this. . . . The only thing he is negative about is that some of the worksheets are pitched at too high a level. . . . He says it is very important that this kind of material goes out continuously. . . . That the school shouldn't buy sexist books even if it is good literature. It's difficult not to feel guilty for not giving Daniel as much feedback as he seems to need, making time and space for him to come and talk to me . . . right then I wanted to hare back to the Institute, there's loads of stuff I could do . . . but I stayed because of a feeling of the need for contact.

This week . . . Tom was much more relaxed, more confident. . . . The pupils were more responsive, made less noise. . . . He had prepared the lesson, introducing it as follows: 'This week we are going on to talk about . . . the kind of jobs women have. How women earn their living is very important. Some girls have been asking me why we have to do this topic, they've been saying it's only me that wants to do it. Well – and girls, I'm speaking especially to you now – you might not think it's important now, but I'm sure you'd all agree women should get as much money as men, wouldn't you?' Shouts of agreement from the girls. 'Well, that's why we're doing this.' The class are reasonably quiet . . . but the girls make comments indicating lack of interest. Tom tries to continue . . . introducing the topic of women as cleaners. . . . There is a general hullabaloo as he hands out the text about a woman cleaner. . . . He insists they get down to work: 'I want absolute quiet for ten minutes.' And they do indeed, set to work, although the group of boys at the back continued a bit of provocation for a while: 'Sir, this is a load of rubbish . . .'. A real discussion begins with the two front 'girls' tables, the boys remaining quiet. . . . The basic point Tom tries to get across is that although it's true that some men can be cleaners, or nurses, it's a matter of what is usually the case. . . . The kids have difficulty understanding this point. . . . Tom is interrupted in mid-flow by further comments and questions, so that he is continually distracted. . . . But both Tom and the girls are really involved in the discussion. However, this means the rest of the class are left to their own devices! . . . Predictably, the lesson ends with Joey being given a detention for shouting and answering back, and after the rest have left, two girls remain, the first quietly plaiting the hair of the second.

Tensions in collaborative action research

Four major areas of potential conflict or difficulty became apparent in the course of the project. First there were a cluster of issues associated with the teachers' work situation, which is typically one of overload and stress, to which we were adding the demands of the project. There was a lack of time to discuss fully the issues involved in the project. Added to this, the differing motivations of working party members led to problems in research relations and implicit or explicit mutual imputations of self-interest.

The political issue, which we had hoped would provide the cement for teacher/researcher relations, was in fact another potential area for conflict. The project was based on positive discrimination for girls, the intention was to work with committed teachers in sympathy with this position, but this was not always the case. In addition and not surprisingly, some members of the school communities, often in positions to impede progress on the project, were overtly hostile towards our aims.

But the crux of the matter is the teacher/researcher relation, the traditional objection of teachers to researchers, and the questioning of the value of educational research. At a very immediate level in our project the issues which lay behind this uneasy relation were related to professional capacity and competence. Were we as researchers competent, was our contribution relevant? And from the teachers' side these issues of competence were exacerbated by the nature of the content of the study – teachers who felt effective in their own subject areas sometimes said they lacked confidence in dealing with what they saw as a new and complex area, that of gender relations. At a more general level the relationship between researchers and practitioners traditionally has been perceived as the relationship between theory and practice. We will pursue at this more general level basic problems which confront the researcher engaged in action research, and then provide illustrations from our experience.[6]

In principle action research is predicated upon collaboration, negotiation and reflexivity, and ideally there should be constant interaction between the research function and the action. Action research, as a site for the generation of grounded theory (Glaser and Strauss, 1967; Glaser, 1978) particularly in the context of education, could provide a mode of inquiry which might narrow the gap between theory and practice. But what are the obstacles to this happy synthesis?

Essentially research activity involves a systematic, rigorous and verifiable investigation and interpretation of events and processes. Within a specified set of assumptions and qualifications, it aims to produce an explanation for some aspect of social reality which is plausible and potentially generalizable. This model presupposes that the researcher has control over the research act. In contrast, action research is engaged and interactive. If genuine collaboration between researcher and practitioner is to take place, control cannot reside in one set of hands. Interestingly enough we might define success as the moment when the researcher sees the research design slipping away and the action taking over. We certainly experienced this on the project.

The focus in action research is on processes rather than objectives. Often outcomes cannot be predicted or perhaps specifically defined in advance, although it is clear that every action research project must have an overall framework of general aims, objectives and desirable outcomes to be worth embarking on. It is the lack of specified behavioural or institutional outcomes, in combination with the case specific nature of the processes under investigation, which is frequently taken as evidence that action research is unproductive and ungeneralizable. It could be suggested, however, that it is *the failure to communicate the outcomes of action research satisfactorily* which is at fault here, and it is at this point that theory becomes important.

As far as *feminist* research is concerned, the 'terrors' of the theory/practice split have led to what has appeared to be an action research imperative (Mies, 1983) and a focus on the nature of research relations, with the emphasis on symmetrical democratic relationships between professional women researchers and their lay research partners (Oakley, 1981; Stanley and Wise, 1983). The debate continues, and it is clear that no easy solutions exist.

The project's experiences

We have said that our intention was to work as equal partners with teachers committed to the overall objectives of the project in the action research process of developing, implementing and evaluating curriculum intervention units. In practice the situation was somewhat different. In some instances the teachers who volunteered for our working parties were indeed deeply committed to the principles on which the project was based, and worked tirelessly towards the realization of our joint aims. But more generally the teachers committed to an individual child-centred approach and to coeducation were wary of using gender as a discriminator for differential behaviour towards the children, and indeed of giving girls something which they were not giving to the boys. For example, we the researchers wished to introduce single sex sessions for some issues, recognizing from a range of studies the value of such sessions for girls.[7] Some teachers had not noticed gender-specific classroom interaction patterns, nor considered the implications of these interaction patterns for the processes of teaching and learning, and regarded single sex activities as divisive. We tried to persuade them to attempt single sex sessions. Ultimately some agreed, if reluctantly, and it was only their own successful experience which served to change their views on the issue.

Issues of power relations and control over the research activity came to the fore when in one school the teachers decided to jettison the research design, one of them voicing the group view:

I want to get it into the regular curriculum and reaching as many kids as possible, not stick to the research design. You know, we can do it on our own now – we just needed something to get us going, and you have done just that.

In the event we reached a negotiated settlement in which we were able to recognize the contributions of each party.

From the researcher perspective, losing 'conventional' control over the action research process can have predictable if unintended consequences. While this was unavoidable in terms of the nature of teacher/researcher relations which had developed, the outcomes frequently also had their positive aspects in the longer term. For example, in the second year of the project, a group of teachers were informed by their female year and school heads that they *must* teach the curriculum units developed by the teacher/researcher working party in the first year. The timing was such that they experienced minimal induction into the ideas involved, despite researcher attempts to create this possibility. Apart from two fully committed women, all of these teachers were men. While implementation of the teaching programme was by no means optimal, in the event these men went through the process of confronting and working through the issues involved in an anti-sexist programme at a personal and pedagogic level while actually teaching it. Just how important it is to provide time for participants to prepare themselves before they leap into anti-sexist curriculum practice became quite clear.

As we have said, consciousness raising for teachers has been an unintended consequence of the project as originally envisaged, and it was certainly never intended that this should take place in the classroom. With a subsequent group of teachers the researchers were able to insist on an intensive period of collaborative work, allowing time for the teachers to consider their own thoughts, feelings and problems the issues raised by the programme aims and content, as well as to plan the programme itself. A further group of predominantly male teachers taught another version of the programme in this school. The first group of men – experiencing fear of incompetence in teaching the content of the curriculum units – had reacted initially with hostility towards the programme and project, and this second group also had difficulty because the material was 'so different from what we are used to'. But the researcher/teacher relationship was such that the issues could be explored; the men were reflective of their own practice, and planned to incorporate what they learned from this experience into their teaching at all levels in the school. They commented for example:

We all like to think we're good, we don't make mistakes, we're not sexist or racist, we're not impatient with the kids, never give them a hard time for no good reason – but a programme like this does make you think.

I think that the real impact of this will be on us, me and other members of staff . . . you could say that my attitude prior to the programme has most definitely changed. I'm more acutely aware of the injustice . . . I really do feel that I have gone beyond making crass statements about sexism and inequality – this experience has changed me, and to some extent the other staff.

In this instance it was the *asymmetry* of research relations in one respect which created change of the kind the project had wanted to happen.

The research team made it quite clear from the beginning that there was a 'pure' research aspect to the project, and that they were sociologists interested in generalizations and theorizing from the findings of this particular piece of research. In line with teachers' ambivalence towards educational research, we were charged on occasion with planning the study purely to create an academic treatise, or with using esoteric sociological abstraction and jargon. But when asked by an outsider whether sociologists are useful in curriculum development with teachers, one of our teachers replied:

Yes, because teachers tend to operate on a practical rather than conceptual level, and they tend to rely on anecdote. Sociologists can give us an overview and a systematic approach. The researchers were able to put our thoughts and enthusiasm into systematic perspective.

We have experienced both separation and combination of action and research. In some cases, in the second year of the project, the teachers supported us throughout in pursuit of our pure research goals, and encouraged the development of the curriculum units, but have increasingly left the actual curriculum development task in the hands of the research team. At first it seemed to us that this was a case of a split between research and action, researchers and teachers. Later reflection suggested that in fact the teachers were facilitating our research input into the school in a context in which they found it difficult to undertake such initiatives directly themselves.

We have, in this section, used our experiences to illustrate some of the likely and possibly inherent tensions of educational action research because it is important to be prepared for these when they arise. We want now to turn to the clearly positive results of our work.

The project's impact

It would be foolhardy to imagine that a ten week anti-sexist curriculum unit could generate dramatic change in patterns of occupational choice when set against the weight of the material conditions and ideological climate in which these children are growing up. Yet recognition of the enormity of the problem in its macro-social context must not preclude attempts to open up pathways to change at the micro level. This is what we have tried to do; and, given a more differentiated and subtle approach to what constitutes success in action research, we have made real progress. In the project schools the curriculum units are now incorporated into the school curricula, whether within specific subject departments, within the pastoral programme, or in careers lessons. *All* those who have been involved with the project have become more critically reflective about their own practice – including ourselves as researchers. It is, furthermore, clear from what we have written that teachers working with us who were not committed to anti-sexist education from the outset either became so or at least moved in the direction of questioning their own positions, as the comments included earlier illustrate. From the teachers' perspective, the project's impact has been undoubtedly positive:

A programme like this can have some impact in helping you to look at other things. It doesn't itself change anything. The danger always is that we're going to overestimate our influence, and the importance of this or any input or any one teacher. Here it's just a spark, sometimes it catches, sometimes it doesn't. . . . I'm not actually adding very much to the girls' power. I don't think you can – they have their own. So it comes down to trying to deflate the worst of what the boys do and occasionally attempting to make spaces for the girls to speak in.

The issue of gender is very close to home for these children. Compared with the other things I've done . . . I've not had the same reaction at all, even when they disagreed. . . . You were touching nerves.

And, most importantly, yes, the pupils did get something out of it all. We certainly did produce an outspoken and independent bunch of third year girls in one school, so much so that the familiar male backlash surfaced with complaints that the girls were getting too much attention.[8]

Kathleen told me today she'd had a 'phone call from a third-year boy's mother complaining that the school is now positively discriminating against boys because of our programme, specifically that the boys are not going on tomorrow's visit . . . Kathleen ducked it by saying we can't help it if some places won't take boys. [She] was astounded that this should have happened . . . this kind of thing is opening her eyes more . . . she wouldn't have believed the strength of people's reactions to attempts to improve girls' lot before.

Seeing women moved in from the periphery is a painful experience for men of all ages. Girls became more confident and mutually supportive of each other in the public face of boys' frequently brutally expressed sexism:

Louise, a teacher who hadn't heard about the project and asked about it, gave me some good news. I told her which class was involved and she said 'Aha! That explains why the girls in that class have become so confident recently. . . . I was really surprised, I was wondering why it's happening.'

The teachers are very clear that what is happening is very positive – they talk of the 'bursting out' that the girls are experiencing. . . . The girls are very enthusiastic. . . . Kathleen [teaching first year children] reports that what has surprised her is the level of anger the girls have about their situation, which exploded in response to the boys' chauvinism in discussion. . . . The boys are already becoming dominant in class discussion, and the girls are colluding with each other to prevent this.

Boys were enabled to show genuine caring towards small children by visiting a nursery without girls around, and to have this quality positively reinforced by both male nursery workers as visitors and by their male teacher bringing his own baby into school, talking about the emotional experience of fatherhood with them:

[At the nursery] Bob and Joe took us to the room for the oldest children, the 3 year olds, and the boys played with the toys and kids eagerly from the beginning. . . . The baby room is definitely where the boys were really getting into helping with the children, picking them up, continually playing and helping – close – much more so than with the older children. Daniel [the teacher] said later 'One boy, David, he was just magnificent . . . he took the role of telling other people in the group what to do and how to look after the babies. Don't do that, how to do this. He was extremely caring and careful. And he's a very macho little boy if you see him in the playground.'

We learned, too, that both girls and boys may appear disinterested and bored by some activities, visits or visitors at the time – but these are remembered later in frequent and enthusiastic discussions:

Mrs Johnson, the ex-bus driver, left a great impression, and I received some fairly graphic explanations of what jobs she had held in London Transport.

For all of us, there was considerable satisfaction in seeing girls who had never handled a saw or lifted a trowel gaining evident pleasure in making a join, building a wall, or doing a touch of spot welding in a women-only workshop:

. . . the girls were interested at once, eager to have a go. When Lizzie arrived she whipped us across to the women's workshop and from that moment onwards there was nothing stopping the girls, grins like Cheshire cats, trying out everything they could get at. The verdict was unanimous – 'Brilliant!' And one girl said later of the programme:

They talked about how there's more opportunities for women if you learn a manual trade. You don't really realize that women could do 'em, but we went round a skillcentre and we saw women doing the jobs like bricklaying and plumbing and all that and realized that it's a better job than being a secretary.

There is no doubt that both girls and boys gained new information about work and adult life, and that they became more aware of gender inequalities. Few will be able to translate this into the patterns of their future lives in any radical way, but they do know more about where the gaps lie between what might be and what usually is:

Most of the time they had no illusions about the future and were realistic if not fatalistic about their future prospects. They were prepared to say that men and women should do the same jobs, have equal pay, share childcare and housework, but did not ultimately believe they had the power to change anything. . . . But I think that if the course at least made them question the way things are or might be then it was worthwhile.

It is these kinds of positive and satisfying outcomes which not only lend a distinct quality to action research of this type, but which also make the (frequently immense) effort worthwhile for everyone involved. We were able to link discovery with action, and we have been rewarded: with greater understanding of gender-specific schooling processes and with the conviction that teachers and researchers, working together, can begin to change those processes to make schooling a more worthwhile experience for girls.

Notes

1 This article draws on Chisholm and Holland, 1986. The project was funded by the ESRC, EOC and ILEA.
2 Holland and Chisholm (1985) give details of the research design, and of the tasks undertaken in each school in each year of the project.
3 Some initial information can be found in Blackman (1986), Chisholm (1986) and Holland (1986).
4 To that extent an objectives model of evaluation can be applied to the study, and we have included pre- and post-tests as one means of assessing change in these areas.
5 Holland *et al.* (1985) give details of the programmes which were developed, some examples of the curriculum materials used, and the views of teachers and their experience of working on the project. Some of the materials and advice on their use will be published as a teachers' pack in 1987 by Blackwell (title unresolved).
6 These issues are discussed more fully in Chisholm (1984).
7 The issue is controversial perhaps ultimately because if we could decide finally that single-sex schooling was best for girls and mixed schooling best for boys what could be done? This is one suggestion, based on criteria of academic achievement for girls and social development for boys. Dale (1969, 1971, 1974) produces evidence in favour of mixed schooling; Spender and Sarah (1980), Shaw (1980), Deem (1984) and Mahony (1985) do so for single-sex schooling. See also ILEA (1985).
8 The following quotes are from field notes and observation and interview reports and recordings.

References

Blackman, S. J., *Doleful schooling: Youth labour market issues*, Girls and Occupational Choice Working Paper 8, London University Institute of Education, 1986.
Byrne, E., *Women and education*, London, Tavistock, 1978.
Chisholm, L. A., *Comments and reflections on action research in education*, Girls and Occupational Choice Working Paper 2, London University Institute of Education, 1984.
Chisholm, L. A., *Gender and vocation*, Working Paper no. 4, Post-Sixteen Education Centre, London University Institute of Education, 1986.
Chisholm, L. A. and Holland, J., 'Girls and Occupational Choice: Anti-sexism in action in a curriculum development project', *British Journal of Sociology of Education*, **7** (4), 1986.
Dale, R. R., *Mixed or single-sex schools?*, vol. I (1969); also vol. II (1971) and vol. III (1974), London, Routledge and Kegan Paul.
Deem, R. (ed.), *Schooling for women's work*, London, Routledge and Kegan Paul, 1980.
Deem, R. (ed.), *Co-education reconsidered*, Milton Keynes, Open University, 1980.
Department of Education and Science, *New Earnings Survey*, London, HMSO, 1984.
Freeman, P. L., 'Don't talk to me about lexical meta-analysis of criterion-referenced clustering and lap-dissolve spatial transformations: a consideration of the role of practising teachers in educational research', *British Educational Research Journal*, **12** (2), 1986, pp. 197–206.
Glaser, B. G. and Strauss, A. L., *The discovery of grounded theory: strategies of qualitative research*, London, Weidenfeld and Nicolson, 1967.
Glaser, B. G., *Advances in the methodology of grounded theory: theoretical sensitivity*, Mill Valley, The Sociology Press, 1978.
Holland, J., *Girls and occupational choice: in search of meanings*, paper for Education and Training 14–18 Conference, St Hilda's Oxford September, 1986.

Holland, J. Blackman, S. J., Gordon, T. and teaching team, *A woman's place: strategies for change in the educational context*, Girls and Occupational Choice Working Paper 4, London University Institute of Education, 1985.

Holland, J. and Chisholm, L. A., *Girls and occupational choice: A brief description of the first eighteen months of the project*, Girls and Occupational Choice Working Paper 6, London University Institute of Education, 1985.

Inner London Education Authority, Report of the Working Party on Single-Sex and Co-education, London, ILEA, 1985.

Macdonald, B. and Ruddock, J., 'Curriculum research and development projects: Barriers to success', *British Journal of Educational Psychology*, **41** (2), 1971, pp. 148–54.

Mahony, P., *Schools for the boys? Coeducation reassessed*, London, Hutchinson, 1985.

Mies, M., 'Towards a methodology for feminist research', in Bowles, G. and Duelli-Klein, R., *Theories of women's studies*, London, Routledge and Kegan Paul, 1983.

Oakley, A., 'Interviewing women: a contradiction in terms', in Roberts, H. (ed.), *Doing feminist research*, London, Routledge and Kegan Paul, 1981.

Pratt, J. Bloomfield, J. and Seale, C., *Option choice: A question of equal opportunities*, London, Nelson/NFER, 1984.

Shaw, J., 'Education and the individual: Schooling for girls or mixed schooling – a mixed blessing', in Deem, R., *Schooling for women's work*, London, Routledge and Kegan Paul, 1980.

Shipman, M. D., with Bolam, D. and Jenkins, D., *Inside a curriculum project: A case study in the process of curriculum change*, London, Methuen, 1974.

Spender, D. and Sarah, E. (eds), *Learning to lose: Sexism and education*, London, The Women's Press, 1980.

Stanley, L. and Wise, S., *Breaking out: Feminist consciousness and feminist research*, London, Routledge and Kegan Paul, 1983.

Stanworth, M., *Gender and schooling: A study of sexual divisions in the classroom*, London, Hutchinson, 1983.

22 Teacher as researcher: a new tradition for research on gender

Val Millman

Since the early 1980s there has been a concerted attempt by both academics and practitioners concerned with gender differences in education to create a mutually respected, mutually useful body of knowledge and experience. This level of collaboration in educational research has been responsible for instigating widespread public debate around gender differences in schools. In turn, many LEAs have been prompted to allocate resources to the promotion of gender equality, at a time of severe constraint in other areas of their budget.

The impact of this collaboration has been mainly achieved by the involvement of teachers in the research process itself. The kinds of questions posed by 'teacher researchers' have had a more practical, classroom based orientation than other forms of research on gender. How were teachers to resolve the day to day behaviour of the girls and boys in their classrooms? What sort of teaching strategies would 'liberate' pupils from their sex-stereotyped perceptions and aspirations? How might teachers adapt their work in order to further the aims of equality of opportunity? The Girls into Science and Technology Project (GIST: 1979–83) and the Schools Council Sex Differentiation Project (1981–3) were both examples of short-term projects which not only engaged teachers in carrying out research but also established centres of school-based expertise capable of sustaining change beyond the lifetime of the project. More recently, LEA advisers with responsibility for promoting sex equality have adopted the teacher–researcher model as a means of identifying and disseminating 'good' practice within their own authorities. This chapter will examine the process of teacher research and focus on the particular opportunities it affords for examining gender differentiation in a variety of educational contexts.

Why teacher as researcher?

An attractive feature of using teachers as researchers for educational decision and policy-making was that it offered considerable scope for professional development. In addition to providing teachers with a clearer understanding of gender issues, school-based research was directed towards developing a range of observational and appraisal techniques which were likely to sharpen teachers' reactions to and understanding of other areas of school life. Another advantage was that the research process itself was likely to heighten self-awareness and reflection not only for the teacher–researcher but for other teachers and colleagues working alongside.

Source: Commissioned.

Teachers became their own researchers and carried out studies in their own schools which they hoped would illuminate their and their colleagues understanding of the ways in which gender differentiation operates. The insights thus gained would lead to action to change where change was needed. Data was collected . . . examined, shared with colleagues and reflected upon. It generated discussion, recognition, amazement – and action (Taylor, H., *Seeing is Believing*, Brent, 1984).

However, a recurring feature of this research tradition was that teachers often felt hesitant about conducting their own research either because they felt them-selves incapable of 'doing research' or because they were sceptical about the validity of the data that they were in a position to gather. Both views, a product of the traditional distance between academics and practitioners (see Chisholm, L., and Holland J. in this volume) were, in part, ameliorated by external support from academic researchers or educational advisers. These were able to help teachers redefine their existing notions of 'research' towards a process more feasible, productive and relevant to the situation in which they found themselves.

A criticism frequently made of small-scale action research is that the data is gathered from such small samples that it can have no statistical significance and no generalisable validity. This, while true, is irrelevant in the context of investigation into individual classrooms. The great value of teacher conducted school focused enquiry is that it illuminates the particular and leads to consideration of how that particular may be improved (Taylor, H., 1984).

Nevertheless some teachers in the Schools Council Sex Differentiation Project thought scientific validity so important in helping them claim the attention of their more sceptical colleagues that they decided to test their findings in examination performance for statistical significance before presenting this evidence to colleagues.

The approach adopted by teachers in the first part of the study arose from their wish to make their research statistically valid. Although there were some departmental staff who had little knowledge of statistical data testing, it was considered important to conduct the study as 'scientifically' as possible. While it was recognized that other approaches had their own validity, it was felt that an investigation of test scores and examination results clearly lent itself to statistical analysis. Staff thought that there were many sceptics who would try to dismiss their research on grounds of subjectivity, so it was important to meet their criticisms with evidence that had validity in their eyes. Later they could move on to obtain more qualitative data which illuminated particular aspects of their study. Staff were assisted in analysing their data by some simple 'guidelines to statistical analysis' prepared by the head of department (Millman, V. and Weiner, G., 1985, p. 29).

There were also differences in research approach dependent on the origins and status of the research study; those teacher–researchers who were collecting data on behalf of an outside research body (GIST, Schools Council) or their LEA were, in the main, unable to determine the objectives and methods of this research. In smaller-scale projects, however, teachers were freer to choose both the topic of their investigation and their method of investigation (e.g. May and Rudduck, 1983).

Of considerable importance in developing successful change strategies and achieving implementation, was the status of the teacher–researchers themselves, as perceived by colleagues at both classroom and senior management levels. Established and respected teachers had considerably more influence on school policy than those on supply or in their probationary year (see Millman, V. and Weiner, G., 1984). Moreover if the school already had a tradition of teacher-initiated debate on general curricular issues, the existing structures of staff and curriculum development were more likely to provide a forum within which research findings on gender could be presented to colleagues.

Strategies were developed to involve members of school management teams in research planning and review at an early stage so that they, too, would feel committed to acting on research findings (May and Ruddock, 1983). In schools where equal opportunities was a new agenda item, it was found that involving immediate colleagues in the research process and setting realistic, if limited, objectives were crucial to the success of the project e.g. aiming to secure a discussion slot at a departmental meeting rather than the radical reformulation of whole school policy.

The research process

What questions or topics were likely to make good starting points for school-based inquiry? For the Schools Council Project, the principal goal of which was 'to help teachers to recognize that sexism in school is a problem', the topic of research was selected on the basis of 'consideration of the elements of school life which were more likely to influence the perceptions and performance of students' *and* suitability for in-depth investigation into the extent of bias in chosen areas (Millman, V. and Weiner, G., 1985).

For those working in the GIST Project the 'action research plan' was more precise.

1 We tested children's spatial ability and their science knowledge on entry to secondary school, and explored their attitudes to science and sex roles. The results were then fed back to schools.
2 We worked with teachers to increase their awareness of the impact of gender on educational achievement and outcomes, and to view it as a pedagogical issue.
3 A programme of visits to schools by women working in science and technology was mounted.
4 On the basis of 2 and 3 above, teachers and schools were invited to mount their own interventions; these included development of more 'girl friendly' curriculum materials, single sex clubs and classes, observation to increase awareness of sex differences in classroom interaction.
5 Children's attitudes to science and to sex roles were again measured for comparison with the initial survey, and their subject options monitored and compared with previous year-groups in each school (Whyte, J. 1985, p. 78).

For teachers establishing their own priorities, feasibility and modesty of scope were of particular importance in their selection of topic. Thus investigating patterns of use of play areas or school dinner safety arrangements (see May and Ruddock, 1983), were easier to pursue than, for example, the extent of influence of the media on young children. It could be argued that this is a serious limitation of the teacher as researcher tradition.

For the Schools Council Project, eight areas of the official and hidden curriculum were selected as potentially suitable for closer analysis.

a *Sex differentiation in whole school areas* – gathering information on option choice, examination entry and results as a preliminary for more focused work.
b *Sex bias in reading schemes, textbooks and teaching resources* – analysing curricular material for stereotyping and irrelevance to pupils' lives.
c *Sex bias in specific subjects or departmental areas* – examining the 'milieu' of a subject or department, for instance, by analysing staffing patterns, examination entry and results, pupil attitudes, option choice, to gain a clear overview of the working of a department.
d *The 'hidden' curriculum* – looking at implicit as well as formal aspects of the curriculum, e.g. assemblies, uniform, out-of-school activities, teacher and pupil attitude and expectation.
e *Classroom relationships* – considering by observation and monitoring the relationship between pupils in the classroom and between pupils and teachers.
f *Careers education* – examining the effects of the content and timing of careers advice.
g *Language use in school* – undertaking studies of language use in all areas of school life, e.g. within the classroom, in the playground, in school booklets and parent publications.
h *The changing curriculum* – looking at changes in the school curriculum brought about by the decline of traditional forms of employment and the growth of computer technology (Weiner, 1985, p. 118).

May and Ruddock (1983), on the other hand, chose projects based on the belief that 'teachers work best with knowledge that is generated from their *own* experiences and that reflects the particularities of their own circumstances' (Preface). So investigations ranged from gathering data on seating patterns at school dinner-time by means of an observation diary to observing free choice activities in an infant classroom.

In selecting the methodology and strategies of school-based research, it became evident that traditional research methods, e.g. statistically valid quantitive data gathering or labour-intensive ethnographies, were not suitable. New questions demanded new answers.

What kinds of inquiry methods are both manageable in the context of school-based inquiry and are likely to yield data that will help teachers to explore the question that is the starting point for their inquiry? When one has gathered data in relation to a question or topic, what does one do with it? (May, N. and Ruddock, J. 1983).

Again the major objective was that methods needed to be selected that were both manageable and productive. For instance, if the research was to be undertaken in the classroom at the same time as the teacher was carrying out normal teaching responsibilities, the more straightforward the method of research selected, the better. In these circumstances it was easier to record general observations in the form of field notes and diary entries rather than for instance, conducting individual or small group interviews without interruptions or comments from other pupils.

Analysis of textbooks proved a popular activity of this kind:

Margaret S was filling a temporary one-term supply post in the modern languages department of an outer London comprehensive school. She aimed to produce evidence of sex-role differentiation in her own subject area which would raise awareness amongst her departmental colleagues. She hoped that in the future this might become a model for other departments to follow. She focused her attention on the textbooks used in the modern languages department, believing that an analysis of the sex bias presented in those books would open up discussion of wider gender inequalities reinforced by the teachers themselves. Here Margaret describes how she carried out her research:

'I have chosen to look at the Longman's Audio-Visual Course books, realizing that these constitute only a few of a large range of books available, but that they are used in a large number of classes learning French both in this and in other schools. Textbooks in French do not have a 'factual' content in quite the same way that, for example, Physics or Home Economics textbooks might have. Some courses in foreign languages appear to have some of their content determined by considerations of what it is appropriate to teach in terms of 'grammar' and 'vocabulary', and some use a more situational approach, but in both cases the story being recounted is invented by the authors. It is a useful exercise to examine the content of the texts that are being used and to see what students may read in, and between, their lines' (Millman, V. and Weiner, G., 1985, p. 26).

Some teachers tried audio-taping class lessons in order to monitor their own and girls' and boys' contributions to class discussion. However, it was found that such material was difficult to transcribe or not sufficiently clear for detailed analysis. Portraying classroom activities, through video-recording, although providing interesting data, was challenged on the basis that it was artificially influenced by the unusual presence of video cameras in the classroom (Millman, V. and Weiner, G., 1985).

Questionnaires, probably the most efficient method of collecting quantitative data, were found to be useful in terms of ease of analysis, administration and in identification of areas needing further and more detailed research. However their limitations were evident in terms of the time required for analysis, accuracy of construction and response rate.

Not only did the usefulness of the findings depend on the skill with which the questionnaire had been constructed but the accuracy of the results also depended on the willingness of the respondents to complete and return the questionnaires (Millman, V. and Weiner, G., 1985, p. 44).

In contrast 'carefully structured interviews, systematically carried out' provided more detailed information than was obtained in the written responses to question-naires, and less structured more open-ended interviews provided room for both interviewer and interviewee to pursue new lines of inquiry and response. Yet often insurmountable obstacles were discovered such as the impossibility of guaran-teeing anonymity, so that interviewees were likely to be less than honest about often highly contentious issues. Also the considerable amount of organization needed, both to conduct the interviews and to analyse the resulting data raised further problems.

Nevertheless teachers in the Schools Council Project were reasonably positive about their experiences:

Analysing loosely structured interview information proved complex and time-consuming. The answers did not fit into neat categories which could be translated into straightforward quantitative statements. Nevertheless, they did reflect the contradictions and inconsistencies that exist in teacher behaviour and that lie at the root of the hidden curriculum. Indeed, the interview process turned out to be as productive as the end results. Initially, many staff interviewed had believed that girls and boys received the same treatment in their classrooms. On closer reflection, they realized that perhaps they were 'less fair' than they would like to think! A summary of the answers to the question 'Do you punish boys and girls in different ways?' illustrates the type of information elicited from the interviews:

One teacher first said, 'no difference' but later said her tolerance level was higher for boys. Everyone thought that the forms of difficult behaviour were often different for boys and girls and therefore the form of discipline could be different. One remarked on girls' emotional upsets needing more careful handling than those of boys, and another said boys were shouted at more than girls. The point that troublesome girls eventually end up with a female Deputy and boys with a male Deputy was made. Only one person said absolutely no differences in punishment occurred (Millman, V. and Weiner, G. 1985, p. 36).

Structured methods of classroom observation provided another fruitful method of research, i.e. using observation checklists with a series of questions pinpointing aspects of school life such as classroom interaction or sex-stereotyping in textbooks. This form of investigation was used in both the GIST and Schools Council Project, yet once again accuracy of recording and the time needed for data analysis provided similar difficulties to those mentioned above.

Whatever the research method adopted, the crucial factor for the teacher–researcher was that findings needed to be shared and discussed with colleagues. Some teachers presented their findings to staff at departmental meetings, others disseminated more widely. For instance, in Enfield, where a group of teachers had worked in collaboration with the Schools Council Project, a booklet with an introduction by the Chief Education Officer was distributed local authority wide. It included information on research studies carried out by teachers in the following areas: analysis of resources through the use of checklists; quantitive analysis of examination entries, subject choices and school-leaver destinations; case studies of pupils on community studies placements; examples of girls' and boys' approaches to school subjects and leisure; examples of school staffing patterns.

Bringing about change

Teachers as researchers have now been drawn into in-service developments at LEA level for some of the reasons mentioned earlier in this chapter, and there are now an increasing number of LEAs within which teacher research into gender differences can be seen to stimulate innovation and influence policy. In the ILEA, where the authority's Research and Statistical Branch has conducted the most detailed monitoring of equal opportunities initiatives, teachers have been actively engaged in the process of data collection, either supplying information about themselves – to contribute to a central analysis of 'Female and Male Teaching Staff in the ILEA' (1982) – or about their schools. Such information has been disseminated in the form of published reports to both teachers and policy-makers. Members of the authority's advisory service have been able to assist teachers in conducting their own monitoring of schools progress towards equal opportunities using some of the techniques outlined in 'Is your school changing?' (Martini,

Myers and Warner, 1984; see also Adams and Walkerdine, 1986; Adams and Arnot, 1986).

Other local authorities with a shorter history of interest in gender issues have worked in co-operation with outside bodies such as the Equal Opportunities Commission (EOC) to initiate teacher research in this area. The EOC publication *Breaking the Mould* (Agnew, 1985) describes how the Sheffield LEA piloted a one-year action research project on careers' education in five of its secondary schools. In addition to monitoring pupils' progress on work experience programmes, for example, in an attempt to 'identify factors which tend to promote and further reinforce sex stereotyped attitudes to work experience placements' teachers analysed the effects of positive interventions in this area.

As with any short-term projects investigated or sponsored by outside bodies, the extent to which the LEA will contrive to support development beyond the project's lifetime will depend on a variety of factors – not least the extent of involvement in the project of those instrumental to the LEA policy-making process. Between 1981 and 1983 the co-ordinator of the Schools Council Sex Differentiation in Schooling Project supported teachers carrying out research in LEAs which had not yet formally recognized the importance of working on gender issues. In most cases the LEA-wide dissemination of school-based research was only just beginning when project funding came to an end. Nevertheless, authorities like Leicestershire have continued to initiate and extend support for investigations begun by the project.

The centrally funded Technical and Vocational Education Initiative (TVEI) has been another short-term project whose 'equal opportunities' criterion has successfully motivated LEAs to take action in this area. Monitoring of projects by the Manpower Services Commission (MSC) subsequent to funding has pressed LEAs to provide visible evidence of progress towards sex equality. Yet, because of insufficient use of the teacher research process, the need for results has often propelled project personnel into forms of action which have been ill-researched and inadequately understood.

In Coventry, approaches developed by TVEI schools have avoided these pitfalls by reflecting on the previous experiences of equal opportunities strategies in which teacher research has played an important part. The following examples illustrate four contexts in which teacher research into gender differences has generated change at both school and LEA level.

Promotion practices for men and women primary teachers
In 1982 teachers as members of Coventry NUT Equal Opportunities Subcommittee carried out a survey of the work histories of primary school teachers. With the help of a member of the Institute of Employment Research at Warwick University, they compiled a questionnaire which was first piloted in nine primary schools and later sent to all primary teachers in the LEA: 466 teachers completed the questionnaire (just under 50 per cent response rate) with women and men respondents proportional to their numbers in the primary teaching force. A thirty-two page report was compiled examining the relative importance of teaching experience, job applications, qualifications, age, career breaks, etc. on women's and men's promotion prospects. There was widespread dissemination of the

report's findings and recommendations both within the LEA and beyond. In addition to school governing bodies now receiving annual breakdowns of female and male teaching staff, wider recognition of the professional development needs of women teachers has been achieved through this survey.

Investigating equal opportunities in a secondary school

In 1983 two women teachers who had attended a series of equal opportunities meetings asked their Head if they could form a school working party to examine gender differences. Members of the working party worked with other teachers to collect a variety of sex equality data which was presented as 'evidence' in a booklet circulated to all teaching staff. The school evidence, which included option choice, examination, career and training data as well as comments and views of girl and boy students, was compared with national statistics and backed up by findings of published research projects. The second half of the booklet entitled 'What can we do?' concludes:

We are well aware that many people are already concerned about this issue. It has been encouraging and exciting to hear about the strategies for change they have adopted. What is needed now is wider discussion of the problem – and more concerted action (Coventry LEA, 1984).

Progress since then has been slow, at times problematic, but sustained by the commitment of those originally involved in the research. A scale point has now been allocated to a teacher with designated responsibility for promoting sex equality, and some in-service training of staff has taken place.

Investigating sex equality in the DES-funded Low Attainers Project (LAP)

A selected group of fourth and fifth year low attaining students from each of Coventry's comprehensive and special schools attended an Occupational Experience Centre under the supervision of their school liaison teacher for one day a week. Students from five or six different schools attended the centre on each day of the week and their liaison teachers worked as a team co-ordinated by a project teacher based at the centre. During the fourth and fifth year each student followed eight nine-week courses run by skilled instructors from a variety of occupational backgrounds. During the project's first year, liaison teachers expressed concern about sex-stereotyped course choice. Project staff agreed to examine these impressions more closely. School liaison teachers were asked to provide a female–male breakdown of students selected for their low attainers group and to monitor the course choices of each of their female/male students.

The day-teams of liaison teachers co-operated in collecting and analysing data. The LEA senior adviser with responsibility for overseeing the project was drawn into discussions and at the end of the project's first year he wrote to school heads asking them 'to review counselling procedures' in order to reduce sex-stereotyped choice.

Discussions of the data collected by liaison teachers also took place within schools and among staff based at the Occupational Experience Centre. This generated changes in practice e.g. in the monitoring of names and the content of some courses. A number of liaison teachers monitored their student's course choices more closely taking particular care that girls and boys did not find themselves in a minority of one or two in occupational workshops. During the second year of the project, in addition to collecting quantitative data, liaison teachers were asked to conduct observations of student interaction in occupational workshops. It was hoped that this would identify less obvious causes of sex-stereotyped choice and encourage teachers to reflect on the 'hidden curriculum' of their own classrooms. Some teachers were reluctant to take part in this; they resented an additional demand being made on their time especially as they could not see 'the point of it'. Others doubted the validity of the exercise or worried about the intrusion on instructors and students. All such concerns were well aired before the observation study finally got off the ground.

It was eventually agreed that the focus would be on student interaction – this was made clear to the instructors with whom the teachers discussed their findings immediately afterwards. Teachers were able to select one of two observation strategies which were discussed with them beforehand. Either they could observe the interaction of a whole group or the behaviour of a single student. In the latter case teachers did not observe a student from their own school.

They were asked to note observations under structured headings as well as add their own comments. Some teachers also carried out interviews with instructors and students. Eventually nearly all liaison teachers conducted observations and reported back their findings to other members of their day team. Their written records were collected centrally and together with an analysis of quantitative data, were summarized in a fifteen-page booklet entitled *DES Special Project: a report of Equal Opportunities*. Copies of the report were distributed to all liaison teachers, project instructors, comprehensive and special school heads, LEA advisers and officers. While the investigations had limited success in encouraging less sex-stereotyped course choice among low attaining pupils, they successfully heightened awareness and initiated a dialogue about gender issues which would not otherwise have taken place.

Investigating classroom interaction and active learning techniques
In 1986 five teachers were appointed to Coventry's TRIST (TVEI Related In-Service Training) team of professional tutors. Sponsored by the MSC, this four-term pilot project aimed to generate the use of active learning techniques among Coventry's secondary school teachers. Each tutor worked alongside individual teachers in a variety of subject areas. The TRIST team held a number of meetings to explore their own professional perceptions of gender differentiation; individual team members read published research in their own area of interest, e.g. media, micro-electronics. They became particularly interested in classroom interaction and the extent to which less didactic teaching styles enable students to take a more active part in shaping their learning. The team decided to carry out observations in the schools with which they were currently working. In bringing their observations together they hoped they would be able to develop active learning approaches which both raised gender issues with pupils and promoted sex equality in classroom interactions.

Each of the five tutors agreed to use a structured classroom observation schedule; in practice, only two tutors adhered to the structured questions, one of whom noted down incidental observations he intended to follow up at a later date. A third tutor abandoned the schedule in favour of making detailed field notes on seating arrangements, girls' and boys' organizing styles, sexist comments and missed opportunities for following up gender issues. The fourth tutor decided not to make formal observations as she felt it would damage her relationship with the class teacher. The fifth tutor, who was working with an all girls group, followed her preliminary observations by devising a card exercise which asked girls to list and rank areas of micro-electronics in which they most needed help. 'Lack of confidence' came top of the list and she was able to follow this up with the girls' class teacher.

Although such lack of uniformity in approach made direct comparison of observations difficult, it was evident that the data collected by the team as a whole was wide ranging, informative and successful in generating a heightened level of awareness. The team subsequently moved on to devise in-service materials on active learning techniques which promoted sex equality in the classroom.

In an evaluation of the teacher–researcher approaches in the four Coventry case studies, the following changes were observed:

a Teachers conducting the research have a sharper and more informed understanding of sex differentiation in education.
b Teachers conducting the research have engaged in dialogues and taken on new roles which have significantly contributed to their own professional development.
c The collection of research data has stimulated the establishment of a central resource base within which details of larger scale research studies are also housed.
d Teaching colleagues, members of senior management teams, pupils, parents and local policy-makers have engaged in discussions of research findings.
e Increased teacher time/staff resources have been allocated to the promotion of gender equality.
f New strategies have been developed through teacher research providing approaches to new developments, e.g. TVEI.

It has not been possible in the space afforded here to give detailed accounts of ways in which teachers have developed research techniques and presented their research findings. These details can be more fully understood from references listed at the end of this chapter. The fact that reports of teacher research into gender are now available in published form reflects the growth in interest that has taken place during the first half of the 1980s. Those attempting to initiate teacher research into gender will be likely to find schools notably more receptive than they would have done five years ago. There are now substantial grounds for optimism based on evidence that such research can raise awareness, influence policy and stimulate educational innovation.

Acknowledgement

Thanks to Gaby Weiner for help in organizing the article.

References

Adams, C. and Arnot, M., *Investigating gender issues in secondary schools*, ILEA, 1986.

Adams, C. and Walkerdine, V., *Investigating gender in the primary school*, ILEA, 1986.

Agnew, D., *Breaking the Mould*, EOC, 1985.

Coventry LEA, *Department of Education and Science Special Project: a report of equal opportunities*, 1985.

Coventry LEA, *Gender and Schooling: towards equal opportunities*, 1984.

ILEA, *Female and Male Teaching Staff in the ILEA: equal opportunity RS833/82*, Inner London Education Authority, 1982.

Kelly, A., Whyte, J. and Smail, B., *Girls into Science and Technology Final Report*, Manchester University, 1984.

Martini, R., Myers, K. and Warner, S., *Is your school changing?*, Inner London Education Authority, 1984.

May, N. and Ruddock, J., *Sex stereotyping and the early years of schooling*, Equal Opportunities Commission/Centre for Applied Research Education 1983.

Millman, V., *Equal Opportunities in TVEI*, Manpower Services Commission, 1986.

Millman, V. and Weiner, G., *Sex Differentiation in Schooling: is there a problem?*, Longman (Schools Council), 1985.

Spender, D., *Man Made Language*, Routledge and Kegan Paul, 1980.

Taylor, H. (ed.), *Seeing is believing: teacher investigations into gender differences in the classroom*, Brent, 1984.

Weiner G., 'The Schools Council and gender: a case study in the legitimation of curriculum policy' in Arnot, M. (ed.), *Race and Gender: equal opportunities policies in education*, Pergamon, 1985.

Whyte, J., 'Girl friendly science and the girl friendly school', in Whyte, J., Deem, R., Kant, L. and Cruickshank, M. (eds), *Girl Friendly Schooling*, Methuen, 1985.

Index

When the index leads to a reference in the notes the number of the note is given in italics.

Index of names